POLITICAL GEOGRAPHY

World-economy, nation-state and locality

Second Edition

POLITICAL GEOGRAPHY

WORLD-ECONOMY, NATION-STATE AND LOCALITY

PETER J. TAYLOR

Department of Geography
University of Newcastle upon Tyne

Longman
Scientific &
Technical
Copublished in the United States with
John Wiley & Sons, Inc., New York

Longman Scientific & Technical,
Longman Group UK Ltd,
Longman House, Burnt Mill, Harlow,
Essex CM20 2JE, England
and Associated Companies throughout the world.

Copublished in the United States with
John Wiley & Sons, Inc., 605 Third Avenue, New York, NY 10158

© Longman Group UK Limited 1989

First published 1985
Second edition 1989

British Library Cataloguing in Publication Data
Taylor, Peter J (Peter James), *1944-*
   Political geography: world economy, nation-state
   and locality. — 2nd ed
   1. Politics. Geographical aspects
   320.1′2

ISBN 0-582-04332-8

Library of Congress Cataloging-in-Publication Data
Taylor, Peter J. (Peter James), 1944–
    Political geography: world-economy, nation-state, and locality /
Peter J. Taylor. — 2nd ed.
      p.   cm.
    Includes index.
    ISBN 0-470-21473-2 (Wiley)
    1. Geography, Political. 2. Geopolitics.   I. Title.
   JC319.T34   1989   89-8354
    320.1′2 — dc20   CIP

Set in Linotron 202 10/12 pt Baskerville
Produced by Longman Group (FE) Limited
Printed in Hong Kong

This book is dedicated to

KARL LIEBKNECHT

1871–1919

CONTENTS

PREFACE TO THE SECOND EDITION

It is indicative of the health of modern political geography that I have felt
compelled to agree to the publisher's invitation to revise this book just four
years after writing it. After the many nice things said by reviewers it might
have been sensible for me to leave well alone. In the event I have decided
upon a very extensive revision of the text. Why?

In writing the first edition I was preoccupied with producing a political
geography on a coherent theoretical foundation. I am reasonably satisfied
that this was achieved. This was a necessary but not sufficient condition for a
good political geography, however. I now feel that I under-valued the
substantive contributions of political geography in my search for a
respectable theoretical structure. Political geography must analyze and
inform the political issues of the day. This was latent in the first edition; in
the second edition I have tried to fulfil this promise in a more explicit
manner. Using a rather gruesome analogy, I have put a little bit more flesh
on the bones on my initial effort. Hence I have kept to the same theoretical
framework but have added much substantive material.

For readers familiar with the first edition it may be useful if I briefly list
the changes I have made on a chapter by chapter basis. In Chapter 1 there
are two new elements: I have chosen to introduce world-systems analysis in a
slightly different way by emphasizing its 'one society assumption', and I have
added a section on the nature of power that treats power in different
institutions of the world-economy. Chapter 2 has the most changes of all the
chapters as geopolitics is 'revived' rather than just 'revisited'. The heritage
has been recast as a political-power or realist perspective on international
relations. The remainder of the chapter is completely rewritten and deals
with the practical geopolitics of politicians in terms of general geopolitical
world order and specific geopolitical codes. In Chapter 3 change is limited to
some minor reordering of material on informal imperialism plus the addition
of a small case study of the largest of the formal empires, that of Britain.

The major organizational departure from the first edition is the division of
the original Chapter 4 'Territory, state and nation' into two chapters
'Territorial states' and 'Nation and nationalism'. In the former the
traditional spatial structure material is reorganized as a discussion of the
making of the world political map and the theoretical material is expanded in
a discussion of the nature of the territorial states. The question of

nationalism is so important that it obviously deserved a chapter to itself. In Chapter 5 I provide a new section on the ideological heritage of nationalism and expand the discussion of theories of nationalism beyond Nairn to alternative arguments for nationalism as resistance.

The final two chapters, now Chapters 6 and 7, both have new sections replacing old. In the discussion of electoral geography the section on ideologies is omitted and two new sections are developed discussing elections in core and periphery, respectively. Some of the material from the first edition is incorporated in the 'core section'; the new material for elections beyond the core is a necessary and long overdue addition to electoral geography. In Chapter 7 the series of case studies with which the first edition concluded are now omitted and replaced by a construction of the new theory of politics in localities that has emerged in recent years.

Despite the addition of substantive material and the updating of ideas, especially in Chapters 2, 5, 6 and 7, this new volume is most certainly not a state of the art presentation of political geography. Such is the revival of political geography that it is no longer possible to write a reasonably comprehensive account of the sub-discipline in a single volume. There are many obvious and important omissions in the new text. The political geography of the law of the sea, analysis of the 'north-south divide' in recent British elections, the geography of war and the rise of nationalisms in the Soviet Union are just four topics where political geographers have made important contributions in recent years that are not adequately recognized in my discussions below. What I do provide is a further explication of the theoretical structure introduced in the first edition. I have continued in my attempt to produce a political geography as an integrated whole while at the same time creating individual chapters that can act as platforms for further study of the major themes of political geography.

This is an exciting time to be a political geographer.

Peter J. Taylor

September 1988

PREFACE TO THE FIRST EDITION

As an undergraduate geography student at Liverpool University from 1963 to 1966 I was not able to attend any lectures on political geography for the simple reason that they did not exist. The Liverpool geography department was by no means exceptional — the 1960s represent the nadir of political geography. This subject was more likely to be kept off honours geography syllabuses than to be put on them. Nevertheless on train journeys back to digs I always made a point of reading those articles in journals to which we had *not* been referred to in lectures. Hence I 'found' political geography. I soon discovered the latest text book, Norman Pound's *Political Geography*, and was fascinated by what were, to me, new topics. I remember enjoying especially the debates concerning the Heartland Theory. But it was soon back to work to earn my degree.

As a post-graduate I carried out a typical piece of quantitative geography research which was fashionably apolitical. One of my research themes, however, led me back to political geography. Regionalization or region-building had as one of its practical examples electoral districting. And so I became hooked on gerrymandering, a concept which neatly linked my spatial analysis interest with political geography. While at Iowa in 1970–71 I was able to follow the redistricting process daily as the Iowa legislature reduced its congressional districts from seven to six. I finished up producing a bibliography on districting as an appendix to a report to the Iowa legislature. Back in England I teamed up with Graham Gudgin with the avowed intention of technically solving the mysteries of the spatial organization of elections. This was further developed in collaboration with Ron Johnston as a more general interest in electoral geography. At the same time I was asked to write annual progress reports on political geography for *Progress in Human Geography* from which I learnt two things: that I had developed a dissatisfaction with current political geography (the reports were more negative than positive) but this was based in large part on my ignorance of the subject-matter. It's a long way from the narrow perspective of electoral geography to the broad vistas of political geography.

These broad vistas were forced upon me when I visited Clark University in 1978–79 as I was assigned to take over Saul Cohen's introductory political geography course. I soon decided that there was no text book suitable for my needs (negative again) but I had no general framework of my own to supersede what I found to be inadequate. The political geography graduates at Clark exposed me on this count and I am continually grateful to them for that. But it was at this time that I was slowly finding a way forward. It seemed to me that Immanuel Wallerstein's world-systems approach provided an answer to many of the questions I had been asking. The last few years have been spent trying to restructure political geography as part of the holistic framework that Wallerstein and his associates have proposed. This book is the result of these endeavours.

In the meantime political geography has shown all the signs of, in Rostow's terms, 'taking off'. International conferences at Lancaster, Haifa and Oxford have allowed me to try out my ideas on my peers drawn from all five continents. As part of this growth I have been involved in launching *Political Geography Quarterly*. As the editor many papers have now passed through my hands and my original fascination with all aspects of political geography has been rekindled. This has had an important effect on this book. Several recent statements on political geography have attempted to distance 'modern' political geography from 'traditional' political geography. Hence capital cities and boundaries are out, social choice theory and location conflicts are in. I feel strongly that we cannot just dismiss our past as if it did not exist. Most of the chapters below start with a 'heritage section' — for geopolitics I discuss an ideological heritage, for imperialism a revolutionary heritage, for electoral geography a liberal heritage and for urban political geography an ecological heritage. These are not meant to be of mere antiquarian interest. Quite simply if you do not know your past you do not understand your present. And of course many themes of the past are of direct relevance today. The neglect of the Heartland Theory in modern political geography in the light of current international tensions is nothing short of criminal. It is not a matter of whether the theory is right or wrong. It is a major component of the world-views of international decision-makers and that makes it real enough for me. I want to survive.

The book is written from a particular viewpoint. I have avoided an approach that reviews and discusses ideas and finishes up sitting on fences after praising the 'best bits' of what are often incompatible theories. My political geography is a world-systems political geography with all that that entails. Ideas are developed in a radical, holistic political-economy framework. Both old and new political geography is reinterpreted in world-systems terms. For instance, capital cities are discussed as core, periphery and semi-periphery political strategies in state management and modern concern for state theory is extended to a theory of *states* since the world-economy by definition has multiple states, not one. I present a definite viewpoint but I hope not an unfair one. I do not use the straw-man technique of debate by setting up a false and simplified view of the ideas of others and then knocking them down. Where I use ideas from other than world-systems work, Stein Rokkan's models for instance, they are only included because I consider them worthy of discussion and criticism. This is how I hope those readers who do not accept my premises will treat this work. It can be used directly as a set of ideas that comprise a political geography to aid teaching or research or it can be used indirectly as a set of ideas against which other ideas can be compared, contrasted and, hopefully, refined or even improved. I have attempted to produce a theoretically respectable political geography which maintains the broad vista and general interest of the best political geographies of the past. I have really enjoyed writing this book. I hope reading it is as enjoyable an experience.

Peter Taylor

November 1983

Chapter 1

A WORLD-SYSTEMS APPROACH TO POLITICAL GEOGRAPHY

WORLD-SYSTEMS ANALYSIS

Historical systems

1. Systems of change
2. Types of change
3. The error of developmentalism

The basic elements of the world-economy

1. A single world market
2. A multiple state system
3. A three-tier structure

DIMENSIONS OF AN HISTORICAL SYSTEM

The dynamics of the world-economy

1. Kondratieff cycles
2. 'Logistic' waves

The spatial structure of the world-economy

1. The geographical extent of the system
2. The concepts of core and periphery
3. The semi-periphery category

A space–time matrix for political geography

POWER AND POLITICS IN THE WORLD-ECONOMY

The nature of power: individuals and institutions

1. Power within households
2. Power between 'peoples'
3. Power and class

The subtlety of power: what is a strong state?

1. Actual and latent force
2. Non-decision making
3. Structural position
4. Power and appearance

A political geography perspective on the world-economy

1. Ideology separating experience from reality
2. World-economy, nation-state and locality

Chapter 1

A WORLD-SYSTEMS APPROACH TO POLITICAL GEOGRAPHY

Cancun is a fashionable holiday resort on Mexico's Yucátan coast. In October 1981 it became the centre of world attention as the venue of a meeting between 'first world' and 'third world' governments. President Reagan led the 'first world' group which included the presidents and prime ministers of all the major 'western' countries. Third World countries were represented by government leaders of seventeen countries from all three 'southern' continents. What transpired at this meeting was referred to as nothing less than 'global negotiations'. Even allowing for journalistic exaggeration, the Cancun meeting is symptomatic of current concern for world-wide perspectives and global thinking. Inkeles (1975: 467) has captured this concern very succinctly:

> The widespread diffusion of this sense of a new, emergent global interrelatedness is expressed in numerous ideas, slogans and catchphrases which have wide currency, such as 'world government', 'the global village', 'spaceship earth', 'the biosphere', and the ubiquitous cartoon of a crowded globe with a light fuse protruding from one end, the whole labelled 'the world population bomb'.

Inkeles sees the 'new sense' as indicating the development of an emerging social structure of the world. His particular approach to studying the global scale is just one of many to emerge in recent years. The Cancun conference itself grew out of pressure resulting from the very influential Brandt Report on North–South differences in material well-being. Other, more radical, researchers have emphasized the existence of a new international division of labour with the industrialization of certain Third World countries. And of course there are the large number of studies of multinational corporations which emphasize the international powers of large private companies. One such study even begins with the assertion that 'The men who run the global corporations are the first in history with the organization, technology, money and ideology to make a credible try at managing the world as an integrated unit' (Barnett and Muller 1974: 13).

World-wide problems and global issues are therefore on the agenda of modern social science. The approach I have chosen to adopt in this study, however, does not emphasize the global uniqueness of the current situation. Present-day global problems and issues are only considered in the light of past processes. For political geographers global concerns are by no means a new theme. The heritage of the various geopolitics and the continuing study of the world political map will make any political geographer wary of the recent 'discovery' of the global scale in both the popular perception and modern social science. Eighty years ago one of the founding fathers of political geography expressed similar global concerns:

> From the present time forth, in the post-Columbian age, we shall again have to deal with a closed political system, and none the less that it will be one of worldwide scope. Every explosion of social forces, instead of being dissipated in a surrounding circuit of unknown space will be sharply re-echoed from the far side of the globe. (Mackinder 1904: 22)

In fact Mackinder was expressing a very common global concern at the turn of the century. Multinational corporation managers may be devising global strategies today but so too were the men who were 'painting the world map pink' in the late nineteenth century to ensure that the sun would never set on the British Empire. There were three rival political ideologies of this period each of which had its own world model. The imperialists adhered to a competitive inter-state viewpoint in which the strong would prosper at the expense of the weak. Such thinking ultimately produced two world wars and twenty-four million battle deaths. Liberals opposed such militarism and suggested an alternative world model of free-trading countries each prospering under its own 'comparative advantage' to produce the goods it exported. They devised international clubs for countries to join and help keep the peace, first the League of Nations and then the United Nations. The socialists were even more explicitly international with their initial emphasis on class rather than country. Their 'Internationals' live on although divided since 1917. Global problems were paramount in many people's minds around the turn of the century at about the time of the emergence of political geography. It is therefore not surprising that political geography has a global heritage. We attempt to maintain this tradition in this study.

We could of course go back further to illustrate earlier 'global concerns'. European colonialism and settlement and the many extra-European wars between European powers before the twentieth century bear witness to the existence of such global conflicts and strategies. In the nineteenth century several European powers were involved in the famous 'Scramble for Africa'. In the eighteenth century Britain and France were fighting on battlefields as far apart as Canada and India. In the seventeenth century the Netherlands were challenging Spain on both sides of the globe in the West and East Indies. And during the sixteenth century Portugal and Spain operated in a global system arranged by Pope Alexander VI and largely confirmed at the Treaty of Tordesillas (1494) in which the non-European world was divided between them along the 47th parallel. Clearly global concerns have a long history.

The question of how far back we trace global concerns is not a trivial one. Any decision on where to start looking for the emergence of the modern world will be based upon a theory, implicit or explicit, about the nature of our modern world. Many studies, such as those briefly referred to at the very beginning of the chapter, involve theoretical frameworks which justify treating the current world situation as distinct from previous situations. In this study we employ Wallerstein's (1979) world-systems approach which provides a much longer temporal perspective. This involves a framework centred upon the capitalist world-economy which emerged in Europe in the period after 1450 and expanded to encompass the whole world by 1900. Both Pope Alexander VI in 1492 and President Reagan at Cancun in 1981 are part of this single story.

Wallerstein's world-systems approach has stimulated a massive literature in recent years. This involves both substantive and theoretical additions to the original ideas and criticisms from a range of alternative perspectives. I do not intend to enter this debate here. In simplest terms my choice of Wallerstein's framework is based on the fact that I have found it to be most useful for ordering and understanding the subject matter of political geography (Taylor 1981a, 1982b). The remaining chapters of this book are an attempt to illustrate this point. The remainder of this chapter describes the world-systems approach and my particular adaptation of it to political geography.

WORLD-SYSTEMS ANALYSIS

World-systems analysis is about how we conceptualize social change. Such changes are usually described in terms of societies that are equated with countries. Hence we talk of 'British society', 'US society', 'Brazilian society', 'Vietnamese society' and so on. Since there are over 150 states in the world today it follows that students of social change will have to deal with over 150 'societies'. This position is accepted by orthodox social science and we may term it the multiple society assumption. World-systems analysis rejects this assumption as a valid starting point for understanding today's world.

Instead of social change occurring country-by-country, Wallerstein postulates a 'world-system' which is currently global in scope. If we accept this 'single society assumption' it follows that the many 'societies as countries' become merely parts of a larger whole. Hence a particular social change in one of these countries can only be fully understood within the wider context that is the world-system. For instance the decline of Britain since the late nineteenth century is not merely a 'British phenomenon', it is part of a wider world-system process which we shall term 'hegemonic decline'. Trying to explain this specific social change by concentrating on Britain alone will only produce a very partial view of the processes that were unfolding at the end of the nineteenth century.

Of course the world-systems approach is not the first venture to challenge orthodox thinking in the social sciences. In fact Wallerstein is consciously attempting to bring together two previous challenges. First he borrows ideas and concepts from the French *Annales* school of history. These historians deplored the excessive detail of early twentieth century history with its emphasis upon political events and especially diplomatic manoeuvres. They argued for a more holistic approach in which the actions of politicians were just one small part in the unfolding history of ordinary people. Different politicians and their diplomacies would come and go but the everyday pattern of life with its economic and environmental material basis continued. The emphasis was therefore on the economic and social roots of history rather than the political facade emphasized in orthodox writings. This approach is perhaps best summarized by Fernand Braudel's phrase *longue durée* which represents the materialist stability underlying political volatility (Wallerstein 1977: 5).

The second challenge which Wallerstein draws upon is the neo-Marxist critique of the development theories of modern social science. The growth of social science after the Second World War coincided with a growth of new states out of the former European colonies. It was the application of modern social science to the problems of these new states which more than anything else exposed its severe limitations. In 1967 Gunder Frank published a cataclysmic critique of social scientific notions of 'modernization' in these new states which showed that ideas developed in the more prosperous parts of the world could not be transferred to poorer areas without wholly distorting the analysis. Frank's main point was that different economic processes operate in different parts of the world. Whereas western Europe and United States may have experienced *development*, most of the remainder of the world experienced the *development of underdevelopment*. This latter phrase encapsulates the main point of this school, namely that for the new states it is not a matter of 'catching up' but rather one of changing the whole process of their development.

The world-systems approach attempts to combine selectively critical elements of Braudel's materialist history with Frank's neo-Marxist development studies, as well as adding several new features, to develop a comprehensive *historical social science*. As Goldfrank (1979) puts it, Wallerstein is explicitly 'bringing history back in' to social science. And, we might add, with the development of Frank's ideas he is also 'bringing geography back in' to social science. Quite simply there is more to understanding the world we live in than can be derived from study of the 'advanced' countries of the world in the late twentieth century, however rigorous or scholarly the conduct of such study is.

HISTORICAL SYSTEMS

Modern social science is the culmination of a tradition that attempts to develop general laws for all times and places. A well-known example of this is the attempt to equate the decline of the British Empire with the decline of the Roman Empire nearly two millenia earlier. Similarly, assumptions are often made that 'human nature' is universal so that motives identified today in 'advanced' countries can be transferred to other periods and cultures. An important example of this is the profit motive in price-fixing markets which is historically limited to modern society. To transfer this motive to past societies is to commit an error which Polanyi (1977) terms the 'economistic fallacy'. The important point is to specify the scope of generalizations. Wallerstein uses the concept of *historical system* to define the limits of his generalizations.

Historical systems are Wallerstein's 'societies'. They are systematic in that they consist of interlocking parts that constitute a single whole but they are also historical in the sense that they are created, develop over a period of time and then reach their demise. Although Wallerstein only recognizes one such system in existence today, there have been innumerable historical systems in the past.

1. Systems of change

Although every historical system is unique, Wallerstein argues that they can be classified into three major types of entity. Such entities are defined by their mode of production, which Wallerstein broadly conceives as the organization of the material basis of a society. This is a much broader concept than the orthodox Marxist definition in that it includes not only the way in which productive tasks are divided up but also decisions concerning the quantities of goods to be produced, their consumption and/or accumulation along with the resulting distribution of goods. Using this broad definition Wallerstein identifies just three basic ways in which the material base of societies has been organized. These three modes of production are each associated with a type of entity or system of change.

A mini-system is the entity based upon the reciprocal-lineage mode of production. This is the original mode of production based upon very limited specialization of tasks. Production is by hunting, gathering or rudimentary agriculture, exchange is reciprocal between producers and the main organizational principle is age and gender. Mini-systems are small extended families or kin-groups which are essentially local in geographical range and exist for just a few generations before destruction or fissure. There have been countless such mini-systems but none has survived to the present, for all have been taken over and incorporated into larger world-systems. By 'world' Wallerstein does not mean 'global' but merely systems larger than the local day-to-day activities of particular members. Two such world-systems are identified by mode of production.

A world-empire is the entity based upon the redistributive-tributary mode of production. World-empires have appeared in many political forms but they all share the same mode of production. This consists of a

large group of agricultural producers whose technology is advanced
enough to generate a surplus of production beyond their immediate needs.
This surplus is sufficient to allow the development of specialized
non-agricultural producers such as artisans and administrators. Whereas
exchange between agricultural producers and artisans is reciprocal the
distinguishing feature of these systems is the appropriation of part of the
surplus to the administrators who form a military- bureaucratic ruling
class. Such tribute is channelled upwards to produce large-scale material
inequality not found in mini- systems. This redistribution may be
maintained in either a unitary political structure such as the Roman
Empire, or a fragmented structure such as feudal Europe. Despite such
political contrasts Wallerstein argues that all such 'civilizations', from the
Bronze Age to the recent past, have the same material basis to their
societies: they are all world- empires. These are less numerous than
mini-systems but nevertheless there have been dozens of such entities
since the Neolithic Revolution.

A world-economy is the entity based upon the capitalist mode of
production. The criterion for production is profitability and the basic drive
of the system is accumulation of the surplus as capital. There is no
overarching political structure so that the basic rule is accumulate or
perish. Competition between different units of production is ultimately
controlled by the cold hand of the market. In this system the efficient
prosper and destroy the less-efficient by undercutting their prices in the
market. This mode of production defines a world-economy.

Historically such entities have been extremely fragile and have been
incorporated and subjugated to world-empires before they could develop
into capital-expanding systems. The great exception is the European
world-economy that emerged after 1450 and survived to take over the
whole world. A key date in its survival is 1557 when both the
Spanish–Austrian Habsburgs and their great rivals the French Valois
dynasty went bankrupt in their attempts to dominate the nascent
world-economy (Wallerstein 1974a: 124). It is entirely appropriate that the
demise of these final attempts to produce a unified European
world-empire should fail not because of military defeat but at the hands of
'international' bankers. Clearly by 1557 the world-economy had truly
arrived and survived its most vulnerable period to become the only
historical example of a fully developing world-economy. As it expanded it
eliminated all remaining mini-systems and world-empires to become truly
global about 1900.

2. Types of change

Now that we have the full array of types of entity within world-systems
analysis we can identify the basic forms that social change can take. It is
worth reiterating the key point that it is these entities that are the objects
of change; they are the 'societies' of this historical social theory. Within

this framework there are four fundamental types of change.

The first two types of change are different means of *transformation* from one mode of production to another. This can occur as an internal process where one system evolves into another. For instance, mini-systems have begat world-empires in certain advantageous circumstances in both the Old and New Worlds. Similarly one world empire, that of feudal Europe, was the predecessor of the capitalist world-economy. We may term this process *transition*: the most famous example is the transition from feudalism to capitalism in Europe in the period after 1450.

Transformation as an external process occurs as *incorporation*. As world-empires expanded they conquered and incorporated former mini-systems. These defeated populations were re-organized to become part of a new mode of production providing tribute to their conquerers. Similarly the expanding world-economy has incorporated mini-systems and world-empires whose populations become part of this new system. All peoples of the continents beyond Europe have experienced this transformation over the last 500 years.

Discontinuities are the third type of change. Discontinuity occurs between different entities at approximately the same location where both entities share the same mode of production. The system breaks down and a new one is constituted in its place. For world-empires the sequence of Chinese states is the classic example. The periods between these separate world-empires are anarchic with some reversal to mini-systems and are commonly referred to as Dark Ages. The most famous is that which occurred in western Europe between the collapse of the Roman Empire and the rise of feudal Europe.

Continuities, the final type of change, occur within systems. Despite the popular image of 'timeless' traditional cultures, all entities are dynamic and continually changing. Such changes are of two basic types — linear and cyclic. All world-empires have displayed a large cyclical pattern of 'rise and fall' as they expanded into mini-systems until bureaucratic- military costs led to diminishing returns resulting in contraction. In the world-economy, linear trends and cycles of growth and stagnation form an integral part of our analysis. They are described in some detail below.

3. The error of developmentalism

We have now clarified the way in which world-systems analysis treats social change. In what follows we will concentrate on one particular system, the capitalist world-economy, whose expansion has eliminated all other systems — hence our 'one society assumption' for studying contemporary social change. The importance of this assumption for our analysis cannot be over-emphasized. It is best illustrated by the error of developmentalism to which orthodox social science is prone.

Modern social science has devised many 'stage models' of development, all of which involve a linear sequence of stages through which societies (=

countries) are expected to travel. The most famous is Rostow's *stages of economic growth* which generalizes British economic history into a ladder of five stages from 'traditional society' at the bottom to 'the age of high mass consumption' at the top. Rostow uses this model to locate different countries on different rungs of his ladder. 'Advanced' countries are at the top whereas most of the new states are on the lower rungs. This way of conceptualizing the world has been very popular in geography where stage models are applied to a wide range of phenomena such as demographic change and transport networks. All assume that the new states can follow a path of development essentially the same as that pursued by the current 'advanced' states. This completely misses out the overall context in which development occurs. When Britain was at the bottom of Rostow's ladder there was no 'high mass consumption' going on at the top.

These developmental models of social change expose the weaknesses of the multiple society assumption. If social change can be adequately understood on a country-by-country basis then the location of other countries on the ladder does not matter: each society is an autonomous object of change moving along the same trajectory but starting at different dates and moving at different speeds. World-systems analysis totally refutes this model of the contemporary world. The fact that some countries are rich and others are poor is not merely a matter of timing along some universal pathway to affluence. Rather rich and poor are part of one system and they are experiencing different processes within that system: Frank's development and development of underdevelopment. Hence the most important fact concerning those countries at the bottom of Rostow's ladder today is that there are countries enjoying the advantage of being above them at the top of the ladder.

Perhaps more than anything else world-systems analysis is a challenge to developmentalism: the simplistic world of an international ladder is superseded by the sophisticated concept of the capitalist world-economy.

THE BASIC ELEMENTS OF THE WORLD-ECONOMY

Now that we have set the study of our world into the overall world-systems framework we can summarize the basic elements of our system which will underlie all our subsequent analyses. Wallerstein identifies three such basic elements.

1. A single world market

The world-economy consists of a single world market which is capitalist. This means that production is for exchange rather than use: producers do not consume what they produce but exchange it on the market for the best price they can get. These products are known as commodities whose value is determined by the market. It is for this reason that the capitalist market is a price-setting institution unlike pre-capitalist markets which are based

upon traditional fixed prices (Polanyi 1977). Since the price of any
commodity is not fixed there is economic competition between producers.
In this competition the more efficient producers can undercut the prices of
other producers to increase their share of the market and to eliminate
rivals. In this way the world-market determines in the long run the
quantity, type and location of production. The concrete result of this
process has been uneven economic development across the world. Since
the Second World War the world-market has been dominated by
multinational corporations.

2. A multiple state system

In contrast to one economic market there has always been a number of
political states in the world-economy. This is part of the definition of the
system since if one state came to control the whole system the
world-market would become politically controlled, competition eliminated
and the system would transform into a world-empire. Hence the
international state system is a necessary element of the world-economy.
Nevertheless single states are able to distort the market in the interests of
their national capitalist group within their own boundaries and powerful
states can distort the market well beyond their boundaries for a short time.
This is the very stuff of 'international politics'. The concrete result of this
process is a competitive state system in which a variety of 'balance of
power' situations may prevail. Since the Second World War the balance of
power has been bi-polar, organized around the United States and the
USSR.

3. A three-tier structure

This third essential element is also 'political' in nature but is more subtle
than the previous one. Wallerstein argues that the exploitative processes
that operate through the world-economy always operate in a three-tiered
format. This is because in any situation of inequality three tiers are more
stable than two tiers of confrontation. Those at the top will always
manoeuvre for the 'creation' of a three-tier structure whereas those at the
bottom will emphasize the two tiers of 'them and us'. The continuing
existence of the world-economy is due in part therefore to the success of
the ruling groups to sustain three-tiered patterns throughout various fields
of conflict. An obvious example is the existence of 'centre' parties between
right and left in many political systems. The most general case is the
promotion of the notion of a 'middle class' between capital and labour. In
other contexts the acceptance of 'middle' ethnic groups such as 'poor
whites' helps ruling groups to maintain stability and control.
Geographically the most interesting example is Wallerstein's concept of
the 'semi-periphery' which separates the extremes of material well-being
in the modern world-economy which Wallerstein terms the core and the
periphery. We define these terms in the next section.

DIMENSIONS OF AN HISTORICAL SYSTEM

If we are bringing history back into political geography the question obviously arises as to 'what history?'. Several recent studies have shared our concern for the neglect of history in geography and have attempted to rectify the situation by presenting brief résumés of world history over the last few hundred years in the opening chapter of their work. The dangers and pitfalls of such writing are obvious: how can such a task be adequately achieved in just a few pages of text? The answer is that we must be highly selective. The selection of episodes to be covered will be directly determined by the purpose of the 'history'. This is nothing new of course; it is true of all history. It is just that the exigencies are so severe for our purpose here.

We are fortunate that our problems has been made manageable by the publication of *The Times Atlas of World History* (Barraclough 1979). Applying Wallerstein's world-systems approach to any subject assumes a level of general historical knowledge which is probably an unreasonable expectation of most students. It is well worth a trip to the library to browse through *The Times Atlas* and obtain a sense of the movement of world history. This is recommended to all readers of this book.

Of course this atlas does not itself employ a world-systems approach. It is divided into seven sections in the following chronological order:

1. The world of early man
2. The first civilizations
3. The classical civilizations of Eurasia
4. The world of divided regions (approximately 600–1500)
5. The world of the emerging west (1500–1800)
6. The age of European dominance (nineteenth century)
7. The age of global civilization (twentieth century)

The product is explicitly global in intent and it avoids the Eurocentric basis of many earlier attempts at world history. Nevertheless it does bear the mark of traditional historiography with its impress of progress from Stone Age to global civilization. Hence Wallerstein's (1980b) conclusion that the *The Times Atlas of World History* represents the culmination of a tradition rather than being a pathbreaker. The seven sectors could be termed Stone Age, Bronze Age, classical Iron Age, Dark Ages, age of exploration, nineteenth-century age of trade and imperialism, and twentieth-century age of global society and world wars, with not too much distortion of the flow of ideas. Wallerstein (1980b) looks forward to a new product in which the waxing and waning of world-empires into and out of zones of mini-systems is gradually replaced after 1450 by the geographical expansion of the capitalist world-economy. That product is not yet available. In the meantime *The Times Atlas* provides an indispensable set of facts catalogued on maps using a traditional model which can be used to bounce world-systems ideas off.

One of the advantages of adopting the world-systems approach is that it enables us to be much more explicit in the theory behind our history. The purpose of this section is to construct just such an historical framework for our political geography which does not simply reflect the weak sense of progress to be found in the other texts referred to at the beginning of this discussion. In place of a linear reconstruction of history we will emphasize the ups and downs of the world-economy. Furthermore the different parts of the world-economy will be affected differentially by these movements. The way we will present these ideas is as a space–time matrix of the world-economy. This is an extremely poor relation to *The Times Atlas* but it does provide a succinct description of the major events relevant to our political geography.

The matrix we generate is not an arbitrary, artificial creation. We are trying to describe the concrete historical entity of the world-economy. Both dimensions of the matrix are calibrated in terms of the system properties of the world-economy. Neither space nor time is treated as in any sense separate from the world-economy. They are *not* space–time containers through which the world-economy 'travels'. Rather they are both interpreted as the product of social relations. The time dimension is described as a social product of the *dynamics* of the world-economy. The space dimension is described as a social product of the *structure* of the world-economy. Our space–time matrix is a simple model which combines the dynamics and structure to provide a framework for political geography.

THE DYNAMICS OF THE WORLD-ECONOMY

One reason for current interest in the global scale of analysis is the fact that the whole world seems to be suffering from an economic recession. It is clear that it is not an American problem or a British problem or the problem of any single state; rather it is a world problem. Furthermore it seems that this is not the first time the 'world' has experienced such a general recession. About fifty years ago similar problems occurred in the Great Depression. As we go back in time such events are less clear but economic historians also identify economic recessions in the late Victorian era and before 1850 — the famous 'hungry forties'. Between each recession there was recovery and growth, the most recent example being the world-wide post-Second World War boom. It is but a short step from these simple observations to the idea that the world-economy has developed in a cyclical manner. The first person to propose such a scheme was a Russian economist, Kondratieff, and today such fifty-year cycles are named after him.

1. Kondratieff cycles

Kondratieff cycles consist of two phases, one of growth (A) and one of stagnation (B). It is generally agreed that the following four cycles have occurred (exact dates vary):

```
  I  1780/90 _____ A _____ 1810/17 _____ B _____ 1844/51
 II  1844/51 _____ A _____ 1870/75 _____ B _____ 1890/96
III  1890/96 _____ A _____1914/20 _____ B _____ 1940/45
 IV  1940/45 _____ A _____ 1967/73 _____ B _____ ?
```

These cycles have been identified in time-series data for a wide range of economic phenomena including industrial and agricultural production and trade statistics for many countries. On this interpretation we are currently experiencing the B-phase of the fourth Kondratieff cycle.

Whereas identification of these cycles is widely agreed the actual causes of their existence are more problematic. They are certainly associated with technological change and the Λ-phases can be easily related to major periods of the adoption of technological innovations. The first A-phase coincides with the original 'industrial revolution' with its steam engines, cotton industry and wrought iron. Subsequent 'new industrial revolutions' also fit the pattern well, consisting of railways and steel (IIA), chemicals (oil) and electricity (IIIA), and aerospace and electronics (IVA). Of course technology itself cannot explain anything. Why did these technical adoptions occur as 'bundles' of innovations and not on a more regular, linear basis? Wallerstein's answer is that cyclical behaviour is inherent in the capitalist mode of production. Contradictions in the organization of the material base mean that linear growth is impossible and intermittent phases of stagnation are necessary. Let us briefly consider this argument.

A basic feature of the capitalist mode of production is the lack of any central control, political or otherwise. The market relies on competition to order the system an competition implies multiple decentralized decision making. Such entrepreneurs make decisions for their own short-term advantage. In good times, A-phases, it is in the interest of all entrepreneurs to invest in production (new technology) since profits are good. With no central planning of investment, however, such short-term decision making will inevitably lead to over-production and the cessation of the A-phase. Conversely in B-phases profits are poor and there will be under-investment in production. This is rational for each individual entrepreneur but it is irrational for the system as a whole. This contradiction is usually referred to as the *anarchy of production* and will produce cycles of investment. After extracting all the surplus value out of a particular set of production processes based on one bundle of technology in an A-phase, the B-phase becomes necessary to reorganize production to generate new conditions for expansion based on a new bundle of technological innovations. Hence the ups and downs of the world-economy as described by the Kondratieff waves.

There is a lot more that could be said about the generation of these cycles, not least the political inputs into the process. These will be the subject-matter of the next chapter and for the time being it is sufficient for us to accept that the nature of the world-economy produces cyclical growth which has been adequately described by Kondratieff waves. This will provide the main part of the metric for the time dimension for our matrix.

2. 'Logistic' waves

What about before 1780? We have indicated that the world-economy emerged after 1450 but we have as yet no metric for this early period. Of course as we go back in time data sources become less plentiful and less reliable, leading to much less consensus on the dynamics of the early world-economy. Some researchers, including Braudel, claim to have found Kondratieff waves before 1780 but such hypotheses for this earlier period do not command the same general support as the sequence reported above. There is, however, more support for longer waves of up to three hundred years which have been referred to as 'logistics'. Just like Kondratieff waves these longer cycles have A- and B- phases. Two logistics of particular interest to world-systems analysis are as follows:

c. 1050 ———— A ———— *c.* 1250 ———— B ———— *c.* 1450
c. 1450 ———— A ———— *c.* 1600 ———— B ———— *c.* 1750

The dates are much less certain than for the Kondratieff waves but there does seem to be enough evidence in terms of land-use and demographic data to support the idea of two very long waves over this general time span.

It will have been noticed that these logistics take us back beyond the beginning of the world-economy. The first logistic is of interest, however, because it encompasses the material rise and decline of feudal Europe, the immediate predecessor of the world-economy. There is a massive literature on the transformation from this feudalism to the capitalist mode of production which is beyond the scope of this text. Wallerstein's (1974a) explanation, however, is relevant since it relates to this first logistic wave and the emergence of the world-economy. The B-phase of the first logistic reflects a real decline in production as indexed by the contraction of agriculture throughout Europe. This is the so-called crisis of feudalism. B-phases terminate when a solution to a crisis is generated. In this case the solution was nothing less than the development of a new mode of production. This emerged gradually out of European exploration and plunder in the Americas, the development of new trade patterns, particularly the Baltic trade, and technological advances in agricultural production. The result was, according to Wallerstein, a new entity or system — the European world-economy based upon agricultural capitalism. This system itself generates a logistic wave of expansion in its emergence in the 'long sixteenth century' followed by stagnation in the 'crisis' of the seventeenth century. However, Wallerstein emphasizes the fact that this second B-phase in agricultural capitalism is different in kind from the B-phase of late feudalism. Unlike the real decline that occurred in feudal Europe, the world-economy B-phase is more one of stagnation. This involved the reordering of the materialist base so that some groups and areas gained while others lost. There was no general decline like the crisis of feudalism but rather a consolidation of the system into a new pattern. In this sense the second logistic B-phase is more like the B-phase of the later Kondratieff waves.

Just as there is a dispute over whether Kondratieff waves extend back before 1780 there is a similar disagreement about whether logistic waves can be extended forward to the present. If either set of cycles is extended then we come across the thorny problem of how they relate to one another. For the purposes of our matrix we will avoid this problem by just using the waves generally accepted in the literature and described above. Our time metric for the world-economy therefore consists of ten units, A- and B- phase for the logistic wave after *c.*1450 and four A- and B-phases in the Kondratieff waves. These two different treatments of time may be thought of as relating to agricultural capitalism and industrial capitalism as consecutive production forms of the world-economy.

THE SPATIAL STRUCTURE OF THE WORLD-ECONOMY

I have dealt with the dynamic property of the world-economy first because the term 'spatial structure' usually conjures up a static picture of an unchanging pattern. The spatial structure we are dealing with here is part and parcel of the same processes that generate the cycles described above. Spatial structure and temporal cycle are two sides of the same mechanisms which produce a single space—time framework. Space and time are separated here for pedagogic reasons so that in what follows it must always be remembered that the spatial structures we describe are essentially dynamic.

1. The geographical extent of the system

Our first task is to consider the geographical expansion of the world-economy. We have mentioned that it emerged as a European world-economy after 1450 and covered the globe by about 1900 but have not indicated how this varying size is defined. Basically all entities are defined in concrete terms by the geographical extent of their division of labour. This is the division of the productive and other tasks which are necessary for the operation of the system. Hence some distribution and trade are a necessary element of the system whereas other trade is merely ephemeral and has little relevance beyond those directly participating in it. For instance, luxury trade between the Roman and Chinese Empires was ephemeral and we would not suggest they be combined to form a single 'Eurasian' system because of this trade. In Wallerstein's terminology China is part of Rome's external arena and vice versa.

Using these criteria Wallerstein delimits the initial European world-system as consisting of western Europe, eastern Europe and those parts of South and Middle America under Iberian control. The rest of the world was an external arena. This included the ring of Portuguese ports around the Indian and Pacific Oceans which were concerned with trade in luxury goods. The development of this Portuguese trade had minimal effects in Asia (they merely replaced Arab and other traders) and in Europe. In contrast Spanish activity in America — especially bullion exports — was fundamentally important in forming the world-economy. For Wallerstein, therefore, Spain was much more important than Portugal in the origins of the world-economy despite the latter's more global pattern of possessions.

From this period on the European world-economy expanded by incorporating the remainder of the world roughly in the order Caribbean, North America, India, East Asia, Australia, Africa and finally the Pacific Islands. These incorporations took several forms. The simplest was plunder. This could only be a short-term process to be supplemented by more productive activities involving new settlement. This sequence occurred in Latin America. Elsewhere aboriginal systems were also destroyed and completely new economies built as in North America and Australia. Alternatively, existing societies remained intact but they were *peripheralized* in the sense that their economies were reorientated to serve wider needs within the world-economy. This could be achieved through political control as in India or directly through 'opening up' an area to market forces as in China. The end result of these various incorporation procedures was the eventual elimination of the external arena.

2. The concepts of core and periphery

The concept of peripheralization implies that these new areas did not join the world-economy as 'equal partners' with existing members but that they joined on unfavourable terms. They were, in fact, joining a particular part of the world-economy which we term the periphery. It is now commonplace to define the modern world in terms of core (meaning the rich countries of North America, Western Europe and Japan) and periphery (meaning the poor countries of the Third World). Although the 'rise' of Japan to core status has been quite dramatic in this century, this core—periphery pattern is often treated as a static, almost natural, phenomenon. The world-economy use of the terms core and periphery is entirely different. Both refer to complex processes and *not* directly to areas, regions or states. The latter only become core-like because of a predominance of core *processes* operating in that particular area, region or state. Similarly peripheral areas, regions or states are defined as those where peripheral *processes* dominate. This is not a trivial semantic point but directly relates to the way in which the spatial structure is modelled. Space itself can be neither core nor periphery in nature. Rather there are core and periphery processes which structure space so that at any point in time one or other of the two processes predominates. Since these processes do not act randomly but generate uneven economic development, broad zones of 'core' and 'periphery' are found. Such zones exhibit some stability — parts of Europe have always been in the core — but also show dramatic changes over the lifetime of the world-economy notably in the rise of non-European areas, first the USA and then Japan.

How does Wallerstein define these two basic processes? Like all core—periphery models there is an implication that 'the core exploits and the periphery is exploited'. But this cannot occur as zones exploiting one another; it occurs through the different processes operating in different zones. Core and periphery processes are opposite types of complex production relations. In simple terms, core processes consist of relations that incorporate *relatively* high wages, advanced technology and a diversified production mix whereas periphery processes involve low wages, more rudimentary technology and a simple production mix. These are general characteristics, the exact nature of which changes constantly with the evolution of the world-economy. It is important to understand that these processes are not determined by the particular product being produced. Frank (1978) provides two good examples to illustrate this. In the late nineteenth century India was organized to provide Lancashire with cotton and Australia to provide Yorkshire with wool. Both were producing raw materials for Britain's textile industry so that their economic function within the world-economy was broadly similar. Nevertheless the social relations embodied in these two productions were very different with one being an imposed peripheral process and the other a transplanted core process. The outcomes for these two countries have clearly depended on these social relations and not the particular type of product. Frank's other example of similar products leading to contrasting outcomes due to production relations is the contrast between the tropical hardwood production of central Africa and the softwood production of North America and Scandinavia. The former combines expensive wood and cheap labour, the latter cheap wood and expensive labour.

3. The semi-periphery category

Core and periphery do not exhaust Wallerstein's concepts for structuring space. Although these processes occur in distinctive zones to produce relatively clear-cut contrasts across the world-economy not all zones are easily designated as primarily core or periphery in nature. One of the most original elements of Wallerstein's approach is his concept of the semi-periphery. This is neither core nor periphery but combines particular mixtures of both processes. Notice there are *no* semi-peripheral processes. Rather the term 'semi-periphery' can be directly applied to zones, areas or states when they exhibit neither a predominance of core nor peripheral processes. This means that the overall social relations operating in such zones involve exploiting peripheral areas while the semi-periphery itself suffers exploitation by the core.

The semi-periphery is interesting because it is the dynamic category within the world-economy. The restructuring of space during recessions involves zones rising and sinking through the semi-periphery. Opportunities for change occur during recessions but these are only limited opportunities — not all the semi-periphery can evolve to become core. Political processes are very important here in the selection of success and failure in the world-economy. Wallerstein actually considers the semi-periphery's role to be more political than economic. It is the crucial middle zone in the spatial manifestation of his three-tiered characterization of the world-economy. For this reason it will figure prominently in much of our subsequent discussions.

A SPACE–TIME MATRIX FOR POLITICAL GEOGRAPHY

The above discussion produces a 10 × 3 matrix involving ten phases of growth and stagnation and three types of spatial zone. In Table 1.1 this framework is used to portray those features of the evolving world-economy that are necessary for understanding our political geography. This table should be read and referred to as necessary for subsequent chapters. It is largely self-explanatory but a brief commentary will illustrate the ways in which this information will be related to our discussion.

The establishment of the world-economy as a system operating from eastern Europe to the New World involved the development of both Atlantic trade and the Baltic trade. The former was initiated from Iberia but gradually came to be financially controlled from the incipient core of north-west Europe on which the Baltic trade was based. Once this core becomes established Iberia is relegated to a 'conveyor belt' for the transfer of surplus from its colonies to the core. It is during the logistic B-phase that the basic elements of the world-economy identified above become consolidated. First, there is a single world-market organized and controlled from north-west Europe. Second, a multiple state system emerges epitomized by the initiation of 'international law' to regulate relations between states. Third, a three-tiered spatial structure clearly emerges and can be identified in the new division of labour for agricultural production: 'free' wage labour developing in the north-west European core; partially free 'sharecropping' arrangements in the Mediterranean semi-periphery and, in the periphery, two different forms of coerced labour — slavery in the New World and the so-called 'second feudalism' in eastern Europe. Despite massive changes in the world-economy since this time these three essential features have remained and are just as important today as they were in the seventeenth century.

Following the consolidation of the world-economy it has grown economically and geographically in fits and starts as described by the four Kondratieff waves. Some degree of symmetry in these changes can be identified from Table 1.1 by designating British and American 'centuries'. These relate to the rise of these two states, defeat of their rivals (France and Germany respectively), their dominance of the world-economy (including their promotion of free trade) and finally their decline with new rivalries emerging (including the rise of protectionism and/or imperialism). We consider such patterns in some detail in the next chapter.

In order to illustrate the rest of the matrix let us highlight the route of today's major states through this matrix. Britain became part of the core by the time of the logistic B-phase when it restructured its state in the civil war. It has maintained that position despite relative decline since the second Kondratieff B-phase. France's early position is similar to Britain's but defeat in the periphery and relative decline in the logistic B-phase led to a restructuring of the French state in the revolution. However, subsequent defeat in the core of the first Kondratieff wave led to a second relative decline but this time within the core. The United States and Germany (Prussia) have had much more volatile histories. Both carved out semi-peripheral positions in the logistic B-phase but their positions were unstable. In the United States peripheralization was prevented by the War of Independence. This victory was consolidated by the civil war in the second Kondratieff A-phase when southern cotton became part of an American periphery (rather than part of a British periphery) in a restructured American state. From this point onwards the United States prospered to become the major power of the twentieth century. Initially its major rival was Germany, which also restructured its state in the second Kondratieff A-phase under Prussian leadership. But subsequent economic prowess was set back in the third Kondratieff wave by military defeat. Today Germany is again a major economic challenger of the United States in the core. The major economic challenger is Japan which only entered the world-economy in the second Kondratieff wave. It also restructured its state, suffered military setbacks but has now finally come through towards economic leadership. Russia, on the other hand, entered the world-economy earlier but declined in the second Kondratieff wave. This was halted by a reorganization of the Russian state as the USSR, which has emerged as a major military power but remains economically semi-peripheral. Finally China entered the world-economy in the periphery at the end of the first Kondratieff wave and has attempted to rise to semi-peripheral status with reorganizations of the state in the third and fourth Kondratieff A-phases. Reorganization as the People's Republic of China has been successful.

This description emphasizes the role of state reorganization in the rise

Table 1.1   A space–time information matrix

		Core
Logistic Curve	A	Initial geographical expansion based on Iberia but economic advances based on north-west Europe.
	B	Consolidation of north-west European dominance, first Dutch and then French–English rivalry
Kondratieff Wave I	A	Industrial revolution in Britain, 'national' revolution in France. Defeat of France
	B	Consolidation of British economic leadership. Origins of socialism in Britain and France
Kondratieff Wave II	A	Britain as the 'workshop of the world' in an era of free trade
	B	Decline of Britain relative to USA and Germany. Emergence of the Socialist Second International
Kondratieff Wave III	A	Consolidation of German and USA economic leadership. Arms race
	B	Defeat of Germany, British Empire saved. USA economic leadership confirmed
Kondratieff Wave IV	A	USA as the greatest power in the world both military and economically. New era of free trade
	B	Decline of USA relative to Europe and Japan. Nuclear arms race

of these states. But we should not imply that a state merely needs to reorder its political apparatus to enjoy world-economy success. By only describing the success stories — today's major states — we omit the far greater number of failures: while Germany and the United States were reorganizing in the second Kondratieff A-phase so too was the Ottoman Empire, but to much less effect. In fact political reorganization has become a way of life in many semi-peripheral states as lack of success in the world-economy brings forth pressure for change again and again. We are now ready to consider power and politics in the world-economy.

POWER AND POLITICS IN THE WORLD-ECONOMY

One common criticism of Wallerstein's approach is that it neglects the political dimension. Zolberg (1981), for instance, claims that politics is the 'missing link' in the world-systems approach. By now the reader should be

Semi-periphery	Periphery
Relative decline of cities of central and Mediterranean Europe	Iberian empires in 'New World' second 'feudalism' in eastern Europe
Declining areas now include Iberia and joined by rising groups in Sweden, Prussia and north-east USA	Retrenchment in Latin America and East Europe. Rise of Caribbean sugar. French defeat in India and Canada
Relative decline of whole semi-periphery. Establishment of USA	Decolonization and expansion — formal control in India but informal controls in Latin America
Beginning of selective rise in North America and central Europe	Expansion of British influence in Latin America. Initial opening up of East Asia
Reorganization of semi-periphery: civil war in USA, unification of Germany and Italy, entry of Russia	The classic era of 'informal imperialism' with growth of Latin America
Decline of Russia and Mediterranean Europe	Expansion — scramble for Africa. The classical age of imperialism
Entry of Japan and Dominion states	Consolidation of new colonies (Africa) plus growth in trade elsewhere (especially China)
Socialist victory in Russia — establishment of USSR. Entry of Argentina	Neglect of periphery. Beginning of peripheral revolts. Import-substitution in Latin America
Rise of eastern Europe and 'cold war'. Entry of OPEC	Socialist victory in China. Decolonization leading this time to 'neo-colonialism'
Entry of 'Little Japans' in East Asia and new regional powers — China, Brazil, Mexico, India. Rise of debts to core	Severe economic crisis and conflict. Expansion of poverty

aware that such criticisms represent a misunderstanding of the framework we have adopted. Quite simply an emphasis upon the materialist base of society as defined by a mode of production does not necessarily mean that politics is ignored or devalued. In the section on basic elements of the world-economy above, two of the three characteristics described were pre-eminently political in nature — the multi-state system and the three-tier structure. It is the purpose of this final section of our introductory chapter to develop the argument concerning politics in the world-economy in order to derive our political geography perspective on the world-economy.

The position we take in interpreting political events in the world-economy is based upon the analysis of Chase-Dunn (1981, 1982). As we have seen, the capitalist mode of production involves the extraction of economic surplus for accumulation within the world-economy. This surplus is expropriated in two related ways. The distinguishing feature of our system is the expropriation via the market. But the traditional expropriation method of world-empires is not entirely eliminated. The use of political and military power to obtain surplus is the second method of expropriation. Of course this second method cannot dominate the system or else the system would be transformed into a new mode of production. But neither should it be undervalued as a process in the world-economy from the initial Spanish plunder of the New World to today's support of multinational, corporate interests by the 'home' country, usually the United States. The important point is that these two methods of expropriation should not be interpreted as two separate processes — or 'two logics' as Chase-Dunn (1981) terms them — one 'political' and the other 'economic'. In our framework they are but two aspects of the same overall political-economy logic. Chase-Dunn (1982: 25) puts the argument as follows:

> The interdependence of political military power and competitive advantage in production in the capitalist world-economy reveals that the logic of the accumulation process *includes* the logic of state building and geopolitics.

Political processes lie at the heart of world-systems analysis but they are not located there separately in isolation.

The argument so far has equated politics with activities surrounding states. While state-centred politics are crucial for understanding the world-economy, they do not constitute the sum of political activities. If we equate politics with use of power then we soon appreciate that political processes do not begin and end with states: all social institutions have their politics.

THE NATURE OF POWER: INDIVIDUALS AND INSTITUTIONS

We can begin by considering power at its most simple level. Consider two individuals A and B who are in conflict over the future outcome of an event. Let us suppose that A's interests are served by outcome X and B's by outcome Y. Then simply by observing which outcome occurs we would infer the power ranking of A and B. For instance, if X occurs we can assert that A is more powerful than B. When we inquire why A was able to defeat B we would expect to find that in some sense A possessed more resources than B. If this were a schoolyard quarrel we might find that A packed the harder punch.

This model provides us with an elementary feel for the nature of power but only that. The world of politics does not consist of millions and millions of conflicts between unequal pairs of individuals. Potential losers have never been naive enough to let such a world evolve. Let us return to our simple example to show how we can move beyond pairwise conflict. Consider conflict occurring in a schoolyard again. The two fighters will inevitably attract a crowd. B, as we have seen, is losing. What should she or he do? The answer is simple — before defeat occurs she or he must widen the scope of the conflict by inviting the crowd to participate. By changing the scope of the conflict B is changing the balance of power. If

B's gang is stronger than A's then it is now in the interests of the latter to widen the scope further — say bring in the school authorities to stamp out gang warfare.

This model of power resolution is derived from Schattschneider (1960), who argues generally that the outcome of any conflict will *not* depend on the relative power of the competing interests but will be determined by the eventual scope of the conflict. Hence it follows that the most important strategy in politics is to define the scope of any conflict. Furthermore since every increase in scope changes the balance of power, weaker interests will inevitably be pushing to widen the scope of their conflicts. Historically this has been illustrated by two opposing political strategies: on the left, collectivist politics are preached; on the right, a much more individualistic approach is favoured. Two important political conflicts of the last century show how this has operated in practice (Taylor 1984). First the extension of electoral suffrage has gradually increased the scope of national politics, culminating in universal suffrage. This has, of course, changed the policies of parties and the practices of governments as politicians have had to respond to the needs of their new clients. Second the rise of trade unions is an explicit means of widening the scope of industrial conflicts. This basic ideology of worker unionism has always been resisted by employers by trying to keep disputes 'local', originally by having trade unions outlawed and subsequently by legal constraints on the scope of their activities. The history of both democratic politics and trade unionism is at heart a matter of changing the scope of conflicts.

The corollary of Schattschneider's ideas is that this 'politics from below' will eventually extend conflicts to a global scale. Such 'internationalism' has a hallowed place in left wing politics and traces its origins to Marx's call in 1848, 'Workers of all countries unite, you have nothing to lose but your chains'. Even today it is noticeable that it is the poorer countries of the world that make most use of the United Nations. But all such internationalism has either come to nothing or is relatively ineffectual. The scope of most politics is decidedly not global. This is because there is a vast array of institutions that have been created between the individual and the ultimate scope of politics at the global scale. The main theme of this book is about understanding how the scope of conflicts has been limited. What are the key institutions in this process?

Out of the multitude of institutions that exist Wallerstein (1984) identifies four that are crucial to the operation of the world-economy. First there are the *states* where formal power in the world-economy lies. States are responsible for the laws that define the practices of all other institutions. We have previously described the importance of this institution and much of the remainder of this book will be devoted to developing themes concerning the power of states.

Second there are the '*peoples*', groupings of individuals that have cultural affinities. There is no single acceptable name for this category of institution. Where a cultural group controls a state they may be defined as

a nation. Where they constitute a minority within a state they are
sometimes referred to literally as 'minorities' or as ethnic groups. Of
course such minorities may aspire to be a nation with its own state, such
as the Tamils in Sri Lanka or the Basques in Spain. To complicate matters
there are some multi-state nations such as the Arab nation. Despite the
complexity of this category of institution the importance of 'peoples'
cannot be doubted in the modern world.

The third category of institution is perhaps less complex but no less
controversial than 'peoples'. The world's population can be divided into
strata based upon economic criteria which we will term *classes*. Wallerstein
follows Marxist practice here and defines classes in terms of location
within the mode of production. Since the latter is currently global it
follows that in world-systems analysis classes are defined in global terms.

At the other end of the scale are the *households*, Wallerstein's fourth key
institution. These are defined not by kin or cohabitation but in terms of
the pooling of income. They are, therefore, small groups of individuals
that come together to face an often hostile world. The basic behaviour of
such a group is the operation of a budget that combines resources and
allocates expenditure. Wallerstein considers such households to be the
'atoms' of his system, the basic building block of the other institutions.
Hence everybody is first of all a member of a household; that household is
liable to the laws of a particular state; will have cultural affinities with a
certain 'people' and will be economically located within a specific class.

Wallerstein (1984) considers these four institutions, as he defines them,
to be unique to the capitalist world-economy. They interact one upon
another in very many ways forever creating and recreating the temporal
and spatial patterns described in the last section. Households are
important, for instance, in maintaining the cultural definitions of peoples,
while 'peoples' fundamentally influence both the boundaries of states and
the nature of class conflicts. This is Wallerstein's 'institutional vortex' that
underlies the whole operation of our modern world-system.

Institutions both facilitate and constrain the behaviour of individuals by
laws, rules, customs and norms. What is and what is not possible will vary
with the power of particular institutions. For each category of institution
the distribution of power will vary both within and between institutions.
For instance we can ask both who controls a particular state and what the
power of that state is within the inter-state system. In this way we can
identify hierarchies of power within and between all four institutions. We
illustrate this below by concentrating on particular aspects of informal
power distributions, leaving the critical case of formal power and the state
to the next section.

1. Power within households

Income pooling may be reduced to daily, weekly or monthly budgets but it entails a continuity that is generational in nature. Households are frequently changing as some members die and others are born, but they typically show a constancy that allows for the reproduction cycle: it is within households that the next generation is reared. This assumes a pattern of gender relations within households. In the capitalist world-economy the particular form that gender relations take is known as *patriarchy*, the domination of women by men.

The notion of income pooling does not, of course, assure equality of access to the resources of a household. The arrangement of work in many different kinds of households across the world provides men with the access to cash and therefore markets, leaving women with 'domestic chores'. In core countries this has generally led to a devaluing of many women's contribution to the household as 'merely housework'. In peripheral countries this has often led to the devaluing of food production as 'women's work' relative to male-controlled cash crop production.

This constitutes a very good example of how the scope of a politics has sustained a particular hierarchy of power. In the case of households we are entering the private world of the family: what goes on between 'man and wife' is not in the public realm. This narrow scope can lead to condoning, or at least ignoring, the most naked form of power — physical violence. 'Outsiders', both public officials and neighbours, have been loath to interfere even in the most extreme cases. To the degree that women are confined to the private world of the family they are condemned to political impotence. There are no trade unions for either housewives or food crop producers.

The patriarchy found within households permeates throughout all levels of the world-economy. Where women do enter wage work they typically get paid less and are less well represented as we move to higher levels of any occupational ladder. This endemic sexism is most clearly illustrated in politics where male politicians dominate the legislatures of all states (Table 1.2). Women are under-represented in all legislatures throughout the world. Nevertheless they are better represented in some countries than others, notably the Scandinavian liberal democracies and some communist states. Women continue to be poorly represented in the major liberal democracies (USA, UK, France, Japan) and the USSR. This is gender inequality even more marked in the executive branch of government in all types of regime — liberal democracies, communist states, military dictatorships, traditional monarchies and so on. The Mrs Gandhis and Mrs Thatchers of this world are conspicuous because of their rarity value.

2. Power between 'peoples'

'Peoples' reflect the diversity within humanity that has always existed. In the world-economy this human variety has been used to create specific sets of 'peoples' to justify material and political inequalities. Three types

Table 1.2 Percentage of women members in fifty-two legislatures, *c.* 1980

Sweden	28%	Canada	4%
Guinea	27	France	4
		New Zealand	4
Finland	26	Syria	4
E. Germany	25	Tunisia	4
		USA	4
Norway	24	Algeria	3
Italy	16	Columbia	3
		El Salvador	3
Albania	15	USSR	3
Czechoslovakia	15	UK	3
Netherlands	14	Argentina	2
Hungary	12	Egypt	2
		Guatemala	2
Switzerland	11	Japan	2
Austria	10	Sri Lanka	2
Belgium	10		
Bulgaria	10	Brazil	1
China	10	Iran	1
Portugal	10	Australia	0
Cuba	9	Lebanon	0
W. Germany	9	Panama	0
Romania	9		
Mexico	8		
Poland	8		
Ireland	7		
Israel	7		
Paraguay	7		
Denmark	6		
Costa Rica	5		
Iceland	5		
India	5		
Luxembourg	5		
Spain	5		
Sudan	5		

Derived from Randall (1982).

of 'people' have been produced — races, nations and ethnic groups — and each relates to one basic feature of the world-economy.

Race is a product of the expansion of the modern world-system. With the incorporation of non-European zones into the world-economy the non-European peoples that survived were added to the periphery. In this way race came to be directly expressed in the division of labour as a white core and a non-white periphery. The South African government recognizes this power hierarchy today when they designate visiting Japanese businessmen as 'honorary whites'. More generally the ideology of racism has legitimated world-wide inequalities throughout the history of the world-economy.

'Nation' as a concept rose to express competition between states. It legitimates the whole political superstructure of the world-economy that is the inter-state system: every state aspires to be a 'nation-state'. By justifying the political fragmentation of the world, nations play a key role in perpetuating inequalities between countries. The associated ideology, nationalism, has been the most powerful political force in the twentieth century with millions of young people willingly sacrificing their lives for their country and its people.

Ethnic groups are always a minority within a country. All multi-ethnic states contain a hierarchy of groups with different occupations associated with different groups. Where the ethnic groups are immigrants this 'ethnization' of occupations legitimizes the practical inequalities within the state. In contrast the inequalities suffered by non-immigrant ethnic groups can produce an alternative minority nationalism to challenge the state.

The concept of 'peoples' covers a difficult and complex mixture of cultural phenomena. We have only scratched at the surface of this complexity here. Nevertheless it has been shown that peoples are implicated in hierarchies of power from the global scale to the neighbourhood. They remain key institutions for the legitimization of inequalities.

3. Power and class

All analyses of power and class start with Marx. At the heart of his analysis of capitalism there is a fundamental conflict between capital and labour. In class terms the *bourgeoisie* own the means of production and buy the labour power of the *proletariate*. In this way the whole production process is controlled by the former at the expense of the latter. Hence this power hierarchy and the resulting class conflict are central to all Marxist political analyses.

Wallerstein accepts the centrality of class conflict in his capitalist world-economy. However since his definition of mode of production is broader than Marx's, it follows that Wallerstein's identification of classes diverges from that of orthodox Marxism. For instance Wallerstein's strata of labour are termed *direct producers* and include all who are immediate creators of commodities — both wage-earners *and* non-wage producers. Hence the proletariate wage-earners are joined by peasant producers, share-croppers and many other exploited forms of labour including the female and child labour often hidden within households.

On the other side of the class conflict are the *controllers* of production who may or may not be 'capitalists' as owners of capital in the original Marxist sense. For instance the typical form of capital in the late twentieth century is the multinational corporation. The executive élite who control

these corporations need not be major shareholders and certainly their
power within the organization does not depend on their shareholding.
Although formally employees of the corporations it would be disingenuous
not to recognize the very real power that this group of people command.
They combine with another group of controllers, senior state officials, who
also command large amounts of capital, to produce the 'new bourgeoisie'
of the twentieth century.

Marx recognized the existence of a middle class between proletariate
and bourgeoisie but predicted that this intermediate class would decline in
size and importance as the fundamental conflict between capital and
labour developed. In fact this has not happened in the core countries of
the world-economy. Instead we have had the 'rise of the middle classes' as
white collar occupations have grown and have numerically overtaken
blue-collar workers. This large intermediate stratum combines a wide range
of occupations with seemingly little connection. Wallerstein interprets
these occupations as the *cadres* of the world-economy. As capitalist
production and organization have become more complex there has arisen
an increasing need for cadres to run the system and make sure it operates
as smoothly as possible. Originally such cadres merely supervised the
direct producers on behalf of the capitalist controllers. Today there is a
vast array of occupations that are required for the smooth running of the
system. These include the older professions such as lawyers and
accountants, and many new positions such as middle managers within
corporations and bureaucrats within state organizations. The end result is
a massive middle stratum of cadres between controllers and direct
producers. This is a classic example of one of Wallerstein's three-tier
structures facilitating the stability of the world-economy.

Finally we need to show how classes relate to states. We have already
noted that since classes are defined in terms of mode of production it
follows that in world-systems analysis today they are global in scope. We
shall term these *objective* classes since they are derived logically from the
analysis. In terms of political practice, however, classes have been most
commonly defined on a state-by-state basis. These *subjective* classes are
parts of our larger objective classes. But not all classes have been equally
national in scope. While the proletariate have had the internationalist
rhetoric, it is the capitalists and the controllers who have been the more
effective international actors — their subjective class actions have always
been much closer to their objective class interests. At the present time this
is demonstrated by the flexibility of multinational corporations in moving
around their production units to reduce labour costs. The direct producers
have no organized strategy to combat the controllers' ability to create new
geographical divisions of labour. Power differentials are particularly acute
in this example and are basic to our political geography.

THE SUBTLETY OF POWER. WHAT IS A STRONG STATE?

Our discussion of power thus far has been based upon the simple
assumption that outcomes will reflect a power hierarchy which, in turn,
indicates the differential resources available to combatants. By changing
the scope of a conflict we alter the power hierarchy. But what if the power
hierarchy is not in fact a sure predictor of success or failure? Some recent
conflicts between states indicate that this is indeed the case. Quite simply
the nature of power is much subtler than we have so far supposed.

   The measurement of the relative power of states has been a perennial
problem in political geography. It is a problem because 'power' is one of
those concepts which cannot be directly measured. The usual solution has
been to identify some salient characteristics of states which are then
combined to produce an index of power for each state. A simple example
is Fuck's index where power is computed by cubing a country's gross
national product and then multiplying the cube by the square root of its
population (Muir 1981: 149). The result provides an intuitively reasonable
measure of power but it is hardly satisfactory. Why use just production
and population variables? Why combine them in this specific manner?
Such questions cannot be answered without explicit recourse to the theory
behind the measurement. We have to go back to the question — what
makes a particular characteristic salient to this measurement problem?

   Most studies of state power have been inductive in nature, to the severe
neglect of theory. The theory implicit in this work is usually some notion
of war potential. But the defeat of the 'super-power' United States by the
'medium-power' of Vietnam has required a complete rethink. Even more
intriguing has been the recent experience of Britain — defeated in a North
Atlantic War by a 'small power' Iceland in the 1970s (the so-called Cod
War), but victorious in a South Atlantic War over a 'medium power'
Argentina in the 1980s. What do we make of these recent exercises of state
power on the international scene? One solution is to lower our sights and
admit that 'it seems unlikely that a complete measure will ever be
obtained' (Muir 1981: 149). We then retreat into 'rough estimates' which
are dependent upon the 'situation' in which the power is employed. Muir
(1981: 150) uses five variables — area, population, steel production, size of
army and number of nuclear submarines — to provide his rough estimates
of power. Again the results are intuitively correct but what use are they if
they imply a US victory in Vietnam or a British triumph over Iceland? It is
not enough to say that state power depends on the situation in which it is
employed.

   We need a completely fresh approach to studying state power. This can
be achieved through the world-economy approach by employing the concepts
of overt and covert power relations. Whereas the former is what we normally
understand by power as reflected in conflict we will argue that covert power,
the ability to forward particular interests without resort to coercion or threat,

is much more pervasive and important. We identify four types of power relations, two overt and two covert.

1. Actual and latent force

Overt power is the political relation observed in conflict as described previously. If the conflict is between states or potential states the outcome may be war but the basic argument is the same: if two states A and B have opposing interests in a situation then whichever interest prevails indicates which of the two states is more powerful. In the American civil war we would say that the north was basically more powerful than the south or that in the Second World War the Allies were ultimately more powerful than the Axis powers. This is a very important demonstration of power as witnessed by the 224 wars each causing more than one thousand battle deaths between 1816 and 1980 listed by Small and Singer (1982).

Overt power need not consist of an actual use of force. Violent coercion can be seen as a last resort after persuasion has been attempted. Such diplomacy does not normally rely on the logic of argument, however, but is backed up by the threat of force. This latent force is especially well illustrated in the Cuban missile crisis of 1962 when Soviet vessels were turned back without any actual use of force. Such brinkmanship is rare but more modest 'gunboat diplomacy' has been a hallmark of both British and American foreign policy at different times in the last two centuries. For instance, Blechman and Kaplan (1978) record 215 incidents between 1945 and 1976, when American armed forces were used politically to further American interests but without appreciable violence — what they call 'force without war'. A typical example would be the visit of the most powerful warship in the US Navy, uss *Missouri*, to Turkey in 1945 at a time of USSR claims on Turkish territory. As Blechman and Kaplan (1978: 2) put it:

> The meaning of this event was missed by no one; Washington had not so subtly reminded the Soviet Union and others that the United States was a great military power and that it could project this power abroad, even to shores far distant.

Blechman and Kaplan identify four periods of American use of latent force which are shown in Table 1.3 along with a geographical allocation of the incidents to eight political arenas. It can be seen that early American concern for Europe in the first period gives way to involvement in East Asia in the second period. In the third period Middle America/Caribbean and South-east Asia dominate the picture whereas the Middle East/North Africa and South-East Asia are the important arenas in the final period. Obviously these peaks of incidents revolve around important crises of the post-Second World War era, notably Berlin in the first period, Korea in the second period, Cuba in the third period, Vietnam in the third and fourth periods and Israel in the third and fourth periods. The interesting point is the quantity of such incidents in comparison to just the two major

Table 1.3 366 examples of latent forces: USA and USSR armed forces used as political instruments 1946–75

Arenas	Time Periods							
	1946–8		1949–55		1956–65		1966–75	
	USA	USSR	USA	USSR	USA	USSR	USA	USSR
Europe/ Mediterranean	15	10	6	24	13	24	5	23
Middle East/ North Africa	3	2	2	2	18	5	15	23
South Asia	0	0	0	0	2	0	1	3
South-east Asia	0	0	4	0	26	5	12	1
East Asia	1	6	8	5	7	3	5	6
Africa south of the Sahara	0	0	1	0	8	3	1	6
Middle America/ Caribbean	2	0	3	0	35	2	6	2
South America	3	0	0	0	9	0	0	0
Total	24	18	24	31	118	42	45	64

examples of actual force employed by the United States in Korea and Vietnam.

Of course, the United States is not alone in 'flexing its muscles' in this way. The foreign policy of the other 'super-power', the Soviet Union, has been studied in a similar manner by Kaplan (1981) who identifies 190 'incidents' when Soviet armed forces were used as political instruments between 1944 and 1979. One hundred and fifty-five of these incidents which occurred between 1946 and 1975 have been added to Table 1.3 for comparative purposes. In this case the data show the emergence of the USSR as a global power. In the first two periods all incidents occurred in arenas adjacent to the USSR but in the final two periods the political influence of USSR armed forces spreads to all arenas except South America. But we are jumping ahead in our argument — we deal with geopolitics in the next chapter. The point of Table 1.3 is to illustrate the existence of latent force and to show its quantitative importance.

2. Non-decision making

The most well-known form of covert power is described by the strange term 'non-decision making'. This derives from Schattschneider's (1960) study of American democracy in which he argued that 'all organization is bias'. By this he means that in any politics only some conflicts of interest will be represented on the political agenda. All other conflicts will be 'organized out of politics' so that they do not become the subject of any overt power relations. Schattschneider's examples relate to political parties and in particular to the rather limited range of options offered to the American electorate. We will consider his ideas in Chapter 6. His work is now most well known as the source for Bachrach and Baratz's (1962) concept of non-decision-making in urban studies. They argue that just to study overt decision-making in urban government misses out the agenda-setting process when what will be and what will not be considered occurs. This is essentially a form of manipulation which allows decisions to be steered along certain directions normally favourable to maintaining the status quo. The power is covert in that 'decisions' on non-agenda matters do not have to be made (hence non-decision making). This view takes us a long way along the road to understanding the strength of the status quo in the world-economy.

A most sustained attempt to change the agenda of world politics occurred at the United Nations after the achievement of a Third World majority in the General Assembly in the wake of the decolonization of the post-Second World War period. The United Nations Conference on Trade and Development has spawned two 'development decades' and we have had the Brandt commission culminating with the Cancun conference in which 'global negotiations' took place. But despite the lip-service paid to development of the poorer countries at Cancun the agenda of world politics has not changed. It is not North—South issues that dominate current inter-state relations, instead the East—West conflict continues at the top of the agenda. UN pressure seems merely to have weakened the position of that body in the eyes of the dominant states, notably the United States. The lesson is simple — once established, agendas are very difficult to shift since they represent the very assumptions upon which politics is based. Both 'old cold war', '*détente*' and 'new cold war' share the same assumptions which omit the massive material inequalities of our world from the main agenda. This is non-decision making because it leaves the status quo untouched by the mainstream of world politics.

3. *Structural position*

Non-decision making is not the only form of covert power relations. It is important for understanding that power games are not played out in some neutral arena but it is only one relatively minor aspect of covert power relations. If indeed the UN was successful in defusing the East—West conflict and focusing all attention on Third World poverty, there is no guarantee that material inequalities will be successfully tackled. Getting an issue on the agenda is a start but only a start. The vested interests of the status quo will have to combat the periphery directly but they need not have to use overt force to maintain their position.

The most important form of power relation is structural. It derives directly from the operation of the world-economy as a system. Consider

the two states of Brazil and Switzerland. On almost every power index
Brazil will appear more powerful than Switzerland — on Muir's criteria it
has more area, population, steel production and soldiers, for instance.
But this is only a war potential measure, and Brazil and Switzerland have
not gone to war with one another and are unlikely to do so in the future:
the Swiss government are not that silly. In fact Switzerland has not gone to
war with anybody since the Napoleonic era. But in the hierarchical spatial
structure of the world-economy, Switzerland is core and Brazil is only
semi-periphery. By definition, therefore, Switzerland can be said to
'exploit' Brazil because the world-economy is structured in such a way as
to favour Switzerland at Brazil's expense. Switzerland does not have to
engage in any overt actions to impose its domination beyond 'normal'
trading relations: Swiss bankers are part of an international banking
community imposing conditions on Brazil to reschedule its debts. And
Swiss multinationals such as Nestlé are involved in profitable enterprises
for the ultimate benefit of Swiss shareholders. Quite simply the operation
of the world market, and Swiss and Brazilian relations to that market,
ensure Swiss predominance and a resulting flow of surplus to Switzerland.
This is a far cry from the original Spanish plunder of the Americas based
on a very overt use of power but it is none the less real for all that. In fact
it is much cheaper and efficient exploitation. It is also very different from
the covert use of power in agenda-setting. The Swiss are involved in no
manipulation of the system; quite the opposite. They are playing the rules
of the game as they are meant to be played. It is just that those rules, the
operation of the world-economy, are in their favour as a state whose
economy is based upon core production relations. With more efficient
production they can call the tune in countries that cannot directly
compete economically with them, such as Brazil.

4. Power and appearance

We can now return to our original question concerning the power of
states. In the world-economy approach, power is a direct reflection of the
ability of a state to operate within the system to its own material
advantage. This depends on the efficiency of its production processes
which is measured by our categories of core, semi-periphery and
periphery. If power is overtly expressed then we can expect a
core/semi-periphery/periphery sequence of success chances in a given
conflict. But most expressions of this power will be covert and structural.
Although this is essentially an 'economic' definition of power it can be
directly related to the notion of the 'strong state' as a complementary
expression of power.

Generally speaking there is a tendency for core states to be relatively
liberal in their characteristics since their power is based primarily on their
economic prowess. The seventeenth-century Dutch state was the first state
to reach such a fortunate position. As a politically weak federation of

counties it never *appeared* to be the most powerful state in the world — but for a short period that is exactly what it was. Britain and America have subsequently become leading 'liberal' states. In Chapter 2 we shall refer to such states as hegemonic. In contrast the semi-periphery tends to be occupied by authoritarian states which *appear* to be politically powerful. The absolute monarchies of the early world-economy right through to the authoritarian regimes of today's semi-periphery (for example, Brazil and Russia) illustrate this characteristic. Their political postures can be interpreted in part as attempts to compensate for their relative economic weakness. Remember that the semi-periphery is the most dynamic category in the world-economy and these states have to employ political processes to restructure the system in their favour. Usually, of course, they are unsuccessful. Finally there are the peripheral states, the weakest element in the system. For much of the history of the world-economy this zone has not been in political control of its own territory but has had colonial status. This is obviously the weakest possible position to hold in the world-economy. Even with political independence, however, economic dependence will remain, leading to concepts such as 'informal imperialism' and 'neo-colonialism' whereby the destiny of the country remains almost wholly outside its own control. The main problem of the state is internal security leading to repression and often ephemeral regimes. Informal imperialism and peripheral states are both dealt with in later chapters. The point to make here is that despite the tanks and guns they are essentially weak states. Overt political power is attempting to compensate for the lack of 'real' power in the world-economy.

Finally what of the classic power anomaly, the failure of the United States to secure victory in Vietnam? As the major core country there is no doubt that the Americans had available far more resources than the Vietnamese. Why did not power prevail?

There are two routes to answering this question. First we need to look at the nature of the Vietnamese challenge. The Vietnamese liberation movement mobilized the Vietnam population to an unusual degree. Quite literally the Americans found themselves in the anomalous position that they could only 'save' Vietnam by destroying it. And this brings us to the second route to an explanation. Whereas the US destruction of Vietnam prevented the success of their 'hearts and minds' campaign to win over the Vietnamese peasantry, it directly furthered Vietnamese efforts to win over 'hearts and minds' within American public opinion. The end result was that the United States was unable to proceed with the destruction of Vietnam and covered its resulting inevitable defeat by a process of 'Vietnamizing' their war effort. Hence the military victory of semi-peripheral Vietnam.

But what is the importance of this anomaly to the world-economy? Its symbolic importance cannot be underestimated for weaker powers in all areas of politics. It is too early to assess its long-term relevance to the future world-economy. But for the Vietnamese at the present time the fruits of victory are not that sweet. The national cohesion that brought military victory has not been marshalled towards economic success. The latter is a much more elusive goal; it requires a completely new strategy. The burden of being a semi-peripheral state is hard enough but when the war devastation is added the immediate future looks bleak. Vietnam is hardly in a position to compete in the world-economy as a rising semi-peripheral state. Like so many other Third World states, Vietnam has found that winning political independence is a hollow victory while economic poverty prevails.

This example justifies our emphasis upon economic dimensions of power at the expense of narrow political and military measures. Any visitor to Vietnam and the United States after the war would be hard put to identify the winner. The recent economic successes of Japan and West Germany also belie the importance of military victory compared to the basic economic processes upon which the world-economy is built. The appearance of power is most vividly expressed in victory celebrations after war. But we know that power is more subtle than simple force: think of Japan and Great Britain since 1945.

A POLITICAL GEOGRAPHY PERSPECTIVE ON THE WORLD ECONOMY

We have described the way in which we will interpret politics in the world-economy but have not dealt with political *geography*. Given our holistic stance we will not be attempting to devise a sub-discipline of political geography with its own subject matter. We recognize only historical social science in the political economy tradition in which there are no disciplines or sub-disciplines. What we offer is a political geography perspective on the world-economy. The only justification for devising this perspective in preference to other viewpoints is that it seems to provide an interesting arrangement of ideas and suggests insights into the operation of the world-economy which have not been so clearly shown elsewhere.

What is this political geography perspective? At its simplest it just involves viewing the world-economy through different geographical scales of analysis. In much of our previous discussion we have treated topics of the international scale. This should not be taken to imply that the world-economy approach deals *only* with global-level activities, however. For the purposes of our exposition it has been convenient to stay largely at this one geography scale. Since the world-economy is a holistic concept, however, it follows that one scale of analysis cannot be hived off and studied separately any more than economic or political processes can be treated in isolation. The world-systems approach must treat activities at all geographical scales.

If we briefly return to our problem examples in the measurement of power we will soon see the need for an integrated approach to

geographical scales. American defeat in Vietnam or the contrasting
fortunes of Britain in the North and South Atlantic conflicts cannot be
properly considered at the level of state power comparisons. These
interstate conflicts must be seen in relation to the overall international
context in which they occurred and in their interactions with intra-state
processes. Obviously American policy in Vietnam in the early 1970s — the
so-called Vietnamization of the war — was a response to internal pressures
on the US government. In order to avoid the separation of foreign and
domestic policy which occurs in much political analysis, the political
geography perspective uses geographical scale as its principle of
organization. In this way continuities across scales can be identified and
assessed.

   Political geographers of the current generation have come to accept
geographical scale as the main way of ordering their studies. Numerous
books since 1975 have employed a framework that employs three scales of
analysis — international or global, national or state level and an
intra-national usually urban metropolitan scale. Although this framework
represents a consensus of opinion it is particularly disappointing that this
position has been reached with no articulation of theory to justify a trilogy
of geographical scales (Taylor 1982a). Two questions immediately arise —
'Why just three scales?' and 'Why these particular three scales?' These
questions have not been answered because they have not been asked.
Instead the three scales are accepted merely as 'given': as one author puts
it these 'three broad areas of interest seem to present themselves' (Short
1982: 1). Well, of course, they do no such thing. These three scales do not
just happen to appear so that political geographers have some convenient
hooks upon which to hang their information. In fact recognition of the
three scales is implicit in many social science studies beyond political
geography (Taylor 1981b). It represents a particular way of viewing the
world which is a subtle form of developmentalism. The scales pivot around
the basic unit of the state — hence the inter*national*, *national* and
intra-*national* terminology. The problem is that if it is taken at face value it
destroys the holism of the world-economy. Hence Short (1982: 1) is able to
write about 'distinct spatial scales of analysis' and Johnston (1973: 14)
even refers to 'relatively closed or self-sufficient systems' at these different
scales. If political geography is to use geographical scale it cannot just
accept this organization as given: the framework must explain why these
scales exist and how they relate one to another.

1. Ideology separating experience from reality

Why three scales? This immediately brings to mind Wallerstein's
three-tier structure of conflict control. We have already come across his
geographical example of core—semi-periphery—periphery. We can term this
a horizontal three-tier geographical structure. Our scales form a vertical
three-tier geographical structure pivoting about the nation-state. The role

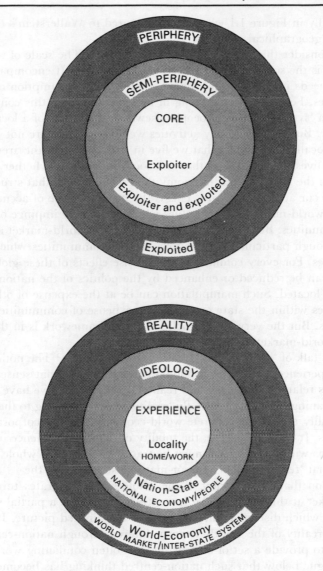

Fig. 1.1 Alternative three-tiered structures of separation and control (a) Horizontal division by area (b) Vertical division by scale.

of all three-tier structures is the promotion of a middle category to separate conflicting interests. In our model, therefore, the nation-state becomes the mediator between global and local scales. We will treat this arrangement as a classic example of ideology separating experience from reality. The three scales therefore represent a national scale of ideology, a local scale of experience and a global scale of reality. This is illustrated schematically in Figure 1.1 where it is compared to Wallerstein's original horizontal geographical structure.

Let us consider this interpretation in more detail. The scale of experience is the scale at which we live our daily lives. It encompasses all our basic needs including employment, shelter and consumption of basic commodities. For most people living in the core countries this consists of a daily urban 'system'; for most people elsewhere it consists of a local rural community. But the day-to-day activities we all engage in are not sustained locally. By the fact that we live in a *world*-system the arena that affects our lives is much larger than our local community whether urban or rural. In the current world-economy the crucial events that structure our lives occur at a global scale. This is the ultimate scale of accumulation where the world-market defines values which ultimately impinge on our local communities. But this is not a direct effect; the world-market is filtered through particular aggregations of local communities which are nation-states. For every community the precise effects of these global processes can be reduced or enhanced by the politics of the nation-state in which it is located. Such manipulation can be at the expense of other communities within the state or else at the expense of communities in other states. But the very stuff of politics in this framework is in this filter between world-market and local community.

But why talk of 'ideology' and 'reality' in this context? The notion of scale of experience seems unexceptional enough but in what sense are the other scales related to ideology and reality? In this model we have very specific meanings for these terms. By 'reality' we are referring to the holistic reality that is the concrete world-economy which incorporates the other scales. It is, in this sense, the totality of the system. Hence ultimate explanations within the system must be traced back to this 'whole'. It is the scale that 'really matters'. In our materialist argument the accumulation that is the motor of the whole system operàtes through the world-market at this global scale. In contrast ideology is a partial view of the system which distorts reality into a false and limited picture. In our model the reality of the world-system is filtered through nation-centred ideologies to provide a set of contrasting and often conflicting world views. We will argue below that such nation-centred thinking has become pervasive in modern politics. This has the effect of diverting political protest away from the key processes at the scale of reality by ensuring that they stop short at the scale of ideology — the nation-state. It is in this sense that we have a geographical model of ideology separating experience from reality.

A simple example may clarify the argument at this point. I have drawn from my own political experience of the late 1970s. Wallsend is a shipbuilding town in north-east England. With the onset of the current recession there was much local concern for the future of the shipyards. As the major employer in the town any closure of the industry would have

major repercussions throughout the local community. This is the scale of
experience. It is at the scale of ideology that policy emerges, however.
Following pressure from, among others, the local Labour Party, the British
(Labour) government nationalized shipbuilding including the Wallsend
yards. But this is ideological because it reflects only a partial view of the
problem. It may protect jobs in the short term but it does not tackle the
problem of Wallsend's shipyards over the long term. These problems
derive from the scale of reality — both supply and demand for ships is
global in scope. The current problem in the industry stems from the fall in
demand for world shipping in the wake of the 1973—74 oil price rise and
the increase in supply with the emergence of new shipyards in other
countries such as South Korea. Clearly a policy of nationalization within
Britain is a long way from solving the problems of Wallsend's ship building
industry. Rather it represents a political solution which stops at the state
scale so that there is no challenge to the processes of accumulation at the
global scale.

Nelund (1978) provides another more general example of this distortion
of politics. In a study of a broad range of thirteen countries, survey
respondents were asked about political issues at various scales. The issue
of war and peace was, not surprisingly, viewed predominantly as one
concerning the world as a whole. But as Nelund points out, this means it
is despatched to a level 'where nobody can reach it'. Hence even if it is of
greatest concern to an individual he or she can do very little about it. War
and peace have been, and remain, largely the concern of politicians and
diplomats. Hence the difficulty of the anti-nuclear peace movement in
breaking into the world of global politics. Nelund (1978: 278) concludes
that

> the national world picture does not provide us with a language which we can
> use in our daily life to deal with our concerns. It is a mental burden, and
> even more it takes us in wrong directions by placing our true concerns
> beyond our reach, involving us in institutional efforts to reach the issue
> which we ourselves have displaced.

This is ideological distortion of not just our experience but that of the
politicians also. United Nations peace efforts, for example, are restricted
to the realm of international politics so that the *internal* politics of states
are largely ignored. And yet such separation of geographical scales of
analysis is a crucial weakness in all peace-keeping efforts. It seems that
the holism of our approach cannot be applied to peace except by a few
elements of protest movements.

Finally we must stress that this model does not posit three processes
operating at three scales but just one process which is manifest at three
scales. In general this process takes the following form — the needs of
accumulation are experienced locally (for example, closure of a hospital)
and justified nationally (for example, to promote national efficiency) for

ultimate benefits organized globally (for example, by multinational corporations paying less tax). This is a single process in which ideology separates experience from reality. There is but one system — the world-economy.

2. *World-economy, nation-state and locality*

This model represents our particular organization of political geography summarized by the sub-title of this book — world-economy, nation-state and locality. Hence we follow the established pattern of using three scales of analysis but treat them in a more analytical manner than other studies. Even though each of the following chapters concentrates largely on activities at one of the three scales they do not constitute separate studies of each scale. For instance imperialism is a concept associated with the global scale but we will argue that it cannot be understood without consideration of forces operating within states. Alternatively political parties operate at the national scale but we will argue that they cannot be understood without consideration of the global scale. In every chapter discussion will range across scales depending on the particular requirements for explanation.

Each chapter follows a similar format. We begin by reviewing past approaches which are evaluated as different 'heritages' in political geography. Some of this heritage is then dismissed as either no longer relevant or even misleading and false. Other parts of our heritage are built upon and developed. And finally some new elements are added to political geography in the application of world-systems logic to the subject-matter. In short we dismiss, develop and generate political geography ideas.

Chapters 2 and 3 are devoted to geopolitics and imperialism respectively. In the former case we identify a largely power-political heritage and in the latter case a revolutionary heritage. Both heritages are largely dismissed on the grounds of being too state-centric. We develop ideas on state-building and political cycles in our presentation of a dynamic model of politics in the world-economy. The particular new elements derived from our world-systems logic concern the role of the USSR in geopolitics and the geographies of imperialism.

In Chapters 4 and 5 we deal with the classic trilogy of political geography — territory, state and nation. The heritage of studies of the territorial state is found to be imbued with developmentalism and functionalism whereas nationalism's heritage is excessively ideological in nature. In contrast we develop ideas on the state as a mechanism of control and the nation as a vehicle for political consensus. Reinterpretations and new ideas from our world-system logic involve the spatial structure of the state, a theory of *states* in the world-economy, and a materialist theory of nationalism.

Chapter 6 stays at the same scale in its treatment of electoral geography. The heritage of these studies involves a very restricted geographical coverage, biased towards core states, due to the liberal theory of elections which has been employed. We employ world-systems logic to interpret elections and the operation of parties in *all* parts of the world. Although electoral geography is one of the major growth areas in modern political geography, we will argue that it is in particular need of a major rethink.

In the final chapter the ecological heritage of urban studies is described and its political implications exposed. When we come to dismiss this past, however, we find that it leads to querying much modern work which treats the 'city' as a separate, operating system. We do not accept the existence of such an entity, hence our use of the term 'locality' to refer to local areas of experience both rural and urban. The first area we develop is the study of neighbourhood effects which we treat more generally as socialization into local political cultures. Finally we introduce some recent ideas on a theory of politics in localities.

The end-result is a political geography which attempts to rethink our studies in world-economy terms. There is some new wine in old bottles but also some old wine in new bottles. Although none of this wine is as yet sufficiently matured, it is hoped that it will not taste too bitter for the discerning reader.

Chapter 2

GEOPOLITICS REVIVED

THE POWER-POLITICAL HERITAGE

Mackinder's heartland theory

1. Political background: from Liberal to Conservative
2. Spatial structure: land power versus sea power

German geopolitics 1924–1941

1. Political background: Nazi connections
2. Spatial structure: global pan-regions

Containment and deterrence: the US world model

1. Containing the fortress: dominoes and Finlands in the Rimland
2. Counterbalancing the Heartland: nuclear deterrence
3. Cohen's model of geostrategic and geopolitical regions

Legacy

GEOPOLITICAL WORLD ORDERS

Cycles of international politics

1. Modelski's long cycles of global politics
2. Cycles of hegemony
3. British and American centuries: the paired Kondratieff model
4. Cycles and geopolitical world orders

The cold war as a geopolitical world order

1. Geopolitical transition to Cold War
2. Phases of the Cold War
3. Cold War as superstructure
4. A world-systems interpretation of the USSR

A new geopolitical transition?

1. Superstates, pan-regions and world classes
2. An ideological fracture?

GEOPOLITICAL CODES

Containment: geopolitical codes of US hegemony

1. George Kennan's geopolitical code
2. Variations in containment codes

Alternative geopolitical codes

1. France's Gaullist geopolitical code
2. Nehru and India's non-alignment code

CHAPTER 2

GEOPOLITICS REVIVED

The demise and rise of geopolitics since World War II has been quite remarkable. For most of the time geopolitics has been virtually abandoned as an academic discourse. One result of this demise has been the cutting-off of political geography from its distinguished heritage of 'founding fathers' such as Friedrich Ratzel in Germany, Sir Halford Mackinder in Britain and Isaiah Bowman in the United States. That political geographers have been willing to take such an extreme step is testimony to the profound impact of German geopolitics in the 1930s on political geography in particular and geography in general. The term 'geopolitics' became an embarrassment to be distinguished from 'respectable' political geography. Saul Cohen has been the major exception among political geographers in keeping global thinking alive in political geography. He understood that geopolitical issues were too important a subject for geographers to abandon. And now he has been joined by many other geographers in an overdue but no less welcome revival of geopolitics.

The revival of geopolitics has taken three distinct forms. First, and perhaps most intriguingly, geopolitics has become a popular term for describing global rivalries in world politics. Hepple (1986) traces this recent usage of the term to the extensive references to 'geopolitics' in former US Secretary of State Henry Kissinger's widely quoted memoirs. From media discussion of Kissinger's ideas the term re-entered popular language so that today it is not unusual to encounter reference to geopolitics in any serious press article on world political issues. In this usage geopolitics seems to be a shorthand phrase to indicate a general process of managing global rivalry to produce a balance of power or equilibrium in world affairs. The general implication is that US politicians need to master this art in the new circumstances of the relative decline of US power.

This popularizing of geopolitics was no doubt important in lessening geographers' inhibitions over their erstwhile wayward child. Hence the second form that the revival has taken is an academic one, a new more critical geopolitics. Critical historiographical studies of past geopolitics have been a necessary component of this 'geographer's geopolitics'. Such revisionist histories have included both reassessment of key figures of the

past, such as Isaiah Bowman (N. Smith 1984) and, of course, fresh
perspectives on German geopolitics (Heske 1986; Bassin 1987). More
generally political geographers have become particularly involved in
researching the geography of war and peace (Pepper and Jenkins 1985;
O'Loughlin 1986; O'Loughlin and van der Wustern 1986; O'Sullivan
1986). But as yet this new geopolitics lacks cohesion. This chapter
attempts to provide a framework for studying global rivalry in political
geography.

Before we embark on this task, however, we need to mention briefly the
third form that the revival of geopolitics has taken. This is associated with
the neo-conservative, pro-military lobby which have added geopolitical
arguments to their 'Cold War rhetoric' (Gray 1977). Such studies talk of
'geopolitical imperatives' and treat geography as 'the permanent factor'
that all strategic thinking must revolve around. This naive treatment of
space as an unchanging stage exposes the basic lack of understanding of
the nature of geography. Many years ago Bowman (1948: 130) provided
the answer to such simplistic reasoning:

> It is often said that geography does not change. In truth geography changes
> as rapidly as ideas and technology change; that is the *meaning* of geographical
> conditions changes.

We will be concerned with such a 'geographer's geopolitics' which charts
the changing meaning of the 'geographical factor'. The simple geopolitics
of Cold War rhetoric will be of interest only insofar as it has influence on
the politics of global rivalry.

This chapter is divided into three parts. We begin by describing the
power-political heritage of geopolitics. Quite simply we cannot expect any
advances in this field until we have come to terms with our notorious past.
We conclude from this section that the practical geopolitics of politicians
and their advisors must be our subject-matter. In part two we begin the
task of analyzing this subject-matter by introducing the concept of
geopolitical world orders. These are the relatively stable structures that
define distinct periods of world politics. We are currently living in the
Cold War geopolitical world order. After setting out the historical
evidence for such world orders this part of the chapter concentrates on the
Cold War. In the final section we look at the more specific geopolitical
codes of particular governments. Following on from the Cold War
emphasis of the previous section, we concentrate on the family of US
geopolitical codes that are known as containment. In both substantive
sections of the chapter we consider geopolitical analyses that go beyond
the Cold War. What are the indications of a geopolitical transition to a
new world order and what form might it take?

Geopolitics is not the only topic in political geography that deals with
the global scale. In Chapter 3 we present a political geography of

imperialisms. Before we deal with either subject we need to distinguish between geopolitics and imperialism.

Although not usually discussed in the same context both terms relate to political activity at an inter-state scale. Current usage distinguishes geopolitics as concerned with rivalry between major powers (core and rising semi-periphery states), and imperialism as domination by strong states (in the core) of weak states (in the periphery). Politically, geopolitics describes a *rivalry* relation whereas imperialism describes a *dominance* relation. Spatially they are currently reflected in 'east-west' and 'north-south' spatial patterns respectively. Although there have been previous definitions, and these are dealt with below, we will employ these current uses of the terms here. The interesting question for political geography is the relation between the two concepts in their politics and in their spatial structure. In world-system analysis geopolitics is about rivalry (currently East versus West) in the core for domination of the periphery by imperialism (currently North over South).

THE POWER-POLITICAL HERITAGE

There have been two major traditions in the study of international relations — realism and idealism. The former has been the dominant tradition and has built upon a series of classical works on statecraft and inter-state rivalry. The sixteenth-century writings of Machiavelli and the nineteenth-century writings of Clausewitz are the most well-known 'classical' international relations works. All such studies emphasize the compelling insecurity of the state and hence advocate policies of power politics. This simply means the stronger state imposing its will on the weaker. War, or at least the threat of war, is therefore central to realist prescriptions for, and interpretations of, international relations. It is for this reason that idealists have condemned realists as amoral.

Many observers interpreted World War I as the inevitable culmination of realist thinking in international relations. Realism represented the Old World's way of conducting international affairs. The entry of the United States into the war signalled the entry of idealism into international relations as the New World's way of organizing affairs of state. President Wilson immediately set about rationalizing US involvement in the war in terms of abstract principles for conducting international affairs. Whereas realism left the strong states to take responsibility for world affairs, the new idealism required the control of such power by means of the collective action of all states. The main product of this type of thinking was the League of Nations set up in the aftermath of World War I to prevent such a disaster ever occurring again. Hence, whereas realism is generally considered to be conservative in its favouring of the strong, idealism is a liberal doctrine that attempts to place international relations on a firm 'constitutional' basis.

Geopolitics has generally been part of the realist tradition of international relations. The key initial statement of geopolitics by Mackinder (1904), for instance, has become one of the classics of realism. But, after 1918, in the new climate of idealist opinion, Bowman (1924) produced his famous world survey, New World, in which old-style realism is expunged from geography. Nevertheless, Bowman's book remains a rare exception to geopolitics' power-political heritage. Even in this case Bowman's arguments do not represent a true international perspective, but rather he views the world very much through American eyes (Smith 1984). In fact both realists and idealists share what is basically a state-centred view of the world (Banks 1986). This makes all such studies liable to biases in favour of an author's own country. In the case of geopolitics it has always been very easy to identify the nationality of an author from the content of his or her writings. We use this feature to illustrate the power-political heritage of geopolitics in this section. We will deal with three such geopolitics from states that dominated the first half of this century, Britain, Germany and the United States.

MACKINDER'S HEARTLAND THEORY

The starting point for almost all discussions of geopolitics is Sir Halford Mackinder's Heartland Theory. Despite its neglect in geography it remains probably the most well-known geographical model throughout the world. Although first propounded in 1904 it continues to inform debate on foreign policy. Walters (1974: 27) goes so far as to say that 'the Heartland theory stands as the first premise of Western military thought'. This remarkable achievement of longevity is the subject-matter of this section.

Mackinder's world model was presented on three occasions covering nearly forty years. The original thesis was presented in 1904 as 'The Geographical Pivot of History'. The ideas were refined and presented after the First World War (1919) in *Democratic Ideals and Reality* where 'Pivot Area' becomes Heartland. Then in 1943 Mackinder, at the age of eighty-two, provided a final version of his ideas. Despite this long period covering two world wars the idea of an Asiatic 'fortress' remains the centrepiece of his models and is largely responsible for its popularity since 1945. Most discussion of Mackinder concentrates on his 1919 work, but here we will be particularly concerned with the origins of his ideas just after the turn of the century. For further details see Parker (1982) and Blouet (1987).

1. Political background: from Liberal to Conservative

Mackinder developed his world strategic views at a crucial period in the world-economy when Britain was losing her political and economic leadership. In the nineteenth century Britain had been the champion of a liberal world-economy which she could dominate. The rise of the United States and Germany in the final quarter of the century dramatically changed the situation. Mackinder had been a leading member of the Liberal Party — the party of free trade — but about 1903 he began to revise his views. Britain's role was changing and he no longer believed that simple accumulation of capital in London would be sufficient to meet the challenge of Germany's massive growth in heavy industry. He converted to a protectionist position which involved changing political parties — the Conservatives were the party of 'tariff reform'. This new position emphasized the need to maintain British industry to face the German challenge. These concerns with current power rivalries are directly expressed in his famous world model (Semmel 1960).

2. The spatial structure: land power versus sea power

Mackinder's original presentation of his model is a very broad conception of world history. Basically he identifies central Asia as the pivot-area of history from which horsemen have dominated Asian and European history because of their superior mobility. With the age of maritime exploration from 1492, however, we enter the Columbian era when the balance of power swung decisively to the coastal powers, notably Britain. Mackinder now considered this era to be coming to an end. In the 'post-Columbian' era new transport technology, particularly the railways, would redress the balance back in favour of land-based power and the pivot-area would reassert itself. The pivot-area was defined in terms of a zone not accessible to sea-power and was surrounded by an inner crescent in mainland Europe and Asia and an outer crescent in the islands and continents beyond Eurasia (Fig. 2.1a).

What had this to do with current (1904) power politics? Well at its simplest this model can be interpreted as a historical-geographical rationalization for the traditional British policy of maintaining a balance of power in Europe so that no one continental power could threaten Britain. In this case the policy implications are to prevent Germany allying with Russia to control the pivot-area and so to command the resources to overthrow the Britain Empire. Mackinder's message in 1904 was that Britain is more vulnerable than before to the rise of a continental power. British foreign policy needs revision to accord with the new post-Columbian situation to supplement a revised trade policy.

In his 1919 revision of this world model he redefines central Asia as the 'Heartland' which is larger than the original pivot-area. This is based on a reassessment of the penetrative capabilities of sea powers. Nevertheless the same basic structure remains and the fear of German control of the Heartland is still central. In fact he is much more explicit in his advice as given in his famous dictum:

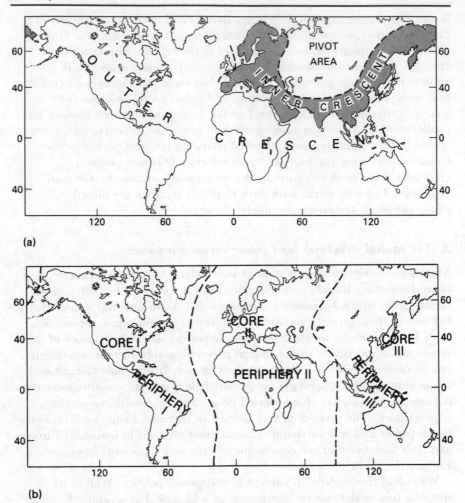

Fig. 2.1   Alternative geopolitical models (a) Mackinder's original model (b) A
model of pan-regions

> Who rules East Europe commands the Heartland
> Who rules the Heartland commands the World-Island
> Who rules the World-Island commands the World.

(The World-Island is Eurasia plus Africa consisting of two-thirds of the
world's lands.) This message was specifically composed for world
statesmen at Versailles who were redrawing the map of Europe. The
emphasis on east Europe as the strategic route to the Heartland was
interpreted as requiring a strip of buffer states to separate Germany and
Russia. These were created by the peace negotiators but proved to be
ineffective bulwarks in 1939.

Mackinder's 1943 revision is more comprehensive but far less relevant to our discussion. It reflected the contemporary short-term alliance of Russia, Britain and America and posited them together as Heartland and 'Midland Ocean' (North Atlantic) to control and suppress the German danger between them. This is a long way from the grand history and basic materialist strategic thinking behind his original world model. We will not consider this final model any further.

A concluding point to make about Mackinder is that he was much more than the geo-strategist portrayed in political geography. By starting with his economic and national political views I have tried to portray him as more of a political economist with a holistic viewpoint lacking in so many of his followers.

GERMAN GEOPOLITICS 1924–1941

German geopolitics is blamed for all manner of things both within geography and without. It is usual to condemn this school in political geography textbooks as forsaking objective science and justifying the aggressive foreign policy of the Third Reich. We cannot join in this accusation of subjectivity and national bias here, however, because this is precisely how we are describing the whole heritage of geopolitics — German and non-German. Nevertheless this national school was associated with a defeated regime who pursued a disastrous foreign policy and some of the retribution stuck to geography and to political geography in particular.

1. Political background: Nazi connections

German geopolitics was centred on the work of Karl Haushofer. He was Professor of Geography at the University of Munich from 1921–39 and he edited the flagship journal of geopolitics, *Zeitschrift für Geopolitik*. Much of our knowledge of Haushofer has been clouded by reports on his work in World War II when many myths were created that political geographers have been too slow in correcting. For instance there never was an Institute of Geopolitics at Munich and Haushofer never commanded 'a thousand scientists' plotting a German victory. In recent years there have been several valuable re-evaluations of Haushofer and German geopolitics which we draw upon here (Heske 1986, 1987; Paterson 1987; Bassin 1987; O'Loughlin and van der Wusten 1988).

Although idealistic ideas dominated most international relations studies in the inter-war years, realist assessments of the world scene prospered in one corner of Europe, defeated Germany. Here idealism was discredited because of its association with what was considered to be the unfair Treaty of Versailles. It is in this context that we must review the rise of German geopolitics. As Paterson (1987) has pointed out, the short-term aim of geopolitics was the revision of the Treaty of Versailles. The key concept for this challenge was Ratzel's *Lebensraum* (literally 'living space') which interpreted Germany's problems as being due to unfair and confining boundaries. The solution was expansion. It is easy to see why such a geopolitics should appeal to Nazi politicians before and after the creation of the Third Reich.

The question of Haushofer's influence on Nazi policy is a controversial one. Certainly it is now generally concluded that he had much less influence than World War II reports suggested. Heske (1986) outlines the current opinion as follows. Haushofer was well known in right wing political circles for his realist policy prescriptions. He was friendly with Hitler's deputy Rudolf Hess from 1919 onwards, meeting him for detailed discussions about once a month throughout this period. He also had contact with other leaders of the Third Reich (von Ribbentrop, Goebbels and Himmler), but much less so with Hitler himself. In the 1930s Haushofer's main link with the political élite seems to have been through his son Albrecht. However, after Hess's abortive peace mission to Britain in 1941 Haushofer lost what influence he had had on the Nazi regime. In 1944 Albrecht was executed for his part in the failed assassination attempt on Hitler.

If we move on from the questions of inter-personal relations to the realm of the ideas themselves, we find further reasons to doubt Haushofer's critical importance at this time. Bassin (1987) has compared geopolitics with National Socialist doctrine and has exposed the fundamental difference in their theories. Whereas geopolitics was derived from Ratzel's scientific materialism, National Socialism promoted ideas of innate human qualities ennobling racial theories of superiority. Despite Haushofer's attempts to avoid this contradiction between the two doctrines (Heske 1987), it is doubtful whether geopolitics could have ever become the leading science of Nazi Germany as its opponents have claimed. Rather it represented a set of realist ideas that could be used when convenient. Similarly, Haushofer was a right-wing academic who was used to ease relations between the Third Reich and academia. The result, according to Heske (1987), was that geography was implicated more than any other science in the legitimation of the Nazi regime and Haushofer must bear the main responsibility for this.

2. Spatial structure: global pan-regions

With the breakdown of the British-led, free trade system of the mid-nineteenth century, the world gradually moved towards a system of economic blocs behind tariff barriers. As we have seen, Mackinder's conversion to tariff reform was to promote the British Empire as an economic bloc — the policy of 'imperial preferences'. The ultimate result of such thinking was autarchy or economic self-sufficiency. Since Germany had lost all her colonies after World War I, autarchy for Haushofer and his associates was originally linked to *Lebensraum* and expansion into eastern Europe. But return of the colonies formed an important aspect of the call to revise the Versailles Treaty and this led to a more global appreciation of Germany's role in the world. The result was an interpretation of global economic regions as pan-regions.

The idea of economic blocs was not original, of course, but pan-regions were distinctive in their sweeping redefinition of economic patterns. Other proposals of economic blocs were careful to follow the current pattern of colonies and spheres of influence (Horrabin 1942). But pan-regions were more than mere economic blocs. They were based upon 'pan-ideas' which provided an ideological basis for the region (O'Loughlin and van der Wusten 1988). The Pan-Americanism implicit in the Monroe Doctrine was the classic pan-idea associated with a pan-region.

In German geopolitics three great pan-regions were finally identified (Fig. 2.1b) based upon Germany, Japan and the United States. This is an interesting geographical organization in that it involves huge functional regions around each core state cross-cutting environmental-resource regions which straddle the earth latitudinally. Hence each pan-region would have a share of the world's arctic, temperate and tropical environments. As political economy units they produce three regions with a high potential for autarchy. If it had so evolved, such a world model would have produced three separate world-systems, each with its own core — Europe, Japan and Anglo-America; and periphery — Africa and India, East and South-East Asia, and Latin America respectively.

The rise to dominance in the world-economy by the United States after World War II ended the general drift towards economic blocs and so made the concept of pan-regions temporarily irrelevant. But with the current demise of US dominance of the world-economy, economic blocs and even pan-regions are returning to the world political agenda (O'Sullivan 1986; O'Loughlin and van der Wusten 1988).

CONTAINMENT AND DETERRENCE: THE US WORLD MODEL

German geopolitics accommodated the United States not as the dominant power but as one member of a set of three dominant powers. Germany's world model can be interpreted as a sort of Monroe Doctrine × 3. With the defeat of Germany the United States emerged as the strongest world power and its interests were far greater than the hemisphere region allocated in the German plan. America required a global strategy and a world model to base it on. This meant a return to Mackinder-type thinking. Although the original thesis had warned of the strategic superiority of land-power in the twentieth century, Mackinder's final (1943) work had been much less pessimistic from a sea-power viewpoint. This position was more fully developed by Nicholas Spykman (1944) who directly perceived post-war American needs as neutralizing the power of the Heartland. As a counter to the Mackinder thesis he argued that the key area was the 'inner crescent', which he renamed the 'Rimland'; control of the latter could neutralise the power of the Heartland. All was not lost therefore for the sea-power in twentieth-century geopolitics. By the end of the war it was clear that in effect the Heartland could be equated with the USSR. Germany's failure to defeat Russia had enhanced Mackinder's reputation. From this point onwards there existed a general world model which we can call the Heartland–Rimland thesis involving land power (the USSR) versus sea-power (the USA) separated by a contact zone (the Rimland). To be sure there were minor variations in terms of definitions and emphases but this three-tier structure originally derived from Mackinder's 1904 paper persisted into the post-1945 era. It survived a barrage of criticisms — Mackinder's initial emphasis on railways seemed pretty antiquated in the age of inter-continental ballistic missiles — but in a sense it does not matter whether the model is an accurate representation of reality; what does matter is that enough people believed it to be true. Therefore the Heartland–Rimland thesis could become an ideological tool of US foreign policy makers.

The application of Mackinder's ideas so many years after they were first propounded is not due to his being some sort of prophetic genius. It relates, instead, to the fact that he provided a simple spatial structure which precisely suited the needs of US foreign policy after 1945. The world was reduced to two super powers with the onset of the Cold War, and the Heartland–Rimland thesis provided an easy way of conceptualising the new situation. The original hydrology basis of pivot-area and Mackinder's concern for German expansion were conveniently forgotten and we were left with a model in which the enemy, the USSR, had control of the 'fortress', the Heartland. Policy was formulated accordingly.

1. Containing the 'fortress': dominoes and Finlands in the Rimland

If the USSR is a fortress then the way to deal with a fortress is to surround it and seal it in. In policy jargon this is known as containment, with the ring of post-war anti-Soviet alliances in the Rimland as the seal — NATO in Europe, CENTO in West Asia and SEATO in East Asia. Where the seal came unstuck intervention was necessary and the Rimland contains the majority of major and minor conflicts in the post-1945 era — Berlin, Korea, the Middle East and Vietnam being the major conflicts. All of this activity is premised on preventing Soviet domination of the World-Island. In its wake containment has spawned more limited but equally simple spatial models to deal with particular sectors of the Rimland. The classic analogy is domino theory whereby the 'fall' of one country will inevitably lead to the defeat of US interests in adjacent countries: the loss of Kampuchea puts Thailand and Malaysia at risk, and so on. O'Sullivan (1982) has demolished this idea of countries lined up like dominoes to be toppled by Communists or held up by US support. The main feature of his theory is that it conveniently avoids all discussion of the *internal* conflicts of the countries and therefore prevents the emergence of alternative theories of unrest that do not blame externally inspired communist agitation. In Western Europe domino theory has been replaced by the notion of Finlandization. This admits that there will be no Soviet military take-over but that USSR influence will nevertheless be extended by insidious control of the domestic politics of the countries involved. Finland is supposed to be the 'model' for this process. Again this simple theory has been demolished in recent political geography (Liebowitz 1983). Quite simply the world is more complicated than these simple spatial analogies allow for. Nevertheless such ideas have lain behind US foreign policy and 'dominoes' have been reappearing in the 1980s in Central America.

2. Counter-balancing the Heartland: nuclear deterrence

Whereas containment policy emphasizes the Rimland, the second policy reflecting the three-tier world model concentrates more on the implications of a Soviet Heartland. Walters (1974) makes a very cogent argument that the policy of nuclear deterrence would never have developed but for the Heartland theory. Quite simply, once it is accepted that the USSR have the superior geopolitical position then nuclear weapons become the necessary salvation of the West. A nuclear arsenal will act as a counterbalance to Russia's basic strategic advantage. *Despite* the Heartland theory, a new balance of power can be created on the basis of the nuclear deterrent and the World-Island can be saved. Hence perhaps the most momentous foreign policy decision of all time — to generate what was to become the nuclear arms race — is based upon a geographical theory which nearly all geographers and political scientists reject. Nevertheless it should not be thought that these ideas are diminishing in importance. The renewal of the Cold War and the rise of conservative politics in domestic affairs have been paralleled by a new belligerent neo-conservative foreign policy lobby (Ajami 1978) where Mackinder again becomes the prophetic genius to stop the Germans . . . er, sorry the Russians. In recent years this has been most forcibly argued by Gray (1977) who claims to remind us once again of the 'lessons of geopolitics'. Some ideas, it seems, never go away — as long as they continue to have an ideological utility.

3. Cohen's model of geostrategic and geopolitical regions

Saul Cohen is the only geographer working in this field who has attempted a complete revision of the Heartland—Rimland thesis. His basic purpose is to question the policy of containment with its implication that the whole Eurasian littoral is a potential battleground. He exposes, once again, the poverty of Heartland—Rimland theory. For instance he points out that by viewing the situation as land-power versus sea-power a containment policy can only be seen as locking the stable door after the horse has bolted, given current Soviet naval strength in all oceans. His revision of strategic thinking consists, therefore, of providing a much more militarily flexible

and geographically sensitive model. His movement away from the
Heartland—Rimland thesis comes in two stages and we will deal with each
in turn chronologically.

In his *Geography and Politics in a World Divided* Cohen (1973) offers a
hierarchical and regional world model. This is based on exposing the
'unity myth' which he believes has misled previous geopoliticians.
According to Cohen there is not a strategic unity of space but rather there
are separate arenas in a fundamentally divided world. He brings forward
the traditional geographical concept of the region to describe this division.
A hierarchy of two types of region are identified depending on whether
they are global or regional in scope. Geostrategic regions are functionally
defined and express the inter-relations of a large part of the world.
Geopolitical regions are subdivisions of the above and they tend to be
relatively homogeneous in terms of one or more of culture, economics and
politics.

Cohen's (1973) use of these concepts to produce a world model is shown
in Fig. 2.2. He defines just two geostrategic regions each dominated by one
of the two major powers and termed 'the Trade-Dependent Maritime
World' and 'the Eurasian Continental World'. Hence his initial spatial
structure is similar to the old geopolitical models. However, he goes a step
further and divides each geostrategic region into five and two geopolitical
regions respectively. In addition, South Asia is recognized as a potential
geostrategic region. Between the two existing geostrategic regions there
are two distinctive geopolitical regions which are termed shatterbelts — the
Middle East and South-East Asia. Unlike other geopolitical regions these
two are characterized by a lack of political unity; they are fragmented with
both geostrategic regions having 'footholds' in the region. They are of
strategic importance to both great powers and it is here where

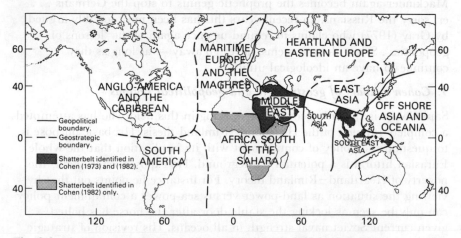

Fig. 2.2 Cohen's geostrategic regions and their geopolitical subdivisions

'containment' must be practised. Essentially Cohen is saying that not all parts of the Rimland are equally important and policy must be sensitive to this fact. Selective containment rather than blanket containment is the policy in line with his geographical 'realities'.

In a revision of his model Cohen (1982) has further emphasized the divisions of the world strategic system. He has modified some of the details of his initial spatial structure — notably the designation of Africa south of the Sahara as a third shatter belt (Fig. 2.2) — but the major change is one of emphasis on 'second order' or regional centres of power. In the original model geopolitical regions were the basis of multiple power nodes and this comes to the fore in the revised model. Three geopolitical regions have developed new world powers — Japan, China and Europe — to join the USA and the USSR. Other geopolitical regions have developed second-order powers which dominate their region, such as India, Brazil and Nigeria. Cohen assesses twenty-seven states as second-order powers and beyond these he defines third-, fourth- and fifth-order states. Definitions are largely based on the scope for influence beyond the states' boundaries. The end result is a multiple-node world with many overlapping areas of influence which is much more dynamic than the old bi-polar model. The key difference is the greater inter-connectedness between regions and between countries on different rungs of the hierarchy. The influence of both the old major powers has declined to be taken over in part by the rise of the new regional powers. This is a far cry from the simplicity of the Heartland–Rimland thesis and is returning towards the traditional complexity of regional geography models.

There is one crucial aspect in which Cohen is similar to the Heartland–Rimland devotees. Like them he is attempting to inform his own country's foreign policy. Cohen's revised model is explicitly intended to counteract the calls for a renewal of containment policy in the wake of the election of conservative Ronald Reagan to the presidency, for instance. Cohen's is very much an American view of the world.

LEGACY

The purpose of this section has not been to 'expose' political biases since they are not particularly well hidden. N. Smith (1984), for instance, has recently shown that Bowman's rhetoric against German geopolitics in the Second World War rings a little hollow today when we remember his own contribution to America's war effort. However, our point is not to be anti-American, or anti-German or anti-British but to recognize generally the national bias that has permeated all geopolitical strategic thinking (O'Loughlin 1984). Nevertheless, the models we have looked at are important in the context of this discussion because they derive directly from traditional political geography. We must come to terms with Mackinder and geopolitics, not by ignoring them but by understanding

these ideas in their historical and national contexts. Only in this way can
we go beyond our distinguished yet notorious heritage.

Although critical historiography of geopolitics is a necessary stage on
the road to a new geopolitics, it is only a first step. We have learnt two
basic lessons. First, geopolitics is not a collection of eternal imperatives.
From Mackinder to Cohen geographers have shown the ever-changing
basis of geopolitics: geopolitics is historical. Second, geopolitics has not
been a neutral science. Geographers and non-geographers alike have
shown their national biases all too clearly.

How do we learn from these lessons? Agnew and O'Tuathail (1988) have
suggested a framework in which we can develop a historically-sensitive
geopolitics that can transcend national biases. They define geopolitics as a
particular form of reasoning that values and orders places in terms of the
security of a single state or group of states. This broad definition allows
them to identify two basic types of geopolitical reasoning. This is the key
step in our argument. First there is practical geopolitical reasoning which
is continually being carried out by state élites, both civilian and military.
They evaluate places beyond their borders as potential threats to their
national security. In this way places are reduced to what Agnew and
O'Tuathail call 'security commodities'.

Second there is formal geopolitical reasoning where the practical ideas
are organized into theories in academic geopolitical writings such as those
discussed above. Formal geopolitical reasoning divides up the world and
argues for differential valuing of the resulting parts. Heartland, Rimland
and shelter belts are concepts that describe archetypal security
commodities which different theorists have designated highest priority.

The importance of identifying these two forms of geopolitics is to
understand the relationship between them. While it is well known that the
formal has influenced the practical as we have documented above, it is
equally clear that the practical has decisively influenced the formal. As
O'Tuathail (1986) has recently pointed out, most geopolitical writers have
wanted to practise geopolitics. This is the reason, of course, that
geopolitics has had such a problematic history. The solution is quite
straightforward. We must make practical geopolitical reasoning the object
of our analysis in formal geopolitical reasoning. This new geopolitics will
attempt to make sense of the past and present geopolitical reasoning of
state strategists. In this way we can realistically hope to transcend the
national biases that have hitherto seemed endemic to geopolitics.

GEOPOLITICAL WORLD ORDERS

Practical geopolitical reasoning produces what Gaddis (1982) calls
geopolitical codes. These are operational codes consisting of a set of
political—geographical assumptions that underlie a country's foreign

policy. Such a code will have to incorporate a definition of a state's interests, an identification of external threats to those interests, a planned response to such threats and a justification for that response. There will, of course, be as many geopolitical codes as there are states.

Although every code will be unique to its particular country such practical reasoning is not conducted in a vacuum. The creation of geopolitical codes is not independent of one another. In fact there has always been a hierarchy of influence within the inter-state system whereby the more powerful impose ideas and assumptions on the less powerful. In particular the so-called 'great powers' have had an excessive influence on the geopolitical codes of other members of the system. So much so that within any one historical period most geopolitical codes tend to fit together to form a single overall dominant pattern. These are geopolitical world orders.

Agnew and O'Tuathail (1988) recognize that geopolitical world orders can be traced back at least as far as the treaties of Westphalia of 1648. They draw on Robert Cox's (1981) concept of world orders and his method of historical structures. The latter is a framework of action combining three interacting forces — material capability, ideas and institutions. The application of this model to world orders can be illustrated by the case of the Cold War whereby the United States had the material *capability* to dominate the post-World War II scene — it advanced liberal, political and economic *ideas* and helped found *institutions* such as the United Nations to provide stability to the new world order. For Cox such world orders combine social, political and economic structures. The Cold War is the political structure of this particular world order. Cox associates his world orders with the hegemony of one state which imposes and then protects its world order. In short, our specific concern for geopolitical world orders cannot be meaningfully separated from a more general concern for the rise and fall of great powers over the history of the world-economy. We must tackle this topic before we attempt to define particular geopolitical world orders.

CYCLES OF INTERNATIONAL POLITICS

The history of the inter-state system can be characterized by the rise and fall of just a few major powers. Some researchers have identified a sort of 'system within a system' covering just these major powers. Levy's (1983) 'great power system', for instance, includes only thirteen states since 1495 and no more than seven at any one time. The story of these powers has recently been told by Paul Kennedy (1988) in his bestselling *The Rise and Fall of the Great Powers*. In many ways this is a classic 'book of its times'. Recent years have witnessed a plethora of studies showing how no one state has been able to maintain its predominance in the world-system. The decline of Britain has long fascinated Americans and since about 1970 there are signs that even this latest colossus is suffering a relative decline. And therein lies the secret of the remarkable success of Kennedy's book. Understanding 'decline' is both topical and relevant. Can we learn from history?

Most studies of the rise and decline of major powers have developed cyclical models of change. Goldstein (1988) has recently described more than a dozen such analyses. We shall concentrate on two of the most well-known here. Modelski provides a model which identified five cycles and four world leaders (Britain 'leads' twice). In contrast, in world-systems analysis just three hegemonic cycles are distinguished with just three hegemonic powers. These differences in numbers of cycles are symptomatic of fundamental differences in the conception of political cycles.

1. Modelski's long cycles of global politics

Gaddis (1982) has divided writers of history into two groups: 'lumpers' and 'splitters'. The former impose order on the past, the latter revel in differences and discrepancies. All writers on cycles of international politics are lumpers by definition. George Modelski is the arch-lumper of this body of work.

Modelski first presented his long cycles model in an article in 1978 and has made several modifications since, culminating in his book *Long Cycles in World Politics* in 1987. Basically, Modelski's work is a reaction against two very different traditions in international relations. First, Modelski is at pains to dismiss realist writers, such as Bull (1977), who argue that the international system is essentially anarchic. Modelski discovers a symmetry to international politics that is the very antithesis of anarchy. Second, Modelski is a major critic of international political economy which he believes devalues political processes at the expense of economic factors. He argues for 'two logics' rather than one, with his global politics being autonomous of the world-economy. The original 1978 article was written to provide an alternative political perspective to Wallerstein's (1974b) introduction of his world-systems analysis. This makes Modelski's long cycle model particularly interesting here, since it enables us to explore the differences between the 'two logics' assumption and our political economy position.

There are many superficial similarities between Modelski's global cycles and the framework we are using. Modelski's global system begins about 1500 and then proceeds to develop in a cyclical manner. Modelski (1978: 218) creates a new type of cycle of just over a hundred years in length — so that we are currently experiencing the fifth such cycle. Each cycle is associated with a world power which is defined as a state which engages in over half the 'order-keeping' function of the global political system. Four such world powers have existed — Portugal, Netherlands, Britain and the United States. These have dominated 'their centuries' — Portugal the sixteenth, Netherlands the seventeenth, Britain the eighteenth and the nineteenth, and currently the United States in the twentieth. Britain is unique in having dominated two global cycles.

The details of these global cycles are shown in Table 2.1. In each case the rise and fall of the world power is indicated through definite steps. A cycle starts with a weak global organizational structure of severe political competition which degenerates into global war. Such wars have a wide geographical range and have global pay offs — the winner is able to order the resulting political system. This phase ends with a legitimizing treaty which formally sets up the new world order centred on the new world power. As no world power can maintain its control, a decline phase sets in. Initially the world order becomes bi-polar and then multi-polar before the system becomes weakly organized again, is ripe for the rise of a new world power, and the cycle starts again. We can be impressed by the symmetry Modelski finds in international politics.

The geographical scope of Modelski's model is initially larger than the world-economy. His international political system is global from its inception. This is not just a matter of geographical definition: it relates to how the role of Portugal is interpreted. For Modelski, by taking over the trading network in the Indian Ocean the Portuguese became the centre of a global system and hence a world power. In contrast Wallerstein places most of the Portuguese activity in the external arena outside the world-economy; Spanish-American colonization is far more important in that it creates a new periphery. For Modelski Spain only operated on the fringes of his system and never developed a 'world outlook'. Here we come to the crux of the difference between the two approaches since the notion of a world outlook in the global sense is totally unnecessary for Wallerstein. His world-system was originally a European world-economy and only became global in scope about 1900.

Why is a world outlook an important criterion for Modelski? The original mechanisms for change in his system are two-fold. First, there is what Modelski (1978: 224) terms 'the urge to make global order'. Once the possibilities of a global order became known an innate will for power becomes expressed as an urge to shape world order. Only a few people may have such a world outlook, but they respond to the inarticulated needs of the many. Second, the nature of international politics as a system means that structures run down and have to be reconstructed. All systems suffer a loss of order and survive by cyclical development. Table 2.1 describes a particular expression of this general process. It is on the basis of these two mechanisms that change has occurred in Modelski's global system.

Clearly, here we have uncovered the weak point of the model. For all its symmetry, its mechanisms of change are inherently disappointing. We can trace this back to Modelski's starting point that the global political system must be functionally distinguished from the world-economy. This is not to

Table 2.1 Long cycles of global politics

Cycles	World powers	World wars	Legitimating treaties	Key institutions	Landmarks of decline
I	Portugal	Italian Wars (1494–1517)	Treaty of Tordesillas	Global network of bases	Spanish annexation (1580)
II	Netherlands	Spanish Wars (1579–1609)	Twelve year truce with Spain (1609)	'Mare librum'	The English Revolution
III	Britain	French Wars (1688–1713)	Treaty of Utrecht (1713)	Command of the sea	Independence of USA
IV	Britain	French Wars (1792–1815)	Paris and Vienna (1814, 1815)	Free trade	Imperialism
V	USA	German Wars (1914–45)	Versailles and Potsdam (1919, 1945)	United Nations	Vietnam War

say that he necessarily underestimates the importance of economic processes — Modelski's politics are about who gets what in the world system — but he treats the two processes as distinct. In our terminology this is a classic illustration of the poverty of disciplines. As we have argued in Chapter 1, the state system and the economic system are integral parts of a single process of development incorporated in the concept of the world-economy. There are not two logics but one. The world-economy could not operate except within the political framework provided by a competitive state system. It is a necessary, though not sufficient, definition of a capitalist world-economy (Chase-Dunn 1982). The implication of this is that the mechanisms of change are not economic or political but both. Instead of Modelski's political framework we need a political-economy framework for bringing history back into our geopolitics.

Modelski's response to such criticism has been to find an alternative holistic framework in which to situate his model. He has found it in the classic work on social systems by Talcott Parsons. Modelski (1987: 118) finds it 'a matter of some satisfaction' that Parsonian terminology 'corresponds' to his own model. The cycles are broken down into four phases in which each generation of world power élites performs one of the classical Parsonian functions of 'latent pattern maintenance', 'integration', 'goal attainment' and 'adaption' in the changing world system. The result is that the sequence of global cycles define a 'learning curve' with each cycle building upon those that have gone before. World powers take on the role of teaching agents.

In many ways this new systems framework is preferable to Modelski's earlier use of general systems concepts in the sense that processes of change are more explicitly specified. But the resulting functionalism would seem to be too much for even the most dedicated 'lumper'. Most important of all his application of Parsonian analysis does nothing to clarify the interrelations between his political processes and the massive economic changes occurring at the very same time. Modelski (1981) has flirted with linking his model to Kondratieff waves, but this has proved most unsatisfactory and has been abandoned in favour of Parsons.

In the final instance Modelski's model must be seen in the context of current US decline. The most unusual feature of the model is the designation of the eighteenth century as Britain's. This sets an important precedent since at the end of her first cycle Britain lost 'a bungled colonial war' (the American War of Independence), which provided the shock and stimulus to start the processes rolling for a second century of world leadership (Modelski 1987; 87). It is but a short step from one bungled colonial war to another (the Vietnamese War of Independence), and a prediction of a forthcoming second 'American century'. If Britain can have two cycles, why not the United States? In short, Modelski provides a very optimistic model for a progressive world system and a powerful America.

2. Cycles of hegemony

In world-system analysis hegemony in the inter-state system is a very rare phenomenon. It has occurred just three times — Dutch hegemony in the mid-seventeenth century, British hegemony in the mid-nineteenth century and US hegemony in the mid-twentieth century. Such hegemonies encompass dominance in economic, political and ideological spheres of activity. But they are firmly based upon the development of an economic supremacy. This has involved three stages. First, the hegemonic state has gained primacy in production efficiency over its rivals. Second, this enables its merchants to build a commercial advantage. Third, the bankers of the state are able to achieve a financial dominance of the world-economy. When production, commercial and financial activities in one state are more efficient than in all rival states, then that state is hegemonic. Such states have been able to dominate the inter-state system, not by threatening some *imperium*, but by balancing forces in such a way as to prevent any rival coalition forming and growing large enough to threaten the hegemonic state's political leadership. Furthermore the hegemonic states have propagated liberal ideas that have been widely accepted throughout the world-system. Hence hegemonic states are much more than world political leaders.

The rise and establishment of a hegemonic state has been followed by its gradual decline. The very openness of the hegemonic state's liberalism enables rivals to copy the technical advances and emulate the production efficiencies. Soon the hegemonic state's lead over its rivals declines first in production and then subsequently in commerce and finance. In practice the two instances of decline have been cushioned to some degree by an alliance between the old declining and the new rising hegemonic state — the Dutch initially became Britain's junior partners, a role Britain took with respect to the United States after 1945. This may both smooth the transfer of leadership and help legitimate the new situation.

The rise and decline of hegemonic states defines a hegemonic cycle. Following Gordon (1980), Wallerstein (1984b) has tentatively related such cycles to three logistic waves of the world-economy. Such cycles involve long-term, world market control of investments that sustain the existence of hegemonic power. These investments are both political and economic, and produce a system-wide infrastructure. For instance, system-wide transport, communication and financial networks are a necessary requirement for hegemony. There is also a need for diplomatic networks and a pattern of military bases around the world. In this way each hegemonic state has built up a hegemonic infrastructure through which it has dominated the system. In each case world wars of approximately thirty years duration culminated in confirming hegemony and restructuring the inter-state system. Hence the Thirty Years' War ending in the treaties of Westphalia of 1648 mark the coming of the Dutch hegemonic system, the

Revolutionary/Napoleonic Wars ending in the Congress of Vienna of 1815 mark the coming of the British hegemonic system, and the twentieth century's two 'world wars' ending in the setting up of the United Nations in 1945 mark the coming of US hegemony.

Cycles of hegemony are not as neat as Modelski's long cycles. The three cycles do not match the symmetry of Modelski's five 'centuries' of leadership. There are broad parallels of timing with Modelski's model over the Dutch long cycle, the second British long cycle and the current US long cycle. But even here differences arise. Modelski, for instance, does not treat the Thirty Years' War in the seventeenth century as one of his 'world wars' (see Table 2.1), but prefers to consider it as a more regional (that is, European) war because of its lack of a major global dimension. The important differences arise, however, in relation to Modelski's Portuguese long cycle and the first British long cycle. We have already discussed the issue of the validity of Portuguese world leadership above. We can merely add here that the additional criterion world-system analysis sets for identifying hegemony completely rules out the candidature of Portugal in the sixteenth century.

Differences over Modelski's first British long cycle in the eighteenth century are much more interesting. This cycle is crucial for regularity in Modelski's model. In the hegemony cycles there is no equivalent regularity since the time span between the first two hegemonies is much longer than that between the last two. This is not only less neat, it is also less optimistic from a US viewpoint since it removes the precedent of Britain's double dose of leadership. In Wallerstein's analysis the eighteenth century represents nothing more than the ending of one logistic, the beginning of another and the intense political rivalry that such circumstances are associated with. The post-Dutch hegemony period of rivalry between Britain and France lasted longer than the post-British hegemony period of rivalry between the United States and Germany, but that does not negate the logic of the model. What is lost in symmetry is more than made up for in the more comprehensive nature of the hegemonic model.

3. British and American centuries: the paired Kondratieff model

Any model that uses logistic waves as its basis immediately brings forward the question of their relationship with Kondratieff cycles. In Chapter 1 we avoided this question by incorporating both types of cycle into our discussion, but for different time periods. Goldstein (1988) has reviewed this debate in relation to political cycles. Here we will consider simply the application of a Kondratieff model to the periods surrounding UK and US hegemony. This is important. First, it links the rise and fall of hegemony to the basic material processes of the world-economy as reflected in Kondratieff cycles. Second, it is a necessary addition to the hegemony model, since it brings the other world powers into the model. Finally, it shows that political mechanisms are an integral part of the overall restructuring of the world-economy that occurs within these cycles. It is this political element that is described here.

Political activity has always been an integral part of the world-economy. State policies are important processes in the changes observed in the world-economy. Since they are neither independent processes nor mere reflections of economic necessities ('economism') it follows that there is some choice available. If there were no choice there would be no need for public institutions such as the state. Public agencies have the role of distorting market forces in favour of those private groups controlling the agency. There has never been a 'pure' world-economy even in periods where free trade has dominated. The power of a public agency and hence its ability to organize the market depends upon the strength of its backers and their material resources. Strong states may promote a 'free market' while less strong states may favour explicit distortion of the market through protectionism, for instance. In this way states can act as a medium through which a first set of production processes (upon which the world-economy operates) are translated into a second set of distribution processes and patterns. Since these intermediate processes tend to favour the already-strong it follows that political activity will often increase the economic polarization of the market (that is helping the core at the expense of the periphery).

The power of a state to organize the market to its own ends is not just a property of that state's resources. The fact that we are dealing with a world-economy and not a world empire (that is, there is a multiplicity of states) means relative positions are more important than measures of absolute power. These state positions are relative not only to other states, however, but also to the gross availability of material resources within the world-economy. The cyclical nature of material growth means that opportunities for operating various state policies vary systematically over time. This is not just a matter of different economic environments being suited to alternative state strategies. At any particular conjunction, specifically successful policies can only work for a limited number of agencies. Quite simply every successful state eliminates opportunities for other states. There will always be constraints in terms of the total world resources available for redistribution via state activities. Given the 'correct' policies it is *not* possible for all semi-periphery states and the periphery to become core-like. Although this is not a zero-sum game in a static sense since the available production is always changing in a cyclical fashion, nevertheless we do have here a sort of 'dynamic zero-sum game'.

If state activity is an integral part of the operation of the world-economy we should be able to model it within our temporal and spatial framework. Just such a model has been proposed by Wallerstein and his associates (Research Working Group 1979). They postulate political activity occurring over a time-period covering two Kondratieff waves.

The rise and fall of hegemonic power relates to 'paired-Kondratieffs' as follows. If we start with a first growth phase, A-1, we find geopolitical rivalry as core states compete for succession to leadership. On hindsight, however, we can see new technological advances are concentrated in one country so that increased production efficiency gives this state a long-term advantage. A-1 is associated with the stage of *ascending hegemony*. In B-1 overall decline of the world-economy leaves less opportunities for expansion but the ascending power now derives commercial supremacy and is able to protect its interests relative to its rivals. By this stage it is clear which state is to be the hegemonic power. B-1 is associated with the stage of *hegemonic victory*. With renewed growth of the world-economy we reach A-2, the stage of *hegemonic maturity*. By this time the financial centre of the world-economy has moved to the hegemonic state which is now supreme in production, commerce and finance (that is, 'true' hegemony). Since the hegemonic power can successfully compete with all its rivals it now favours 'opening' the world-economy. These are periods of free trade. Finally, *declining hegemony* occurs during B-2 when production efficiency is no longer sufficient to dominate rivals. This results in acute competition as new powers try to obtain a larger share of a declining market. These are periods of protectionism and formal imperialism as each rival attempts to preserve its own portion of the periphery.

According to Wallerstein's research group the four Kondratieff cycles from the industrial revolution can be interpreted as two 'paired Kondratieffs' (Table 2.2). The first pair covering the nineteenth century correspond to the rise and fall of British hegemony and the second pair describe a similar sequence of events for the United States in the twentieth century. There is no need to consider this table in great detail except to note how several familiar episodes neatly fit into the model.

In terms of our discussion of state involvement in the operation of the world-economy, phases A-2 and B-2 are particularly important. In A-2 the hegemonic power imposes policies of open trade on the system to reap the rewards of its own efficiency. In the mid-nineteenth century Britain proclaimed 'free trade' backed up by gunboats and a century later a new world-policeman, this time with aircraft carriers, was going through the whole process of liberalizing trade once again. These policies certainly contributed to the massive growth of the world-economy in the A-2 phases and were imposed through a mixture of negotiation, bargaining and bullying. Options for non-hegemonic powers were highly constrained and they largely went along with the hegemonic leadership.

All this changes with the onset of the B-2 phase, however. As production efficiencies spread, economic leadership deserts the hegemonic power. These are key periods because of the opportunities that declining hegemony provides for other core and semi-periphery states. The imposition of free trade is no longer taken for granted as various states work out new strategies for the new circumstances. In the late nineteenth century Britain entered the Depression as hegemonic power and came out

Table 2.2   A dynamic model of hegemony and rivalry

	Great Britain	USA
	1790/8	1890/6
A_1 **Ascending Hegemony**	Rivalry with France (Napoleonic Wars) Productive efficiency: industrial revolution	Rivalry with Germany Productive efficiency: mass production techniques
	1815/25	1913/20
B_1 **Hegemonic Victory**	Commercial victory in Latin America and control of India: workshop of the world	Commercial victory in the final collapse of British free trade system and decisive military defeat of Germany
	1844/51	1940/5
A_2 **Hegemonic maturity**	Era of Free Trade: London becomes financial centre of the world-economy	Liberal economic system of Bretton Woods based upon the dollar: New York new financial centre of the world
	1870/75	1967/73
B_2 **Declining Hegemony**	Classical age of imperialism as European powers and USA rival Britain. 'New' industrial revolution emerging outside Britain	Reversal to protectionist practices to counteract Japan and European rivals
	1890/96	

behind Germany and the United States in terms of production efficiency. B-2 phases are clearly fundamental periods of restructuring in the world-economy in which geopolitical processes play an important role. We are currently living through just such a phase.

4. Cycles and geopolitical world orders

We are now in a position to identify geopolitical world orders within our models of world political cycles. The world orders refer to the specific system-wide arrangements for organizing the power hierarchy in the world-economy. The clearest examples are to be found during the brief phases of hegemony. In each case the Treaty of Westphalia, the Congress of Vienna and the aftermath of World War II produced new world orders that politically eliminated the previous threats to the new hegemonic power (Habsburg domains, France and Germany). However, with the decline of hegemony this world order begins to disintegrate and during the long periods of rivalry the situation is usually much less clear. But there is world order, of course, even after a hegemonic power has lost its ability to singly dominate the inter-state system. In the periods of rivalry between hegemonic phases anarchy does not prevail, rather the great powers have to accommodate one another's needs in patterns that may be much less stable than under hegemony. Nevertheless, geopolitical world orders transcend the special case of hegemony.

Let us consider in this light the period between British and US hegemony. The Congress of Vienna presided over the defeat of France and instituted a conservative international regime in Europe. This particularly suited Britain for two reasons. First, with the demise of France there was no European power that could threaten Britain's world-wide interests. Second, Britain could pursue a balance of power policy in Europe so as to prevent a coalition of states emerging to challenge Britain. Thus British hegemonic world order survived until the establishment of the German Empire under Prussian leadership in 1870. At this time we can identify what we may term a *geopolitical transition*, a changeover from one world order to another. Such transitions quite literally separate two distinctly different political worlds.

Prussian military successes against Austria in 1866 and France in 1870 completely transformed the situation in Europe. Following on from the earlier Anglo–French defeat of Russia in the Crimea, the new German Empire was clearly the pre-eminent power in continental Europe. In these circumstances Britain's balance of power policy was no longer viable. This in turn opened up the question of Britain's pre-eminence in the world beyond Europe. There were now two 'world cities' at the centre of international politics—London and Berlin. And it was in the latter in 1885 that all the major powers attended the famous conference that led to a sharing out of the spoils of the new imperialism. In this period of rivalry there were no firm alliances, but rather a fluid geopolitical pattern around a bi-polar centre. We may term this the British–German geopolitical world order.

Another important geopolitical transition occurs just after the turn of the century. The fluidity gives way to a new stability. In 1904 the British–French entente is signed and three years later Britain agrees a similar *entente* with France's ally Russia. In this way British foreign policy is completely transformed from its post-Congress of Vienna position of not having any committed alliances on continental Europe. Now, Britain was linked in alliance with her two traditional enemies against the new great rival Germany. (It is, of course, no coincidence that this is the time Mackinder produces his classic paper.) Europe was now divided into two power blocs which were to form the basis of the two sides in both world wars. We may term this the geopolitical world order of the British succession. The succession finally falls to the United States in 1945 and we arrive at a new hegemony and a further geopolitical world order.

THE COLD WAR AS A GEOPOLITICAL WORLD ORDER

There is no doubt that in 1945 by any reasonable criteria the United States could claim to be hegemonic. Germany, Japan and Italy were defeated, France had been occupied, Russia was devastated and Britain was bankrupt. In contrast, America's economy had expanded during the war. By 1945 she was responsible for over fifty per cent of world production. It would seem the US hegemony was even more impressive than the two previous hegemonies. And yet, in geopolitical terms, US hegemony was in no sense as successful as Britain's a century before. US hegemony has been 'spoilt' by the existence of a major ideological and military challenger, the USSR. Whereas Britain's balance of power policy involved staying on the outside and diplomatically manipulating the other great powers, the United States is an integral part of the new balance of power situation and has been continually involved in a massive and dangerous arms race. The Cold War is not what we have come to expect of a hegemonic geopolitical world order. How did this come about?

1. Geopolitical transition to the Cold War

The short period after World War II is a classic example of a geopolitical transition. If we take the world situation either side of the transition we soon appreciate the immensity of the change that took place. This is symbolized by two world events only a decade apart and both occurring in German cities. In 1938 at Munich, Britain and Germany negotiated to stave off a world war. In 1948 at Berlin the USA and the USSR confronted each other in what many believed would lead to another world war. In only a decade everything had changed — new leaders, new challengers, a new geopolitical world order.

It surprised many observers at the time how quickly the victorious allies of 1945 split to produce a new confrontation. By 1947 the Cold War was evident for all to see. In fact we have already observed how previous geopolitical transitions have also involved relatively rapid turn arounds — this seems to be the norm. But for those involved this rapid production of new enemies was a mystery requiring a 'solution'. Hence a huge literature has been produced on the creation of the Cold War. Two main schools of thought have emerged producing contrary conclusions. The so-called 'orthodox' school blames USSR expansionism that left the United States with no alternative but containment policies. After the United States' Vietnam experience a revisionist school emerged that blamed the United States. In this argument the USSR was ostracised for not succumbing to the USA's hegemonic world strategy. Today, both of these positions are considered to be too simplistic. There are now numerous post-revisionist

positions that analyze the complexity of early post-World War II
international relations. From a geopolitical perspective the most
interesting are those that emphasize the role of Britain in the making of
the Cold War (Taylor, forthcoming).

In 1945 the geopolitical situation was very fluid. The Big Three victors
had very different priorities. The United States had clear economic
priorities to open up the world for American business. Britain had political
priorities to remain a major power. Although Britain had effectively
mortgaged her future in loans to win the war, she remained the largest
empire in the history of the world. The USSR's priority was clearly to
safeguard its western flank in Eastern Europe through which she had been
invaded twice in twenty years. At first these various interests seemed to be
compatible with one another in the goodwill generated by war victory.
This was summarized in President Roosevelt's vision of 'one world' and
symbolized by the creation of the United Nations. In this idealistic
conception of the world the divisive power-politics of the past was
banished and replaced by a world of friendship and co-operation.

What went wrong? The problem power among the Big Three was Great
Britain. The other two members of the triumvirate were clearly
super-powers of continental proportions. Britain was a small island with a
scattered empire whose loyalty could no longer be relied upon. It is not
surprising, therefore, that the main priority of British politicians at this
time was the devising of policies to maintain Britain in the top rank
alongside the United States and the Soviet Union. And it was soon
appreciated that this would require outside financial aid. The British
economy was in such dire straights that bankruptcy could only be avoided
by negotiating an emergency loan for which the United States was the only
source. The loan that was successfully negotiated in December 1945 had
commercial and financial strings attached to it. In simple terms, the
British Empire was being prised open for American business. Despite the
support of the latter the agreement was very difficult to sell to the
American public. Why should they foot the bill to prop up the British
Empire? In the event the agreement passed through Congress in the wake
of the first post-war bout of anti-Communism in the United States. Hence
Britain was not supported because it was necessary for US business, rather
Britain was supported as a bulwark against the threat of expanding
communism. According to Kolko and Kolko (1973), US foreign policy
moved from negotiation to crusade.

Not unnaturally Britain encouraged and supported the new crusade.
The USSR became isolated and Britain moved into a position of chief ally
of the hegemonic power. In the two years after World War II Britain
undermined the international relations based on the Big Three concept in
numerous ways (Taylor, forthcoming). Britain's Foreign Secretary, Ernest
Bevin, worked assiduously against the USSR in the regular meetings of
foreign ministers (Deighton 1987). Sir Winston Churchill gave his Fulton

speech in 1946 in which he used the famous phrase 'Iron Curtain' to
signify a division of Europe (Harbutt 1986). In 1947, Britain informed the
United States that it could no longer maintain its troops in Greece and
Turkey. This precipitated President Truman's speech in which the United
States promised to support free peoples everywhere. The Truman Doctrine
was clearly targeted at the USSR and marks the formal beginning of the
Cold War.

From Britain's perspective this represented a major diplomatic success:
the United States had finally come to recognize its hegemonic
responsibilities. Britain played a leading role in 1948 in operating the
Marshall Plan, giving US aid to Western Europe. Then, in the next year
Britain again played the leading role in the formation of the North
Atlantic Treaty Organization. A new world was created under US
leadership with Britain having a 'special relationship' as the trusted
deputy while leaving the USSR out in the cold. In short, Britain had
solved, at least for the time being, its post-war crisis of power. It is not
surprising, therefore, that some authorities have concluded that the Cold
War was in reality a 'secondary effect' of Britain's prime objective to
remain a first rank power (Ryan 1982).

This interpretation of the making of the Cold War has the advantages of
accounting for the rapidity of change from 'one world' to the bi-polar
situation of 1947. It is, nevertheless, only a partial explanation, but it does
highlight part of the political process in what was a most definitive
geopolitical transition.

2. *Phases of the Cold War*

Whatever the importance of Britain's role in the making of the Cold War,
it is certain that the subsequent developments definitely focused on the
two superpowers: the Cold War is the responsibility of the United States
and the Soviet Union from 1947 to the present time.

The phrase 'Cold War' is a very unusual one in that it has been
associated with two different 'opposites'. When Walter Lippman first
coined the phrase in 1947 it was to contrast the contemporary USA−USSR
differences with the recent 'hot war' with Germany. In this sense 'cold' is
the opposite of 'hot'. Cold War implies a 'stand off' situation rather than
direct conflict. Subsequently, a rather different alternative to Cold War
has emerged, which emphasizes accommodation between the
super-powers. In this case the Cold War is said to have 'thawed'. These
temperature analogies are confusing because both 'hot' and 'thaw'
themselves represent opposite political outcomes − war and *détente*.
Nevertheless, these terms are now etched into our political language with
relations between the super-powers being described as sometimes 'blowing
hot and cold' and at other times 'thawing'. Hence Halliday (1983) uses
these concepts to divide the Cold War into four phases. We will use his
periodization to show how the original pattern of conflicts, mimicking

Mackinder's Heartland theory, has gradually evolved into a broader global pattern. In Halliday's first period, what he calls the 'First Cold War' from 1947 to 1953, all the major super-power confrontations occur in the Rimland. This is a period when super-power relations run hot and cold — from the original crisis in Greece and Turkey in 1947, through the Berlin blockade of 1948 to the real hot war in Korea. The next period of 'oscillatory antagonism' from 1953 to 1969 is a mixture of crises and summits combining hot, cold and thaw elements. Rimland conflicts move to the Middle East and South-East Asia. But now we get the first major confrontation beyond the 'world-island' in Cuba. From 1969 to 1979 we come to the third period, when the thaw dominates. *Détente* represents a concerted effort to produce a negotiated settlement of differences. Conflict continues in the Middle East, but now differences are appearing also in southern Africa and central America. After 1979 a new phase begins, Halliday's, 'Second Cold War', in which the thaw disappears. Although important Rimland confrontations remain in the Middle East, southern Africa and central America come to play as important a part in super-power relations. By this time the Cold War has lost its 'Mackinderesque' pattern and has become pervasive across the globe from Nicaragua to Afghanistan. Since 1985 a new thaw has occurred but the Cold War geopolitical world order remains firmly in place as world security continues to be viewed as a matter for just the two super-powers — the United States and the Soviet Union.

3. Cold War as superstructure

How do we interpret this geopolitical world order as a superstructure in world-systems analysis? Basically the Cold War is a political structure based upon two contrary relations between the super-powers — opposition and dependence (Cox 1986). Most theories of the Cold War emphasize one relation at the expense of the other. We will try and achieve a better balance between the two.

Theories of opposition are generally concerned to apportion blame, building upon the 'orthodox' and 'revisionist' schools in the making of the Cold War literature. Hence the Cold War is either the result of the Soviet threat or a reflection of US imperialism. In either case the world is viewed as facing a climactic conflict between two opposing world views — communism and capitalism. These alternative ways of life based upon completely different values are incompatible. In Halliday's (1983) terms this is 'The Great Contest', which may be seen as an ideological battle or, more fundamentally, as global class conflict.

This view of the Cold War interprets the geopolitical world order on the terms set out by the adversaries. It is quite literally the Cold Warriors' version of the Cold War. The world is divided into just three types of place 'ours', 'theirs' and various disputed spaces. The conflict is unbridgeable; the end result is either a communist or capitalist world.

We should, of course, always be wary of those who set the political agenda. We know from Schattschneider that agenda setting can never be a neutral process. There is nothing natural or inevitable about the Cold War. It is a particular world order that favours some issues at the expense of others. We must ask ourselves, therefore, what issues are organized off the political agenda by the Cold War. Presumably these are matters that are not the prime concern of either super-power. In short, they are dependent on each other in maintaining a world order that highlights super-power politics.

In this sort of argument the Cold War acts as a diversion from alternative politics. Such diversions have been identified at three geographical scales. At the domestic level for each super-power the Cold War has been instrumental in mobilizing their populations behind the state in its confrontation with its enemy. It has enabled narrow definitions of loyalty to be used to marginalize alternative politics within each country. In the United States the main example is the anti-communist hysteria of the early 1950s led by Senator McCarthy. This produced a consensus on US foreign policy that was maintained for a generation before the Vietnam debacle fractured public opinion. In the USSR the Cold War has allowed the persecution and marginalizing of various 'dissident' groups.

Beyond their own countries the Cold War has enabled both super-powers to maintain a firm control on their allies. Each super-power leads a bloc of countries whose foreign policy options are severely curtailed. The most naked examples of the constraints are to be found in Eastern Europe and Latin America. In the former the Soviet Union has militarily intervened to prevent liberal or revisionist regimes appearing, and in the latter the United States has intervened to stop radical or socialist regimes appearing. In fact, one of the most remarkable features of the Cold War has been the success of both super-powers in maintaining bloc cohesion.

Finally, beyond the blocs the Cold War can be interpreted as deflecting attention from the North—South issue of massive global material inequalities. We have already discussed this briefly in Chapter 1 in terms of the decline of the United Nations as a major actor in the world-economy as its focus has moved away from East—West issues towards North—South issues. In this argument the Great Contest is in reality the Great Conspiracy.

There is no doubt that the super-powers have used the Cold War to bolster their own positions (Wallerstein 1984a). For instance, the 'Second Cold War' phase can be understood as a reaction to the relative economic decline of the United States. By concentrating on the military sphere the United States temporarily side-stepped its economic difficulties and re-established its leadership. There is no doubt that the United States remains number one in the West as a political power. In this sense the

United States has used the Soviet Union in its competition with rival friendly states. But, on the other hand, there is no doubt that the Soviet Union has represented a genuine challenge to the United States, both militarily and ideologically. It is the Soviet Union that has made the Cold War geopolitical world order so unusual. The role of the USSR in the world-economy is a completely novel one — it combines a semi-peripheral economy with a super-power political status. We cannot possibly understand the Cold War without coming to terms with this mismatch between economics and politics.

4. A world-systems interpretation of the USSR

We have seen that the traditional approaches to geopolitics treat the USSR as a land-power threat to the traditional dominance of sea powers. To balance the picture we will start our discussion by giving the Soviet view of its world position. In contrast to the expansionary motives assumed in western strategy, the USSR interprets its position as essentially defensive. This viewpoint in based upon two invasions since its inception in 1917 — first, US and Western European support for White Russians in the Civil War of 1918−21 and second, the German invasion of 1941−44. Hence the Soviet Union is the protector of the socialist world surrounded by a hostile capitalism. One country's containment is indeed another country's expansion!

For our argument here the most relevant part of the Soviet model is the notion of *two* world-systems operating contemporaneously, a capitalist one and a socialist one. This notion stems from Stalin's attempt to build socialism in one country between the world wars. It was expanded with the institution of COMECON after the Second World War as a 'co-operative division of labour' in Eastern Europe, in contrast to the capitalist competitive division of labour in the West. An attempt has been made by Szymanski (1982) to integrate this orthodox Marxist position with Wallerstein's framework. He claims that there are indeed two separate world-systems and economic transactions between them constitute luxury trade rather than essential trade. In this sense the two systems co-exist in the way other contemporaneous systems (Roman and Chinese world-empires, for instance) have done before. This conception of two separate economic systems that compete politically is, of course, the mirror image of American geopolitics. We will show that both positions provide less insight than a world-systems interpretation of a single world-economy.

Charles Levinson (1980) has provided a wealth of evidence to expose what he terms 'the ideological façade' of both US and USSR geopolitics. The following selection of some of the information he has compiled will give an indication of the basis of his argument. He shows that the largest forty multinational corporations all have co-operative agreements with one or more of the eight Eastern European states with communist regimes —

thirty-four of them with the Soviet Union itself. He lists 151 corporations from fifteen different countries which have offices in Moscow. There are 108 multinational corporations from thirteen countries listed as operating in Bucharest alone. In the other direction, 170 acknowledged multinational joint-ventures by the USSR in nineteen Western countries are tabled. It is not surprising therefore that by 1977 one-third of USSR imports and one-quarter of USSR exports were with Western countries. Levinson's conclusion is that although it is international politics which makes the news it is these crucial economic transactions which steer international politics. Hence, *détente* followed trade, and *not* vice versa. This is what Levinson calls the 'overworld' of economic dealings which have seen USSR and Eastern Europe become inexorably integrated into the world-economy. It is epitomized by the Pepsi Cola Corporation's deal to sell cola drink in Russia and to market vodka in the West — hence the title of Levinson's book *Vodka Cola*.

Gunder Frank (1977) has provided further evidence for the same process, which he terms *trans-ideological enterprise*. He charts the massive rise in East—West trade especially since the death of Stalin in 1954 and discusses the various bartering arrangements and other agreements which have made this growth possible. The motives for all this activity are very traditional. For the corporations there is an extension of the geographical range of their profit-making. This is particularly important at a time of world-wide recession. The Eastern European states provide a source of relatively cheap, yet skilled, disciplined and healthy labour. And, of course, there is the vast raw material potential of the Soviet Union. For the latter the motive is equally straightforward. Co-operation with Western corporations was the only solution to a technology lag which the Soviet Union has suffered in the wake of the rise of electronic industries in the West. Increasing integration into the world-economy is the price the USSR has to pay for keeping up with its ideological competitors.

Wallerstein interprets all this evidence as placing the Soviet Union and its Eastern European allies in the semi-periphery. Gunder Frank (1977) shows that the Soviet Union lies in an intermediate position between 'west' and 'south'. For instance, East—South trade is used to pay for East—West trade in numerous multilateral arrangements. In short, the USSR exploits the South but is itself exploited by the West in terms of trade arrangements. (This process of unequal exchange in trade is explained in Chapter 3 under 'informal imperialism'.) This places the Soviet regime economically on a par with other non-socialist semi-peripheral countries such as Brazil or Iran. Although it can be argued that *within* COMECON, trade is not capitalistic — prices are not set by the world market — trade is influenced by world market prices. Furthermore this production is for exchange, and ultimate use of production is grossly distorted by the world-economy as a whole through its aggressive inter-state system. With our single political economy logic the current situation of the USSR and its allies cannot be interpreted as anything other than as an integral part of the world-economy.

If the Soviet Union represents an example of an aggressive upward-moving semi-periphery state where does this leave its socialist rhetoric? According to Brucan (1981), Eastern Europe provides a model for development strategy rather than for socialism. From the very beginning, with Lenin's New Economic Policy of 1921, the essence of Soviet policy has been to 'catch up' and this involved all-out mobilization of national potential. The original heavy industry 'import substitution' phase of protectionism or autarchy has given way to an export orientation in the 1970s which Frank and Levinson have charted (Koves 1981). In fact the original ideology of the revolution had to be developed to invent the intermediate state of 'socialism' between capitalism and communism to cover the period when the USSR was 'developing the forces of production'. All this seems very much like mercantilism in new clothing (Frank 1977; Wallerstein 1982 and Chase-Dunn 1982). The United States, Germany and Japan have in their turn been aggressive, upwardly mobile, semi-peripheral states who have used political means (protectionism, public investment in infrastructure and other support) to improve their competitive position in the world-economy. Soviet 'socialism' seems to be a classic case of a modern semi-periphery strategy.

But, of course, the USSR is more than just another rising semi-periphery state. The establishment of the Soviet state in 1917 was the culmination of a revolutionary movement whose internationalism was stemmed but which nevertheless represented, and still represents, an ideological challenge to the capitalism of the world-economy. With the revolution initially limited to Russia, Stalin had no option but to build 'socialism in one country' — to catch up before the new state was destroyed. From this point onwards the logic of the world-system placed the USSR in a 'Catch 22' situation. In order to survive the state needed to compete with other states but this competition involved playing the world-economy game by capitalist rules. This has come to a head in the current recession. There have always been policy conflicts within the Soviet bloc between fundamentalists who emphasize their socialist credentials and the technocrats who emphasize efficiency. This 'red versus expert' conflict has been recently resolved in the latter's favour under the pressures of the current world recession. This can be seen throughout Eastern Europe and is particularly obvious in post-Mao China.

The fact that the world-revolutionary movement — Wallerstein terms it anti-systemic forces — is currently in the vice of the world-economy does not lessen the unique nature of the USSR challenge to US hegemony. Never before has a semi-peripheral state had the world-wide impact that the Soviet state has had. Unlike other semi-periphery states the USSR is *not* a regional power in Cohen's term, but is truly a political super-power of global proportions. During its period of hegemony the USA has been challenged by the USSR on all continents. This is because the socialist ideology of the USSR has been more compatible with peripheral liberation movements than the USA's liberalism. Nearly all national movements in the second half of the twentieth century have employed socialist rhetoric even if they have been unable to practise fully these ideas. The result has been that the challenge to the USA's hegemony has been on two fronts — political and ideological by the USSR, and with the downturn of the current Kondratieff wave, economic by Europe and Japan.

A NEW GEOPOLITICAL TRANSITION?

For most people born since World War II the Cold War geopolitical world order must seem immutable (Thompson 1987). Their only experience of global politics has been of the USA versus the USSR. The Great Contest can appear to be almost natural and eternal. Even the changes brought about during the 'thaw' periods of *détente* reinforce the same world order — a dangerous Cold War becomes a safe Cold War. When we talk of a geopolitical transition we are thinking of much more fundamental changes than that envisaged by the advocates of *détente*. A geopolitical transition would mark the end of the Cold War. The Great Contest would disappear and the world would be organized in an altogether different way. The two world politics would be as different as those between Munich in 1938 and Berlin in 1948.

Brunn (1981) has provided ten scenarios for the twenty-first century in which different geopolitical themes are explored. One of his scenarios represents the chilliest way of ending the Cold War. Global nuclear war and the Armageddon scenario has haunted the Cold War geopolitical world order throughout its history, generating opposition and providing a rationale for *détente*. However, a failure to prevent nuclear war would produce not so much a geopolitical transition as a biological transition between species as *homo sapiens* eliminate themselves. Unfortunately, we have to acknowledge the Armageddon scenario as a real possibility. Nevertheless, we shall proceed on the assumption that the Cold War will not culminate in global disaster and that to search for a geopolitical transition is a realistic undertaking.

The simplest alternative scenario is to use our paired-Kondratieff model to predict a 'Japanese century'. As US hegemony winds down the question of a successor naturally arises and on almost all economic criteria Japan seems to be the most likely hegemonic candidate. This is certainly the most discussed scenario and Paul Kennedy's (1988) success is most certainly based on his raising of this possibility. His model postulates that all great powers overstretch themselves militarily and this becomes a particularly acute problem when economic decline sets in. Hence the demise of great powers from the Habsburgs to the British Empire. Is the United States the latest great power to succumb to this process? What makes Japan look so good as successor in this sort of discussion is that its economic prowess is unencumbered by any military commitments. Here, surely, is a new hegemonic state in the making.

There is another way of reading the history of hegemonic states, however. In the three cases so far each new hegemonic power has been substantially larger than its predecessor. In this light Japan as a medium-sized state does not look the part to take over from the United States. We will emphasize this size criterion in our discussion of future geopolitics.

1. Super-states, pan-regions and world classes

The replacement of American hegemony by a new era of rivalry is now generally accepted — as long ago as 1971 President Nixon recognized the new 'multi-polarity'. Five poles are usually identified: the USA, the USSR, Western Europe, Japan and China. These are obviously derived first from the disintegration of the eastern bloc with the Sino–Soviet split and second from what Kaldor (1979) identifies as a 'disintegrating west' reflecting Japanese and European economic rivalry with the United States. But these 'poles' cover only about one half of the world's population. Here we will extend the discussion to the remainder of the world by using Galtung's (1979) model of the territorial structure of the world.

In Fig. 2.3a we have presented a simplified version of Galtung's model portraying the world as ten 'super-states'. The model is arranged in approximate geographical order so that it can express both East–West and North–South political conflicts. Five regions of the South are added to the original five 'poles' in Galtung's diagram. Our complete list of super-states now reads United States plus Canada, European Community plus the rest of Western Europe, Soviet Union plus Eastern Europe, Japan, Africa, Middle East, India plus the rest of South Asia, South-East Asia with Oceania, and finally Latin America. Clearly, these potential super-states display a wide range of levels of economic and political unity. Nevertheless, they have all experienced some moves towards political and/or economic co-operation in recent years: the United States is joining with Canada in a trade bloc; the European Community has expanded to incorporate almost all of Western Europe, and this process seems set to continue; the Soviet Union and Eastern Europe are already tied together in COMECON; Japan is a nation-state; Africa has its Organization of African Unity; the Middle East has its Arab League and is the focus of OPEC; SARC is the South Asian Association for Regional Cooperation; China is a nation-state, South-East Asia has its Association of South-East Asian Nations; and finally, there is the Latin America Free Trade Association. Although these organizations vary immensely in their success in mobilizing economic and political power, they all reflect a tendency towards the growth of larger political actors on the world scene.

Galtung (1979) proposes several alternative future geopolitical scenarios.

a) Super-states

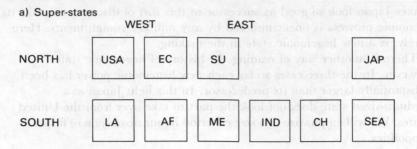

b) Pan-regions

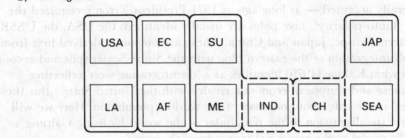

c) World-classes

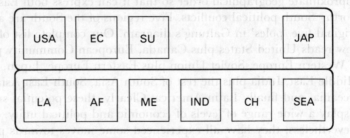

d) Ideological fracture

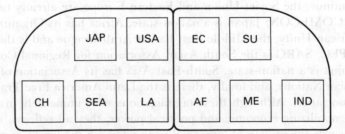

Fig. 2.3   Alternative geopolitical scenarios

One is the development of super-state rivalry based upon these ten units. In this scenario these ten super-states will exist in a perennial world of trading wars as each super-state vies for economic advantage. In these battles ideological differences become unimportant and Cold War alliances collapse.

A second Galtung scenario takes the super-state thesis a stage further, with each unit trying to protect its economy by promoting autarchy. The end result of such a process is the re-discovery of pan-regions as northern super-states combine with their southern neighbours (Fig. 2.3b). Since there are only four northern super-states this produces four pan regions which may or may not include India and China.

In a third scenario Galtung pits North against South (Fig. 2.3c). He terms these 'world classes'. This represents a 'Third-worldist' view of world politics represented in the past by China's claim to be leader of the Third World against the combined might of the United States and the Soviet Union. This sort of thinking is closely related to the social analyses from which world-systems analysis derives. The revolt of the periphery against the core is a central political and/or economic project of dependency theory. We will discuss this further in Chapter 3, under 'imperialism'.

2. An ideological fracture?

In world-systems analysis a rather different scenario to a simple clash of 'world classes' in suggested. Since the relative decline of the US economy is the fundamental change of the late twentieth century, it follows that we must search for a geopolitical transition in the reorganization consequent to that decline. So far this economic pressure has been mainly reflected in a sporadic willingness to negotiate arms reductions. Wallerstein (1984a: 65–6) speculates that we shall see a far more fundamental effect that will create a new geopolitical world order.

We must go back to the Sino–Soviet split of 1962 to begin the story. This ideological split divided the Communist bloc. The question is whether the split will eventually extend to divide the capitalist camp in the same way. If this happens it may produce a new world where a 'Greater Europe' faces a combination of 'Pacific Rim' powers (Fig. 2.3d).

The first steps in this transition occurred with US–Chinese rapprochement during the *détente* of the 1970s. Although this move was within the logic of the Cold War — breaking up the Communist monolith — it nevertheless represented a political agreement across the 'two worlds'. The next step will need to be an economic *rapprochement* with Japan. If trade wars can be prevented there are major advantages to both Japan and the United States to share a combined technological leadership in most leading sectors of the world-economy. Wallerstein points to the Toyota-General Motors co-operation deal as an indicator of this process. The result could be a formidable world bloc centred upon China, Japan and the United States. If this were to materialize it would represent the final victory of the (US) West Coast pro-Asia lobby over the Eastern Establishment Europhiles.

But what would this mean for Europe? Although the super-powers are essentially extra-European, Europe has always been at the centre of the Cold War geopolitical world order. The Pacific Rim power bloc threatens to displace Europe from the centre of world affairs to a side-show location. Western Europe can only retaliate with a European *détente* — accommodation with the Soviet bloc (Wallerstein, 1988). By re-uniting eastern and western Europe this could form the basis of a new Greater Europe bloc incorporating Africa, the Middle East and even India.

What would this new bi-polar world order represent? The key point is that it cuts right across the ideological justification for the Cold War. Both sides are focused on communist-capitalist accommodations. Hence, from the point of view of current geopolitical assumptions, Wallerstein's scenario is ideologically absurd. But that, of course, is the nature of any geopolitical transition — the absurd becomes the obvious.

GEOPOLITICAL CODES

We have already defined geopolitical codes as the set of strategic assumptions a government makes about other states in forming its foreign policy. They are closely related to what Henrikson (1980) calls 'image-plans'. Such operational codes involve evaluation of places beyond the state's boundaries in terms of their strategic importance and as potential threats. Geopolitical codes are not just state-centric, they involve a particular single state's view of the world. They are by definition, therefore, highly biased pictures of the world. Nevertheless, we must come to terms with them and understand them as the basic building blocks of geopolitical world orders.

Geopolitical codes operate at three levels — local, regional and global. The local level code involves evaluation of neighbouring states. Governments of all countries, however small, must have such a code. Regional level codes are required for states who aspire to project their power beyond their immediate neighbours. The governments of all regional powers and potential regional powers need to map out such codes. Finally, a few states will have global policies and their governments will have appropriate world-wide geopolitical codes. Hence, all countries have local codes, many countries have regional codes and a few countries have global codes.

Some simple examples will help fix these ideas. Bartlett gives a very clear example of one major power's three levels of concern in World War I. For Germany 'the war is one of defence against France, prevention against Russia but a struggle for world supremacy with Britain' (Bartlett

1984: 89). Sometimes a regional code will be in conflict with a local code. The best example of this is the traditional local hostility between Greece and Turkey, which contrasts with their sharing a similar regional code set by membership of NATO. In fact, treaties are a good indicator of codes, especially at the regional level. The change round of Australia and New Zealand from being part of Britain's global code to having their own regional (Pacific) code is marked by the establishment of the ANZUS pact just after the end of World War II. Australian and New Zealand troops fought in Europe in both world wars, but it is unlikely that they will do so again — Europe is now beyond their geopolitical codes.

In the discussion below I will concentrate upon global geopolitical codes, but this does not necessarily mean that I believe the other code levels to be unimportant. Quite the opposite, in fact. Local codes, for instance, are implicated in the vast majority of wars. In the large scale quantitative analyses by political scientists conducted to find the causes of war, the results have been disappointing save for one consistent finding: war is more likely between any two states where they share a border (Zinnes 1980). Political geographers have followed this up with their own analysis of the spatial contiguity of war and have confirmed the findings of the political scientists (O'Loughlin 1986). Although the spectacular world wars by definition involve all geographical levels of activity, most wars occur only between neighbours with conflicting local geopolitical codes.

Even by restricting our concern to global-level codes we are still unable to even approach a comprehensive review of such a massive topic. We will concentrate, therefore, on recent US codes for which there is good documentation and treat in less detail aspects of French and Indian global codes to indicate some of the variety beyond US views of the world.

CONTAINMENT: THE GEOPOLITICAL CODES OF US HEGEMONY

US foreign policy since World War II is often summarized by the term 'containment', implying a defensive posture against an expanding Soviet enemy. We have previously used this concept as a general term to describe modern US geopolitics, but as we move to the level of operational codes we soon find that containment has meant rather different things at different times. There is no single 'containment code', rather there are a family of geopolitical codes to which the general term 'containment' has been applied. These codes are very different from one another and have fundamentally different implications for foreign policy. We will concentrate on George Kennan's original formulation of containment as our illustration of this type of geopolitical code before showing how it has been crucially modified as a blueprint for US foreign policy since 1950.

1. George Kennan's geopolitical code

Kennan's geopolitical code must be seen, first and foremost, as a reaction against the idealistic thinking in US foreign policy in the period surrounding World War II. Kennan was an opponent of such universalistic thinking, especially as it applied to the Soviet Union which was his specialist area of expertise. In 1945 the USA was pursuing a 'one world' policy by trying to entice the USSR as a partner in a new world order. This 'containment by integration', as Gaddis (1982: 9) calls it, was failing in its objectives when Kennan sent his famous 'long telegram' from Moscow in February 1946, explaining why such integration was impossible. Quite simply the USSR was playing a different sort of game — universalistic prescriptions were therefore useless.

Although well received, the telegram did not signal a new coherent US policy. For the next year a 'harder' line was taken in Soviet relations — the so-called 'patient and firm' stand — which culminated in the Truman Declaration of March 1947. Although this is usually taken as a fundamental point of departure for a new foreign policy — containment no less — Gaddis (1982) argues that this interpretation hides the continuing incoherence of US foreign policy in early 1947. The speech to Congress was forced on the President by Britain's planned withdrawal from Greece and Turkey. Its purpose was to get congressional support and its rhetoric was designed accordingly. Hence the apparent world-wide pledge to support 'free peoples' everywhere. This universalistic rhetoric to achieve particular ends was just the sort of policy statement Kennan deplored. What was the use of promising what could not be delivered? The Truman Doctrine created a massive credibility gap based upon a mismatch of ends and means. Between 1945 and 1947, US armed forces had been reduced from 12 million to 1.5 million. An equivalent reduction in the defence budget had accompanied this demobilization. Hence the globalist rhetoric could not be translated into its corollary, what we might term a blanket containment policy. Kennan's containment policy was a much more subtle argument following traditional power-political precepts.

In 1947, Secretary of State George Marshall appointed Kennan to a new position as director to his Policy Planning Staff. At the same time the famous 'Mr X' article appeared in the journal *Foreign Affairs*; the article analysed Soviet foreign policy and its implications for the United States. As a government employee Kennan tried to remain anonymous, but he was soon revealed to be 'Mr X'. This article was important because it introduced the term 'containment', which now began to be used as a general description of government policy in the new circumstances of the Cold War. Unfortunately, the article is somewhat confusing as a statement of Kennan's views and we are indebted to the careful researches of Gaddis (1982) who used other documents, especially those reporting Kennan's speeches and lectures at this time, to reconstruct the geopolitical code Kennan was advocating.

Since Kennan's first premise was that 'not all parts of the world were equally vital to American security' (Gaddis 1982: 30) his initial task as advisor was to attempt to order places in terms of their importance for US security. He began by identifying three broad zones — the Atlantic community from Canada to Western Europe, the Mediterranean and Middle East as far as Iran, and the Western Pacific covering Japan and the Philippines. He further refined his argument to produce four vital power centres. These were identified in terms of their industrial potential to sustain a modern war against the United States. Britain, Germany, Japan and the USSR are so identified, and with the USA these constitute Kennan's five power nodes of the modern world. In 1947 only one of these power centres, the Soviet Union, was hostile to the United States. The problem was to limit hostility to just one power centre and prevent a repeat of World War II when two of these power centres, Germany and Japan, together threatened US security. The means of achieving this end was a traditional balance of power strategy. This meant that power vacuums could no longer be allowed to exist in Germany and Japan. These had to be converted to friendly powers alongside Britain.

Once these vital power vacuums were filled, however, Kennan did not envisage any further interference in the internal affairs of these or any other countries. This was to be a classical hegemonic balance of power policy, with the United States on the outside using diplomatic and other means to prevent a threatening hostile alliance emerging:

> It should be noted that what Kennan was advocating was not an American sphere of influence in Europe or Asia, but rather the emergence of centres of power in these regions independent of both Soviet and American control. (Gaddis 1982: 31)

Hence US policy was to bolster friendly powers with economic rather than military aid. Kennan was a strong supporter of the Marshall Plan for western Europe and insisted that the economic aid should be administered by Europeans not Americans.

The Soviet threat was viewed as being political rather than military. The Marshall Plan was to prevent economic collapse in Europe from which only the Soviet Union would make political gains. Kennan sometimes referred to the Soviet threat as 'psychological' since its aim was to 'demoralize the democracies'. But here lay an important difficulty in operationalizing this code. Demoralization could occur because of events outside the five power centres — if communist forces took control of a neighbouring country, for instance. Hence, Kennan identified important non-industrial areas around the five power centres that were important though not vital. Such areas had to be safeguarded because their demise may change the politics of an adjacent power centre. Here we see the origins of the domino theory. For this reason Kennan supported Truman's pledge of support for Greece and Turkey. It should be emphasized though that this did not mean he supported anti-communist wars everywhere — he was against intervention in China for instance.

This geopolitical code is genuinely hegemonic in nature and can be compared with Britain's policy of a century earlier. There are three key elements of similarity: a diplomatic use of a balance of power strategy to prevent any powerful hostile alliances emerging; no major military entanglements and no land wars; but a willingness for limited intervention in key locations to maintain the balance of power. Unlike Britain's hegemonic code that lasted half a century, the US limited containment code survived only two years. Ironically, it became a victim of the Cold War and was converted into a series of much more comprehensive containment strategies in later years.

2. Variations in containment codes

Kennan's containment code was the first of a family of such codes. Gaddis (1982) identifies four distinctive geopolitical codes between 1949 and 1979. Although each new code shared a common presumption of the Great Contest between the USA and the USSR, they had different assumptions concerning the nature of that conflict and hence produced different policy prescriptions. Geopolitically they diverged from Kennan's balance of power model in two main ways: instead of isolating the enemy, the enemy is either surrounded or pursued.

After 1949 the focus of world affairs seemed to move from Europe to Asia. Kennan's containment code did not survive the 'fall' of China and the coming of the Korean War. This precipitated a security policy rethink which produced the famous document NSC-68. The fundamental difference with Kennan was that whereas he saw US interests served by diversity, NSC-68 favoured uniformity to produce a more predictable world. Furthermore, since the Soviets now represented a world-wide threat, there was a need for a world-wide reply. The result was a blanket containment model to surround the enemy. The geopolitical implications were clear: NSC-68 proposed 'a perimeter defence, with all points along the perimeter considered of equal importance' (Gaddis 1982: 91). Instead of defending selected strongpoints, NSC-68 claimed that 'a defeat of free institutions anywhere is a defeat everywhere' (Gaddis 1982: 91).

Perimeter containment concedes a third of the world's population to communism. In the anti-communist fever in the USA of the 1950s this was not acceptable to many right-wing politicians. They demanded a bolder foreign policy where the USA took the initiative. The concept of 'roll-back' entered the political volcabulary. The new Republican administration of 1953 accused the previous Democratic government of 'abandoning' millions of people to communism. Under Secretary of State John Foster Dulles, a 'New Look' foreign policy was proclaimed. This incorporated assumptions completely at variance with previous containment codes. The Soviet threat was interpreted ideologically as a great world-wide communist menace. Whereas Kennan considered communist ideology a tool of the Soviet state, Dulles thought the Soviet state to be a tool of the

communist movement. This changed the whole nature of the Great
Contest. Threat of nuclear retaliation became the prime means of stopping
communism. Geopolitically the key development was the massive
extension of covert activity by the CIA under the Secretary of State's
brother Allen Dulles. This involved direct intervention in the affairs of
other states. Activities that have come to light include the overthrow of
two foreign governments (Iran in 1953 and Guatemala in 1954),
assassination plots against unfriendly foreign leaders (Chou En-lai and
Fidel Castro, for example), paramilitary operations inside China and
North Vietnam and the infiltration of refugees into Eastern Europe to
provoke disorders (Gaddis 1982: 158). All this aggression was, of course,
directly counter to Kennan's thesis that US interests were best served by a
diversity of regimes across the world.

With the election of John Kennedy in 1960 there was an early indication
of a return to balance of power concepts and diversity. This came to be
known as the doctrine of 'flexible response'. But under the influence of
Walter Rostow, competition between the ideals of communism and
capitalism came to the fore again, this time as alternative development
goals for Third World countries. In this context the new containment soon
developed into a rather more general concept than that suggested by the
phrase 'flexible response'. Kennedy, in 1963, for instance, proclaimed that:

> I know full well that every time a country, regardless of how far it may be from
> our borders . . . passes behind the Iron Curtain, the security of the United States
> is thereby endangered. (Gaddis 1982: 211)

Vietnam became the symbol of US resistance to communism in a very
inflexible response to a communist threat. President Johnson continued
Kennedy's foreign policy echoing NSC-68: 'surrender anywhere threatens
defeat everywhere' (Gaddis 1982: 211).

After the disaster of Vietnam, US foreign policy advisors were ready to
turn away from the crude containment codes of the post-Kennan era. The
dominant strategist in the Nixon administration after 1969 was Henry
Kissinger, a historian specializing in the European power politics of the
nineteenth century. He understood the advantages of Kennan's original
balance of power arguments. The social scientists who had dominated
foreign policy-making under Kennedy and Johnson were now viewed as
superficial thinkers who had concentrated on political processes at the
expense of the outcomes. In a very telling phrase Kissinger called for a
'philosophical deepening' of the policy-making process (Gaddis 1982:
277). Only then would it become possible to understand the paradox that
although diversity in the world was the normal premise for US interests
the outcome was typically to press for uniformity.

The 'maturity' that Kissinger brought to American foreign policy was
very geopolitical. As we have seen he is credited as being responsible for
the rehabilitation of geopolitics. The moral crusade against communism

was replaced by pragmatic power-political exercises. The basic insight of this approach was that 'shared geopolitical interests' could transcend 'philosophies and history' (Gaddis 1982: 279). Hence, communism was not a monolithic threat but could be divided. The precedent of Tito's Yugoslavia splitting from the USSR in 1948 was now replicated by the great US coup of coming to agreement with China at the expense of the USSR. Containment seemed to have come full circle from Kennan to Kissinger in terms of both approach and outcomes. In fact Nixon's multi-polar world of USA, USSR, Western Europe, China and Japan is close in concept of Kennan's five power centres. The result was the *détente* phase of the Cold War.

The pragmatic power politics of Kissinger is in the classical realist tradition and is thus strictly amoral. This is most clearly demonstrated in relations with the Third World. Kissinger understood that it was naive to assume that improving conditions in Third World countries would automatically improve the USA's position in the competition with the USSR. Increased material benefits might well lead to further demands, increasing unrest and more radicalism. Since the essence of the power-political approach is national self-interest, it follows that the numerous but weak countries of the Third World could be ignored except where they impinged upon perceived US interests. The classic case of the latter was the democratic election of the socialist Salvador Allende in Chile in 1971. The United States immediately began covert action to destabilize and overthrow this regime. They were successful, Allende was assassinated in the coup that destroyed his government in 1973. As Kissinger is reported to have commented:

> I don't see why we have to let a country go Marxist just because its people are irresponsible. (Gaddis 1982: 338)

Democracy has to be destroyed to be saved! Clearly the diversity envisaged by Kissinger was not without its limits. As in all power political strategies the weak suffer at the expense of the strong: balance of power is everything and small countries cannot be allowed to upset it.

The 1980s have witnessed almost a repeat of the sequence of 'containments' Gaddis describes for 1949−79. The ideological interpretation reappears in the form of the 'evil empire' so that 'roll-back' returns to the political agenda. The Reagan doctrine involves supporting rebel groups fighting communist regimes on three continents, especially in Angola, Afghanistan and Central America. The last has been crucial. Kissinger's rehabilitation of geopolitics has made it available for use in combination with the new moral crusade against communism to produce a quite potent mix. The language of geopolitics is now available to justify policies that are far removed from Kissinger's balance of power model. O'Tuathail (1986) has described this 'new geopolitics' to telling effect for the case of US−El Salvador relations.

By the later 1980s, US containment codes had turned full circle once again with the new friendly relations with the USSR. This second *détente* leaves Cold War geopolitics in place, of course. Power politics is focused even more on the two super-powers as arms reductions are negotiated. But the thaw means little to the minor powers in the inter-state system. Nicaragua continues to struggle not to become the Chile of the new *détente*.

ALTERNATIVE GEOPOLITICAL CODES

Since the United States has been the hegemonic power in the Cold War geopolitical world order it follows that its operational codes have had a dominant influence on the nature of recent world politics. The geopolitical codes of other countries normally have had to adjust to the US view of the world in some way. Even the USSR, for instance, has generally had to conform to geopolitical codes that are the obverse of the US codes.

In this final section we describe two geopolitical codes that have been specially chosen because they directly challenge the geopolitics of the US codes. Both are associated with particular governments dominated by a major world statesman. In France the government of de Gaulle operated a distinctive 'European' code and in India the government of Nehru developed a distinctively 'Third World' code. In their different ways both geopolitical codes were anti-USA. The reputations of both de Gaulle and Nehru were built upon their distinctive geopolitics. And these reputations were well deserved since they provided early precursors of possible geopolitical transitions to new world orders such as those we have described previously.

1. France's Gaullist geopolitical code

Charles de Gaulle was President of France from 1958 to 1969. He gave his country a very distinctive geopolitical code which represented an early ideological fracture in the Cold War geopolitical world order. In Western Europe the buttress of this world order is NATO. From a Cold War perspective it is to be expected that internal threats to NATO will come from politicians of the left. And yet, the only country ever to withdraw from NATO is France under de Gaulle. Whatever political label we may use to describe the French President, he is certainly not of the left. Hence, when NATO headquarters were moved from Paris to Brussels in 1965 it was clear that the political processes operating were not consistent with the assumptions of the dominant world order.

The Gaullist geopolitical code was derived from traditional French codes focusing on the German threat on the Rhine at the local level, manoeuvering against Russia at the regional (European) level, and competing with Britain at the global level. In de Gaulle's view of the world the United States had replaced Britain at the global level. France's overwhelming concern in the twentieth century had been the security threat from Germany, but by the 1960s, with the success of the European Community, of which both France and West Germany were founder members, and with the 1963 Franco—German friendship treaty, this problem had finally been solved. This left de Gaulle the luxury of being able to concentrate on the regional and global levels, on relations with the USSR and the USA.

De Gaulle was first of all a French nationalist. He held a mystical view of France as the hexagon at the centre of European politics facing Britain, Germany, Italy, the Mediterranean, Spain and the Atlantic (Menil 1977). His sense of history thus incorporated France's unique geography and he quoted approvingly Napoleon's dictum that 'The policy of a state lies in its geography' (Menil 1977: 19). In 1960 France detonated her first nuclear bomb, confirming her world power status by joining the USA, the USSR and Britain as nuclear powers. But de Gaulle realized that an independent nuclear capability was not enough in a world of super-powers. The relative decline of France as a world power was part of the broader decline of Europe in the world. For the first time in the history of the modern world the major centres of power were beyond Western Europe. The NATO option that had linked Western Europe to one of the outside super-powers represented a betrayal of Europe. Hence, de Gaulle supported a form of European unity but without integration. This would leave France able to lead a Western European power bloc to rival the USA and the USSR. NATO membership was incompatible with this vision. Furthermore, he vetoed British membership of the European Community on the grounds that Britain was essentially an oceanic power rather than a European one. Once in the European Community Britain would act as a Trojan horse for the United States.

The positive policy implications of this geopolitical code was the promotion of a 'European *détente*' rather than a 'super-power *détente*' (Menil 1977: 163). From a Gaullist viewpoint it was nothing less than a scandal that two outside super-powers should negotiate about the future of Europe without Europeans being present. But de Gaulle's attempt to open the Iron Curtain came to an abrupt halt with the Soviet invasion of Czechoslovakia in 1968. After de Gaulle's resignation in 1969 a form of European *détente* (*Ostpolitik*) took place under the leadership of West Germany in the 1970s. But this initiative was conducted in parallel with super-power *détente* and so posed no direct threat to the Cold War geopolitical world order.

Although France remains formally outside NATO, de Gaulle's geopolitical code promoting an independent Europe has not been rigorously pursued since his fall in 1969. France did not veto Britain's third application to join the European Community in 1973, for instance. Nevertheless, there is a Gaullist vision of Europe that survives to be regenerated into a new politics at an appropriate time. If the ideological fracture that Wallerstein predicts comes about it will owe much to the Gaullist geopolitical code.

2. *Nehru and India's non-alignment code*

Nehru was Prime Minister of India from Independence in 1947 until his death in 1964. In the 1950s the focus of international politics moved to Asia and Nehru came to be widely regarded as the prime spokesman for Asia and as the world's leading peace-maker. Not surprisingly Nehru dominated Indian politics and gave it a very distinctive geopolitical code.

The three levels of this geopolitical code were very clearly demarcated. At the local level India offered a sort of informal protectorate over the small Himilayan Kingdoms (Nepal, Bhutan) and a paternal attitude to Sri Lanka. At the regional level there was an acute rivalry with Pakistan in South Asia and with China at a larger Asian continental scale. Globally, India had pretentions to being a world power. This was centred on Nehru's status as a world statesman and his role in the establishment of the non-alignment movement.

Initially Nehru developed Indian foreign policy along idealistic lines, combining a Ghandian moralist tradition with a social democratic idealism derived from contacts with British Labour leaders. In 1954 India launched a moral propaganda offensive offering the *Panchsheel* as a solution to the world's political problems (Willets 1978: 7). Initially this set out the principles on which India and China decided to settle their differences over Tibet. Basically it was a declaration that disputes be settled peacefully by mutual agreement with the ultimate aim of generating a world of peaceful co-existence. The Cold War trend towards collective security by military alliance was now challenged by the notion of collective peace without military alliances. In three years India made 18 bi-lateral agreements with other countries endorsing *Panchsheel*, culminating in its partial incorporation into a United Nations resolution in December 1957 (Willets 1978: 7).

Parallel with this moral crusade India began the task of organizing what were coming to be known as the new 'developing countries'. In 1949, fifteen Asian countries met in New Delhi to protest at the colonial policy of the Netherlands in Indonesia. The next year India convened the first *ad hoc* Afro—Asian caucus at the United Nations. The real breakthrough came in 1955 with the Bandung Conference, a general Afro—Asian meeting of states attended by 29 countries. This included a broad cross-section of Afro—Asian states including both communist states (for example, China and North Vietnam) and pro-western states (for example, Japan and the Philippines). In the event this meeting was of more importance for symbolic reasons than for what it achieved. Of much more importance was the first meeting of the non-aligned movement six years later in Belgrade.

The non-aligned movement was the joint product of three outstanding statesmen: Nehru of India, Tito of Yugoslavia and Nasser of Egypt. With the invasion of Egypt by Britain and France in 1956 at Suez, Nehru denounced Britain and supported Egypt. At the same time Tito was attempting to forge an independence from the Soviet Union in Eastern Europe. Hence, for both Egypt and Yugoslavia, their interest in a non-aligned movement was to find broad global support in their efforts to remain independent of the Cold War powers. India, on the other hand, had no such immediate threat and saw the movement as a vehicle for playing its role as a world power.

The Belgrade conference brought together only 26 countries since states in alliance with either super-power were not invited. This rule immediately eliminated India's two regional rivals, communist China and pro-western Pakistan. Under Tito's tutorage India's idealistic foreign policy was severely modified in the non-aligned movement. Non-alignment did not equate with neutrality. The movement was actively involved in supporting anti-colonial revolutions and was vehemently against the Cold War assumption that all countries had to choose sides in the Great Contest. It represents a genuine precursor to a geopolitical transition to Galtung's 'World Classes' world order (Fig. 2.3c).

Since the death of Nehru, India has not played such an important role on the world stage. She has continued to be an important member of the non-aligned movement but the emphasis has gradually moved away from the peace ideals of Nehru towards concern for the overwhelming material inequality in the world. As such the movement has become part of a much broader protest that includes all of the Third World. But, for India, Nehru's legacy is still important in terms of the original non-alignment principle. South Asia is a distinctive region of the world that continues to be 'outside' the Cold War. Despite Pakistan's close links with the United States and the Soviet war in nearby Afganistan, South Asia remains an oasis in the Cold War geopolitical order. As Cohen has recognized in his geopolitical modelling, South Asia constitutes a separate geostrategic region (Fig. 2.2).

Both Nehru's non-alignment code and de Gaulle's European code brought strong criticism from the United States. There was no place for non-alignment in Dulles' containment code, and Kennedy and Johnson's flexible response did not envisage the break-up of NATO. Nevertheless, it is worth noting as a final point that both the Indian and French challenges to the orthodox Cold War thinking of their time would not have violated the original containment assumptions of George Kennan. Quite simply, after 1949 the independent power centres that Kennan advocated were taken off the political agenda. Any geopolitical transition away from the Cold War must begin by building on geopolitical codes — such as those of Nehru and de Gaulle — that advocate a return to Kennan's independent power centres.

Chapter 3

GEOGRAPHY OF IMPERIALISMS

THE REVOLUTIONARY HERITAGE

The rise and fall of the classical theory

1. Imperialism as geopolitics
2. The Hobson–Lenin paradigm
3. Despatching imperialism to history

A world-systems interpretation of imperialism

1. Transcending Robinson and Gallagher
2. Transcending the classical theory

FORMAL IMPERIALISM: THE CREATION OF EMPIRES

Two cycles of formal imperialism

1. The cumulative number of colonies
2. Establishment: creation, reorganization and transfer
3. De-colonization: geographical contagion and contrasting ideologies

The geography of formal imperialism

1. Core: the imperial states
2. Periphery: the political arenas

The economics of formal imperialism

1. The sugar islands of the Caribbean
2. 'Islands of development' in Africa

Where the sun never set

1. Hegemony and empire
2. Imperial geopolitical codes
3. The imperial ideology

INFORMAL IMPERIALISM: DOMINANCE WITHOUT EMPIRE

The international relations of informal imperialism

1. Free trade and the hegemonic state
2. Protectionism and the semi-periphery
3. The choice for the periphery

Informal imperialism as a structural relation

1. The rise of social imperialism
2. The key mechanism: unequal exchange

Informal imperialism today

Chapter 3

GEOGRAPHY OF IMPERIALISMS

The rise of geography as a university discipline in the late nineteenth century was closely related to imperialism (Hudson 1977). The systematic parts of the discipline that were developed at this time — political geography, commercial geography and colonial geography — all covered fields of study that were useful to those engaged in imperial activities be they politicians or soldiers, traders or settlers. Outside the universities, geographical societies flourished as vehicles for providing advice to would-be imperial actors (McKay 1943). Contemporaries who wanted to find out about the imperialism of their age turned to geography for the facts. Lenin, for instance, used a work of the German geographer A. Supan, *The Territorial Development of the European Colonies,* for information on the extent of late nineteenth-century European expansion. Geography and imperialism were intimately entwined.

Just as geopolitics was found to be an embarrassment to geography after World War II, so a generation earlier links to imperialism were found to be an embarrassment to geography in the aftermath of World War I. In the interwar period (1919–39), according to Bowle (1974: 524), 'the main intellectual fashion (was) set strongly against Empire'. And of course this intellectual trend was confirmed by the disintegration of the European empires after 1945. As a result imperialism was largely removed from both the political and academic agendas as a matter of little or no contemporary relevance. World-systems analysis is part of a new trend that is reversing this agenda setting. Imperialism is a central concept in our political geography. As with geopolitics, we are not in the business of endorsing this form of global politics, rather we treat it as an object of study necessary for understanding our modern world.

Today, despite its obvious political and geographical characteristics, the topic of imperialism is a neglected theme in political geography. This is not just a problem of political geography, however, but is more to do with the nature of modern social science as a whole. It relates directly to what is referred to as the poverty of disciplines. The term 'imperialism' is a classic political-economy concept which cannot be properly defined in either political or economic categories alone (Barratt Brown 1974: 19). Hence the neglect of imperialism has spread far beyond political geography. One of the most cogent criticisms of the whole 'modernization'

and 'development' schools of modern social science, for instance, is that
they seem to conveniently 'forget' or at least 'ignore' the contribution of
imperialism to the modern world situation.

The geographical extent of European political control in the periphery is
shown in Fig. 3.1. All areas that were at some time under core control are
shown and can be seen to include almost all the periphery. The major
exception is China but even here the leading core states delimited their
'spheres of influence'. In geographical terms the result of this political
control was a world organized as one huge functional region for the core
states. This has been, and we shall argue remains, the dominant spatial
organization of the twentieth century. And yet until recently this subject
was considered so unimportant that it was largely left to historians to
debate it outside the social sciences.

In our world-systems approach, of course, imperialism is much more
than a problem of history. 'Bringing history back in' means opening up the
issues of imperialism once again. One of the achievements of the new
neo-Marxist perspectives on social science is the rediscovery of the
revolutionary heritage of imperialism. Of course the concept has not been
neglected just because it is difficult to fit into the modern disciplines of
political science and economics; imperialism has been neglected because it
is part of a classical revolutionary theory which modern social science was
designed to circumvent. We cannot understand imperialism, in a
world-systems or any other framework, without first understanding its
revolutionary heritage. The first section of this chapter describes this
heritage and the subsequent interpretations of historians who could safely
label these issues as concerns of the past.

This chapter is primarily descriptive in nature. The neglect of our theme
means that we must start our political geography studies at a stage where
ordering of information is our dominant concern. This is achieved by

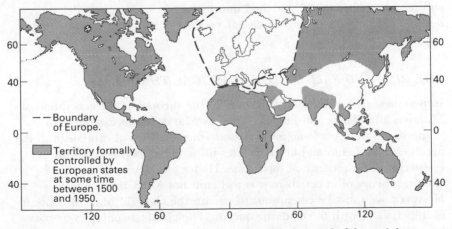

Fig. 3.1 The geographical extent of European political control of the periphery

using the dynamic model of hegemony and rivalry presented in the previous chapter. These descriptions are divided into two sections, the first dealing with formal imperialism and the second with informal imperialism. Both imperialisms are characterized by the dominance relation between core and periphery, the distinction between them being that the former involves political control of periphery territory in addition to economic exploitation.

THE REVOLUTIONARY HERITAGE

One of the problems in dealing with a concept like imperialism is that its meaning has changed over time. We are using it in this study in its current meaning as indicating a dominance relation, but in considering the heritage of our study we must understand past meanings. In fact imperialism, unlike the terms 'imperial' and 'empire' from which it derives, is of fairly recent origin. Its initial use was as a term of abuse to describe French Emperor Louis Napoleon's foreign policy in the mid-nineteenth century, the implication being that the policy was aggressive and reckless. By the end of the century imperialism was associated with aggressive expansion by core countries and was a major concern of domestic politics — both the British general election and the American presidential election of 1900 had imperialism as a major campaign issue for instance. From this contemporary debate one contribution stands out as being of continuing significance — J. A. Hobson's (1902) *Imperialism: A Study*, written in the aftermath of the British imperial war in South Africa. As a polemic against imperialism this was to become a source for Lenin's theory and we consider these surprising links between English liberalism and Russian Marxism in our outline of the revolutionary theory below. This is followed by a description of how the subject-matter became despatched into history before we consider the development of new theory which has become part of the world-systems approach.

THE RISE AND FALL OF THE CLASSICAL THEORY

Imperialism had a central role to play in the theories of the generation of Marxists after Marx and Engels. Whereas Marx did not use the term 'imperialism' and made no general study of the effects of capitalism in the periphery, for Lenin and his associates imperialism had become the essence of the capitalism of their time. Hence when we refer to the classical theory of imperialism it is to Lenin not Marx that we refer. However, we must be careful not to equate the classical Marxist concept of imperialism with the modern concept. The classical concept was both broader and more akin to our geopolitics than is often realized. The various meanings of the concept will become clear as we look at the different theories.

1. Imperialism as geopolitics

Lenin's famous pamphlet on imperialism was written during the First World War as part of an on-going debate in Marxist circles on the meaning of the war. It was avowedly polemic and popular and represents a position that subsequently became orthodox Marxism rather than an original contribution (Brewer 1980: ch. 5). That is to say he draws upon the work of other authors, reorders some ideas, changes the emphases to suit his debating position but adds little to the argument. Lenin particularly draws on the work of Hilferding, an Austrian Marxist, and the British liberal writer Hobson.

According to Brewer (1980), Hilferding is the real founder of the Marxist theory of imperialism. He used the term imperialism to mean inter-core rivalry which incorporated dominance over the periphery but which did not make this its primary characteristic. Rather he emphasized the rise of finance capital in a new monopoly era when industrial and financial capital are fused into one system. He was particularly impressed by the power of the banks and their relations to industry and the state in pre-1914 Germany. He concluded that finance capital needed strong state support in terms of economic protection and obtaining territories for investment, markets and raw materials. But he remained concerned largely with the internal developments of core countries rather than the 'spillover' effects into the periphery. These ideas are developed in Bukharin's (1972) *Imperialism and the World Economy* of 1917 in which the idea of imperialism as the geopolitics of a particular stage of capitalism — Bukharin's finance monopoly capitalism — is proposed. Lenin takes this argument one step further and defines imperialism as a stage of capitalism, the 'highest', in fact. By this he meant that the competitive capitalism that Marx had described in the mid-nineteenth century had been replaced by a monopoly capitalism. This was the final stage of capitalism because the contradictions of the system were reflected in inter-state rivalries which had produced a world war as the beginning of the revolution. For Lenin the First World War represented the death throes of capitalism.

2. The Hobson–Lenin paradigm

The other major source for Lenin's ideas was, as we have indicated, Hobson's non-Marxist anti-imperialism. For Hobson the 'taproot' of imperialism was surplus capital generated in the core looking for investment outlets in the periphery. Hobson collected data on overseas investment, areas and populations of colonies and dates of acquisitions and concluded that 1870 was a vital turning point in European history. Lenin reproduced this information in his own pamphlet and Wallerstein (1980b) feels it is reasonable to talk of the Hobson–Lenin paradigm. This has three basic positions: (i) within states there are different interests between different sectors of capital; (ii) a monopoly, finance sector was emerging as the dominant interest which could steer the state into imperial ventures for its own interests but against the interests of the other sectors; and (iii) despite much popular support these ventures were against the real interests of the working classes in these countries. Wallerstein terms this a paradigm because of its influence in setting the agenda for all subsequent studies of imperialism. In this sense, whether we agree with Hobson and Lenin's theses or not, we remain a 'prisoner' of their ideas as long as they continue to be the starting point of discussions on imperialism.

Wallerstein (1980b) emphasizes the similarities between Hobson and Lenin on imperialism. This is important because their association has given Lenin's revolutionary theory a respectability in Western thought which it might not otherwise have received. But there are, of course, fundamental differences between the two men. As an English liberal, Hobson's anti-imperialism pointed towards reformist solutions of free trade and raising domestic consumption. Lenin's theory was intended as a contribution to overthrowing the capitalist system. By understanding the stage that capitalism had reached, revolutionary forces could seize the opportunity that the world war offered and create a new system. This was not a prediction but a statement of the theoretical rationale for revolutionary strategy and practice. In the end the practice was only partially successful, producing a successful revolution in Russia alone. But the theory remained to be refined and updated by sympathizers and criticized and dismissed by opponents. The best way of achieving the latter is to take the subject off the political agenda. This was done by despatching the topic to history where the final stage of capitalism becomes converted into the harmless 'age of imperialism'.

3. Despatching imperialism to history

After the First World War these 'classical' theories of imperialism became used as raw material in debates on the causes of the First World War and/or growth of European empires. They became simplified as 'single-cause' theories, as economic determinism, to be refuted by careful, scholarly historical research. This begins with Schumpeter's (1951) assertion in 1919 that imperialism, far from being the highest stage of capitalism, is essentially anti-capitalist and reflects the militarism of the pre-capitalist European nobility. Schumpeter therefore dismisses economic motives and brings social and political causes to the fore. Subsequent historical interpretations have emphasized narrow, political causes. These are the 'balance of power' theories (Foeken 1982) which view imperialism as a vehicle of European diplomacy in the late nineteenth-century rivalry between Germany, France and Britain. This is most fully developed by Mansergh (1949) and represents the antithesis of the classical theory, emphasizing as it does the decisions of a few political leaders at the expense of any general political-economy process.

Since the Second World War there has been a reaction against such narrow historical interpretations. In a series of studies Robinson and Gallagher have attempted to rethink the whole debate. Their critique is of particular relevance to our study on two counts. First, they challenge the whole idea of an 'age of imperialism' in the late nineteenth century (Gallagher and Robinson 1953). They emphasize the continuity of policy throughout the nineteenth century and do not accept that 1870 represents a fundamental watershed in modern history. After all, India, 'the jewel in Britain's imperial crown', was obtained before the age of imperialism and continued to be by far the most important imperial possession throughout the age of imperialism. Second, they queried whether the causes of European expansion could be found solely in processes — economic or political or both — operating in the core (Robinson, Gallagher and Denny 1961). As studies of imperialism began appearing from the periphery it became clear that the timing, nature and form of dominance relations were often conditioned by local circumstances in the periphery. Robinson (1973) has elaborated this into a theory of collaboration whereby certain peripheral élites interact with core states to help produce imperialism. This explains why European powers could control so much of the periphery with relatively little military involvement. Clearly British control of India would have been impossible without collaboration. In short, the classical debate was hopelessly Euro-centric. Hence we can say that Robinson and Gallagher were steering the temporal and spatial co-ordinates of the debate in the direction of the framework adopted for this study.

A WORLD-SYSTEMS INTERPRETATION OF IMPERIALISM

Robinson and Gallagher help us to break out of the Hobson—Lenin paradigm but they do not chart a new theory. By extending the debate beyond the 'age of imperialism' they leave the way open for other historians to commit what we have termed the myth of universal law whereby imperialism is a general political process based on motives of expansion and conquest. Lichtheim (1971), for instance, considers the 'imperialism' of the Roman Empire and other world-empires alongside modern imperialism. Within our world-systems framework — the time limit is quite explicit — imperialism is a dominance relation in the world-economy and therefore is not found prior to the sixteenth century. Previous political expansions are based on fundamentally different political-economy processes and require a separate term to describe them.

Of course, if we can extend Robinson and Gallagher's concern for the nineteenth century backwards to the origins of our system we can also bring the concept forward to the present. It was not just historians who were taking note of new studies of the periphery in the period since the Second World War. As pointed out in Chapter 1, dependency theory was developed and extended to become the world-systems approach. In political terms de-colonization put imperialism back on the agenda with concepts such as Ghanaian leader Kwame Nkrumah's concept of 'Neo-Colonialism' as another stage of capitalism. The time was ripe for a second set of revolutionary theories to emerge to inform and direct the periphery in their relations with the core (Blaut 1975). Here we briefly describe the world-systems theory of imperialism.

1. Transcending Robertson and Gallagher

Wallerstein (1980b) follows Robinson and Gallagher in breaking out of the Hobson—Lenin paradigm. In world-systems terms this paradigm is a classic example of the error of developmentalism taking as it does countries as units of change and identifying stages through which they pass. But we go beyond Robinson and Gallagher's theses by transcending their dichotomies of continuity versus discontinuity and core versus periphery.

The continuity — discontinuity debate is subsumed under our cyclical property of the world-economy. Imperialist activity will vary with the political opportunities afforded to states during the uneven growth of the world-economy. Our paired-Kondratieff model in the last section illustrates how formal imperialism is part of an unfolding logic interacting with periods of hegemony when informal imperialism is prominent. Hence imperialism is a relation that has occurred throughout the history of the world-economy. But this continuity does not preclude identification of particular phases when different strategies prevailed. Hence the very real differences between mid nineteenth-century British hegemony and the late nineteenth-century 'age of imperialism' are incorporated but without any suggestion of a particular 'stage' in a linear sequence.

In a similar manner the world-systems approach can incorporate both sets of arguments in the 'core versus periphery' debate on causes of imperialism. We will use part of Johan Galtung's (1971) 'structural theory of imperialism' to model a range of sub-relations through which the overarching dominance relation of imperialism operates. We will simplify our argument to just two types of state, core (C) and periphery (P), and two classes in each state, dominant (A) and dominated (B). This provides for four groups in the world-economy: core/dominant class (C_A), periphery/dominant class (P_A), core/dominated class (C_B) and periphery/dominated class (P_B). From this we can derive four important relations: *collaboration*, C_A–P_A, whereby the dominant classes of both areas combine to organize their joint domination of the periphery; *social-imperialism*, C_A–C_B, in which the dominated class in the core is 'bought off' by welfare policy as the price for social peace 'at home'; *repression*, P_A–P_B, to maintain exploitation of the periphery by coercion as necessary; and *division*, C_B–P_B, so that there is a separation of interests between dominated classes, that is, the classic strategy of divide and rule. In our approach therefore, Robinson's (1973) collaboration is just one sub-relation of a broader set of relations of imperialism.

2. Transcending the classical Marxist theory

In transcending Robinson and Gallagher we have simultaneously highlighted a key difference between world-systems analysis and classical Marxist theories of imperialism. Whereas the latter consists of various theories of linear change (stages), Wallerstein postulates long-term cyclical change.

There are two further fundamental differences that should be understood. First, world-systems analysis implies a new geography of revolution. This is partly expressed in the different definitions of imperialism, with the traditional theory incorporating much more than core-periphery relations. But it is much more than a matter of definitions. Brewer (1980) shows that the classical theory's relative neglect of the periphery was no accident but a reflection of a theory of revolution which expected transformation to occur in the core where the forces of production, and hence the contradictions of capitalism, were most developed. Indeed in the classical view penetration of the periphery by core countries could be seen as beneficial since 'progressive' capitalism would free the area from the shackles of feudalism just as it had done earlier in Europe. As we have seen, the neo-Marxist view interprets such penetration in a completely different manner with capitalism in the periphery never having a progressive liberating role but rather being regressive from the beginning — what Frank terms the development of underdevelopment. The so called progressive elements of capitalism, therefore, are geographically restricted to the transformation from feudalism to capitalism in the core. From the world-systems perspective this results in a geographical re-alignment of revolutionary forces in terms of core versus periphery with the latter becoming a major focus of future revolt and change. This is the political argument of the radical dependency school and is usually termed 'Third-worldlist' because of its geographical emphasis. It is most closely associated with Mao Tse Tung and his theory of global class struggle. We represented it in Chapter 2 as the 'world classes' future geopolitical scenario (Fig. 2.3c). From a world-systems perspective Wallerstein's ideological fracture scenario (Fig. 2.3d) is a medium-term outcome that may pave the way for a long-term revolt of the periphery.

The second difference between classical Marxist theories and world-systems analysis is related to arguments about the reasons for imperial expansion. Viewing this activity over the long term, Wallerstein comes to a different conclusion concerning its purpose.

Many non-Marxist critics of imperialism, Hobson for instance, have argued that formal imperialism is uneconomic for the core states concerned, benefiting only that small group directly involved in the imperial ventures. As we have seen, this line of argument leads on to the notion of economic dominance by large monopoly or finance capital and the identification of imperialism as a 'stage'. But formal imperialism existed as a major aspect of the world-economy for over four hundred years, starting with the activities of state-licensed charter companies. The problem with such strict economic evaluations of formal imperialism is that they have emphasized trade and the search for new markets for core production. But, as Wallerstein (1983: 38−9) points out, this explanation just does not accord with the historical facts: 'by and large it was the capitalist world that sought out the products of the external arena and not the other way round'. In fact non-capitalist societies did not need products from the core states and such 'needs' had to be 'created' *after* political take-overs. Certainly the search for markets cannot explain the massive imperialist effort on the part of core states over several centuries. Instead Wallerstein suggests that the search for low-cost labour forces is a much better explanation. This switches emphasis from exchange to production. Incorporation of new zones into the periphery invariably led to new production processes based upon the lowest labour costs. In the first instance, therefore, imperial expansion is about extending the division of labour that defines the boundaries of the world-economy. Imperialism, both formal and informal, is the process that created and continues to recreate the periphery.

FORMAL IMPERIALISM: THE CREATION OF EMPIRES

The formal political control of parts of the periphery has been a feature of the world-economy since its inception. From the early Spanish and Portuguese Empires through to the attempt by Italy in the 1930s to forge an African empire, formal imperialism has been a common strategy of core domination over the periphery. Of course, this process must not be confused with the concept of the world-empire as an entity with its own division of labour. Even the British Empire, on which the sun really did not set for over a century, was not a world-empire in our terms but rather a successful core state with a large colonial appendage. In this section we describe the rise and fall of such 'appendages' within the framework of the dynamic model of hegemony and rivalry described in Chapter 2. This description is organized into four parts. First we look at imperialism at the system scale to delineate the overall pattern of the process. Second we consider the imperialist activities of the core states who created the overall pattern. Third we turn to the periphery and briefly consider the political arenas where this dominance relation was imposed. Finally we look at how the two sides of the imperial relation fitted together in a case study of the British Empire.

THE TWO CYCLES OF FORMAL IMPERIALISM

If we wish to describe formal imperialism the first question that arises is
how to measure it. Obviously, figures for population, land area or 'wealth'
under core political control would make ideal indices for monitoring
imperialism but such data is simply not available over the long time
period we employ here. Instead we follow Bergesen and Schoenberg (1980)
and use the presence of a colonial governor to indicate the imposition of
sovereignty of a core state over territory in the periphery. These
personages may have very many different titles (for example, high
commissioner, commandant, chief political resident) but all have
jurisdictions signalling core control of particular parts of the periphery.
Obviously the size of such territorial jurisdictions varies widely in terms
of population, land area and wealth but the presence of governors does
provide a constant unit of measure over five hundred years. As Bergesen
and Schoenberg (1980: 232) admit, there is 'no clear cut way to measure
colonialism.' But this direct measure of political control does provide a
reasonably sensitive index of formal imperialist activity at the world-scale.
   Bergesen and Schoenberg obtain their data from a comprehensive
catalogue of colonial governors compiled by Henige (1970). He identifies
412 colonial jurisdictions and provides a listing of governors for all such
territories from their establishment to de-colonization. Bergesen and
Schoenberg identify two clear 'waves of colonial expansion and
contraction' from this data. We will rework the data here to order it in
terms of our time metric and to identify more than just the period of
colonial control in a territory. Our analysis differs from that of Bergesen
and Schoenberg in two respects, therefore. First the data is classified in
terms of time periods compatible with our space–time matrix. The metric
we have used is a simple 50-year sequence from 1500 to 1800, and a
25-year sequence from 1800 to 1975. This provides for some detail in
addition to the long A- and B-phases in the original logistic wave plus an
approximation to the A- and B-phases of the subsequent Kondratieff
waves. Second we record more than merely establishment and
disestablishment of colonies. From the record of governorships we can also
trace reorganizations of existing colonized territory and transfer of
sovereignty of territory between core states. Both of these are useful
indices in that they are related to phases of stagnation (and hence the
need to reorganize) and core rivalry (expressed as capturing rival
colonies). In the analyses that follow the establishment of colonies is
divided into three categories: creation of colony, reorganization of territory
and transfer of sovereignty.

1. The cumulative number of colonies

We can start by replicating Bergesen and Schoenberg's study. By
cumulating the number of colonies created and subtracting the number of

de-colonizations, the total amount of colonial activity can be found for each time period. The results of this exercise are shown in Fig. 3.2 which reproduces Bergesen and Schoenberg's two long waves of colonial expansion and contraction. There is a long first wave peaking at the conclusion of the logistic B phase and contracting in the A-phase of the first Kondratieff cycle. This largely defines the rise and fall of European empires in the New World of America. The second wave rises through the nineteenth century to peak at the end of the 'age of imperialism' and then declines rapidly into the mid-twentieth century. This largely defines the rise and fall of European empires in the Old World of Asia and Africa. Hence the two waves incorporate two geographically distinct phases of imperialism. This simple space—time pattern provides the framework in which we investigate formal imperialism more fully.

2. Establishment: creation, reorganization and transfer

The 412 colonies identified by Henige (1970) have been classified into three types as indicated above. All three categories are shown in Fig. 3.3 and we will describe each pattern in turn.

Where governors are imposed on a territory for the first time we refer to the creation of a colony. Since this is one political strategy of restructuring during economic stagnation we expect colony creation to be associated with B-phases of our waves. This is generally borne out by Fig. 3.3. The major exception is the imperialist activities of Spain and Portugal in the original A-phase in the emerging world-economy. This followed the Treaty

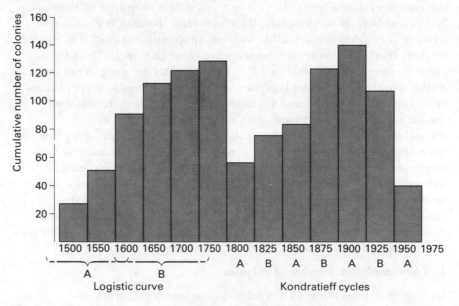

Fig. 3.2   The two long waves of colonial expansion and contraction

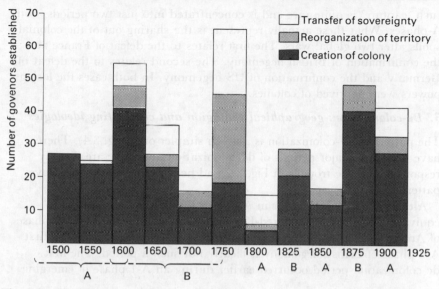

Fig. 3.3 Establishment of colonies, 1500–1925

of Tordesillas when the Pope divided the non-European world between these two leading states. This curtailed the usual rivalry associated with colony creation and it seems that the world-economy was not yet developed sufficiently to enable informal imperialism to operate outside Europe. With the onset of the seventeenth-century stagnation phase, colonial creation expanded with the entry into the non-European arena of north-west European states. From this first peak of colony creation the process slows down until a minor increase during the period of British–French rivalry at the end of the logistic B-phase. During the Kondratieff cycles colony creation goes up and down with the A- and B-phases, but the most notable feature is the 'age of imperialism' clearly marked by the late-nineteenth-century peak. Hence we incorporate both the continuity and the discontinuity arguments by viewing colonial activity as a cyclical process.

Reorganization of territory should be particularly sensitive to periods of stagnation. Such periods involve pressures on states to cut back public expenditure and in the time-scale we are dealing with here this is reflected in attempts to make colonies more 'efficient'. Hence the reorganizations shown in Fig. 3.3 are generally associated with B-phases. The major peak here is at the end of the logistic B-phase when the relative decline of Spain and Portugal meant that their colonies were becoming acute burdens to the state exchequers.

Transfer of sovereignty is a direct measure of inter-state rivalry in the periphery. This is mainly a feature of the logistic B-phase when this type of activity was relatively common. With the onset of the Kondratieff cycles such 'capture' is quite rare and is concentrated into just two periods, both A-phases. What these actually represent is the sharing out of the colonial spoils after two global wars. The first relates to the defeat of France and the confirmation of British hegemony. The second relates to the defeat of Germany and the confirmation of US hegemony. In both cases the losing powers were deprived of colonies.

3. De-colonization: geographical contagion and contrasting ideologies

The pattern of de-colonization is a much simpler one (Fig. 3.4). There have been two major periods of de-colonization and these are directly responsible for the troughs in Fig. 3.2 and hence generate the two-wave pattern.

Although both peaks occur in A-phases they do not correspond to equivalent phases in our paired-Kondratieff model: the second A-2 phase of American hegemony is a period of major de-colonization but the first A-2 phase of British hegemony is clearly not such a period. The first de-colonization period occurred earlier during an A-1 phase of emerging

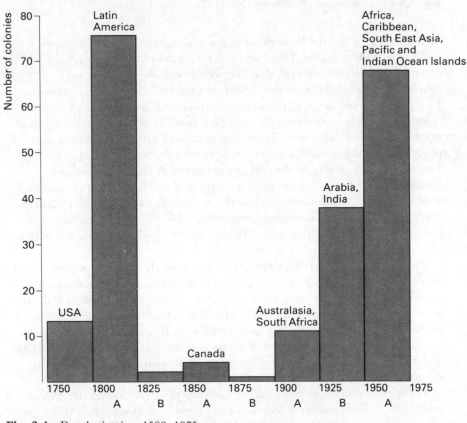

Fig. 3.4   Decolonization, 1500–1975

hegemony. This is best interpreted as the conclusion of the agricultural capitalism of the logistic curve. The de-colonization involved the termination of Spanish and Portuguese colonies in Latin America; by this time the colonizing powers had long since declined themselves to semi-peripheral status. For the competing core powers in this period of emerging British hegemony there were obvious advantages to freeing these anachronistic colonies. This was particularly recognized by George Canning the British Foreign Secretary in his oft-quoted statement of 1824 that a free South America would be 'ours' (that is, British). This de-colonization set the conditions for British 'informal imperialism' in Latin America in the mid-nineteenth century which is discussed in the next section.

One feature of the de-colonization process is its geographical contagion. De-colonization is not a random process but is spatially clustered at different periods. The de-colonization of the Americas, for instance, did not affect existing colonies in the Old World. This spatial contagion shows the importance for de-colonization of processes operating in the periphery. The American War of Independence served as an example for Latin America in the first de-colonization phase; Indian independence led the way for the rest of the periphery in the second de-colonization period. At a regional level political concessions in one colony led to cumulative pressures throughout the region. In this sense the independence awarded to Nkrumah's Ghana in 1957 triggered the de-colonization of the whole continent in the same way that Bolivar's Venezuelan revolt of 1820 led the way in Latin America.

One final point may be added to this interpretation. The rhetoric of the colonial revolutionary leaders in the two periods was very different. The 'freedom' sought in Latin America was proclaimed in a liberal ideology imitating the American Revolution to the north, whereas a century and a half later the ideology is socialist, mildly at first in India, but much more vociferous in Ghana and in the many subsequent wars of national liberation. It is for this reason, of course, that the first de-colonization (Latin America) was more easily re-aligned in the world-economy under British liberal leadership than the second de-colonization with its numerous challenges to American liberal leadership. In broad terms we can note that the first de-colonization period is a liberal revolution at the end of agricultural capitalism whereas the second period encompasses socialist-inspired revolutions at the end of industrial capitalism, which have been much more anti-systemic in nature.

THE GEOGRAPHY OF FORMAL IMPERIALISM

Imperialism is a dominance relation between core and periphery. Our discussion so far has stayed at the system level and we have not investigated the geography of this relation or 'who was "dominating" whom where?' We answer this question below by dealing first with the core and then with the periphery.

1. Core: the imperial states

Who were these colonizing states? In fact they have been surprisingly few in number. In the whole history of the world-economy there have been just twelve formal imperialist states and only five of these can be said to be major colonizers. Fig. 3.5 shows the colonial activity of these states in graphs that use the same format as Fig. 3.3. Seven graphs are shown: separate ones for Spain, Portugal, the Netherlands, France and Britain/England; and combined ones for the early and late 'minor' colonizing states. The early states consist of the Baltic states of Denmark, Sweden and Brandenburg/Prussia; the 'late-comers' are Belgium, Germany, Italy, Japan and The United States. The graphs show the individual patterns of colonial activity of the states that created the total picture we looked at above.

In the logistic A-phase before 1600 all colonial establishment was by Spain and Portugal. The onset of the B-phase brings the Netherlands, France, England and the Baltic states into the fray. This is complemented by a sharp reduction in colony creation by both Spain and Portugal — the location of the core of the world-economy had moved northwards and this is directly reflected in the new colonial activity. As the B-phase progresses all of these new states continue their colonial activities but at a reduced scale except for England/Britain for whom colony-capture is as important or more important than colony creation. As we move into the Kondratieff cycles the Netherlands almost totally cease establishment of colonies so that in the mid-nineteenth century all colonial creation is either British or French. In the classical 'age of imperialism' these two old-stagers are joined by the five late-comers.

Fig. 3.5 enables us to define four periods of colonial activity by imperial states:

1. The first non-competitive era occurs in the logistic A-phase when only Spain and Portugal were imperial states.
2. The first competitive era occurs in the logistic B-phase when eight states were involved in imperialist expansion.
3. The second non-competitive era of the mid-nineteenth century coincides with the rise and consolidation of British hegemony. In this period there are only two states involved in imperial expansion, Britain and France.
4. The second competitive era is the 'age of imperialism' and coincides with the decline of British hegemony. In this period seven states were involved in imperial expansion. We shall use this division of core-state activity in our discussion of peripheral arenas.

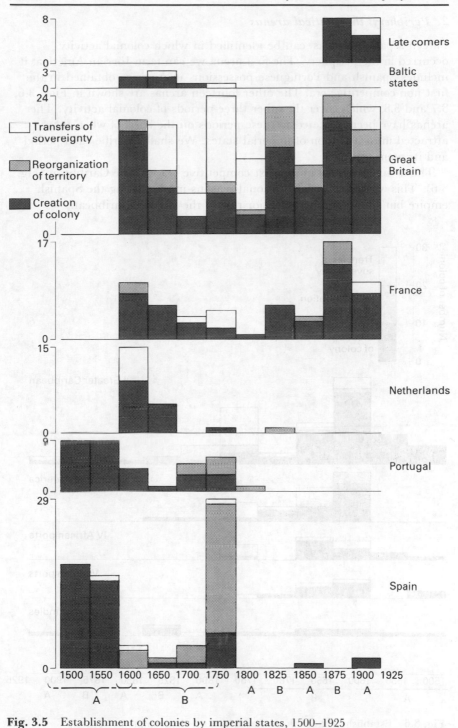

Fig. 3.5 Establishment of colonies by imperial states, 1500–1925

2. Periphery: the political arenas

Fifteen separate 'arenas' can be identified in which colonial activity occurred in the periphery. The first arena we can term Iberian America; it includes Spanish and Portuguese possessions in America obtained in the first non-competitive era. The other fourteen arenas are shown in Figs. 3.6, 3.7 and 3.8, which cover the other three periods of colonial activity. The arenas have been allocated to these periods on the basis of when they attracted most attention of imperial states. We shall describe each period and its arenas in turn.

The dominant arena of the first competitive era was the Caribbean (Fig. 3.6). This was initially for locational reasons in plundering the Spanish empire but subsequently the major role of the Greater Caribbean

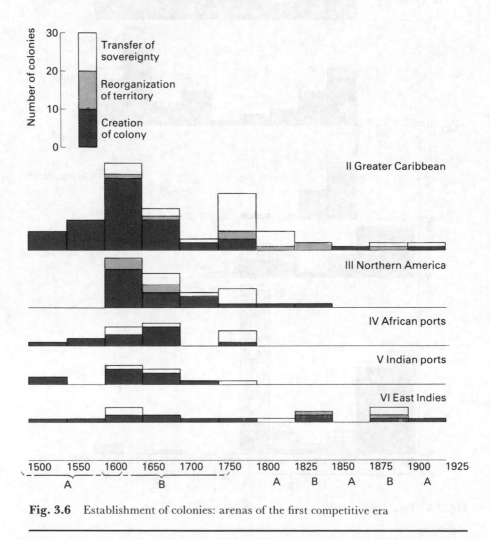

Fig. 3.6   Establishment of colonies: arenas of the first competitive era

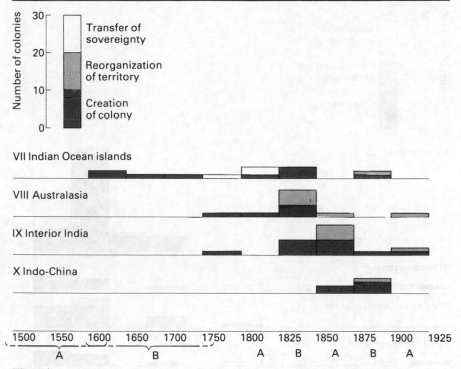

Fig. 3.7 Establishment of colonies: arenas of the second non-competitive era

(Maryland to North-east Brazil) was plantation agriculture supplying sugar and tobacco to the core. Of secondary importance were the Northern America colonies who did not develop a staple crop and effectively prevented themselves becoming peripheralized. This was to be the location of the first major peripheral revolt, of course. The other important arena for this period was the African ports which formed the final apex of the famous Atlantic triangular trade. It is this trade and the surplus value to be derived from it that underlay the colonial competition of this era. The final two arenas were much less important and related to the Indies trade which Wallerstein doubts was integral to the world-economy until after 1750.

In the second non-competitive era colonial activity was much reduced, but four arenas did emerge as active in the mid-nineteenth century (Fig. 3.7). There was no competition among core states within these arenas which were consequently divided between France and Britain. Although without the authority of the Papal Bull legitimizing the earlier Spain–Portugal share-out, Britain and France managed to continue some colonial activity while avoiding each other's ambitions. The Indian Ocean Islands (including Madagascar) and Indo-China were 'conceded' by

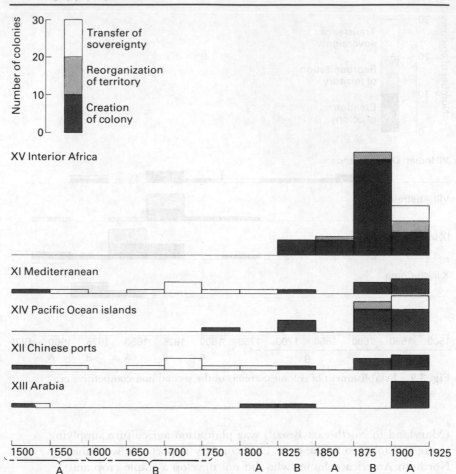

Fig. 3.8 Establishment of colonies: arenas of the second competitive era

Britain as French arenas, and the latter left India and Australasia to the British.

This peaceful arrangement was shattered in the next competitive period during a series of 'scrambles', the most famous being that for Africa although similar pre-emptive staking out of claims occurred in the Mediterranean arena, Pacific Islands and for Chinese ports (Fig. 3.8). With the collapse of the Ottoman Empire there was a final share-out of Arabia after the First World War. The brief take-over of this last arena completes the pattern of formal core control of periphery as depicted by Fig. 3.1.

THE ECONOMICS OF FORMAL IMPERIALISM

The pattern of formal imperialism is now clear. In two major cycles over four hundred years a small group of core states took political control in fifteen separate arenas covering nearly all the periphery. Why? Because of the dominance of the Hobson—Lenin paradigm on this debate most discussion has focused on the second cycle's 'age of imperialism'. This has produced a rather unnecessary debate pitting economic causes against political ones. Foeken (1982) has reviewed these arguments in relation to the partition of Africa and shows that neither set of causes can be sensibly dismissed. What is required is a political economy view of the situation where complementary aspects of the various theories are brought together to produce a more comprehensive account (Foeken 1982: 140). This would bring analysis of the second cycle into line with that of the first cycle, where it has never been doubted that economics and politics are intertwined in the era of mercantilism.

In world-systems analysis, as we have seen, formal imperialism is interpreted as the political method of creating new economic production zones in the world-economy. From the original production of bullion in the Spanish colonies in the sixteenth century to the current production of uranium from Namibia, the last large colony, formal imperialism has been the prime means of ensuring the transformation of external arenas into the world-economy's division of labour. We will illustrate this process using the two 'classic' imperialisms of the first and second competitive eras respectively — the Caribbean and Africa.

1. The sugar islands of the Caribbean

The original Spanish colonization of the Americas largely by-passed the islands of the West Indies. Some larger islands were secured but their main function was only to protect the trade generated on the mainland. As can be seen on Fig. 3.6, all this changed in the logistic B-phase. In the period 1620—70, twenty-five colonies were created in the 'greater' Caribbean by the Netherlands, France and England. In addition England captured three colonies from Spain, and the Netherlands captured three from Portugal. This zone from north-east Brazil to south-east North America was converted after this 'scramble' into 'plantation America' based on the production of tobacco and especially sugar. These two crops represented new 'tastes' of core consumers which provided a buoyant market even in a stagnation era (Wallerstein 1980a).

Sugar production was labour-intensive and ecologically damaging. Soil exhaustion had led to production migrating westward from Mediterranean islands, to Atlantic islands and to north-east Brazil in the late sixteenth century. From there the Dutch introduced it to Barbados, the English to Jamaica and the French to St Dominque. By the late seventeenth century it had overtaken contraband as the main function of the Caribbean islands. Its labour demands were first met by indentured labour but by 1700 African slaves were the dominant source. Caribbean sugar, based upon African slaves, became the major product of the Atlantic trade.

Sugar production was so profitable that even semi-peripheral states joined in the business in the seventeenth century with Denmark, Sweden and Brandenburg/Prussia all obtaining their sugar islands. With highly organized production based on cheap labour, the sugar plantations have sometimes been viewed as the precursors of the organization that was to become the factory system in the industrial revolution in the core. Clearly, in the Caribbean incorporation into the periphery was a process which directly increased the total *production* of the world-economy.

2. 'Islands of development' in Africa

At the other end of the slave trade the European states only secured 'stations' on the West African coast (Fig. 3.6), where they exported slaves received from local slave-trading states. Originally this trade was only a luxury exchange with an external arena. By 1700, however, Wallerstein (1980a) considers it to have become integral to the restructured division of labour occurring during the logistic B-phase. However, as West Africa becomes integrated into the world-economy the production of slaves becomes a relatively inefficient use of this particular sector. Hence British abolition of the slave trade in 1807 reflects long-term economic self-interest underlying the moral issue. Gradual creeping peripheralization of West Africa throughout the nineteenth century is accelerated by the famous 'scramble for Africa' in the age of imperialism (Fig. 3.8). In the final quarter of the nineteenth century colonies were being created in Africa at the rate of one a year. This enabled the continent to be fully integrated into the world-economy as a new periphery.

The spatial structure of this process was very simple and consisted of just three major zones (Wallerstein 1976b). First there were the zones producing for the world market. Every colony had one or more of these and the colonial administrators ensured that a new infrastructure, including ports and railways, was developed to facilitate the flow of commodities to the world market. This produced the pattern which economic geographers have termed 'islands of development'. These 'islands' were of three types. In west Africa peasant agricultural production was common — the Asante cocoa-growing region is a good example. In central Africa company concessions for forest or mineral production were more typical, such as the concessionary companies in the Congo which devastated the area in what was little more than plunder. In east Africa and south Africa production based on white settler populations was also found. In all three cases production was geared towards a small number of products for consumption in the core.

Surrounding each 'development island' was a zone of production for the local market. These were largely peasant farming areas producing food for the labour attracted to the first zone. The remainder of Africa became and still is a large zone of subsistence agriculture which is integrated into the world-economy through its export of labour to the first zone. One of the key processes set in motion by the colonial administrators was a taxation policy which often forced peasants outside the two market zones into becoming wage labourers to provide for their new need for money. Labour migration continues today with the massive flows of labour from the Sahel to the coast in west Africa and from central Africa to south Africa. Every island of development has its own particular pattern of source areas for labour. This international migration incorporates all the advantages to capital of alien labour. It is cheap; it has few rights; the cost of reproduction is elsewhere; and it can be disposed of easily as necessary in recession. The third zone, the labour zone, is at the very edge of the world-economy — the periphery of the periphery.

It is ironic but not surprising that huge tracts of Africa are merely producers of cheap labour for the world-economy. This is where Africa entered the story and although the legal status of this labour has changed, it is the same basic process which relegates most of Africa to the very bottom of the world order. This has continued despite the granting of independence to nearly all of Africa in the post-Second World War era. The migration goes on unabated although now it is between independent states instead of between colonies. Formal imperialism may have been an effective strategy for setting up this situation but it is clearly not a necessary criterion for its continuation: imperialism is dead; long live imperialism! The alternative imperialism, the informal variety, is the subject matter of the final section of this chapter, but before we unravel the intricacies of this 'hidden imperialism' we need to consider how our previous discussions of core states and peripheral arenas, and the geography and the economics of imperialism, fit together in a single empire.

WHERE THE SUN NEVER SET

Although there have been five major imperialist states in the modern world-system one stands out as pre-eminent above the others (Fig. 3.5). By the late nineteenth century the British Empire was not only viewed as the most powerful state in the world, it was widely regarded as the greatest empire the world had ever known. One quarter of the world's lands and population were formally controlled from London (Fig. 3.9). The empire reached its widest extent after World War I when it took over former German colonies and Ottoman territories as mandates from the League of Nations. But they merely represented some late spoils of military victory. The empire reached its true zenith at the end of Queen Victoria's reign. As 'queen-empress' she was a symbol of Britain 'winning the nineteenth century'. The celebration of the Queen's Diamond Jubilee in 1897 centred on a great imperial pageant through the streets of London and this is usually taken as the occasion which marks the high point of British imperialism (Morris 1968). Within two years Britain was embroiled in the

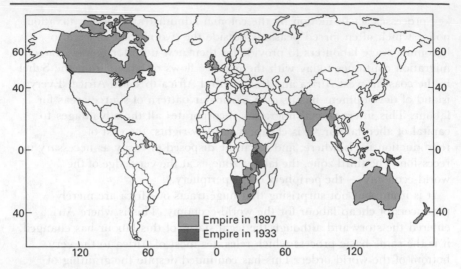

Fig. 3.9 The British Empire in 1897 and its extension in 1933

Boer War and British self-confidence in its right to rule over so much of the world began its long decline

Although there is nothing typical about British imperialism in relation to other imperialisms, we describe it in this section as our case study of formal imperialism because it contributed so much to the making of our modern world. We deal with three themes: the relation of the empire to British hegemony, the geopolitical codes that were created for empire and the ideology that attempted to hold the whole structure together.

Hegemony and empire

Hegemony implies an open world-economy; empire involves the closing off of part of the world-economy from rivals. Hence, as we have seen, imperial expansion is not associated with hegemonic strategies of dominance. But, of course, Britain did not give up her empire on achieving hegemony and in fact continued to extend it, albeit at a slower rate (Fig. 3.5). India became the great exception to British foreign policies of the mid nineteenth century. The crude mercantilist restrictions of the eighteenth century continued in India unabated. As Hobsbawm (1987: 148) has noted, India was

> the only part of the British Empire to which laissez faire never applied . . . And the 'formal' British Empire expanded in India even when no other part of it did. The economic reasons for this were compelling.

India imported 50 per cent of Lancashire cotton textiles and provided 50 per cent of Chinese imports in the form of opium; with government charges and debt interest, 40 per cent of Britain's deficit with the rest of the world was covered by payments from India. No wonder it was called the jewel of the empire!

Despite hegemony, therefore, Britain was the major imperial power in the world before the general expansion of imperialism in the late nineteenth century which marked the decline of that hegemony. Since Britain remained politically the world's most powerful state she gained most from the 'new imperialism' thus creating the mammoth empire so lavishly celebrated in 1897

But what was this imperial creation? Great empires of the past had usually been compact land empires not disconnected pieces of territory spread all over the globe. There was certainly never any overall imperial strategy to produce the particular pattern of lands that ended up coloured pink on the world map. That is why people joked that the empire had been acquired 'in a fit of absence of mind' (Morris 1968: 37). But, of course, it was much more than that. Although not centrally directed, the empire was created in a series of minor and major conflicts with other European powers and local populations over a period of 400 years. Hence it was fragmented because it reflected events in the periphery as much as those of the core.

The problems of geographical fragmentation were exacerbated by the *ad hoc* nature of the administration of the Empire. The Colonial Office directly administered the Crown Colonies. Other colonies were self-governing (the white-settled territories). Much of the empire consisted of 'protectorates' which were technically still foreign countries and were controlled from the Foreign Office which also ran the Egyptian government although the country was never formally British. India was again the exception having its own department of state, the India Office. No wonder Morris (1968: 212) has concluded, 'It was all bits and pieces. There was no System'.

For the imperialist politicians in London geographical fragmentation could be overcome by the new technologies of travel and communications. Contemporary geographers emphasized the decline of distance as an obstacle of separation and discovered the concept of 'time-distance' to replace simple physical distance (Robertson 1900). In the new analysis the world was shrinking and the far-flung empire was converted into a viable political unit. In particular the steamship and the imperial postal service were seen as bringing the empire together. Even more dramatic, by the 1890s the electric telegraphy was producing almost instantaneous links between all components of the Empire. Britain had laid thousands of miles of submarine cables in the late nineteenth century and in 1897 Queen Victoria's Jubilee message was sent in a mere few seconds to all corners of the empire by telegraph. In this new world it seemed that Britain was in the process of producing a new sort of world state. Instead of 'old fashioned' *laissez faire*, new institutions like the Imperial Federation League and the United Empire Trade League supported by geographers such as

Mackinder were formulating and promoting plans for a British imperial federated state. Since it would cover all parts of the world the 'imperial harvest' would be a continuous one. Hence self-sufficiency was a practical goal that was both feasible and which might become necessary as inter-state rivalries heightened. Britain may have lost her hegemonic superiority but here was a chance to create an alternative way of maintaining world dominance. For Britain's imperial politicians there was one important black cloud on the horizon of their new world. The strategic defensive problems of such a fragmented world state were immense. This was Mackinder's major concern, as we have seen. Imperial geopolitical codes were required to make sense of this problem.

2. Imperial geopolitical codes

Britain's haphazard creation of an empire had required a whole series of local geopolitical codes. In every arena local British military and civilian officials had to compete with other European states and come to terms with local populations. After the defeat of, or accommodation with, the former, strategies of control had to be devised for the latter. This meant the identification of collaborators. The basic British strategy was divide and rule. It was at this time that British governors throughout the world 'officially' recognized various cultural groups in order to play one off against another. Official designation in administrative documents such as the census turned these groups into political strata competing for the favours of the Empire. Quite literally the British Empire was the great creator of 'peoples' throughout the world. The legacy of this policy remains with us today in such political rivalries as Hindus, Moslems and Sikhs in India, Tamils and Sinhalese in Sri Lanka, Greeks and Turks in Cyprus, Indians and indigenous Fijians in Fiji, Jews and Palestinians in Israel/Palestine, Chinese and Malays in Malaya plus numerous ethnic rivalries in the former British colonies of Africa.

Divide and rule could help keep control of particular colonies or protectorates but it did not help in global strategy required to defend the Empire as a whole. As a sea empire Britain's strategy was based on its navy. In the nineteenth century government policy operated a two to one rule whereby the Royal Navy was kept twice as large as the combined fleet of its two main rivals. Furthermore the Royal Navy was the only navy with truly global range based upon coaling stations on islands and key ports at intervals of three thousand miles or less on all the major shipping routes.

The route to India was the 'main street' of the Empire. Originally around Africa via the Cape, after the opening of the Suez Canal in 1871 the new route to India became the focus of Britain's imperial strategy. The Mediterranean and Red Sea became vital to British interests with the canal viewed as the 'jugular' of the Empire — hence the need to oust France from Egypt and take over the government of Egypt. But even more important than rivalry with France in the Mediterranean was the threat from Russia to the north-west of India.

At the same time that Britain had been extending its position in India, Russia had been expanding its land empire into central Asia inevitably provoking a clash of interests between the two powers. The result was the Great Game of the nineteenth century, the intrigue and threats between Russia and Britain in a zone extending from Turkey, through Iran to Afghanistan and the north-west frontier of India. This Victorian Cold War, as Edwardes (1975) has called it, rarely erupted into 'hot war' but was an underlying concern of Britain's global imperial geopolitical code. It was this Great Game that Mackinder extended to become the Heartland Theory and which the United States finally inherited as containment in the 'real' Cold War.

3. The imperial ideology

Finally it must be emphasized that the supposed unity of the British Empire was not based solely upon physical facilities such as coaling stations and telegraph offices. Imperialism was not a derogatory term in the late nineteenth century; quite the contrary it was an official and popular ideology. Although we can agree with Morris (1968: 99) that 'one imperial end was basic to all others: profit' and that this was always 'profit for the few', the glory that was Empire could be shared by the many. All Britons both high and low could be proud to be members of the country with the greatest ever empire. They were an 'imperial people' with a 'civilizing mission' for the world. It is here that we can find the ultimate contradiction of formal empire and which was to signal its end within a couple of generations of its zenith.

Basically Britain's imperial ideology incorporated two incompatible principles. First there was the 'imperial philosophy of equality' (Huttenback 1976: 21) sometimes known as 'the High Victorian concept of fair play' (Morris 1968: 516). In theory all the peoples of the colonies were subjects of the Queen and therefore enjoyed the Queen's justice irrespective of colour or creed. Hence 'the rule of law was the one convincingly unifying factor in imperial affairs' (Morris 1968: 195). But alongside this principle was a second principle of racial superiority — Cecil Rhodes's 'visionary project' of 'the world supremacy of the Anglo-Saxon peoples' (Bowle 1974: 359). These two principles clashed most acutely where coloured immigrant labour came into contact with white labour in the settler colonies.

In the creation of new production zones for the world-market large numbers of people were moved to form new labour forces. For tropical crop-production Indians and Chinese were transported all around the world from Fiji to Trinidad. In the more temperate parts of the Empire, European immigration had produced another labour force that was organized into unions and was relatively high-waged. Such 'labour problems' could be 'solved' by using coloured contract labour to replace expensive white labour. In the self-governing colonies the latter were powerful enough to prevent this happening. But if all the Queen's subjects were equal under the law how could this cheap labour be kept out of Australia, Canada, New Zealand and South Africa?

This political problem confronted the chief ministers of the self-governing colonies who met in London at the Jubilee celebrations under the chairmanship of Joseph Chamberlain the Colonial Secretary. He advised adoption of what had come to be known as the 'Natal formula' (Huttenback 1976: 141). This involved the use of a European language test to prevent entry to a colony. Since all immigrants were liable to take the same test it preserved the first principle of equality while enacting the second principle of racial discrimination. Huttenback (1976: 194) sums it up thus: 'The "Natal formula" was simply a means for keeping unwanted immigrants out of a colony through the use of a mechanism which seemed innocuous in legislation'. In short it provided a veil of decency to cover the racialism. Within a year the Australian colonies began enacting the required legislation to produce the 'White Australia' policy while retaining the 'principles of empire'.

Imperialism's claim to the high moral ground — the European 'civilizing mission' — and Britain's particular reputation for fair play was disputed and soundly defeated in the twentieth century. Gandhi in India more than any other individual exposed the contradictions of Empire and won the high moral ground for the anti-imperialists. Imperialism became unfashionable and doomed. Political freedom still had to be won, by physical resistance in many colonies but, after 1945 no European power, not even Britain, could stem the floodtide of independence. In the new world of US hegemony and the Cold War there was no room for an anachronism such as the British Empire.

INFORMAL IMPERIALISM: DOMINANCE WITHOUT EMPIRE

In his *The Geography of Empire* Keith Buchanan (1972) does not discuss the formal imperialisms of the past but concentrates solely on the contemporary dominance of the United States in the world-economy. In what he terms 'the new shape of empire', he points out that whereas the de-colonization process has provided formal independence for colonies from a single imperial state it has not provided independence from the imperial system as a whole (Buchanan 1972: 57). In world-economy terms what we have is a change of strategy by core states from formal to informal imperialism. This is not a new phenomenon. In our model of hegemonies and rivalries the former were associated with informal imperialism. Hence we expect the rise of each hegemonic power to lead to a period of informal imperialism similar to that described by Buchanan for American hegemony. In fact this is exactly what we find. There have been only three hegemonic powers in the history of the world-economy and each is associated with one of the three classic examples of informal imperialism. First, in the mid seventeenth century Dutch hegemony was based, in large part, on the Baltic trade whereby eastern Europe remained politically independent while becoming peripheralized. Dutch merchants dominated the trade but there was no Dutch political control. Second, in the mid nineteenth century Britain employed the 'imperialism of free trade' when Latin America became known as Britain's 'informal empire'. Finally, in the mid twentieth century American hegemony has been associated with de-colonization, to be replaced by neo-colonialism — political independence of the periphery tempered by economic dependence.

Informal imperialism is a much more subtle political strategy than formal imperialism. For this reason it is much less amenable to the descriptive, cataloguing approach employed in the last section. Buchanan (1972) produces numerous interesting maps on topics such as US support for indigenous armies and police to control their own populations — which he terms Vietnamization — but he is unable to capture the basic mechanism of informal imperialism through this empirical approach. Here we develop our argument in two stages. In the first place we show that informal imperialism is no less 'political' despite its emphasis on 'economic' processes. This involves a discussion of trade policy not as a part of economic theory but as alternative state policies within different sectors of the world-economy. But political intervention in the world market cannot change the structural constraints of the world-economy. In the final part of the chapter we describe the basic mechanism of unequal exchange which generates and maintains uneven development throughout our world.

THE INTERNATIONAL RELATIONS OF INFORMAL IMPERIALISM

The mainstream of economic thought traces its origins back to Adam Smith's *Wealth of Nations* written in 1776. This book criticized the policy of mercantilism as generally practised at that time and instead advocated a policy of *laissez-faire*. Ever since Smith, free trade has been a basic principle of all orthodox economics. In the early nineteenth century Ricardo added the idea of comparative advantage to the theory. This claimed that with each state specializing on what it could best produce, free trade would generate an international trade equilibrium to everyone's mutual advantage. Free trade was therefore the best policy for all states, and any political interference in the flow of commodities in or out of a country was neither in the interests of that particular country nor of the system as a whole.

There are two related paradoxes in this orthodox economics. The first is

that it simply does not work out in practice. In the three cases which we
have identified as informal imperialism the peripheral states did not gain
from the openness of their national economies — Eastern Europe still lags
behind Western Europe, Latin America is still a collection of periphery or
semi-periphery states, and Africa and Asia are part of a 'South' periphery
in which mass poverty is increasing during the current recession. As we
shall see, states that have 'caught up' have employed very different
policies. This leads on to the second paradox concerning free trade which
is that most politicians in most countries at most times have realized that
it does not work. Although they have not always had theoretical
arguments to back up their less than orthodox economics, most politicians
have found that the interests of the groups they represent are best served
by some political influence on trade rather than simply leaving it all to the
'hidden hand' of the market. I suppose we can ask, who is right —
'economic theorists' or 'practical politicians'? The answer is that they both
are . . . sometimes, it all depends on the world-economy location of the
state in question.

1. Free trade and the hegemonic state

We can interpret the orthodox economic advocacy of free trade as a
reflection of the structural advantage of core powers, in particular
hegemonic core powers, in the world-economy. As the most efficient
producers of commodities such states can promote free trade in the
knowledge that their producers can beat other producers in any open
economic competition. The market favours efficient producers and the
efficient producers are concentrated in the hegemonic state by definition.
In such a situation it is in the interests of the rising hegemonic power to
present free trade as 'natural' and political control as 'interference'. But,
of course, there is nothing natural about free trade, the world market, or any
other man-made institution. 'All organisation is bias' is Schattschneider's
(1960) point, as we have discussed in Chapter 1, and orthodox economics
represents a classic case of attempting to organize non-hegemonic
interests off the political agenda. The question we ask of any institution,
however, is 'What is the organization of bias in this institution?' (Bachrach
and Baratz 1962: 952). In the case of the world market it is clear that the
bias is in favour of core states and hegemonic core states in particular.
The whole history of the world-economy is testimony to this fact. The
purpose of inter-state politics is either to maintain this bias or to attempt
to change it. The former political strategy is the free trade one which is
associated with informal imperialism. This is neither more nor less
'political' than protectionism, mercantilism or formal imperialism which
attempt to change the status quo. The former is political non
decision-making, the latter political decision-making in Bachrach and
Baratz's (1962) terms. Of course politics is so much easier when the
system is on your side.

2. *Protectionism and the semi-periphery*

The practical politicians who have generally failed to adhere to the orthodox prescriptions for trade have not been without their economic champions, of course. The most famous is the mid nineteenth-century German economist Friedrich List. The world-systems approach is much closer to his analysis than Adam Smith's. For List there was no 'naturally' best trade policy; rather tariffs were a matter of 'time, place and degree of development' (Isaacs 1948: 307). List even admitted that had he been an Englishman he would have probably not doubted the principles of Adam Smith (Frank 1978: 98). But List realized that free trade was not a good policy for the infant industries of his own country, Germany. Hence he advocated a customs union — the famous *Zollverein* — with a tariff around the German states under Prussian leadership. List rationalized his unorthodox position by arguing that there are three stages of development, each of which requires different policies. For the least advanced countries free trade was sensible to promote agriculture. At a certain stage, however, such policy must give way to protectionism to promote industry. Finally, when the latter policy has succeeded in advancing the country to 'wealth and power' then free trade is necessary to maintain supremacy (Isaacs 1948). In world-systems terms List's theory can be translated into policies for periphery, semi-periphery and core countries respectively. Since the Germany of his time was semi-peripheral, he advocated protectionism. In fact we can identify protectionism or, more generally, mercantilism as the strategy of the semi-periphery. Both modern champions of free trade — Britain and the United States — were major advocates of mercantilist policies *before* their hegemonic period: Britain against the Dutch, the United States against Britain. In fact, US Secretary of State Alexander Hamilton's famous *Report on Manufactures* in 1791 remains a classic statement on the need to develop a semi-peripheral strategy as defined here (Frank 1978: 98–9).

3. *The choice for the periphery*

Friedrich List advocated free trade as the tariff policy of the periphery. In fact there have been and continue to be disputes within peripheral countries on the best policy. Gundar Frank has described this for mid nineteenth-century Latin America as a contest between the 'American' party and the 'European' party. The former wanted protection of local production and represented the local industrialists. The latter were liberals who favoured free trade and were supported by landed-interests who wished to export their products to the core and receive back better and cheaper industrial goods than could be produced locally. Generally speaking the 'European party' won the political contest and free trade triumphed. It is in this sense that Frank talks of local capital in allegiance with metropolitan capital under-developing their own country. This is the collaboration relation in informal imperialism epitomized by nineteenth-century Latin American liberals. In contrast, in the United States the 'American party' (notably Republican protectionism) was triumphant and the country did not become under-developed.

Frank's political choices for Latin America a century ago can be identified in the two other classic cases of informal imperialism. Of course his terminology is no longer appropriate — we shall rename his positions peripheral strategy (the European party) and semi-peripheral strategy (the American party). In Eastern Europe we have already noted that the counter-Reformation represents the triumph of Catholic landed-interests over local urban interests. In our new terms the landed interests of eastern Europe adopted a peripheral strategy and opened up their economy to the Dutch.

The current pattern of informal imperialism provides modern political leaders in the periphery with the same basic choice. In any particular state which strategy is adopted will vary with the internal balance of political forces and their relation to core interests. This has been somewhat obscured, however, by the same ideological façade which confuses the geopolitics previously described. In Africa, for instance, Young (1982) distinguishes between states in terms of the self-ascribed ideology of their governments. The two most common categories are 'populist socialism' and 'African capitalism'. In our framework these represent semi-periphery and periphery strategies respectively. Ghana provides a good example of a country where both options have been used. Nkrumah's development policy of using cocoa-export revenues to build-up the urban-industrial sector is a typical semi-peripheral approach which only officially became 'socialism' towards the end of his regime. Nkrumah's great rival Busia, on the other hand, led a government which adopted a liberal trade policy to the advantage of the landed-interests behind the cocoa exports, what we would term a peripheral policy. Hence the overthrow of Nkrumah was not a defeat for socialism, and the overthrow of Busia was not a defeat for capitalism. In world-systems terms, in the case of Ghana both semi-peripheral and peripheral strategies failed politically and economically. Success in the world-economy depends on much more than politicians, however charismatic.

INFORMAL IMPERIALISM AS A STRUCTURAL RELATION

The above argument can be summarized as saying that core states, especially hegemonic core states have a *structural* advantage in the world-economy. By 'structural' we mean that the advantage is built into the whole operation of the world-economy. This is more than a mere cumulative advantage — the system relies on this inequality as part of its functioning. Hence there are no solutions to overcoming world inequalities within the world-economy but there are state strategies which can aid one state at the expense of the others. Wallerstein (1979) uses Tawney's tadpole philosophy to illustrate this. Although a few tadpoles will survive to become adult frogs most will perish not because of their individual failings but because they are part of an ecology which limits the total number of frogs. Similarly if all countries adopt 'perfect' policies for their own economic advance, this does not mean that all will rise to membership of the core. To have a core you need a periphery and without both there would be no world-economy. In this situation it is easier to maintain a core position than to rise upwards.

But what is the mechanism which maintains the core-periphery structure? The exact process has changed over the history of the world-economy and here we will concentrate upon the period of industrial capitalism. Our discussion is based loosely on Emmanuel's (1972) concept of unequal *exchange* in which we will emphasize the political process. Emmanuel's work is an attempt to explain the massive modern inequalities of the world-economy. Whereas before the mid nineteenth century wages were not very different across the various sectors of the world-economy, currently wage differences are very large (Fig. 3.10). Why this change in the intensity of the core–periphery structure? The answer to this question provides us with the basic mechanism of informal imperialism.

1. The rise of social imperialism

Emmanuel's starting point is the concept of a labour market. The rise of the world-economy initially produced 'free' labour in the core countries, where men and women were able to work for whom they pleased. But this freedom was a very hollow one when there were insufficient jobs or when wages were set by employers. In fact 'free' labourers were no better off than their predecessors in feudal Europe and their lack of security might mean that they were worse off. The labour market operated initially on an individual basis with the result that the more powerful party to the agreements — the employer — could force the lowest wages on the worker. In this situation subsistence wages were the norm with wage levels

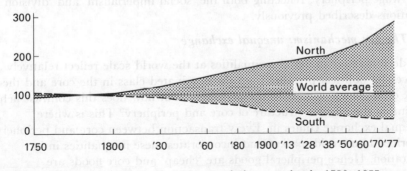

Fig. 3.10 The growing 'North–South' gap: relative wage levels, 1750–1977

reflecting the price of bread which would form up to half a labourer's expenditure. The purpose of wages was to sustain and reproduce the worker and no more. In classical economics subsistence wages were just as 'natural' as free trade but, unlike the latter, this part of our economics heritage has not remained orthodox, at least in the core countries. Quite simply economists were not able to keep wages off the political agenda.

Wages could rise above subsistence levels under certain circumstances. For instance, relative scarcity of labour would tip the balance of negotiations in favour of labour. Hence in the mid nineteenth century the highest wages were not in the European core but in the new settler colonies — notably Australia — with their labour shortages. Marx also mentioned a 'historical and moral element' beyond the market and it is this idea that Emmanuel develops. Marx had used this concept to cover such things as differences in climate and in consumption habits which lead to different levels of subsistence wage. Emmanuel adds a political dimension. Where workers combine they can negotiate from a position of strength in the labour market and obtain more than subsistence wages. This was recognized by politicians, of course, who legislated against unions — in England the Combination Acts of the early nineteenth century. Thompson (1968) argues that after 1832 in England a working-class politics emerged to challenge the state. Although initially unsuccessful, in the mid nineteenth-century period of economic growth, unions consolidated their position and made economic gains for their members. Subsistence wages were no longer 'natural', the issue of wage level was negotiable. Although originally restricted to skilled workmen — Lenin's labour aristocracy — unionism gradually spread to other workers. With the extension of the voting franchise, governments began to make further concessions to workers, culminating in the establishment of the welfare state in the mid twentieth century. This process was also going along in different ways but essentially the same direction in other countries, but only in core countries. Political pressure to increase the well-being of the dominated class has only been successful in core and a few semi-peripheral countries. The end result has been a high-wage core and a low-wage periphery, reflecting both the 'social imperialism' and 'division' relations described previously.

2. The key mechanism: unequal exchange

Modern massive material inequalities at the world scale reflect relatively successful political pressure from the dominated class in the core and the lack of any such success in the periphery. But how does this contrast help maintain the current structure of core and periphery? This is where unequal exchange comes in. Every transaction between core and periphery is priced in a world market that incorporates these inequalities in its operation. Hence peripheral goods are 'cheap' and core goods are 'expensive'. When a German consumer buys Ghanaian cocoa, low

Ghanaian wages are incorporated into the price. This is not just a matter of different technology levels, although these are interwoven with unequal exchange; the essential difference is in social relations at each location — the relative strength of the German worker compared to his Ghanaian equivalent. For 1966, for instance, it has been estimated that the peripheral countries trade of $35 billion would have been 'worth' $57 billion if produced under high-wage conditions (Frank 1978: 107). The shortfall of $22 billion is the result of unequal exchange. Needless to say this is very much greater than all aid programmes put together. It is the difference between social imperialism and subsistence wages.

We have now reached the crux of our argument. The interweaving of class conflict at a state scale and the core—periphery conflict at the global scale through the process of unequal exchange produces the uneven development so characteristic of our world. And the beauty of this process is that it goes on day after day unrevealed. Unlike free trade and subsistence wages which have been victims of political action, the world market remains off the political agenda. It cannot be otherwise in a world divided into many states where each has its own separate politics. Unequal exchange is an integrated mixture of inter-state and intra-state issues which conventional international politics cannot deal with. The world market appears to be based upon the impersonal forces of supply and demand which determine prices. The only issues that arise are the terms of trade or the balance of prices between core and periphery goods. The fact that these terms do not reflect the hidden hand of the market but are defined by centuries of imperialisms producing global differentials in labour costs is conveniently forgotten. This non-decision-making represents a major political achievement of the dominant interests of the modern world-economy.

INFORMAL IMPERIALISM TODAY

Conor Cruise O'Brien (1971) has asked whether imperialism is still a useful term in an age when empires have all but disappeared. I hope we have shown that, though the process is less overt than in the past, imperialism as a global dominance relation continues to be relevant to our understanding of the modern world. We must be careful however in use of the term for, as O'Brien (1971) points out, today it is more likely to be used for propaganda purposes than as a theoretical concept: both the USA and the USSR condemn each other's 'imperialism'. In the case of the western use of the term, O'Brien (1971) dismisses the idea of Soviet imperialism as an 'intellectual gimmick', merely a clever label for anti-communist propagandists to attach to the USSR. Soviet use of the term to describe US activities does have the advantage of continuity with the old imperialism with, for instance, US intervention in Vietnam following on from prior French imperialism in that country. Nevertheless both uses of imperialism are very narrow in their emphasis on political activities. From our previous discussion it will be self-evident that the prime form that imperialism takes today is informal. Hence we can steer clear of the propaganda battle and concentrate on economic relations that constitute the bulk of contemporary imperialist activity. In relation to the Cold War debate we may merely note that since it is the United States that has been hegemonic it has been the most active state in informal imperialism since 1945. However, in its role as a semi-periphery state the USSR contributes to this informal imperialism. As Harding (1971) has pointed out, to the extent that world prices are used as a basis for trade between communist states exploitation automatically occurs through the unequal exchange mechanism. Informal imperialism is pervasive to the contemporary world-system.

The main economic agents of today's informal imperialism are the 'multinational corporations' that produce and trade across several states. These have been the major economic feature of US hegemony and the decline of that hegemony has been marked by a consequent rise of European and Japanese corporations. The relationship between these economic enterprises and the states they operate in is a very important question that we will deal with in some detail in Chapter 4. Here we concentrate on the way in which informal imperialism operates below the scale of the state and corporation. Individuals organize their lives through households and the question arises as to how this institution relates to informal imperialism. In fact households are integral to the operation of unequal exchange.

For unequal exchange to occur we require two zones where direct producers obtain very different levels of remuneration for their labours. We have already considered how high wage and low wage zones come about, but how are they sustained? What are the mechanisms that enable core and periphery to be re-produced in the day-to-day activities of individuals? The answer is that in each zone different types of households have been created to accommodate different levels of resources. In this way the households become part of the structure through which imperialism continues.

Wallerstein (1983) has introduced the concepts of proletarian and semi-proletarian households to describe the different institutions in core and periphery. Proletarian households derive most of their income from waged work. They evolved out of the social imperialism and welfare state developments in the core states in the first half of the twentieth century. As the direct producers obtained higher wages a new form of household, centred upon the nuclear family, was created. Older forms of household covering a larger extended family could be displaced when a single wage became large enough to maintain the immediate family of the wage-earner. In the ideal form of this new household the husband becomes the sole 'breadwinner', the wife becomes a 'housewife' and the children are full-time at school. This produces a patriarchy where women are relegated to the private sphere of the home so that their work is unwaged and largely unrecognized. This leaves men with their wages as the providers of all necessary items from outside the household. Their role as head of household is therefore predictable and almost seems 'natural'.

This household form expanded with US hegemony. The 1947 Ford Motor Company—Auto-Workers Union deal is usually seen as symbolic because the corporation conceded the high wages to sustain the new proletarian household. The suburban way of life for direct producers was born and John Galbraith (1957) announced that we had now entered a new sort of society, the 'affluent society' no less. As the Kondratieff boom spread to Europe after 1950 so too did the affluent society. But this is only the first part of only half the story.

Meanwhile in the periphery economic changes were reinforcing a very different form of household. These are termed semi-proletarian because wages constitute only a minority of household income. In this low wage zone it is not possible for one person to be the sole 'breadwinner'. Hence other members of the household have to contribute various forms of income for their survival. An example will help clarify the situation. In the spatial division of labour we have described in Africa, for instance, households straddle the different geographical zones producing a distinct sexual division of labour. The different zones provide contrasting opportunities for men and women. In the 'islands' producing commodities for the world-economy, for instance, much of the labour is carried out by male migrants who originate from the subsistence zone. These direct producers provide the main wage component of a household income. The other members of the household remain in the subsistence zone where most of the labour is female and unwaged. This form of patriarchy is superficially similar to that described for the proletarian household, with the man controlling the cash; but in this case the cash is much less important to the household. Money from the migrants is necessary for payment of taxes and buying a few items in the market. But the bulk of a household's day-to-day needs are produced within the household. It is this subsistence activity that enables low wages to be paid to the migrant males. In effect the women of the subsistence zone are subsidizing the labour of the world-economy production zones.

Such migrant-labour households are common throughout the periphery but they constitute just one of several semi-proletarian household types. Their common feature is that they transfer reproduction costs away from the production costs for the world market. Hence necessary activities, such as rearing children for the next generation of labour and the looking after of the previous generation of labour after their working lives, are not costed in the pricing of commodities originating from the periphery to the same degree as for commodities from the core. Hence buyers of core goods in the periphery pay a price that contributes to the welfare of direct producers in the core while buyers of periphery goods in the core do not make the same contribution to the welfare of direct producers in the periphery. Hence patriarchy has been moulded in different contexts to generate unequal exchange.

There have been important changes in recent years that have modified the simple pattern of household structures we have just described. In the core the 'ideal' proletarian household based upon one wage has been severely eroded by the massive increase of women in the labour force. The patriarchy represented by the notion of a male 'breadwinner' has been undermined by the ideas generated by the women's movement from the late 1950s onwards. Simultaneously the spread of mass production techniques created a need for additional labour that women could fill. Hence proletarian households in the core have become even more 'proletarian' as they typically rely on more than one wage to maintain their standard of life. This has meant a higher level of commodity consumption by core households which has contributed to the maintenance of the vast material differences between core and periphery.

Meanwhile in parts of the periphery new developments have also been occurring involving bringing more women into the waged labour force. Since the 1960s there has been appreciable growth of industrial production outside the core. This is sometimes referred to as the new international division of labour. In South-east Asia, for instance, a massive electronics industry has grown up employing large numbers of women. Interpretation of this industrial growth has been confused by a general assumption that industry is a property of core countries, leaving the periphery to produce agricultural goods and raw materials. The new international division of labour represents a very different new world in which this assumption has been turned upside down — a 'de-peripheralization' no less. This is not the interpretation of world-systems analysis, however. Core production processes involve relatively high-wage, high technology activities irrespective of the commodity produced. Throughout its hegemony and beyond, the United States has been the major *agricultural* exporter on the world market, for example. The important point is how the production is organized — the social relations of production — not what happens to be produced. Hence peripheral production processes are compatible with industrial activity where the latter is relatively low wage and low technology. Electronics components production can be either core-like or periphery-like depending upon the social relations of production. In South-East Asia the components are produced in a periphery production process that uses the patriarchy of the region in a new way. A labour force of young women has been created whose gender subordination is translated into 'docile, subservient and cheap' labour (Momsen and Townsend 1987: 79). Hence the increased proletarianization of households is not resulting in appreciable increases in the affluence of the households. The low wages ensure that despite industrialization of the periphery, unequal exchange continues unabated.

Chapter 4

TERRITORIAL STATES

CHAPTER 4

TERRITORIAL STATES

The heyday of political geography was the inter-war years of 1918 to 1939.
Geographers were advising at the Peace Conference in Versailles in 1919
and in subsequent years Mackinder, Haushofer, Bowman and others
became important figures beyond the confines of academic geography. As
we have seen, the retreat from this geopolitics in geography was rapid after
1945. Political geography as a whole was devalued in geography and
geopolitics was downgraded within political geography. This change of
emphasis in scale of analysis is most clearly seen in the chapter on
'Political geography' in the semi-centennial publication of the Association
of American Geographers in 1954 entitled *American Geography: Inventory and
Prospect*. In this chapter Hartshorne (1954) makes the now familiar lament
of political geography's 'underdevelopment' within the wider discipline.
Most instructive is his discussion of methods in political geography. Broad
international themes are replaced by emphasis on 'area studies', 'political
division of the world' and above all the 'political region'. This was not
new; Hartshorne was able to draw on previous and current studies, but it
confirmed a political geography in which world strategic views were
conspicuous by their absence.

Political region was nearly always translated into a territorial state, that
is, one of the sovereign units that make up the world political map. Hence
political geography became locked into a particular geographical scale.
Claval (1984) blames this narrow focus as much as the excesses of
geopolitics for the demise of the sub-discipline in the period before 1970.
Nevertheless this political geography of the state did produce interesting
models of the spatial aspects of state structures. Two particular
approaches dominated — the spatial evolution of states and the spatial
integration of states. This produces two relevant heritages for our
consideration of territorial states, developmental and functional, and these
are described in the first section of the chapter.

In the second section of the chapter we use several themes from these
heritages and reorder them to show how the world political map has been
created. Basically we take topics from traditional political geography and
integrate them into a world systems analysis of the inter-state system.
Understanding the creation of the world political map is only a
preliminary stage for such an analysis, however. In the final section we

look at more fundamental questions concerning the nature of the states themselves. The recent debates within Marxist theories of the state are briefly reviewed as a prelude to developing a world-systems theory of the states, that is, of the inter-state system as a whole.

TWO HERITAGES: DEVELOPMENTALISM AND FUNCTIONALISM

Developmental and functional approaches to the political geography of the state have always been closely related. Both can trace a lineage back to Friedrich Ratzel who is generally recognized to have the best claim to the title 'father of political geography'. In keeping with the intellectual milieux of the late nineteenth century Ratzel (1969) developed a theory of the 'organic nature' of the state which consisted of seven laws of spatial growth. Developmentalism and functionalism have been central to traditional political geography thinking ever since. We concentrate on the most influential examples of each here — Pound's model of state development and Hartshorne's functional approach to political geography.

DEVELOPMENTALISM

Biological analogies were common in all parts of geography in the first half of the twentieth century. William Morris Davis's cycle of physical landscape evolution was even more famous than Ratzel's theory of the state. The influence of the Davisian cycle can be found in political geography in the terminology of van Valkenburg's (1939) cycle theory of the state. In this, model states, like river valleys, are deemed to pass through four stages of development — youth, adolescence, maturity and old age. For instance, the United States passed through the first stage from 1776 to 1803 when it consolidated its internal structure; the second stage lasted from 1803 to 1918 when the country expanded; and since that time the country has been 'mature' in its peaceful quest for international co-operation. Many European states had reached old age and were declining, according to van Valkenburg, in the 1930s. De Blij (1967: 104) has provided us with a more up-to-date version of the cycle theory where European states have returned to maturity! This is self-evidently an extreme case of developmentalism — all states are autonomous entities that proceed along parallel paths but from different starting times and at different speeds. The rest of the world only exists to possibly 'interrupt' the sequence.

What this model shows is that developmentalist thinking was to be found in political geography, and in fact in human geography in general (see Taylor 1957), long before the great burst of such theorizing in the social sciences in the 1950s and 1960s. It is these that Wallerstein (1979) attacks; here we will concentrate on political geography examples.

The most influential in recent years has been Norman Pounds's core-area model.

1. The core-area interpretation of state development

The core-area model was originally devised as an explanation of the development of the European state system by Pounds and Ball (1964). They begin by defining two categories of state, 'arbitrary' and 'organic', the latter term obviously reflecting Ratzel's influence. In fact no organic analogy is intended; rather a distinction is made in the way in which territory is allocated to a state. In the arbitrary category the territory is allocated on some preconceived geographical frame as the result of a political settlement, whereas in the organic case the territory evolves slowly by accretions around a core-area. It is the latter process which Pounds and Ball attempt to delineate for Europe.

Pounds and Ball (1964) argue that in order to become the germinal area of a modern state, core-areas must have some initial advantage over neighbouring areas. To become a viable core-area a district must have been capable of generating an economic surplus at an early date. This would provide the resources first to defend itself against conquest and second to expand its domination over less well-endowed neighbours. In feudal Europe this involved fertile soil for agricultural production plus nodal location for trade in materials not available locally. This environmental argument is illustrated by describing the development of the expansion of the authority of French kings from 987 when they merely controlled the area around Paris. The practical power of the kings was gradually extended by a variety of means both military and dynastic. The result was an accretion of territory beyond the core-area so that by 1360 royal authority extended to the Atlantic in the west and the Pyrenees in the south. The eastern boundary of the state was then gradually pushed outwards to approximately its present location by 1789. Pounds and Ball (1964) consider this example of core-area accretions to be the 'prototype' of a general process. Nineteen modern European states are identified that approximate the model (Fig. 4.1).

2. Critique

The simplest criticism to make of this model is that it is an exercise in 'post-diction'. Since we know which states exist today then identification of their core-areas does not mean that we have an adequate explanation of processes operating in the past. Pounds and Ball's core-areas are not the only possible districts with the necessary geographical characteristics to become the germinal areas of modern states. In fact the core-areas shown in Pounds's (1963) text book differ slightly, Norway for instance has lost its core-area in this version (Fig. 4.1). Even the prototype has come in for criticism. Burghardt (1973: 225) argues that there was no predestined French unity that the French monarchs were fulfilling, rather it was they

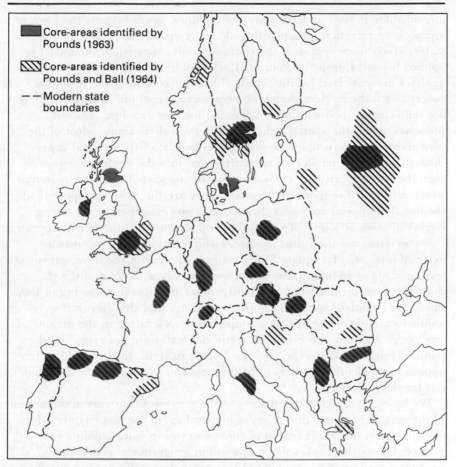

Key:
- Core-areas identified by Pounds (1963)
- Core-areas identified by Pounds and Ball (1964)
- – – Modern state boundaries

Fig. 4.1 Core-areas of European states

who first created the unity. Finer (1974: 96) even concludes that 'territorially speaking, France is quite improbable'!

Burghardt (1969) has further criticized the model because of an inconsistency in definition of the concept of core-area. He identifies three distinct concepts:

1. nuclear core as a germinal area around which accretions of territory have produced the modern territorial state;
2. original core as a germinal area but which failed to obtain accretions of territory; and
3. contemporary core as the current area of greatest political and economic importance in a state.

Burghardt argues that Pounds and Ball's designation of European core-areas confuses nuclear and original cores. The core-areas that are

identified for Poland and Hungary, for instance, never became the basis of
a process of accretion although they do represent historic cores of modern
states. Much more serious is the confusion that arises when the model is
applied beyond Europe by Pounds (1963) and by de Blij (1967). These
analyses are criticized by Burghardt (1969) for confusing the historical
concept with the modern notion of a core-area. From our perspective they
not only confuse political processes over time, they confuse political
processes across the spatial structure of the world-economy. Most of the
core-areas of modern non-European states consist of the original zones
through which the territory was incorporated into the world-economy. As
such the vast majority are coastal or else are associated with raw materials
which attracted European penetration. They are therefore the opposite of
the initial European core-area. Instead of a process generating a strong
territorial state as a unit of security and opportunity, in the non-European
case core-areas are the vulnerable areas which provide opportunities for
external interests. To equate European core-areas with the development of
territorial states in other parts of the world is a typical error of the
developmentalism described previously. Most peripheral states began their
history as colonial appendices of imperial states and this constitutes
another example of the neglect of imperialism as a factor in the making of
our world. Modern non-European territorial states are not repeating the
political processes that generated the European state. In the world-systems
approach we identify two sets of broad mechanisms, one for the core and
one for the periphery.

We have already considered some of the processes that carved out states
in the periphery in our discussion of imperialism in the last chapter. Here
we will return to the discussion of core processes in state-building in
Europe. Of course it takes much more than geographical conditions to
produce a modern state, as Tilly (1975) emphasizes. We need to specify
what the nature of the society that existed in these core-areas was so that
the processes underlying their political successes can be understood.
Hechter and Brustein (1980) have recently attempted such an exercise for
western Europe. They argue that the key core-areas in Spain, Portugal,
France and England enjoyed a particular form of organization which
balanced urban merchant and landed interests. Elsewhere in Europe one
or other of these interests dominated. In the four key core-areas, however,
a political division existed that could be exploited by the central authority
of the state. This is the same power basis of the territorial state identified
by Smith (1978). The end-result was the creation of medium-sized states
in western Europe that contrasted with the merchant dominated city states
and landed-interest dominated empires in central and eastern Europe
respectively.

The Hechter and Brustein model highlights the essential deficiency of
the traditional core-area model. It is not the search for core-areas that is at
fault but the theoretical framework in which this has been pursued.

Instead of identifying a general class of core-areas that all produce the same outcome, a modern state, Hechter and Brustein produce a specific process for the four states that contributed most to the original growth of a world-system based upon western Europe. The subsequent core processes that allowed the survival of these four states and the creation of further modern European states are bound up with the geopolitics we described in Chapter 2 and the mercantilism we discuss below.

FUNCTIONALISM

The basic elements of a geographical theory of the state were developed in the early 1950s by Gottmann (1951, 1952), Hartshorne (1950) and Jones (1954). Gottmann analyzed the political partition of the world and concluded that it was based upon two main factors — movement which causes instability and iconography which causes stability. In this approach, movement includes all exchanges throughout the world whether of peoples, commodities or ideas. Iconography is a system of symbols in which people believe, encompassing elements of national feeling from the state flag to the culture transmitted through the state's schools. These two forces oppose one another, and the world map at any one time is the balance achieved between stability and instability. Hartshorne's (1950) 'functional approach to political geography' developed this idea of two opposing forces more fully.

For Hartshorne the fundamental purpose of the state is to bind together its various social and territorial segments into an effective whole. This integration function can be carried out 'vertically' for social groups and 'horizontally' for territorial groups. Vertical integration is not the concern of political geography except where it is related to territorial differences, according to Hartshorne. He produces, therefore, what we may term a theory of territorial integration.

1. Hartshorne's theory of territorial integration

Territorial integration depends upon two sets of forces — centrifugal forces pulling the state apart and centripetal forces binding it together. Gottmann's movement and iconography are important examples of centrifugal and centripetal forces respectively. Hartshorne's approach now involves a listing of both types of forces and a discussion of their operations. We will briefly describe each set of forces in turn.

The centrifugal forces typically emphasized by political geography are the physical characteristics of a state's territory. The size and shape of a country may be important, for instance. De Blij (1967: 42–5) discusses such issues in some detail but it seems that physical factors vary greatly in their importance as centrifugal forces. Although the original physical separation of Pakistan into east and west is obviously relevant to the ultimate disintegration of the original state in 1971 into a new Pakistan in

the west and Bangladesh in the east, this contrasts with the ease with
which the United States has been able to integrate its forty-ninth and
fiftieth states, Alaska and Hawaii, respectively. Similarly, land-locked
states in Africa suffer serious problems of dependence threatening their
viability, whereas this seems much less important to land-locked
Switzerland and Austria. Obviously these contrasts reflect, once again,
differences between core processes and periphery processes in the
world-economy in which these spatial characteristics have a different
importance. Hence Hartshorne is correct to warn us to be wary about
placing too much weight on such factors *per se* since they are all less
important as centrifugal forces than what he terms the diversity of the
character of the population of a state. This diversity may be expressed in
many ways. Language, ethnic and religious differences are the most
common cause of territorial conflict in states but other features such as
political philosophy, education and levels of living varying by region may
be disruptive. Short (1982) considers the last diversity — regional
inequality in material well-being — to be the most salient centrifugal force
in the modern world. We will return to this point when we discuss
materialist theories on nationalism in Chapter 5.

All of the above features have been associated in different states with
civil wars and sometimes partition. But partition does not always result
and there are, in any case, many states that have never experienced a civil
war based on territorial divisions. What binds states together, therefore?
Hartshorne identifies one basic centripetal force of overwhelming
importance — the state-idea. Every state has a *raison d'être*, a reason for
existence, and it is the strength of this 'idea' which counteracts the
centrifugal forces. In the modern world this state-idea, like Gottmann's
iconography, is closely associated with nationalism and we will consider it
as such in the next chapter. We can note here that it is easier to define
when it is lacking — for instance, it has been said of both the Central
African federation and the West Indian federation that they failed to hold
together because each lacked a widely held state-idea (Dikshit 1971a; Muir
1981: 109).

Hartshorne's theory of territorial integration provides a model for
analyzing particular cases. It has been further developed by Jones (1954)
in his 'unified field theory' of political geography. Hartshorne's concept of
state-idea is extended to form a chain of five related concepts:
political-idea, decision, movement, field and political area. In the case of
modern states the political-idea is the *raison d'être* and the decision is the
specific treaty recognizing the viability of the idea. Movement is
Gottmann's concept as required in operationalizing the decision to
produce a field as the arena in which the movement occurs. Finally a
political area is defined as the territory of the state. Jones gives the
example of the establishment of Israel as follows: Zionism is the idea, the
Balfour Declaration of 1917 is the decision permitting movement

(migration), which produces a field (the immigrant settlement pattern) generating war which defines a state of Israel out of Palestine. When the chain is completed, as in this case, the centripetal forces have triumphed; when the chain is broken, centrifugal forces are deemed to be too strong. In either case we are left with what is essentially a check list for studying the establishment of states.

2. Critique

These ideas of Gottmann, Hartshorne and Jones dominated political geography for over a generation, being faithfully reproduced in many text books. Hence they cannot be merely dismissed as inconsequential; they must be reviewed and evaluated to produce a critical understanding of their strengths and weaknesses.

The basic problem with all functional theories in all fields of inquiry is that they are essentially conservative in nature. That is to say they assume a status quo and neither question how the system got to its current position nor how it might move away from that position. Burghardt (1973: 226) has voiced this criticism succinctly for the theories we have reviewed:

> American functionalist political geographers, following the example of Hartshorne, have tended to treat (territory) as given and have focused their attention on the forces that seem to draw a (state) together or pull it apart. Similarly, Gottmann's emphasis on circulation and iconography appears to presuppose the existence of a state of stable territorial dimension.

Functional analysis can ask some interesting questions but can only provide partial answers. Hence we do not totally dismiss this approach here but in the case of these political geographical analyses there are further important problems that limit their usefulness.

There are two particular criticisms we can make of the theory of territorial integration. First it focused attention on the individual state. We are presented with some relatively abstract concepts to be applied to case studies. Such state-by-state analysis undervalues the existence of the interstate system. Hartshorne (1950) incorporates the 'external functions' of a state in his analysis but provides no overall conception of the external environment in which these functions exist. Obviously in our world-systems analysis below we will consider territorial states as integral parts of an inter-state system.

The second criticism relates to Hartshorne's assertion that integration — the organization of a territory — is the fundamental purpose of the state. It is treated as self-evident that the state operates for itself. But the balance of forces that are provided to explain the success or failure of a state in its prime purpose are abstracted out of the social formation in which the state exists. At this point of the argument it is useful to repeat Schattschneider's dictum that 'all organization is bias'. The establishment and disestablishment of states represent victories for some social groups and defeats for others. It is for this reason that we cannot banish 'vertical' integration of social groups from our political geography as Hartshorne proposes. The state can only be understood as a response to the needs of certain groups at the expense of other groups. Integration is a process that can be looked back at with pride by the winners but we should not forget the losers in such conflict. Marxist theories of the state explicitly recognize social conflicts and this is the reason they have become popular in political geography in recent years. We introduce such conflict theories of the state when we consider the nature of the state more fully below. But first we reconsider some of the important topics to be found in traditional political geography which have been treated in a developmentalist and/or functionalist manner.

THE MAKING OF THE WORLD POLITICAL MAP

Probably the most familiar map of all is the one showing the territories of the states across the world. This world political map is the simple geographical expression of the inter-state system. The minimum requirement for any political geography is to understand this map. And yet the map itself is quite misleading since it gives an impression of stability that is completely false. The map provides a snapshot of states at one point in time; the reality is that this pattern is forever changing. The world political map must be interpreted as a series of patterns that have changed drastically in the past and which may have equally major changes in the future. Our concern is to understand how the world political map became the pattern we see today

In 1500 Europe possessed a cultural homogeneity but was politically highly decentralized. Tilly (1975: 24) has estimated that there were 1500 independent political units in Europe at this time. By 1900 there were just 20 states in Europe and it had imposed its inter-state system on the rest of the world. This massive feat of political construction must not lead us to assume that there was anything inevitable about this outcome. Looking at the world from the vantage point of 1500 Tilly believes there were five possible alternative futures for Europe — continued decentralized feudal arrangements, a new decentralized trading network of cities, a Christian theocratic federation, a political empire or an inter-state system. In hindsight we can see that the last was most compatible with economic changes occurring at that time and provided windows of opportunity for the emergence of capitalism. We consider this more fully in the next section on the nature of the states. Here we concentrate on the inter-state system as a dynamic spatial structure.

Changes in the world political map have often been the outcome of wars and conflicts associated with major geopolitical transitions. The world political map was redrawn at Westphalia after the Thirty Years War in

1648, at Vienna after the Napoleonic Wars in 1815 and of course in this century after both world wars. Each new map provides the underlying political geography framework for a geopolitical world order. But the world political map is a matter of direct concern for more than the major powers in their geopolitical rivalries. All states are concerned with their corner of the world map and minor changes occur within a world order as the result of wars and conflicts between the lesser powers. Hence, in the space available here, it is impossible to trace the huge number of changes that have taken place to create today's world political map. We attempt no such inventory but concentrate on the key features of the changing system. The whole structure is premised on two concepts, territory and sovereignty, and we start our discussion with them.

TERRITORY AND SOVEREIGNTY

Jean Gottmann (1973: 16) has described the origins of the concept of territory. It derives from the Latin, and was originally applied to a city's surrounding district over which it had jurisdiction. Its initial application was to city-states in the Classical World and it reappeared to describe the jurisdictions of medieval Italian cities. It was never applied to the whole Roman Empire or medieval Christendom with their universal pretentions. 'Territory' implies a division of political power. In modern usage its application to cities has become obsolete; it is now applied to modern states. A territory is the land belonging to a ruler or state. This meaning has been traced back to 1494, approximately to the birth of the world-economy.

The modern meaning of territory is closely tied up with the legal concept of sovereignty. In fact this is a way in which it can be distinguished from the original city-scale definition. Sovereignty implies that there is one final and absolute authority in a political community (Hinsley 1966: 26). This concept was not evolved in the classical Greek world — city territories were not sovereign. Instead Hinsley traces the concept back to the Roman Empire and the emperor's *imperium* over the Empire. This is a personal political domination with no explicit territorial link given the Empire's universal claims. It is this concept that was passed on to medieval Europe in Roman Law and is retained in modern language when a king or queen is referred to as the sovereign of a country. But medieval Europe under feudalism was a hierarchical system of power and authority, not a territorial one. The relations of lord and subject were personal ones of protection and service and were not territorially based. It is the bringing together of territory and sovereignty which provides the basis of the modern inter-state system. This emerged in the century after 1494 and was finalized by the treaty of Westphalia of 1648. This is usually interpreted as the first treaty defining modern international law. It recognized that each state was sovereign in its own territory: that is,

interference in the internal affairs of a country was the first offence of
international law. The result was a formal recognition of a Europe
parcelled up into some three hundred sovereign units. This was the original
territorial basis of the modern inter-state system — the first 'world political
map'.

1. Territory: security and opportunity

This first mosaic of sovereign territories was a direct result of the strife
resulting from the religious wars in Europe in the wake of the Reformation
and Counter-Reformation. The crucial political issue of the day was order
and stability, or rather the lack of it, and the territorial state emerged as
the solution to the problem of security (Herz 1957). The legal concept of
sovereignty was backed up by a 'hard shell' of defences which made it
relatively impenetrable to foreign armies so that it became the ultimate
unit of protection. Herz (1957) provides a technical explanation for this
development — the gunpowder revolution in warfare which made individual
city ramparts obsolete. The original 'hard shell' of the walled city was
replaced by the sovereign state and new defences based upon much larger
resources. Such new warfare required a firm territorial basis, not the
personal hierarchy of the medieval period.

   Herz's explanation is a good one in that it incorporates an important
dimension in the origins of modern state formation. But it is only a partial
explanation. Tilly (1975) introduces other factors in the 'survival' of these
states and the inter-state system. Security provides a stability in which a
territory's resources can be mobilized more completely. The territorial
state is associated with the rise of absolute monarchs in Europe with their
centralized bureaucracies, taxation and large armies. In a world-systems
perspective, however, we need to go beyond these 'political' factors. We
follow Gottmann (1973) in identifying two basic functions of the territorial
state — security and opportunity. The former relates to the origins of the
inter-state system, the latter to the emerging world market.

   The rise of a world-economy provided different opportunities for
entrepreneurs in different locations. In the agricultural world-economy
described by Wallerstein (1974a, 1980a) the major groups contesting for
advantage in the new world market were the agricultural landed interests
on the one hand and the urban merchants on the other. According to
Smith (1978) this conflict is directly related to the rise of the modern state
with the landed aristocracy giving up their medieval rights in return for
the sovereign's support against the new rising urban class. But this initial
alliance between landed interests and the new managers of the state
apparatus soon had to give way to a more flexible 'politics'. In a
competitive state system security requires more than recognition of
sovereignty. It requires keeping up with neighbouring states in economic
terms. Hence the emergence of mercantilism which we have briefly
discussed in previous chapters. Mercantilism was simply the transfer

of the commercial policies of the trading city to the territorial state (Isaacs
1948: 47–8). The scale of territorial restrictions on trade was enhanced to
become a major arm of state-making. Mercantilism was based on the
premise that each state had to grab as much of the world market as it
could by building its industry and commerce at the expense of other
states. The power of the state ultimately depended on the success of its
mercantilism. The exact nature of different states' policies in the world
market reflected the balance of power between the landed and merchant
interests. The former succeeded overwhelmingly in eastern Europe to
produce its peripheralization; in the rest of Europe the balance varied with
merchants most successful in the two most successful states of the
Netherlands and England. In all cases this commercial policy beyond the
confines of cities was the product of the new territorial state and the
inter-state system. Security and order, opportunity and mercantilism were
all premised on the territorial state.

2. *Sovereignty as international capacity*

Territory is the platform for engaging in international relations;
sovereignty provides the legitimation. Quite simply:

> Sovereignty is the ground rule of inter-state relations in that it identifies the
> territorial entities who are eligible to participate in the game. (James 1984: 2)

Hence not all territories are sovereign states.

Before this century when there were still regions outside the
world-economy, political entities of the external arena were not recognized
as having any political rights. The Iroquois in North America, the Zulus in
southern Africa and the Marathas of central India were all equally
unrecognized as legitimate actors in the inter-state system. This had the
effect of making their territories available for incorporation into expanding
sovereign states. Small and Singer (1982) call the resulting wars
'extra-systemic'. Such formal imperialism was therefore a legitimate
activity in international law since it violated no recognized sovereignties.

Today, as in the past, it is not possible to become sovereign just by
declaring yourself thus. Sovereignty is never a matter for a single state, it
is an inter-state arrangement because sovereignty can only exist for 'states
who reciprocally recognise each other's legitimate existence within the
framework and norms of the inter-state system' (Wallerstein 1984a: 175).
Hence the Bantustans declared independent by South Africa as part of the
apartheid policy are recognized by no other states as sovereign and cannot
therefore be said to be part of the inter-state system. Similarly the republic
set up in the northern half of Cyprus following the Turkish invasion of
1974 has obtained no recognition beyond Turkey. Since 1945 recognition
of sovereignty has been confirmed usually by acceptance into membership
of the United Nations. Hence the very first task of the new post-colonial
states of Africa and Asia was to apply to join the UN to prove their entry

on to the world stage. In short, sovereignty gives territories an international capacity in the world-economy.

James (1984) points out that territorial sovereignty is a feature of the modern state system that distinguishes it from previous political systems. For Wallerstein (1984a: 33) this is vital:

> It is the fact that states in the capitalist world-economy exist within a framework of our inter-state system that is the *differentia specifica* the modern state, distinguishing it from other bureaucratic polities.

Hence the historical continuities that are sometimes traced between modern states and medieval polities (Portugal, France and England are the main examples) are misleading at best and confusing at worse. In the fourteenth century Portugal was not a sovereign state operating in a competitive inter-state system and neither was England or France. They operated a different politics in a different world-system. Reciprocated sovereignty is only found in the capitalist world-economy.

3. Conflicting territorial claims

The operation of the twin principles of territory and sovereignty as the basis of international law has an important corollary: states have become the 'collective individuals' around which laws are framed. Hence the 'rights of states' have priority over the interests of other institutions. This is enshrined in Article 2 of the United Nations Charter which upholds the territorial integrity of member states and outlaws intervention into their domestic affairs (Burghardt 1973: 227). This produces a further corollary, international law is essentially conservative in nature preserving as it does the status quo in the inter-state system. But we have already noted that stability has not been the norm for the world political map. Changes occur when political claims for territory override legal conservatism; how are they justified?

Burghardt (1973) reviews several types of political claims and concludes that just three have had any major influence on the make-up of the world political map. Ranked in order they are 'effective control', 'territorial integrity' and historical/cultural claims.

Effective control as a criterion for accepting a state's right to a territory is used to legitimate armed conquest. In the international sphere as in national courts, 'possession is nine tenths of the law'. For all the idealism of the United Nations and other world bodies, power politics still lies at the root of international relations. Hence nobody today disputes India's incorporation of Goa into its territory after the successful invasion of the Portuguese colony in 1962. Sovereignty is normally accepted once effective control of a territory is demonstrated. This was the principle that was applied for the partition of Africa among European powers after the Berlin Conference in 1884.

Territorial integrity can be used to challenge the right of a state that has effective control over a territory. Geographical claims can be at any scale. The most famous is the US concept of 'Manifest Destiny' which justified ocean-to-ocean expansion of the USA. (Burghardt 1973, 236). Most claims are much more modest. Currently the most well-known is the Spanish claim to Gibraltar. Despite British effective control and the wishes of the Gibraltarians to keep their link with Britain, the United Nations voted in 1968 for the transfer of Gibraltar to Spain. The fact that Gibraltar was part of the Iberian peninsular provided the basis for the territorial integrity claim (Burghardt 1973, 236).

Historical and cultural claims are much more varied in nature. Historical claims relate to either priority or duration of occupation. The former was reduced to nothing more than 'discovery' by European explorers in the partition of Africa. (The priority of occupation by those in the external arena was not recognized, of course — they had no sovereignty). Other historical claims have usually been associated with national claims to territory under the heading of 'national self-determination'. We deal with the problems surrounding this concept in Chapter 5. One interesting example of historical priority is worthy of mention here, however. With few exceptions today's independent African states have the same boundaries as the colonial territories they superseded. Hence the boundaries of Africa drawn by European powers after 1884 have largely survived intact. This is a very good illustration of the conservatism inherent in the inter-state system succeeding in blocking change in the pattern of the world political map. Generally the new states do not support the division of another state because it would likely lead to questioning the integrity of their own inherited territory. Hence when Biafra attempted to secede from Nigeria in the civil war of 1969–71 she obtained little or no political support from other African states. Today most African boundaries are older than European boundaries!

The last example exemplifies the basic conclusion of this discussion: the making of the world political map has been the result of power politics. It is a map of the changing pattern of winners and losers. Territory provides a platform, sovereignty a justification, but neither is an adequate defence for a state against a successful action of power politics by a rival bent on its elimination from the world stage.

Before we leave the issue of competing territorial claims mention must be made of the important question of sovereignty over the seas. In 1982 the United Nations produced a new Convention on the Law of the Sea which was signed by 159 countries but not by the United States. For a discussion of the political geography of the new law reference can be made to Glassner (1986) and Blake (1987).

BOUNDARIES AND CAPITALS

If territory and sovereignty are the two most important concepts for understanding the world political map, boundary lines and capital cities are the two artifacts that most demand our attention. For most of the history of the world-economy, states were rarely experienced by most of their subjects. Day-to-day activities continued with little or no interference by the state. Boundaries and capitals represent the two major exceptions to this rule. Boundaries and capitals are associated with the growth of two new important forms of behaviour and eventually led to two distinctive types of political landscape.

The two forms of behaviour are smuggling and diplomacy. The political map provided opportunities for entrepreneurs in their continual search for profit. Buying cheap and selling dear could now be achieved by avoiding customs duties when entering territories. Contraband was a major aspect of capitalism from the very beginning of the world-economy and was an extension of the traditional fraudulent practices of avoiding city tolls by earlier traders (Braudel 1984). The new boundaries produced a patchwork of larger markets and varying levels of taxes. It is not surprising, therefore, that smugglers have entered the folklore of border areas throughout the world-economy. Diplomats on the other hand are to be found in the capital cities of the new states. The inter-state system was an expensive one to survive in. The medieval European practice of moving government with the personage of the King had to give way to a permanent location of government business. Furthermore the leading states of the system needed access to information on their rivals' activities and wanted, if possible, to provide input into their decision making. Diplomacy was born as governments despatched permanent representatives to the capital cities of their rivals.

In time both boundaries and capitals came to be the two locations where the state could be seen to impinge directly on the landscape. Border landscapes with customs houses and associated controls, and varieties of defensive structures, have become distinctive locations in the modern world. Similarly, capital cities have come to represent their states symbolically with a variety of distinctive grand architectures. In boundaries and capitals we have the two most explicit products of the inter-state system.

We cannot deal with the details of the variety of borders and capitals that have been produced in the making of the world political map. Rather we describe typologies of this detail as they relate to the workings of the world-economy.

1. Frontiers and boundaries

Frontiers and boundaries have probably been the most popular topic in political geography. However, as long ago as 1963 Pounds (1963: 93–4) noted a decline of interest in this subject matter. This reflects the lessening of boundary disputes in the areas where political geography was largely practised — Europe and North America. This contrasts with the first

half of the twentieth century in Europe when boundary issues were central
to international politics. Furthermore many of the early geographers of
this century (for example, Sir Thomas Holdrich) were themselves
boundary drawers and surveyors in the imperial division of the periphery.
Hence concern for boundaries has waxed and waned with the changing
interests of the core countries. Of course, boundary issues continue to be a
vital ingredient of politics beyond Europe and North America. Good
reviews of the early work on boundaries are available in Minghi (1963),
Jones (1959) and Prescott (1965). Here we shall reinterpret some of this
vast quantity of material in world-systems terms.

The usual starting point in this subject-area is to distinguish frontiers
from boundaries. This is necessary since the terms are commonly used
interchangeably. Kristof (1959) uses the etymology of each term to derive
their essential difference. Frontier comes from the notion of 'in front' as
the 'spearhead of civilization'. Boundary comes from 'bounds' implying
territorial limits. Frontier is therefore outward-orientated and boundary
inward-orientated. Whereas a boundary is a definite line of separation, a
frontier is a zone of contact.

These definitions fit very neatly into our world-systems framework. A
frontier zone is the area between two social systems or entities. In the case
of world-empires this can be between other world-empires or their
juxtaposition with outside mini-systems. Classic cases are the frontiers of
China and Rome. Although in each case they built walls between their
'civilization' and barbarians, the walls were part of a wider frontier zone.
In Roman Britain, for instance, Hadrian's Wall was just part of the
fortifications of the highland military zone or frontier which separated the
civilian south and east from the non-Roman north and west. With the rise
of the world-economy a frontier emerged between this system and the
systems it was supplanting. The history of imperialism is about pushing
forward the frontiers of this new world-system. It produced the 'classic'
frontier in the American west, but also other similar frontiers in Australia,
South Africa, North Africa, north-west India and Asiatic Russia. The
frontier ended with the closing of the world-system at the beginning of this
century. We now live in a world with one system so that there are no
longer any frontiers — they are now phenomena of history.

Frontiers everywhere have been replaced by boundaries. Boundaries are
a necessary component of the sovereignty of territories. Sovereignty must
be bounded: a world of sovereign states is a world divided by boundaries.
Boundaries therefore are an essential element of the modern
world-economy. But of course the process of boundary making is very
different in the various sections of the world-economy. Jones (1959)
identifies five types of boundary concepts — 'natural', 'national',
'contractual', 'geometrical' and 'power-political'. These categories are not
exclusive to one another: from our perspective, for instance, we would
identify all boundaries as reflecting the power-politics of their respective

producers. Nevertheless these are useful concepts which, as Jones is able to show, reflect the different ideas of the state in the evolving world-economy. The idea of 'natural' boundaries is a product of the strength of the French state in eighteenth-century Europe and its use of the new rationalist philosophy to claim a larger 'natural' territory (Pounds 1951, 1954). In contrast the idea of 'national' boundaries is the Germanic reaction to French expansionist ideas. We will consider this reaction further in our discussion of 'nation' below. These two ideas are rationalizations of particular power-political positions in the core and semi-periphery of the world-economy. In the periphery, also, two types of boundary emerged. In non-competitive arenas in the nineteenth century, such as India and Indo-China, the boundaries reflect the expansion of one core state at the expense of weak pre-capitalist social formations. This is where frontiers are extended and then converted to boundaries. The limits are finally achieved when two powers begin to approach one another's peripheral territory. This may lead to the formation of a buffer state in the periphery as in the cases of Afghanistan between Russia and British India, and Thailand between French Indo-China and British India. In competitive arenas the boundaries are usually far more arbitrary as they reflect contractual arrangements between competitors. It is in these areas that 'clear' international boundaries are necessary to prevent disputes. Hence such boundaries commonly follow physical features such as rivers or else are simply geometrical lines usually of longitude or latitude. Examples of such 'contractual' boundaries are, of course, the USA's western boundaries to north and south along the 49th parallel and the Rio Grande respectively. The most competitive arena of all, Africa in the late nineteenth century, has the most 'contractual international boundaries'. Here the concepts of 'natural' or 'national' boundaries had no relevance as ethnic groups and river basins were divided up in complete contrast to the boundary processes then evolving in the core. Once again, we find contrasting processes in core and periphery which are the hallmark of the world-systems approach.

2. Capital cities as control centres

One of the features of core-areas is that they usually have the capital city of the state located within them. Paris and London are obvious examples of this. This has led some political geographers to identify 'natural' and 'artificial' capital cities with the former represented by those in core-areas. As Spate (1942) pointed out long ago, any such distinction is to misunderstand the nature of politics in our society. London is no more 'natural' than Canberra: they are both the result of political decisions, albeit over very different time horizons. Spate rightly dismisses this old dichotomy but retreats into case studies as his own approach to capital cities. Whereas case studies are invaluable for understanding the nature of capital cities they are not sufficient for a full appreciation of the role of these localities in the territorial state. They are, after all, the control centre of the territory, the locus of political decision-making, the symbolic centre of the state and often very much more. As well as the complexity that Spate identifies, which leads him to emphasize their differences, there are important similarities which we will draw upon here.

Many European observes have remarked that Washington DC is an unusual capital in that it is not one of the largest cities in its country. Lowenthal (1958) even calls it an 'anti-capital' reflecting as it does initial American 'anti-metropolitan' revolutionary politics. Henrikson (1983) has reviewed this literature and concludes, not surprisingly, that it manifests a Euro-centric bias. Like Spate before him, Henrikson can find no justification for treating Paris and London as 'ideal models' which the rest of the world should follow. Instead Henrikson identifies two models of the capital city: the European concept of the capital as the opinion-forming centre of the state dominant in political, cultural and economic spheres and the American concept of a responsive centre which specializes in politics. Fifer (1981) for instance refers to Washington DC as 'a company town'. Henrikson is more poetic — 'a small, cozy town, global in scope'.

These two concepts do not cover all cases, however. In a famous paper Mark Jefferson (1939) described a 'Law of the Primate City' in which he propounded the 'law' that a country's capital city is always 'disproportionately large'. This law 'fits' the European concept but is obviously at variance with the American concept. The reason why it is still quoted is because it fits so many countries in the periphery. In most Latin American, African and Asian states the capital city is truly primate — Buenos Aires, Lima, Dar es Salaam, Dakar, Djakata and Manila, to name just two from each continent. This should not be read as meaning that they employ a 'European concept' in the definition of their capital since their position is so very different. In the same way as we dismiss the European core-area model for peripheral states we also avoid using the 'European concept' to cover most peripheral capital cities.

We can reconcile these problems of definition and add to our analysis of capital cities by employing the world-systems approach. There are three types of capital city — one the result of core processes, one the result of peripheral processes and a third reflecting semi-peripheral political strategies. We will describe each type in turn.

The capital cities resulting from core processes are what Henrikson terms the European concept. The rise of the classic examples of this type are part of the initial economic processes that led to Europe becoming the core of the world-economy. The mercantilist competition of the logistic wave involved the development of vastly increased political involvement centred on the historic capital city. The new bureaucracies were located there and these cities grew rapidly to dominate their territories. They became the political control centres that were attempting to steer the emerging world-economy in directions beneficial to their particular territory.

In contrast, in the periphery new cities emerged or particular old cities grew where they were useful to the exploitative core—periphery relation. Most commonly these were ports directly linked to the core. They were the product of peripheral processes and have often been likened to 'plug holes' sucking out, as it were, the wealth of the periphery. In formal imperialism political control was directly associated with this process so that these 'parasitic cities' became 'colonial capitals'. Many of them retained their political status following independence and they remain the most extreme examples of Jefferson's primate cities.

But not all colonial administrative centres have remained as capital cities. Some governments have recognized the imperialist basis of their inherited capital city and have relocated their 'control centre' elsewhere. This is part of a conscious semi-peripheral strategy to break the core—periphery links symbolized and practised through the old capital. Often it is expressed as a 'nationalist' reaction as capitals are moved from the coast inland to the old 'core' of a pre-world-economy social formation. A good example of this can be found in the relocation of the Russian capital. In the original incorporation of Russia into the world-economy, the capital was moved from Moscow to a virgin site on the Baltic Sea where St Petersburg was built as 'a window on the west'. After the revolution the capital returned to Moscow as the new Soviet regime retreated from this outward stance in its attempt to break with the peripheralizing processes of the past. Other similar examples of relocation are from Istanbul to Ankara in the centre of Turkey's territory, from Karachi inland to Islamabad in Pakistan, inland from Rio de Janeiro to central Brazil in Brazilia, and currently Nigeria is moving its capital from the colonial port of Lagos inland to a new site at Abuja in central Nigeria. In all cases we can interpret the relocation as part of a semi-peripheral strategy which is attempting to lessen peripheral processes operating in the country.

The semi-peripheral strategy tends to produce what Henrikson terms the American concept of a capital city, in effect a political 'company town'. The case of Washington DC is also the result of an attempt to prevent peripheralization in the creation of the United States of America. It represents the dominance of 'national politics' over the needs of the world-economy and has been the model for other federal capitals, some of which we have already mentioned. As a compromise between the sectional interests of North and South its closest parallels are the cases of Ottawa (between French (Quebec) and English (Ontario) Canada) and Canberra (between the two largest cities in Australia, Sydney and Melbourne). Washington DC, Ottawa and Canberra all represent part of a strategy for mobilizing a new territory for competition in the world-economy.

In summary, therefore, we can identify three types of capital city reflecting world-economy processes: the initial core processes in Europe and the peripheral processes in Latin America, Africa and Asia, both of which generate 'primate cities', and capital cities which have developed as part of a conscious semi-peripheral strategy and which tend to be located in past and current semi-peripheral states.

3. Dividing up the state

Capital cities may be the control centres of the world political map but the territorial states are certainly not the equivalent of the city states of the past. The territory between capital city and state boundary has never been totally controlled from the centre. Quite simply the territories of the inter-state system have been too large for such elementary central organization. Rather the territories have had to be divided up with authority delegated to agents of the state in the communities and regions beyond the capital.

In Europe the states inherited local and regional divisions from their medieval predecessors. In England for instance the 'shires' or counties were originally the areas controlled by sheriffs (shire = sheriffdom'). In France the accretions of the medieval period produced a wide range of sub-state units with many different degrees of central authority. Political revolution has provided opportunities to eliminate traditional divisions and to reconstruct the structure of the state in the image of the new rulers. Typically the new boundaries had two purposes, to provide for more rational units and to undermine traditional loyalties. In 1789, for instance, the Abbé Sieyès drew up a completely new spatial structure for the French state which wiped away all the traditional provincial institutions. A series of regular shape and equal-area spatial units were created which cut through old social patterns of life. The delineation of these departments was an exercise in spatial-social engineering to break loyalties to the old provinces. To reduce local identification further, the names of the departments avoided any reference to historical, social or economic patterns of life. Instead the departments were named after 'neutral' physical features such as rivers and mountains. This strategy has become quite common. Poulsen (1971: 228) describes how the Yugoslav government established nine regions in 1931, 'neutrally named after river basins in order to weaken the nationalisms of the major ethnic groups'. Probably the best example of this is King Carol's reorganization of Roumania in 1938 into ten completely new districts. These were specifically designed to cut across the traditional ethnic and historical provinces so as not to provide rallying points for sectionalism (Helin 1967: 492–3). Once again these were named after rivers, mountains and seas to avoid new regional identities emerging. This is another example of local government units contributing to the Napoleonic ethos of a 'unified and indivisible nation state'. Clearly, dividing up the state is not a neutral technical exercise but an essential political policy for all territorial states.

Originally state territories were divided for administrative and defence purposes. This association has continued into this century. The 'standard regions' of England for instance, originally devised as civil defence regions in the event of invasion, remain the basis for the administrative regions of all British Government departments today while retaining their original purpose. In the event of a nuclear attack on Britain that destroys communications to and from London, these regions will become new sovereign units whose 'capitals' will be underground control centres.

With the increase in activities of the states in the nineteenth and twentieth centuries, divisions of the territories have been required for more than just administration and defence. With the state taking on additional economic and social responsibilities, for example, special policy regions have been designated. Perhaps the two most famous are those associated with the Tennessee Valley Authority in the United States and the regional policy of Great Britain. The regionalization of the state, integral to the state planning of the Communist regime of Eastern Europe, has been much more comprehensive.

One of the original major pressures for the increased state activity in the social sphere is to be found in the extensions to the franchise for electing governments. With the gradual moves towards 'one person, one vote' in Europe and North America, there was a concomitant need to update the electoral divisions or districts. We deal with this topic in Chapter 6. At the same time, democratizing local government produced another tier of divisions that were independent of the state's administration and defence. We deal with this topic in Chapter 7.

Policy regions, electoral districts and local government areas all share one property: they are divisions of the state's territory that do not impinge in any manner on the state's sovereignty. This is not the case with all divisions of the state. Federal divisions of the state and partitions of the state are different in kind from other divisions. The former involves a 'vertical' split in sovereignty, so that it is 'shared' between different geographical scales. The latter is a 'horizontal' or geographical split in sovereignty that produces two or more states where there was one. Federalism and partition are both central processes in the making of the modern world map and were identified as such by traditional political geographers in their concern for state integration. We conclude this section of the chapter, therefore, by concentrating on these two topics.

FEDERALISM AND PARTITION

In terms of political integration we can identify four forms of sovereignty. The first is the *unitary state* where sovereignty is undivided. Britain and France are usually considered to be the archetypal unitary states. In Britain, for instance, sovereignty is traditionally held by 'the crown in parliament', providing for the pre-eminence of the latter. With the creation of the European Community, Britain and France are no longer such 'ideal' examples of unitary states. Second, *federal states* have sovereignty split between two levels of government as we have seen. Hence in the United States the fifty states and the federal level share sovereignty. In federal states the constitution is the enabling document that divides power between the two levels. Third, in *confederal associations* states are legally bound in a much looser arrangement. The key difference with federalism is probably to be found in the lack of opportunity in the latter for states to leave the union. In confederal arrangements states give up some of their sovereignty to a supra-national authority. In the European Community, for instance, the executive Commission routinely take decisions that are binding on the member states of the Community. Nevertheless the European Community is far from being the 'United States of Europe' its founding fathers wished for. The most important limitation of the Community's sovereign powers is in the field of defence — the constituent states retain the basic function of defending their territories. Finally, *partition* represents a situation where it it not possible to maintain sovereignty over a territory. The most famous is probably the partition of the Austro-Hungarian Empire after World War 1 into several new states.

1. Federalism: opportunity and diversity

A federation is, according to K. W. Robinson (1961: 3) 'the most geographically expressive of all political systems'. It is hardly surprising, therefore, that it has attracted much political geography research (Dikshit 1975; Paddison 1983). Generally, federalism is interpreted as the most practical of Hartshorne's centripetal forces in that it has to be consciously designed to fit a particular situation of diversity. A sensitive and carefully designed constitution which is perceived as fair and evenly balanced can contribute to the viability of the state and may even become part of the state-idea as has been the case for the United States. The problem with this domination of the Hartshorne model is that the internal diversity of territories has been emphasized much more than the external pressures to produce federations. Historically it has been the latter that have been the major stimulus to federation. For instance, whereas France and England exemplify the development of unitary states in the early world-economy, Switzerland and the Netherlands represent pioneer experiments in federal structures. Both were defensive combinations of cantons and counties to resist larger neighbours in the era of mercantilist rivalry. Hence we can reasonably argue that we need a more balanced discussion of the internal and external factors behind federalism.

Geographers and political scientists have attempted to specify the conditions under which federalism is the chosen state structure; Paddison (1983: 105) lists four sets of such ideas. Obviously the reasons are many and various given the many examples of federated states. But one thing does emerge. There must be a powerful group of state-builders who are able to convince the members of the territorial sub-units of the benefits of union over separation. The basis of such arguments returns to

our original discussion concerning territories in the world-economy. It
must be shown that security and opportunity are greater in the larger
territory than for separate smaller territories. This requires an alliance
between the state builders and the economic groups who will benefit from
the larger territorial arrangement. This is very clearly seen in the
American case as Beard (1914) has argued and Libby (1894) illustrated.
Both Fifer (1976) and Archer and Taylor (1981) use the latter's maps of
support for the American federal constitution in 1789 to show distinct
differences between different parts of the new colonies. It is not a
north-south sectionalism that emerges but a commercial versus frontier
cleavage that dominates. In the urban areas and commercial farming areas
which were firmly linked into the world-economy, support for federation
was very strong. In the more isolated areas with their more self-sufficient
economy the advantages of federation were far less obvious. Suspicion of
centralization prevailed and these areas tended to reject the federal
constitution. The world-economy linked majority finally prevailed and the
United States was formed on a constitutional basis for its economic
groups to challenge the world-economy order using mercantilist policies
through the federal government. Although the nature and balance of
American federalism has changed over time, it has contributed to the
survival and rise of the state and is now very much part of the American
'state-idea'.

   To contrast with the successful example of the United States we can
consider the case of Colombia in the nineteenth century. In Chapter 3 we
noted the competition between 'American' parties and 'European' parties
in Latin America; in Colombia this translated into Conservatives and
Liberals (Delpar 1981). The latter claimed to represent a cluster of
'modern' and 'rational' ideas. Hence their preference for a federal system
of government was accompanied by a secular anti-clerical outlook and
support for economic *laissez-faire*. Centralism was equated with despotism
(Delpar 1981: 67). By the 1850s the Liberals were able to begin to
implement federal ideas and after a civil war they created a Federal
Constitution in 1863. Parallel with these constitutional moves this
'European' party implemented an economic policy of *laissez-faire*. But
federalism was to become a victim of its association with this economic
strategy. As Delpar (1981: 71) points out, in Colombia 'private enterprise
could not manage without state help'. Quite simply by the 1880s economic
freedom had not been delivered. After another civil war a Conservative
victory in 1886 produced higher tariffs and a new constitution. A 'unitary
republic' was created with the federal states being converted into
administrative departments. The demise of federalism in Colombia,
therefore, contrasts with the success of the US federation after the victory
of its 'American' (protectionist) party (the Republicans) in the US civil
war from 1861–5. What these two examples clearly show is that federation

can never be considered in isolation from the other political issues that affect the success of the state in the world-economy.

Today federalism is associated with the larger countries of the world such as the United States, the Soviet Union, Canada and Australia. It is considered the appropriate constitutional arrangement to cope with the inevitable social and economic differences that large size brings. But this is not the only reason for modern federations. After World War II both Britain and France insisted that the constitution for West Germany should be federal because this was thought to produce a weaker state that would be less of a threat in the future. This seems to be the centralization-despotism link hypothesis again.

In the periphery, federalism is again associated with larger states which often have particular problems of cultural diversity. The example of India shows how federalism has had to be modified to cope with cultural pressures. On independence India was divided into twenty-seven states in a federal constitution that carefully separated powers between the different levels of sovereignty. The new states were combinations of pre-independence units and had no specific relation to the underlying cultural geography of India. As late as 1945 the Congress Party had called for the creation of boundaries based on language but now that they were in power they changed their policy (Hardgrave 1974). A special commission was set up to investigate the matter and warned that defining states by language would be a threat to national unity. 'Arbitrary' states were favoured because they provided no constitutional platforms for language-based separatists. But this political strategy of the central state builders was a dangerous one, for the states also provided no basis for a popular politics that could aid in the political integration of the country. The constitution was not generally accepted as fair and balanced since it produced a situation where nearly every cultural group had a grievance against the federal state. Change was not long in coming. In 1955 a States Reorganization Commission conceded the need for the states to more closely match the cultural geography of the country and produced a new federal structure of 14 language-based states. This structure has been further refined so that today India is a federation of twenty-two states that broadly reflect the cultural diversity of its territory. The original fears for the national unity of the state have been found to be largely unsubstantiated: Indian federalism has operated as a centripetal force.

One particular feature of the India case is the ease with which the boundaries of the states could be altered: the 1955 reforms required only a majority vote of the federal parliament. This contrasts with federal arrangements in core states where the constituent units of the federation cannot be so easily changed. This obviously reflects a balance of power in the Indian situation that is biased towards the centre. On some definitions of federalism this would rule out India as a federal state. But this ease of

producing constituent units in a federation is shared by other peripheral
states. In Nigeria, for instance, it has been developed into a strategy for
economic development (Ikporukpo 1986). On independence in 1963,
Nigeria inherited a territory divided into four administrative regions. In
1967 it became a federal state with 12 constituent units. Since then there
have been further divisions to produce more and more states. By 1983
Ikporukpo (1986) reports 29 states in existence with 48 outstanding
proposals, some of which have since been accepted. Each state is a 'forum
for development' and each new state capital a potential economic growth
centre. This seems to be a unique experiment in the use of a federal
constitutional framework to try and produce an even spatial pattern of
development with every area having the opportunity of implementing its
own development plan. This is a new form of state-led economic
development. It reminds us once again of the profound differences in
circumstances between core and periphery with, in this case, a peripheral
state using its constitutional territorial arrangements in a most innovative
fashion.

2. Creating new states by partition

Not all federal arrangements have been successes. In the final stages of the
dismantling of their empire, the British colonial administrators tried to
produce several federations by combining colonies to produce larger and
possibly more viable independent states. But by and large this did not
work. The West Indian, Central African and East African federations
collapsed and Singapore seceded from Malaysia. In traditional political
geography terms there was no state-idea to build upon so that centrifugal
forces overwhelmed the new creations. Put another way, if you remove
'rule' from the British imperial tradition of 'divide and rule', all you are
left with is 'divide'. This process was to be seen in its most spectacular
form in British India where the partition of 1947 produced Pakistan and
India after the loss of one million lives and the transfer of twelve million
people.

   In established states partition represents a general threat to the status
quo. It is for this reason that separatist movements usually command very
little support in the international community, as we noted in the case of
Biafra. In contrast the separation of Bangladesh from Pakistan in 1971 was
quickly accepted by the international community after its creation in the
Pakistan civil war, by Indian armed intervention. There had always been
doubts about the territorial viability of Pakistan when it consisted of two
units, west and east Pakistan separated by several thousand miles of
territory of a hostile neighbour. But the key factor in international
acceptance for the partition in 1971 was the failure of the old Pakistan
state to accept an election result that put the reins of government in the
hands of a political party from the more populous east Pakistan. This
brought to a head grievances concerning the way in which the old Pakistan

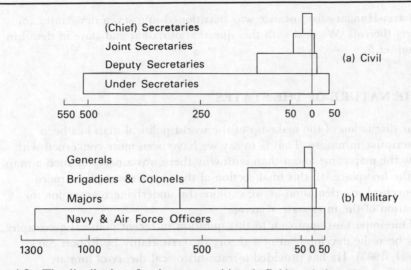

Fig. 4.2   The distribution of senior state positions in Pakistan before 1971 between west Pakistan (on the left)and east Pakistan (on the right)

state had favoured west Pakistan at the expense of east Pakistan. Fig. 4.2 shows how the state apparatus, both military and civilian, was firmly in the hands of just one part of the country. The state promoted centrifugal forces when it needed to develop very strong centripetal forces to survive as two separated territorial units. When partition came, therefore, it was not interpreted as the result of a typical separatist movement, but as a particular and necessary correction of post-colonial boundaries: Bangladesh was an exception that would not affect the status quo. Within three years the new Pakistan (formerly west Pakistan) recognized the new state of Bangladesh (formerly east Pakistan).

In political geography Waterman (1984, 1987) has considered the processes of partition in some detail. Following Henderson and Lebow (1974), he identifies two very different processes in operation which are termed *divided nations* and *partitioned states*. In the former the state has a cultural and linguistic unity before partition. Examples are Germany, Korea, Mongolia, China and Vietnam from 1955 to 1974. These partitions are the result of outside forces and are not considered permanent by their populations. Hence Vietnam was reunified and in the other cases there remains the concept of one nation despite the two states.

Partitioned states on the other hand are usually considered to be permanent. Here partition is the result of internal pressures. It is a way of solving a destructive diversity within a country. Examples are India—Pakistan, Palestine—Israel, Cyprus and Ireland. The main period of success for this type of partition came at the end of World War I when national self-determination was accepted as a criterion for state formation leading to the partition of the old multi-national empires.

Austria-Hungary for instance was partitioned into seven new states (or parts thereof). We deal with this question of nation and state in detail in Chapter 5.

THE NATURE OF THE STATES

Our discussion of the make-up of the world political map has been descriptive in nature. That is to say we have been more concerned with how the map came about than with why there was a need for such a map in the first place. In this final section of the chapter we will be more theoretical in orientation as we explore the underlying reasons for the creation of the inter-state system.

One important approach to this question in recent political geography has been the development of a theory of territoriality by Robert Sack (1981, 1983). He has provided a trans-historical theory of human behaviour in which territorial behaviour is a particular strategy of control over a specific geographical area or territory. This general theory of power can be applied to all geographical scales and may be observed in all societies. It is therefore a highly abstract theory. In our discussion below we will concentrate on less abstract theories whose scope is limited to the capitalist world-economy. The thesis that Sack generates can be applied to the processes that operate in the modern inter-state system, as to any other system, but they do not help us identify the particular role of the state in our modern system. For this we have to turn to specific theories of the state.

THEORIES OF THE STATE

The notion of sovereignty assumes the existence of the state. But this is a two-way relationship. At the simplest level the state is defined by its possession of sovereignty. This distinguishes it from all other forms of human organization. As Laski (1935: 21–2) points out, this sovereignty amounts to nothing less than supreme coercive power within a territory — the state 'gives orders to all and receives orders from none' inside its recognized boundaries. Invasion by a foreign power or internal insurgency aiming at creating a new state is a violation of a state's sovereignty. If not defeated the state no longer has a monopoly of coercion in its territory and faces extinction. The division of Poland between Germany and the USSR in 1939 is an example of extinction by external violation of sovereignty.

It is important to distinguish between state and government at the outset of this discussion. Again using Laski (1935: 23), government can be interpreted as the major agent of the state which exists to carry out the day-to-day business of the state. Governments are short-term mechanisms for administering the long-term purposes of the state. Hence every state is

served by a continual succession of governments. But governments only
represent the state, they cannot replace it. A government is not a sovereign
body: opposition to the government is a vital activity at the very heart of
liberal democracy; opposition to the state is treason. Governments may try
and define themselves as the state and hence condemn their opponents as
'traitors' but this is a very dangerous game. If this strategy fails the state
may find itself challenged within its boundaries by what McColl (1969)
terms the *insurgent state* with its own core-area, territory and claims to
sovereignty. In this case the fall of the government can precipitate
overthrow of the state as happened, for instance, in Vietnam in 1975.

It has been suggested that this distinction between state and
government is not of practical interest because all state action must
involve some specific government action acting in its name (Laski 1935:
25). The important point, however, is that this distinction is a theoretical
one and it is at this level that this section is pitched. One of the major
problems of much political science and political geography is that they
have considered government action without understanding the wider
context in which it occurs. That framework can only be provided by
developing a theory of the state separate from the particular actions of
particular governments. That is the purpose of this section; we return to
a consideration of governments in Chapter 6.

Quentin Skinner (1978: 352—8) has described the origins of the modern
concept of the state and once again we find that a basic concept in our
modern world first appears at the same time as the emergence of the
world-economy itself. The word state comes from the Latin *status* and its
medieval usage is related to either the 'state' or condition of a ruler or the
'state' of the realm. The idea of a public power separate from ruler and
ruled which is the supreme political authority in a given territory does not
occur at this medieval period or earlier periods. The modern concept
develops from this medieval usage in the sixteenth century first in France
and then in England. Skinner (1978) argues that this is because these two
countries provided early examples of the properties that make up the
modern state — a centralized regime based on a bureaucracy operating
within well-established boundaries. By the end of the sixteenth century
Skinner claims that the modern concept of the state is well established in
these two countries and modern political analysis focusing on the nature
of the state can be said to begin from this time onwards.

We are indebted to Clark and Dear (1984) for the most comprehensive
discussion of modern theories of the state in geography. They identify
eighteen different theories which they reduce to two modes of analysis —
theories of the state in capitalism and theories of the capitalist state. The
former mode treats capitalism as a given and concentrates on the
functions of the state. These are generally described as liberal or
conservative theories of the state. Identification of the 'capitalist state' in
the second mode of analysis indicates that the economic relations of

capitalism are brought into the political analysis. These are Marxist theories of the state.

1. Theories of the state in capitalism

In the core states of the world we all experience *the state as a supplier of public goods* (Clark and Dear 1984: 18—19). Tietz (1968) provides a brief catalogue of our uses of the state from birth to death showing how much our modern way of life is dependent on public goods — schools, hospitals, police, fire prevention, waste disposal, postal services, etc. Theories of the state as a supplier of public goods are concerned with the efficiency of this provision. Political geographers, for instance, have been concerned to produce models of the most desirable service areas for the provision of public goods (Massam 1975).

Equally important to our modern way of life is *the state as a regulator and facilitator*. This is the second theory Clark and Dear (1984: 19) identify whereby the state operates macroeconomic and other policies to support the economy within its territory. Johnston (1982a: 13) adds the role of the state producing the physical infrastructure for the smooth running of the economy — roads, railways, power transmission lines, etc. Political geographers have been concerned with these processes as they relate to spatial integration.

Undoubtedly the most important theory of the state in capitalism is *the state as arbiter* (Clark and Dear 1984: 21; Johnston 1982a: 12, 13). In this theory the state is deemed to be above the endemic conflicts of society and therefore can act as a neutral umpire in adjudicating disputes. This theory underlies most political activity within the core states of the world-economy. Political parties in countries with competitive elections, for instance, normally assume the state to be a neutral institution. After all, the prize of winning control of government would be a rather hollow one if the state hindered or prevented implementation of policies. Coates (1975: 142) provides a nice illustration of this assumption for the British Labour Party. Harold Wilson, the Labour Prime Minister of the 1960s and 1970s, used the analogy of the state as a car. Whoever won an election got the ignition keys and was therefore able to sit in the driving seat and turn the car either left or right. In their most sophisticated form these ideas form a pluralist theory of the state which we discuss further in the next section.

One reason why parties of the left have accepted theories of the state in capitalism is because they have been relatively successful in putting many of their policies into practice. Clark and Dear (1984: 20) call this *the state as social engineer*. This concerns the role of the state in ensuring some degree of distributional justice within its territory. The product is usually termed the welfare state and, as we have seen, the process of its creation can be social imperialism from the top as well as social pressure from below. Welfare geography, concerned with spatial inequalities, has been a major growth area of modern political geography (Cox 1979).

Johnston (1982a: 12) adds a category of *the state as protector* which combines Clark and Dear's public goods and social engineering roles but with more explicit reference to the 'police function'. This is of interest because theories of the state in capitalism generally ignore or underplay the coercive function of the state. However, as we have previously noted, it is precisely this function that distinguishes the state from other social institutions. In the states of the periphery, of course, this particular function is far more obvious as the state is commonly involved in activities of repression. This highlights a very important limitation of these theories — their implicit bias to the activities of states in the core. Furthermore this is symptomatic of a more fundamental criticism. Theories of the state in capitalism are relatively superficial descriptions of state functions. It is not that these functions are not real but rather that their enumeration does not advance our understanding very far. In Marxist terms they remain at the level of appearances without engaging with the social reality underlying those appearances (Clark and Dear 1984: 18).

2. Theories of the capitalist state

It is well known that Marx himself never developed a theory of the state. It was a project that he set himself but never completed. Hence Marxist theories of the state are products of his many followers and this has inevitably led to alternative interpretations of what such a theory should say: there is not *a* Marxist theory of the state but many Marxist *theories* of the state. In this discussion we will consider both the differences and similarities of a small number of these theories which have recently entered political geography. We begin by briefly describing the original orthodox Marxist position before moving on to review three debates surrounding recent attempts by Marxists to update their theory. Finally we introduce one set of ideas which are particularly related to our political geography perspective.

In Marx's voluminous political writings there is much raw material for his followers to use to construct theories of the state. Two ideas have dominated Marxist political thinking. The first, from *The Communist Manifesto* of 1848, dismissed the state as nothing more than 'a committee for organizing the affairs of the bourgeoisie'. The second, which can be found in several writings, consists of a 'base-superstructure model' of society where this engineering analogy is used to depict a foundation of economic relations upon which the ideological and political superstructure is constructed. These two simple ideas are difficult to accommodate to the complexities of the modern state. If they are taken at face value they lead to a reduction of all politics and the state to a mere reflection of economic forces. Such crude reductionism is termed *'economism'*. Hunt (1980: 10) provides a good example of this type of thinking in his criticism of Lenin's contribution to state theory. Lenin proposed a strict relationship between stages of economic development and types of state. Hence parliamentary democracy is the form of state for competitive capitalism, the bureaucratic-military state emerges with monopoly capitalism and, of course, socialism replaces these with 'the dictatorship of the proletariat'. In modern orthodox Marxist theory, economics and politics are fused in another stage known as state monopoly capitalism (Jessop 1982). By directly equating the form of the state with the economic base, Lenin provides a simple explanation which we now identify as economism. Of course, this model is every much as developmentalist as the cycle theory of states or even Rostow's stages of economic growth (Wallerstein 1974b). Most modern Marxists distance themselves from such simplistic analyses (Hunt 1980). Nevertheless this is the heritage for modern Marxist theories of the state and in what follows we show how modern Marxist theorists have attempted to avoid such economism.

In the social science of the English-speaking world recent concern for Marxist theories of the state can be said to begin with Ralph Miliband's *State in Capitalist Society* (1969) which was written to counter the prevailing *pluralist* theory of the state in political science in which the state is an umpire adjudicating between competing interests. Since modern society consists of very many overlapping interests — labour, farmers, business, home owners, consumers, and so on — no one group is ever able to dominate the state. The balance of interests served will vary as governments change but the state will remain pluralist in nature and able to respond to a wide range of interests. This is quite obviously the opposite of the Marxist class theory which in these terms is strictly a non-pluralist account of the state.

There are two fundamental properties of pluralist and related non-Marxist theories of the state. The first is that the state is treated as neutral; it is a body above the day-to-day politics of its constituent institutions. This property is vital to social-democratic strategies in Western European states since it assumes that if a Labour or Social Democratic party wins control of the government in an election, it can use the state to carry out its 'socialist' reforms. The state is 'up for grabs', as it were, in electoral politics. The second property of such theories is that they treat the political sphere as separate from the economic sphere. This is the basis of the whole notion of a 'political science', of course, so that no problem is envisaged in the relations of politics and economics. They are separate, though often related, processes that can be adequately studied as autonomous systems. We met this argument in discussing inter-state politics in Chapter 2 and it is repeated at all scales of analysis. From the perspective of this study, pluralist theories of the state represent an important example of the poverty of disciplines.

Economism and pluralist theory can be seen as opposite ends of a scale measuring the autonomy of the political from the economic. At the economism end there is no autonomy. At the political science end there is absolute autonomy. In between we can identify different degrees of 'relative autonomy' where politics is not determined by economic processes but is not independent of them either. Most modern Marxist analyses have located themselves in the relative autonomy sector of this scale and it is from just such a position that Miliband (1969) launched his attack on the pluralist theory.

The bulwark of the pluralist theory is the existence of elections. In 1848 the state may have looked very much like a one-class institution but with franchise reforms the modern liberal-democratic state looks very much like the pluralist model. We deal with liberal democracy in some detail in the next chapter and here we will only show how Miliband attempts to uncover the class nature of the apparently pluralist state. Miliband's method is to marshal data on the social, political and economic élites of the modern state and to show that they all come from the same class background. By showing the many inter-linkages in terms of family, education and general economic interests, Miliband is able to paint a picture of a single dominant class in which pluralist competition is a myth. This dominant class is able to manipulate the state apparatus irrespective of which party is in government. This has come to be known as the *instrumentalist* theory of the state. It restates the class basis of the state and completely undermines the neutral pluralist view.

Miliband's thesis stimulated a debate with Poulantzas (1969) upon how to construct a Marxist theory of the state. Poulantzas argued that Miliband's empirical approach, while useful and interesting, was seriously flawed because it involved analyzing the state on terms laid down by non-Marxist theory. It is not that empirical analysis is wrong in itself but the way in which it is integrated with theory is important. Miliband's study reduces to a description of particular roles within the state apparatus and investigation of links between people carrying out these different roles. The inevitable result is an emphasis on interpersonal relations which is reminiscent of the original pluralist thinking. For Poulantzas the class nature of the state is not a matter of empirical verification or falsification. A state is not capitalist in nature because a dominant class with capitalist links manipulates the state for capitalist ends. The state is capitalist because it operates within a capitalist mode of production. This sets constraints on the range of action that is possible so that the state has no option but to conform to the needs of capital. The introduction of liberal democracy does not change this fundamental property. This is a *logical* argument for which empirical proof is unnecessary. Such a *structuralist* position need not reduce to economism; Poulantzas shares Miliband's relative autonomy assumption with the state dependent on the economic base only 'in the last instance'.

The Miliband–Poulantzas debate was introduced into geography by Dear and Clark (1978). At about the same time, however, the work of West German Marxists was just becoming available (Holloway and Picciotto 1978) and this completely cut across the arguments that separated Miliband and Poulantzas. This *derivation* school rejected the notion of relative autonomy and so undermined the arguments of both protagonists. By assuming relative autonomy any theory implicitly accepts the separation of the economic from the political. By doing this the proponents of such theories cut politics off from the main motor of change in capitalist society, the accumulation process. For the derivationists, therefore, the key question is not about the *degree* of separation between the political and economic but why does it *appear* this way in capitalist society. The Marxist political analyses, developed by Miliband and Poulantzas in their different ways, cannot adequately answer this question because they have forsaken the holism of political economy.

For these West German theorists the solution was simple: a Marxist theory of the state must be derived from the mechanisms and concepts described by Marx in his basic theoretical work, *Das Kapital*. To the need for competition in the economic sphere they add the need for co-operation in the political sphere. The state becomes necessary to counter the self-destructive processes of unbridled economic competition. This may even involve political processes that appear to be anti-capitalist. The evolution of the welfare state, for instance, involves ensuring the reproduction of a skilled and healthy labour force for the long-term interests of capital. In this role of co-ordinating capital and reproducing labour the state may appear neutral and above the political conflict between capital and labour. This is why non-Marxist theories of the state appear so reasonable and are so widely and easily accepted.

Following Gold *et al.* (1975), Dear and Clark (1978) introduced a further Marxist approach to the state which they term 'ideological'. All Marxist theories incorporate some notion of ideology in their formulation but Gold *et al.* (1975) refer in this context to theories that specifically emphasize the state as a form of mystification whereby class conflicts are hidden behind a national consensus. This is very close to the conception of the state as the scale of ideology that we introduced in the Chapter 1. In the Marxist literature it is most closely associated with the work of Gramsci and his followers (Jessop 1982). Gramsci is most well-known today for his concept of hegemony. This derives from Marx's original argument that the ruling ideas in a society are the ideas of the ruling class. In Gramsci's work hegemony is the political, intellectual and moral leadership of the dominant class which results in the dominated class actively consenting to their own domination (Jessop 1982: 17). Hence alongside the coercive state apparatus (police, army, judiciary, and so on) there is the ideological state apparatus (education, mass media, popular entertainment, and so on) through which consent is generated. Notice that these ideological functions need not be carried out by public agencies — in this theory the state is much more than just the public sector. Historically the vital battle for state sovereignty involved subjugation of other authority within the state's territory, both local magnates and the universal ideas of the church. In the latter case the issue centred on education and the state's attempts to 'nationalize' its population by converting religious education into a state ideological apparatus. The successful combination of coercion and hegemony will produce an 'integral state'. Here we have a parallel with our territorial integration theory and the concept of state-idea and iconography. The notion of hegemony, however, is much more pervasive and directly derives from the class-basis of the state. In this argument Marx's original 'committee' assertion of 1848 remains broadly true: the difference between then and now merely relates to the changing relative balance between coercive and ideological means of control.

It is, of course, very difficult to summarize such a vigorous and expanding field of enquiry as Marxist theories of the state in just a few pages (Short 1982: 109). We are not able to do justice to the ideas of even the few theorists we have mentioned. Miliband's (1969) original study includes an interesting discussion of dominant class ideology, for instance and we have only dealt with Poulantzas in his response to Miliband, whereas Jessop (1982) considers his work to be the most impressive of the recent spate of new theory. For a comprehensive discussion of this field the reader is referred to Jessop (1982). Clark and Dear (1984) provide a discussion of the state apparatus.

We started this discussion with a description of Lenin's economism. The modern theorists have countered this problem in different ways but they have not tackled the problem of Lenin's developmentalism. Although we have brought the argument a long way forward from simple economism all the analyses described above remain rooted at the state level. For our assessment of their utility within the framework of this book it is necessary to review them in the context of the world-economy.

THEORY OF THE STATES

The political sphere that we deal with in this study is not the single state but the whole inter-state system. Hence we need a theory of *states* where the multiplicity of states is a fundamental property of the theory. Clearly none of the above offers this type of theory. Nevertheless the various themes highlighted above do provide pointers towards provision of our need and our approach does clarify some of the contentious issues. In this discussion we begin, in a preliminary way, the bringing together of theories of the state and the world-systems approach.

1. One economy, many states

The basic empirical problem confronting the Marxists was that the same economic system — capitalism — was producing different state forms. Although the United States and Italy were both capitalist states, for instance, they exhibited very different politics. It is this variety of politics which was to be the subject matter of Marxist political analysis (Miliband 1977; Scase 1980). The break with economism was obviously necessary and relative autonomy was a very attractive concept upon which to base these new analyses. As we have seen, the derivationists have cast severe doubt on the validity of this position but they have not replaced it with another means for accounting for the variety of politics under capitalism. The world-economy approach provides a simple explanation of this variety which makes the concept of relative autonomy unnecessary.

The notion of relative autonomy is implicitly based upon the idea that both state and economy cover the same territory. In Scase (1980), for instance, the issue of the relation between economics and politics is treated on a state-by-state basis for Western Europe. When viewed in this manner it is easy to see how the problem of relating one national economy to one state polity emerges. But this whole issue disappears with the world-systems perspective and its multi-state system. Instead of a one-to-one problem there is a one-to-many situation — one world-economy and many states. Hence we do not have to appeal to a relative autonomy argument to explain the variety of political forms that states take under capitalism. Instead there are numerous fragments of the world-economy each with its particular sovereign states. Since these 'fragments of capitalism' differ from one another there is no reason to suppose that the forms that the states take should not differ from one another. Quite simply, different fragments of capitalism are associated with different state forms. The variety of politics remains to be understood but there is no need to resort to relative autonomy for explanation.

Dismissal of relative autonomy brings us into line with the state derivation position. But we soon find that there are problems in applying this theory to our framework. In its initial form we have seen that the state is derived to overcome the anarchic consequences of a 'free' capitalism. If we translate this to a world-economy then this theory predicts a world government to compensate for global anarchy. This is, for course, quite the opposite to the capitalist world-economy as conceived by Wallerstein. As we have seen, multiple states are necessary for manoeuvre by economic actors on the world stage. Production of a world government would therefore signal the end of capitalism as a mode of production.

2. A new instrumentalism

In this new analysis we replace the relative autonomy of the state as a separate entity by the manoeuvrability of states as institutions within the world-economy. These are the particular institutions of the system that wield formal power; they make the rules and they police them. States as the repositories of this power are, therefore, instruments of groups who use the power for their own interests. We can *derive* an instrumental theory of states from the inter-group conflicts within the capitalist world-economy.

Let us start with the prime logic of the modern world-system, ceaseless capital accumulation. From Chapter 1 we know that this is organized through class institutions with the controllers of capital attempting to maximize their particular shares of the world surplus. This surplus is ultimately realized as profits on the world market. Controllers have two basic strategies for increasing their profits — they can either raise prices or lower costs. The former requires some degree of pseudo-monopoly, the latter directly involves the direct producers. In both strategies controllers of capital have used the states as important instruments in their struggle for the world surplus.

States can be used first and foremost to control flows across their borders. It is through such restrictions on finance, trade and migration that pseudo-monopolies can be created and prices of commodities maintained. The limiting cases are autarchy (or closed national economy) and pure free trade (or open national economy), but in reality states have always pursued policies between these extremes. Whatever policy is adopted it will favour some controllers of capital at the expense of others. Hence it is hardly surprising that in the late nineteenth century state politics was dominated by the free trade versus protection issue. Today this conflict continues in many realms of policy including repatriation of capital and immigration. This use of the state is integral to intra-class competition within the strata that control capital.

States can be used in a second crucial way to set the legal rules that govern the social relations of production within territories. It is through this means that costs of production can be kept to a minimum. Laws covering wage bargaining, corporation responsibilities for employee welfare and rights to trade union membership are all examples of how state actions can directly affect production costs. Laws restricting or banning trade union activities are common in peripheral states and constitute a key part of the informal imperialism mechanism. This use of the state is integral to inter-class conflict between controllers of capital and direct producers.

Hence we can derive two politics from the two strategies of controllers of capital — raising prices produces an intra-class, inter-state politics and reducing costs produces an inter-class, intra-state politics. It is not suggested that these are the only politics operating in the world-economy but they are the most crucial because they relate to the heart of the system, the capital accumulation process.

Like the world political map, the world market is never simply a given constituent of the world-economy. It is forever being fought over and remade to favour some groups over others, and states are central to this process. We can now return to the question of the variety of state forms by treating them as instruments in the struggle for the world's surplus.

3. The variety of state forms: a space—time introduction

The form that states take depends upon the particular combination of economic, social and political forces in their territory in the past and at the present time. Hence strictly speaking every state form will be unique. But we can generalize in terms of the space—time structures previously discussed. Particular combinations can be aggregated into a simple 3 × 2 matrix with time represented by A- and B-phases of growth and stagnation and space apportioned between core, semi-periphery and periphery. We should then be able to discuss the form that states take within each of these six positions allowing for further variation due to different histories or past positions. In all cases the states will have to carry out two basic tasks: (i) provide the conditions for accumulation of capital and (ii) maintain legitimation of the system. O'Connor (1973) identifies these two basic functions of the state in his study of the fiscal crisis with specific references to USA. Here we will extend his ideas, based as they are on German derivationists, to states generally within our space—time categories of the world-economy. In particular we will consider the legitimation function as a varying balance between forces of coercion and consensus.

Core states are the most stable and consensus has been far more important than coercion in maintaining control. This is because the capitals of core states are strongly placed in the world market and can pass on some of their surplus to core labour. This is the process of social imperialism described in the previous chapter. It is much more than simple bribery, however, and involves the incorporation of labour into the system. These are the truly 'hegemonized' states. But the strength of this hegemony varies between A- and B-phases. In periods of growth more resources are available to keep the system stable. These are periods of building hegemony in the wake of union successes, social-security advances and finally the welfare state. With the onset of stagnation, pressures to maintain conditions for accumulation lead to cut-backs in public expenditure with resulting dangers in the loss of legitimacy. In core states, however, the hegemony has coped remarkably well with the current B-phase.

The opposite situation obtains in peripheral states where instability dominates. Here there is no surplus to buy off labour, which is largely left to fend for itself while being coerced into submission. The result is an 'over-developed superstructure' relative to the economic base, according to Alavi (1979). But this does not represent strength, it reflects the weakness of peripheral states in the world-economy. As before in our arguments, overtly 'strong' states deceive by their appearance. Alavi (1979) argues that in post-colonial societies a military-bureaucratic group emerges to oversee the interests of three exploiting classes: (i) the metropolitan core interest, (ii) the local urban-industrial interest, and (iii) the landowning interest. These three 'capitals' have a common interest in maintaining order as the basic condition for accumulation. But they compete in terms of relations of the state to the world-economy. Generally speaking metropolitan core interests and local landowners favour an open economy whereas local industrial interests favour protection. This is the peripheral/semi-peripheral strategy dichotomy discussed in Chapter 3 and illustrated using Frank's discussion of 'American' and 'European' parties in nineteenth-century Latin America. To the extent that urban industrial groups are able to have their interests promoted by the military-bureaucratic regime the state becomes more like a semi-periphery state. But such promotion can fail, of course, and the state will sink even lower into the periphery. The case of Ghana and the failure of Nkrumah's 'African socialism' is an example of this (Osei-Kwame and Taylor 1984). It is a matter of the pattern of opportunity existing for advance in the world-economy which varies with A- and B-phases, of course.

Finally we come to the most interesting examples — the semi-periphery states. As we argued in Chapter 1 this is the dynamic sector of the world-economy where political actions by states can affect the future structure of the system. According to Chase-Dunn (1982) this is where class struggle is greatest, where the balance between coercion and consensus is most critical. State governments in this zone specialize in strategies which emphasize accumulation, as we have previously indicated. Semi-peripheral economic policy is all about 'catching up', it is the zone of protection in particular and mercantilism in general. This will make legitimation difficult so that much of the semi-periphery is associated with dictatorial regimes. But coercion itself is a very expensive form of control and will stretch resources to the extent of hindering the 'catching up'. Hence the semi-periphery is also associated with powerful consensus forces, specifically Fascism and Communism, and generally nationalism. These are strategies for mobilizing the state's population behind the dominant classes without the greater material expenses of the social imperialism of the core.

THE TERRITORIAL STATES TODAY

According to many commentators today, states are suffering from some form of crisis. For Deutch (1981) the entry of the world into the 'nuclear age' in 1945 means that states can no longer even perform their most basic function, the defence of their people. Brown, in his provocatively titled book *World without Borders* (1973), provided an 'inventory' of problems for humanity that transcend the territorial state such as the environmental crisis, the population problem and the widening of the rich-poor gap. He highlights the growing economic interdependence of the world and claims that 'national sovereignty is being gradually but steadily sacrificed for affluence' (1973: 187). Is the end of the territorial state and the inter-state system in sight?

The contemporary world is sometimes portrayed as consisting of a great competition in which large private corporations are in the process of undermining the traditional territorial states. One common way of expressing this competition is to rank countries and corporations together in terms of their gross domestic product and total sales respectively.

Brown, for instance, finds that General Motors is economically larger than most states, ranking twenty-third in his combined 'league table'. He concludes enthusiastically that 'Today the sun does set on the British Empire, but not on the scores of global corporate empires' (1973: 215–6). If the territorial states are facing demise, therefore, the consensus would seem to be that large corporations will be their replacement.

The argument for the corporations winning this competition is based upon their greater geographical manoeuverability compared to territorial states. With the end of formal imperialism, the state's economic location policies are internal ones. These can be regional policies to maintain the territorial integrity of the state for legitimation reasons or policies of free-trade enclaves to promote capital accumulation in the state's territory. In either case state strategy is limited to operating its economic policies within its own boundaries. Corporations, on the other hand, can develop economic policies across several territories. In their investment decisions they can play one country off against another. Once production starts they can control their overall tax bills by the method of transfer pricing. This involves the pricing of components being transferred between plants in different countries but *within* the corporation to produce the effect of declaring large profits for plants in low-tax states and small profits or losses in high-tax states. Here we have an economic version of the strategy of divide and rule. The ultimate victory of the corporations seems inevitable.

Of course it is not as simple as this. There is one important characteristic that corporations do not possess and that is *formal* power, the right to make laws. The properties of all corporations are guaranteed in the last instance by the property laws of the states in whose territories their property is located. Hence the notion of competition between state and corporation covers only part of the relation between them. More generally state and corporation exist in a sort of symbiotic relationship with each needing the other. Every state requires capital accumulation within its territory to provide the material basis of its power. Every corporation requires the conditions for accumulation that the state provides.

If the corporation is not replacing the state what does the rise of the large trans-state corporation since 1945 represent? For many Marxists it represents a new stage of capitalism: we have reached a new age of global capitalism where production transcends the barriers of the state. In world-systems analysis it represents a secular trend of increasing concentration of capital but it does not mark any fundamental new process or mechanism. In the capitalist world-economy production has always transcended state boundaries: remember the world-economy is defined in terms of a system-wide division of labour. The system-wide organization of capital has been structured in different ways at different times — charter companies in the first imperialism, investment portfolios in British hegemony and corporations in US hegemony — but these are each merely alternative means to the same end. The world-economy continues to develop in the same cyclical manner as before. Despite all the claims of new powers that the corporations were deemed to possess (see, for example, Barnett and Muller 1974), they were powerless to prevent the downturn of the world-economy in the 1970s. Like all other actors in the system they had to react and adapt to the new circumstances to survive. The fact that many did so successfully to produce a new series of even larger corporations (Taylor and Thrift 1982) represents a further deepening of the same mechanisms of capital concentration. But it is not at all certain that the balance between state and capital has tilted towards the latter. For example, none of today's enterprises would seem to be powerful enough to bankrupt the two leading states as happened to Spain and France in 1557.

In world-systems analysis the inter-state system is integral to the operation of the world-economy. Without multiple states the economic enterprises would not have their windows of opportunity from state control that has allowed them to expand. Hence the ambiguous relationship between the territorial states and capital. To use Deutch's (1981: 331) phrase, the states are 'both indispensable and inadequate' today and throughout the history of the world-economy. Without the territorial states there would be no capitalist system.

Chapter 5

NATION AND NATIONALISM

THE IDEOLOGICAL HERITAGE

A world of nations

1. Primordial origins
2. Culture and politics
3. The doctrine of nationalism

Nationalist uses of history

1. Poetic landscapes and golden ages
2. Inventing traditions: Dutch tartans and English kilts
3. History by rediscovery: Englishness

NATIONALISM IN PRACTICE

A typology of nationalisms

1. National self-determination: plebiscites
2. National determinism: Jovan Cvijic's language maps of Macedonia

State and nation today

1. Nation against state
2. The rights of indigenous peoples

MODERN THEORIES OF NATIONALISM

Nationalism from above

1. Nationalism and uneven development
2. Nations as imagined communities

Nationalism as resistance

1. National struggle as class struggle
2. National struggle as an anti-systemic movement

Chapter 5

NATION AND NATIONALISM

There is an interesting paradox in the treatment of nationalism in political
geography that David Knight (1982) has identified. Nationalism is
generally considered to be the most geographical of all political
movements and yet it has been neglected as a research topic. Traditional
political geography was largely organized around the trilogy of
territory-state-nation so that behind every successful territorial state there
was a vibrant nation. Hence territory becomes national 'homeland' or even
'fatherland' imbued with the symbolic significance of nationalism, and the
state becomes the 'nation-state' as the ideal expression of the political will
of nationalism. It is surprising, therefore, to have to report a dearth of
studies of nationalism *per se* in political geography: there is no equivalent
to Mackinder's contribution in geopolitics or Hartshorne's on the
territorial state.

The paradox of neglect of such a central concept is initially quite
mystifying. It has not been ignored like imperialism, in fact quite the
opposite. Political geography has been imbued with nationalism. The idea
of 'nation' permeates political geography studies to such a degree that the
concept has been seen as largely unproblematic. Nation and nationalism
are a 'given'; they are part of the assumptions of analysis that are not
investigated. And we have not been alone in perpetuating this peculiar
form of neglect. Until recently it was commonplace for social scientists in
general to bemoan the paucity of research on such an important topic
(Smith 1979). All this has changed in the last decade or so with the
development of new theories of nationalism, including important
contributions from political geographers. The idea of the nation and
associated nationalism is no longer considered unproblematic.

Nation and nationalism continue to be central to our understanding in
political geography. This is because they are both explicitly territorial in
nature. As Anderson (1986: 117) points out, nations do not simply occupy
space like other social institutions or organizations, they claim association
with a particular geographical location. They share this property with the
modern sovereign state and this shared territoriality is expressed in the
concept of the nation-state. This is the pivot of our political geography
framework of ideology separating experience from reality, described in
Chapter 1. The territorial state as nation-state represents our scale of

ideology. In the first section of this chapter we expand on this notion by investigating the ideological heritage that lies behind our studies of nationalism. We conclude that nationalism is not an eternal expression of nations through the ages but consists of a family of political practices that are barely two hundred years old. In the second section of the chapter we look at the major outlines of these particularly modern political practices. In the final section we consider in some detail the debates surrounding modern theories of nationalism and how they relate to our world-systems analysis.

THE IDEOLOGICAL HERITAGE

The vast majority of writings on nationalism have been undertaken by self-conscious nationalists. The result is a body of literature extolling the virtues of this nation or that, with little or no comparative perspective. According to Smith (1986: 191) the intellectuals who have produced this material have failed to adhere to the canons of scientific research, indeed 'objectivity is not their main concern'. They have produced a tradition of thinking in which nationalism is interpreted as an autonomous and natural force operating throughout history. This is, as it were, a view of nationalism through the lenses of nationalism. It has assumed a dominant position in interpretations of nationalism both popular and academic (Agnew 1987a). It is the purpose of this section to reveal the basic limitations of this heritage to help free political geography from its deadening grasp.

A WORLD OF NATIONS

We will try and be a little bit more objective in our treatment of nations. Why is the existence of nations taken for granted? Why do nations appear to be as natural as families and kinship groups? We must start with these questions in order to begin to understand why we live in 'a world of nations'.

1. Primordial origins

We all belong to one nation or another. We do not choose which nation to join, it is ascribed to us: We are born *into* a nation. This is the natural basis of nationalism. The word nation comes from the Latin *nasci* meaning to be born. Nations would seem to be historical communities, therefore, that share a common ancestry. Hence the origins of today's 'nations' are to be found in yesterdays 'tribes'. This produces an evolutionary view (see, for example, de Blij 1967) that culminates in a world of nations each with its own particular and unique genealogy.

   A. D. Smith (1986) describes this view as 'primordialist' because of its insistence on the primordial ties of ethnicity and language. For primordialists ethnic communities emerged out of prehistoric times and entered history as the basic units of human experience. For instance, the German people first enter history as the Germanic-speaking tribes fighting the Roman armies along the Rhine frontier. In this view nations are natural and perennial. The human species is genetically divided into a limited number of kin-related groups of individuals. These groups have always existed although may not have always expressed themselves as forcibly as in the very recent past. Hence all periods of history will contain nations and some of these will have survived migrations, assimilations and conquests to form the origins of modern nations: the Babylonians and Assyrians have not survived, the Germans and Chinese have.

2. Culture and politics

Nobody doubts that ethnic communities of one sort or another have existed before the modern era. The important question is the relationship between these communities and the nations we see around us today. Smith (1982) has proposed that we view nations as a particular form of ethnic community that merges cultural identity with political demands. It is this link that is very recent. Breuilly (1985: 5) gives a very revealing example to make this point. In the Middle Ages Dante identified an Italian 'nation' in terms of language. He wanted this language to be the literary language of all Italian poets. He also wrote about politics and defined his ideal form of government. But there was no cross-referencing between these works. Nation was a cultural phenomenon, government a political one and Dante saw no reason why they should be related one to another.

Nationalism provides the link between culture and politics. Nationalism as a term only emerged in the late nineteenth century. As an idea, though, it can be traced back to the earlier concept known as the 'principle of nationality' (Hobsbawm 1987: 142—3). This principle was a very simple and powerful one — every nation has the right to its own state. This idea emerges in the eighteenth century, becomes a major force in world politics in the nineteenth century and has come to dominate the politics of the twentieth century. It was originally associated with the rationalism of the eighteenth century, especially the rejection of the personal authority of the monarch as the source of a state's sovereignty. Instead sovereignty lay with the 'people'. This notion is given political expression in the famous opening sentence of the American Constitution of 1887: 'We the people . . .' The specific idea that 'the people' constitute a 'nation' appears in the French Revolution with the setting up of a National Assembly in 1789 and the French proclaiming themselves 'la grande nation' in 1790 (Rustow 1967: 21, 27). By 1815, at the Congress of Vienna, the novel idea that state should coincide with 'nation' was first expressed; Greek independence in 1821 represents the first direct result of this idea. Revolutions between 1830 and 1848 became 'national' revolutions and the concept finally

triumphed at the Peace Conference in Versailles in 1919 when national
self-determination was recognized as the prime criterion of the new
European political order. Whatever the doubts about 'nation',
'nationalism' is most clearly an ideology of our modern world.

We shall treat nation and nationalism from a 'modernist' rather than
'primordialist' position, to use Smith's (1986) terms. But although the
primordialist heritage is more concerned with justification than
explanation it cannot be ignored. Like the power-political heritage of
geopolitics it is necessary to know this heritage in order to develop an
understanding of the political geography of our modern world. Following
Breuilly (1985) we will emphasize nationalism as a political strategy so
that the activities of nationalist politicians and intellectuals are our object
of study. For the moment we will stay with the latter and their role in
making the general public take the world of nations for granted.
Collectively they have produced what we may term the common doctrine
of nationalism.

3. The doctrine of nationalism

We should never underestimate the ideology of nationalism. As Smith
(1979: 1) so rightly says: 'No other vision has set its stamp so thoroughly on
the map of the world and on our sense of identity'. In fact the idea of nation
is so embedded in our consciousness that it is even reflected in the use of
terms that describe counter-national arrangements: 'supra-national, 'multinational' and 'trans-national' all assume the prior reality of nations (Tivey
1981: 6). Similarly the two great liberal organizations of states in the
twentieth century have found it unnecessary to mention the states themselves
— we have had successively the League of Nations and the United Nations.
Of course 'nations' that do not possess states, such as Kurds or Armenians,
cannot join these organizations but states without nations such as most
newly independent African states do join immediately to reinforce their
sovereign status. Both the League and the UN are or were special clubs for
states not nations. Their ambiguous titles merely reflect the strength of the
doctrine of nationalism in the twentieth century.

But what is this 'doctrine', this ideal that all nationalists subscribe to? It
is more than a simple theory linking an individual to the nation of his or
her birth. It provides a national identity to an individual but it is premised
on a wider acceptance of a world of nations. It provides for much more
than a simple 'them and us' dichotomy such as between a civilized 'us'
and a barbarian 'them' in the former world-empires. In the world made by
nationalism there are multiple 'thems' and 'us.' Numerous other nations
and nationalisms are recognized as equal to and the equivalent of 'our'
nation and 'our' nationalism. This has been expressed most clearly by a
member of the Kach vigilantes, a group of Israeli nationalists who are
usually considered to be at the extreme end of Israel's political
spectrum:

> I personally have nothing against the Arabs. We in Kach do not hate Arabs. We
> love the Jews. The Arabs are a danger to us. If they were Chinamen I would
> fight them too. If I was in the place of the Arabs I would do the same as them.
> It's only natural that they support the PLO, its their liberation organization. I
> understand it. But I won't let them kill Jews.

This statement of mutual respect from such an unlikely source tells us a
lot about the world according to nationalism. We can describe it in terms
of the following propositions drawn from Tivey (1981: 5−6) and Smith
(1982: 150), and related successively to our three scales of analysis.

A1: The world consists of a mosaic of nations.

A2: World order and harmony depends upon expressing this mosaic in a
system of free nation-states.

B1: Nations are the natural units of society.

B2: Nations have a cultural homogeneity based upon common ancestry
and/or history.

B3: Every nation requires its own sovereign state for the true expression
of its culture.

B4: All nations (rather than states) have an inalienable right to a territory
or homeland.

C1: Every individual must belong to a nation.

C2: A person's primary loyalty is to the nation.

C3: Only through the nation can a person find true freedom.

We can term this list the common doctrine of nationalism. It has justified
the following scale effects. The world is politically divided rather than
unified. The state as nation-state is the basic arena of politics. The local
scale is bypassed as experiences are transcended by 'higher' and more
remote ideals.

The effects on social relations are no less profound. Other political
ideologies have had to adapt or be crushed by nationalism. According to
Smith (1979: 8) nationalism split with liberalism at the time of the 1848
revolutions. The simple individualism of classical liberalism had to give
way to a 'national' liberalism in order to survive. At the other end of the
scale the internationalism of socialism was fundamentally defeated at the
outbreak of the First World War in 1914. Worker fought worker under
their different national banners. Like liberalism the various brands of
socialism have had to adapt to the political reality of nationalism in order
to survive. Liberal individualism and socialist internationalism counted for
little against the doctrine of nationalism. The result is our three-tier scale
structure of the world-economy pivoting around the nation-state.

This common doctrine is general to all nationalisms. But every nationalism is based on particularism. Each has its own character. These are what Smith (1982: 150) terms special secondary theories. Since every one is different a brief description of just a single example will have to suffice.

Watson (1970) quotes approvingly from a letter written in 1782 which lists eight features of American society which were to become American 'national characteristics'. These are: 'a love of newness', 'nearness to nature', 'freedom to move', 'the mixing of peoples', 'individualism', 'a sense of destiny', 'violence' and 'man as a whole'. The first four reflect American history, especially frontier history. The next two features are key ideological props of 'the American way of life'. Individual competition to achieve personal success — log cabin to White House —is the basis of American liberal ideology. Manifest destiny has set national goals originally continental in scope and latterly global. The final two features are contradictory as they contrast conflicts in US society with the idealism of belief in rational accommodation. Together these eight features add up to what Watson calls 'the myth of America'; in our terms they are the special secondary theory of American nationalism.

Clearly it is at this level of theory that we can identify the various elements that political geographers have studied in the past — raison d'être, iconography, state idea, and so on. It has been the concentration of effort at this level of symbolism that has prevented political geographers breaking through to the general doctrine in understanding nation and nationalism. This is because nationalism is based upon a series of myths embodied in the secondary theories. These myths consist of distorted histories concerning society/ethnic origins, past heroic ages and betrayals and the 'special' place of the nation in world history. There may well be only one deity but he or she has certainly been generous in designating 'chosen people'!

NATIONALIST USES OF HISTORY

The entry of the 'people' onto the political stage produced a change in the historical requirements of the state. In the absolutist states legitimation was vested in the sovereign whose right to rule rested on his or her lineage. Like the world-empires of the past, the most important history was the monarch's family tree. This was hardly appropriate for the new world of nations. The people, and not just a symbolic head, have to have a link with the past.

One of the inventions of the new national histories was the ascribing of special significance to particular dates. Centenaries became celebrated for the first time, for instance (Hobsbawm 1987: 13). Both centennials of the American and French Revolutions were celebrated with international expositions in 1876 and 1889, respectively. Other nations proclaimed

anniversaries of their foundations in a dim and distant past. Hungarian
patriots found their nation to have its origins in the invasion of Magyars in
896 just in time to celebrate the millenium in 1896. Similarly the Swiss
chose 1291 as the date of the foundation of Switzerland for appropriate
celebrations in 1891 (Anderson 1983: 117). More recently in Poland,
in the early 1960s, other patriots traced the origins of the Polish nation to
its conversion to Christianity in 966 again just in time for a millenial
celebration. We can be sure there were no celebrations in Hungary,
Switzerland or Poland in 1796, 1791 or 1766 respectively for the simple
reason that this was before the need for new histories. Quite simply there
was nothing to celebrate.

The essence of celebrations of such anniversaries is their appeal across
the whole national community. The past is shared by everybody in a
display of national unity. The meaning for the nation is profound: 'history
is the precondition of destiny, the guarantee of our immortality, the lesson
for posterity' (Smith 1986: 208). Without history there can be no nation.

1. Poetic landscapes and golden ages

Smith (1986: 178) identifies three forms of national histories. Where the
new nation has had a formal political existence over a long period there
will be more than a sufficiency of historical material. In this case the
history is produced by *rediscovery*, selecting a new amalgam of facts for the
new history. Where the new nation is less well endowed with material the
history has to be created by conjecture in a process of *reconstruction*. In rare
cases the history may be produced by simple *fabrication*. All such histories
consist of different balances between what Anderson (1986: 130) calls the
'rich amalgam of fact, folklore and fiction'.

Each historical drama has two major components — a story of continuity
that fills in the gap from the origins of the nation to the present and a
small number of symbolic tableaux depicting key events that the whole
nation can identify with. The two most famous are probably William Tell
shooting the apple off his son's head and Joan of Arc being burnt at the
stake (Smith 1986: 180). Both stories evoke the innocence of a patriot
fighting devious and foreign threats to the nation.

National histories both define and direct. First they provide the
space—time co-ordinates of the nation. In the romantic tradition they
create what Smith (1986: 182) terms a poetic space and a golden age. The
former defines the place of the nation, its landscape, its sacred sites and
historical monuments. This can eulogize both the capital city with its
monuments and the ordinary landscape that represents the true habitat of
the people — for England both the historical sites of London and the
thatched cottage on the village green.

This geography is interwoven with the national history. Typically all
such histories include what we may term the Sleeping Beauty complex.
That is to say every nation has its golden age of heroes since when it has

suffered decline but now, like Sleeping Beauty after the kiss, the nation is reawakening to reclaim its former glories. This is the central drama in the series of eight myths that Smith (1986: 192) describes as typical of any national mythology. The whole process is undertaken to generate a vision of the past to shape a direction for the future.

Any selection of historical facts will tend to favour one particular future action over another. For instance national histories of Greece have two alternative golden ages on which the national mythology may hinge. One looks back to the glories of Byzantium, the preservation of Greek culture in the Orthodox Church and Greece as a major eastern Mediterranean power centred on Constantinople as the 'second Rome.' The second possible golden age is that of classical Greece, the rationality of the city states and Greece as a nation-state in the territory of the peninsular. Promoting the former mythology commits the Greek nation-state to a policy of intervention in Anatolia. The second mythology treats the Byzantium episode as an alien Roman interlude and promotes a policy of nation-building within a much smaller Greek territory. After the defeat by Turkey in 1923 the latter mythology has prevailed. The point is, however, that different histories suit different presents and imply alternative futures. Whatever else national histories are primarily about, it is not the past.

2. Inventing traditions: Dutch tartans and English kilts

We have noted that complete fabrications in the creation of national histories are rare. Nevertheless such exercises do illustrate the lengths that nationalists may go to in order to provide a suitable antiquity for a modern nation. This dubious activity by forgers and confidence tricksters can be amazingly successful when taken up by other innocent nationalists.

The national costume of Scotland is perhaps the most widely known of all European nations. All readers will associate tartan kilts with Scottish clans. The general assumption is that they represent the ancient clothing of Scottish kinship groups. It will come as a surprise to many readers, therefore, to find out that the tartan originates from Holland, kilts from England and there were no 'clan tartans' before 1844. This is a tradition that has been invented as part of a fabricated Scottish history.

Trevor-Roper (1983) has carefully documented this invention. He traces three stages in the making of the new history. In the first stage a highly distinctive culture for Celtic Scotland was created. This required reversing the cultural dominance of Ireland over highland Scotland in the medieval period. This was achieved in the eighteenth century by forging an 'ancient epic poem', the *Ossian*, that portrayed great Scottish cultural achievements in which the true Celtic culture core, Ireland, was relegated to a cultural backwater.

The second stage was the creation of new Highland traditions. This centred on the tartan kilt. Tartan designs were imported into England and

Scotland from Holland in the sixteenth century. Quite separately, in 1727, a Lancashire weaver invented new clothes designed for tree felling based on the old Saxon smock. At the time of the Great Rebellion of 1745 therefore, kilts were a very recent invention for labourers and clan tartans did not exist in the Highlands. After the defeat of the rebellion the Highlands became a major source of men for the British army and tartan kilts gradually became the uniforms differentiating the new regiments. Their transfer from lower class and soldier wear to upper-class clothes was a subsequent product of the Romantic movement of the late eighteenth century. In 1778 the Highland Society was established in London and in 1820 the Celtic Society in Edinburgh. In 1819 demand for tartans was so great that the first pattern book was published. By the time George IV paid a state visit to Edinburgh in 1822 the new Highland traditions were an accepted part of Scottish life and the ceremony was dominated by tartans and kilts.

The third stage saw the adoption of the Highland tradition by the Lowland region where the vast majority of the Scottish population lived. This was achieved by another forgery. Two brothers claiming to be descended from the royal Stuart family produced a document, *Vestiarum Scotium*, which purported to show that medieval clans each had their own tartan pattern. This document was published as a historical source in 1842 and two years later the brothers reported its contents in their book *Costume of the Clans* which was suspiciously similar to the earlier commercial pattern book. This allowed all Scots people to find their clan tartan from their surname. Highland tradition soon became popular in the Lowlands and a new large clothing business was created. Since this time Scots people across the world have celebrated their Scottishness in the tartan kilts of the Highland tradition.

3. History by rediscovery: Englishness

The mythical Scottish Highland tradition could be created and accepted because so little was known of pre-modern societies in northern Scotland. At the other end of the information spectrum came the old established states where historical data was plentiful. It should not be thought that a surfeit of information ensures a 'true' objective history, however. In these situations national histories are highly selective of what is included and emphasized.

Most of the 'old traditions' of England date from the late nineteenth century (Dodd 1986). This was the crucial period for the British state when relative economic decline was politically compensated by the new imperialism. This new situation required new traditions and a new history. Important institutions such as the National Theatre, the National Gallery and the Dictionary of National Biography date from this time. In short, a vibrant national culture was being reconstituted to give England a great future and not just a great past such as that conceded to the Celts.

The landscape image of this new culture was rural, in particular the thatched cottages and fields of southern England. At the time England was, of course, the most urbanized country in the world but these cities and northern industrial England were associated with all the problems of modern society. Rural areas, for all their poverty, became the representatives of an idyllic past, a 'Merrie England', where contemporary problems were conspicuous by their absence. The golden Elizabethan age was rediscovered as the authentic site of Merrie England (Hawkins 1986).

The choice of the late sixteenth century as the 'golden age' was not a chance one (Colls 1986). Throughout most of the nineteenth century the golden age was to be found in the late seventeenth century, at the Glorious Revolution of 1688 when the absolutist pretensions of the Stuarts were defeated by Parliament. In the liberal England of British hegemony it was the establishment of these 'liberties' that was celebrated in the national history. With the coming of the new imperialism the origins of 'Englishness' is moved back a century to the beginning of English overseas expansion under Elizabeth. From the original liberal perspective, Elizabeth was a more absolutist monarch than the Stuarts but by the end of the century the continuity that is traced is not that of 'liberties' but that of imperialism. Englishness has moved from an insular territorial stage to a world stage. This national history, like all national histories, is a product of a particular present for the purpose of promoting a particular future.

NATIONALISM IN PRACTICE

If nationalism is the dominant ideology of the world-economy we must always remember that this has not always been the case. We have already indicated that this political use of the idea of nation really dates from the French Revolution and no earlier. In the two or three centuries before 1800 the world-economy evolved without a politics based on nationalism. There were states to be sure but, as Wallerstein (1974a: 102) points out, these were anti-national where regional ethnic powers stood in the way of the absolute state's centralization. There was 'statism' or mercantilism as we have seen, but until the nineteenth century no nationalism. Since that time however, we have experienced a wide variety of different nationalisms. The first task of our discussion below is to put some order into this diversity by presenting a typology of nationalism. We then consider contrasting interpretations of these particular political practices.

A TYPOLOGY OF NATIONALISMS

The most recent description of the variety of nationalism is by Orridge (1981). Our typology below is largely drawn from his discussion of the sequence of various nationalisms. We identify five basic types —

proto-nationalism, unification nationalism, separation nationalism, liberation nationalism and renewal nationalism. We consider each in turn.

Proto-nationalism. This is the nationalism of the original core states, the medium-sized states of Western Europe. This nationalism is the source of much dispute over the timing of the emergence of nation and nationalism. Gottmann (1973: 33–6), for instance, is able to trace the idea of *pro patria mori* — dying for one's country — back to about 1300 so that by 1430 Joan of Arc could freely employ such sentiments to mobilize the French knights against English encroachment on French soil. The statements of English nationalism to be found in Shakespeare's plays of the late sixteenth and early seventeenth century are even more familiar examples of this early 'patriotism'. But these are both examples of loyalty to monarch or state or even country but not to the collective idea of a people as a nation incorporating all sections and classes. Nevertheless the centralizing tendencies of these states within relatively stable boundaries did lead to a degree of cultural homogeneity by 1800 which was not found in other areas of comparable size. England and France are the key examples here but similar nation-states were emerging in Portugal, Sweden, the Netherlands and, to a lesser extent, in Spain. In all of these cases state preceded nation and it can even be said that state produced nation. The result was what Orridge (1981a) terms proto-nation-states. The 'people' were entering politics but nationalism as an ideology was not fully developed until later in the nineteenth century. Hence we can say nation preceded nationalism.

Unification nationalism. For the full development of the ideology of nationalism we have to look elsewhere. In central Europe such medium sized states had been prevented from evolving under the contradictory pressures of small (city-scale) states and large multi-ethnic empires. In particular Germany and Italy were a mosaic of small independent states mixed with provinces of larger empires. After 1800 the Napoleonic wars disrupted this pattern which had been imposed a century and half earlier at the Treaty of Westphalia (1649). Although the Congress of Vienna in 1815 attempted to reconstitute the old Europe, new forces had been unleashed which were to dominate the rest of the century. Nationalism was the justification for uniting most of the German culture area under Prussian leadership into a new German nation-state and transforming Italy from a mere 'geographical expression' to an Italian nation-state. These are the prime examples of unification nationalism and are generally considered to be the heartlands of the ideology.

Separation nationalism. Most successful nationalisms have involved the disintegration of existing sovereign states. In the nineteenth and early twentieth century this nationalism lay behind the creations of a large number of new states out of the Austro-Hungarian, Ottoman and Russian Empires. Starting with Greece in 1821 a whole tier of new states were created in eastern Europe from Bulgaria, through the Balkans to

Scandinavia. Surviving examples are Norway, Finland, Poland,
Czechoslovakia, Hungary, Roumania, Bulgaria, Yugoslavia, Albania and
Greece. Ireland also comes into this category. This type of nationalism
was, until recently, considered to be a phenomenon of the past at least in
core countries. However in the last two decades there have been further
'autonomous' nationalisms appearing in many states. Some of the most
well-known are found in Scotland, Wales, Basque country, Corsica,
Quebec and Wallonia. None of these has at the present time been
successful in establishing its own nation-state but all have been granted
political concessions within the framework of their existing states. We
discuss this 'new' nationalism further below.

Liberation nationalism.   The break-up of European overseas empires was
described in Chapter 4 but is of interest here as representing probably
the most common form of nationalism. Nearly all such movements for
independence have been 'national liberation movements'. The earliest was
the American colonists in 1776 whose War of Independence finally led to a
constitution giving sovereignty to the 'people'. The Latin American
revolutions after the Napoleonic wars were more explicitly 'nationalist' in
character. These can be considered liberal nationalist movements. In the
twentieth century such movements have invariably been socialist
nationalist movements, varying in their socialism from India's mild version
to Vietnam's revolutionary version. Another way of dividing up liberation
nationalism is between those based upon European settler groups and
those based upon indigenous peoples. In the former case we have the United
States and Latin American plus the original 'white' Commonwealth states
of South Africa, Canada, Australia and New Zealand who negotiated
independence without liberation movements. In the latter case there are
the states of Africa and Asia which have become independent since 1945.

Renewal nationalism.   In some parts of the periphery 'ancient' cultures
withstood European political capture for a variety of reasons and were able
to emulate the proto-nationalism of the core often using a politics similar
to unification nationalism. These countries had a long history as ethnic
communities upon which they could easily build their new nationalism.
National renewal to former greatness became the basic cry. Hence Iran
could rediscover its Persian heritage. Turkey after losing its Ottoman
empire could concentrate on its Turkish ethnicity. The classic cases of this
type of nationalism are to be found in Japan and China.

This form of nationalism can also occur as part of a process of creating
a new state identity which attempts to redefine the relations of the state to
the world-economy. As such this renewal is associated with modern
revolutions. Stalin's 'socialism in one country' had many of the trappings
of a renewal of the Russian nation for instance. Other renewals have
occurred in Mexico, Egypt, China and most recently in Iran.

These five types and their various sub-types seem to provide a
reasonable cover of the variety of nationalisms that have existed. The

sequence from the early types to their emulation in the later ones illustrates, according to Orridge (1981a), the basic process of copying and adaption which had lain behind the strength of the ideology. Political leaders in a wide range of contexts have been able to appeal to the nationalist doctrine to justify their actions. This has led to a curious ambivalence in how nationalism is perceived. On the one hand it is a good thing, a positive force in world history as when it is associated with weak states freeing themselves from foreign oppression. But it also has a dark side, the negative force associated with Nazism and Fascism in Europe, and militarism throughout the semi-periphery and periphery. It is, as it were, both good and bad. This is most clearly seen in attitudes to nationalism after the two world wars in the twentieth century. In 1919 the First World War was blamed on the suppression of nationalism; in 1945 the Second World War was blamed on the expression of nationalism (Rustow 1967: 21). Nairn (1977), in a particularly apt analogy, calls nationalism 'the modern Janus' after the famous Roman god who looks in two directions at once, both backwards and forwards. For Nairn this is the essence of the ideology, a simultaneous appeal to both progress and tradition.

We have packaged nationalism into five neat bundles in our typology and this is a necessary step towards explanation. But, by definition, any parsimonious description misses out most of the detail. The problem in the case of nationalism is that it is this very detail — the difference in language, folklore and other traditions — which is the essence of the ideology in practice. There is no room here to present a catalogue of such materials but what we can do is consider related case studies to illustrate difficulties of applying the doctrine in practice. The examples we take are from the political negotiations of the Peace at Paris in 1919. This is chosen for two reasons. First, it represents the apogee of the recognition of nationalism as a legitimate force in world politics. The League of Nations was largely based upon the doctrine of nationalism presented above. Second, nationalism is easier to define as a doctrine than it is to define on the ground. The negotiators at Paris had the task of redrawing the map of central and eastern Europe. The difficulties of their task and different means used to achieve their ends illustrate the two sides of nationalism in a very concrete manner. In short we present some aspects of the geography of nationalism at the peak of its influence.

During the First World War national self-determination gradually came to be regarded, especially after the entry of United States, as the principal war aim of the allied forces. By the time the Paris Peace Conference was convened new states had already been created out of the territories of the defeated states of Germany and Austria-Hungary (Cobban 1969: 556). Hence the peace negotiators spent most of their time putting boundaries around existing political creations. *National self-determination* provided a simple guide to this process — states should be formed around nations as

determined by the people. In strict terms the people decide which
nation-state they belong to. Such choice was rare in practice and was
replaced by the very negation of choice — people were allocated to states
on the basis of some cultural characteristic, usually the language, of the
area they lived in. We may term this process *national determinism*. Let us
consider each process in turn.

1. National self-determination: plebiscites

It follows logically from one nationalist tradition that if sovereignty does
indeed lie with the 'people', then the people should be consulted in any
proposed changes in sovereignty. This is the principle of national
self-determination which requires the use of plebiscites for changing state
boundaries. Wambaugh (1936) defines three periods when plebiscites were
used to decide such matters: (i) in the aftermath of the French Revolution
in Savoy, Nice, Geneva and Belgium to legitimize the extension of the
French state; (ii) between 1848 and 1870 notably as a tool in the
conversion of the Kingdom of Sardinia into the Kingdom of Italy and (iii)
resulting from the Paris Peace conference of 1919. However, use of this
method was surprisingly infrequent given the Allies' war aims: only six
plebiscites were carried out, four to define parts of the new Germany's
border and two to define parts of the new Austria's border.

One of the reasons for the infrequent use of plebiscites in 1919 was the
difficulty in agreeing the ground rules. Which areas are polled and how
the vote is aggregated and interpreted will affect the result. In the event four
different ways of organizing the plebiscites were employed, each implying
a rather different result. The simplest method is the majority method
whereby a province is polled and the whole area is allocated on the basis
of which rival state obtains most votes. On this basis in 1921 Sopron was
allocated to Hungary despite many localities voting to join Austria. The
creation of such 'national minorities' can be lessened by defining different
zones in a province and allowing majorities in the different zones to opt
for different state membership. This was applied in Schleswig where one
zone voted to join Germany and the other to join Denmark. Also in the
Klagenfurt Basin this method was adopted but here both zones opted
for Austria in preference to Yugoslavia. A more sensitive method is to
allow minor border adjustments on the basis of the polling returns. This
was done in Allenstein and Marienwerder in locating the boundary
between Germany and Poland. Finally an attempt was made to draw the
German–Polish boundary through industrial Upper Silesia on a
commune-by-commune basis. Such a partition involving by far the largest
poll led to many problems. Simple voting returns indicated numerous
enclaves, for instance. In the end the boundary was drawn by a special
commission using the plebiscite results only as a guide.

Clearly nationalism in practice was not as simple as the theory of
national self-determination implies. If the rules for Sopron had been applied

to Upper Silesia, for instance, the whole province would have gone to Germany. But there were many more problems which we can only begin to appreciate this far away in time and space. Perhaps the most basic question is who is entitled to vote in such plebiscites? War and its aftermath lead to much migration, some of it forced — should former residents have the vote? In Upper Silesia there were 150,000 such 'out-voters'. In contrast in the Schleswig plebiscite voters had to be domiciled in the province since 1900. In any case can a plebiscite ever be entirely fair when one of the two competing states has recently had sovereignty over the province being polled? In Schleswig, for instance, there had been a vigorous programme of Germanization in schools, courts and other state institutions. Similarly in the Klagenfurt Basin, Yugoslavia complained about fifty years of Austrian propaganda deceiving the Slavonic voters. In fact one of the most interesting features of these minor boundary exercises was the lack of correspondence between poll results and language patterns. In the Klagenfurt Basin, with its large majority of Slovene-speakers, the people voted to join German-speaking Austria. Similarly in Allenstein, Marienwerder and upper Silesia, voting to join Germany was higher than would be expected from the language distribution. Clearly, past political mobilization was cutting across current language status but this was not allowed to happen elsewhere.

2. National determinism: Jovan Cvijic's language maps of Macedonia

According to Cobban (1969) there was a change of emphasis in the practice of nationalism in the second half of the nineteenth century. Annexations occur on nationalist grounds but without asking the 'people'. The expansion of Germany is the prime example with the incorporation of Schleswig and Lorraine by conquest. Here we have a different conception of the politics of nationalism whereby people are designated members of a nation usually on the basis of the language they speak. It is this concept of national determinism which dominated the boundary drawing at Paris in 1919. But even if the language criterion is accepted as a legitimate indication of national preference, and as we have seen plebiscites do not support this assumption, there remain the problems of defining national languages and mapping their distribution. Without the prior existence of nation-states there are no 'standard' languages (except German) but rather various mixtures of dialects. This situation led to a plethora of alternative interpretations of languages and their distribution mostly reflecting the nationality of the 'language-expert'. Here we will concentrate on one such author to show how his language maps change over time to reflect the increasing ambition of his own state. Our source for this discussion is H. R. Wilkinson's (1951) *Maps and Politics*, possibly the most underestimated book ever written on political geography. In this study he looks at seventy-three ethnographic maps of Macedonia from 1730 to 1946. This area is interesting because it lies between Yugoslavia/Serbia, Bulgaria, Greece and Albania. Numerous counter-claims as to its national affiliation occurred until it was finally allocated to Yugoslavia in 1919. The geographer Jovan Cvijic played an important part in legitimizing Serbian, and subsequently Yugoslavian claims, on Macedonia. We consider four of his maps here (Fig. 5.1).

Jovan Cvijic was a distinguished physical geographer who had made his name studying the karst scenery of the Balkans. As head of the Department of Geography at the University of Belgrade his reputation was world-wide. At that time geographers were generalists rather than specialists so that it was normal for individuals to study all sections of the discipline. Cvijic, therefore, wrote books on the human geography of the Balkans and it is his ethnographic maps in these studies that concern us here. His first ethnographic map appeared in 1906 and did not attempt to distinguish between Serbians and Bulgarians, classifying both as simply Slavs. However he did tentatively introduce the term 'Macedo-Slav' at this time to indicate that the Slavs of this region were neither Serbians nor Bulgarians. This was counter to most current thinking which extended the

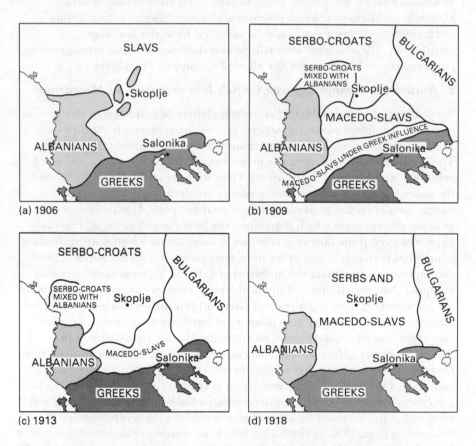

Fig. 5.1 Cvijic's language maps of Macedonia (a) 1906 (b) 1909 (c) 1913 (d) 1918

Bulgarian nation across Macedonia. Cvijic's new concept was widely criticized and not generally accepted. Cvijic first depicted Macedo-Slavs on his 1909 map which Wilkinson (1951: 163) terms 'revolutionary'. The distribution of Serbs is extended to south of Skopje and south of them a broad band of Macedo-Slavs are identified. In contrast the Bulgarian distribution is very limited and they are all but excluded from Macedonia. The political significance of identifying these areas as Macedo-Slav rather than Bulgarian is that it gave them *no* national affiliation so that the area was open to future Serbian claims.

This future was not far away. In the Balkan wars (1912–13) Serbia extended its territory southwards and Cvijic's cartography responded accordingly. His 1913 map shows further extensions of Serbs southwards. This does not represent migration but simply Serbian political interests. On this map Serbia gains at the expense of Albanians rather than Bulgarians to reflect the outcome of the wars — Bulgarians now occupied some territory depicted Macedo-Slav in 1909. The latter group remained, however, as a neutral ethnic mixture transitional between the Serbs and Bulgarians. But for Cvijic they were always what Wilkinson terms 'incipient Serbs'

In 1918 Cvijic produced his most influential map in his book on the human geography of the Balkans. The book was hailed a masterpiece and his ethnographic map was reproduced in the prestigious French *Annales de Géographie* and *American Geographical Review*. In Britain Cvijic was awarded the Patron's Gold Medal of the *Royal Geographical Society* in part for his work on the Balkans. Hence he was able to influence the Peace Conference as a most distinguished geographer and expert on ethnic distributions in the Balkans. In the 1918 map this 'expertise' now extended Serbian ethnicity into areas formerly depicted as Bulgarian. Although in hindsight Wilkinson (1951) has been able to show the continual biases of Cvijic's work, he was accepted at the Peace Conference as impartial. Whereas in 1913 Serbian annexation of parts of Macedonia was widely interpreted as usurping Bulgarian rights, by 1919 Cvijic had succeeded in justifying Serbia's right to retain Macedonia on nationalist grounds. Despite maps by genuine neutrals portraying Macedonia as largely Bulgarian (Wilkinson 1951: 204), the concept of Macedo-Slav entered the British and American political vocabulary. Of course the Bulgarians protested and requested a plebiscite but their claims were rejected. The Macedo-Slavs were not a nationality and so were not awarded minority rights in the peace settlement. By 1924 when the first post-war census was published, Macedo-Slav had become a mere dialect of Serbo-Croat. Hence in the ethnic maps published in Bowman's (1924) *New World* and *Geographical Review* in 1925 the Serbs have finally incorporated the former 'Bulgarians' who had become 'Macedo-Slavs' on the basis of one man's work. Bulgaria captured Macedonia in 1942 but was again on the losing side in 1945 so that the province remains Yugoslavian to this day.

We have considered this example of national determinism in some detail because it illustrates so clearly the paucity of the theory of national self-determination which underlay the peace conference and most subsequent thinking on the nation-state. 'Nations' do not exist as neatly packaged bundles of people waiting for a state to be drawn around them. No less than states, nations are created and reflect the politics in which they are made. Any theory of nationalism cannot, therefore, be merely a theory of ethnic distribution, rather it must be a theory of the political construction of nations. The final boundaries of states in Macedonia reflect the power politics in the region in the first half of this century as interpreted and promoted by Jovan Cvijic. There is probably no other example of one man influencing national definition so completely as Cvijic but this extreme case clarifies the general process.

STATE AND NATION TODAY

The reorganization of the world political map after World War I is generally considered to be the apogee of nationalist politics because it represents the culmination of the nineteenth century European nationalist movements. But this standard interpretation does not look so clear cut from the perspective of the late twentieth century. Today we see the fruits of nationalist movements beyond Europe that have produced far more states since 1945 than were created after World War I. Although we have previously considered these as the collapse of the European imperialism, this was engineered, of course, by new national liberation movements throughout the world. The result is that by far the majority of states that appear on today's world political map have been created since 1945. It is clearly time to take a fresh look at state and nation from a global rather than a purely European perspective.

Gunnar Nielsson (1985) has investigated the question of the relation between today's states and ethnic groups — 'nations' and 'national minorities'. He produces data for 164 states and 589 ethnic groups covering the whole world. The fact that there are three times as many ethnic groups as states does not augur well for finding an ideal world of nation-states. In fact Nielsson produces a typology in which a range of relationships between state and nation are identified.

In his search for the nation-state Mikesell (1983) claims to find only one authentic example — Iceland. All other states have a degree of mixed population that makes their credentials as nation-states doubtful. In the real world of politics we do not expect the 'cultural purity' that Mikesell places on the concept of nation-state. Following Nielsson (1985) we will define nation-states as those states where over sixty per cent of the population are from one ethnic group: 107 of the 164 states qualify on this very loose definition. These can be divided into two main types. First, there are those where the ethnic group is dispersed across several states.

The best example is the Arab nation which dominates seventeen nation-states. We shall term these *part-nation-states*. There are fifty-two such cases. Egypt and Syria are typical examples, along with the 'divided nations' we described in Chapter 4 — the two 'Koreas' and two 'Germanies'. Second, there are the *single-nation-states* where an ethnic group dominates only one state. On a few occasions the ethnic group contributes more than ninety-five per cent of a state's population. These are closest to the nation-state ideal and there are twenty-three such cases. Iceland, Japan and Somalia are typical examples. It is more common where one ethnic group dominates the state, but not to the degree of the 'ideal' category of single nation-states. There are thirty-two such cases. Great Britain and the United States are examples of this category, along with Nicaragua, Sri Lanka and Zimbabwe.

Nielsson (1985) identifies fifty-seven *non-nation-states* where there is no single ethnic group that has sixty per cent of the state's population. These can be divided into three types. An *intermediate-non-nation-state* type occurs where there is a single dominant ethnic group in a state but it constitutes only about half the population (40−60 per cent in Nielsson's definition). There are seventeen such states with examples being the USSR, the Philippines and Sudan. *Bi-nation-states* are identified by Nielsson (1985) where two ethnic groups provide a combined percentage of a state's population of over sixty-five per cent. There are twenty-one cases and Belgium, Peru and Fiji are typical examples. Finally there are nineteen cases of what Nielsson (1985) terms *multinational states* with a high degree of ethnic fragmentation so that they do not fall into any of the above groups. India, Malaysia and Nigeria are typical examples.

In Table 5.1 we show how these types of state are distributed across five continents. The geographical pattern is as we would expect. The two continents with the oldest modern states, Europe and the Americas, have the most single-nation-states of both categories. Part-nation-states are most common in Asia, which reflects a fragmentation of their large nations. Multination-states and bi-nation-states are most common in Africa, reflecting the arbitrary boundaries imposed on the continent in the colonial division. But we can also note that most types are found on all continents. The major exception is the dearth of multination-states in Europe which reflects their dismantling after World War I. We can conclude, therefore, that nation-states of one sort or another form the majority of the world's states but that the nation-state ideal as reflected in single-nation-states has not managed to dominate even in its 'heartland' of Europe. The non-national states are obviously susceptible to nationalist challenges from within their boundaries. Governments in these states have to be very sensitive to the needs of the range of ethnic groups in their territory. In Chapter 4, for instance, we showed how the Indian government conceded a language-based federal structure to contain ethnic discontent. But we should not think that ethnic challenges are limited to

Table 5.1 Geographical distribution of nation states and non nation-states

| | Nation-states | | | Non-nation-states | | |
	Part-nation-states	Single-nation-states Over 95% one ethnic group	60–94% one ethnic group	Intermediate non-nation-states	Bi-nation-states	Multi-nation-states
AFRICA	7	4	3	9	9	14
AMERICAS	7	6	11	1	5	3
ASIA	22	2	6	6	3	2
EUROPE	12	9	9	1	2	0
OCEANIA	4	2	3	0	2	0
TOTAL	52	23	32	17	21	19

the non-nation-states. Our loose definition of nation-state allows for important minority ethnic groups to reside in the single nation-state category and it is in these states that some of the main examples of 'ethnic resurgency' have been found in recent years.

1. Nation against state

The resurgence of minority nationalisms within European states from the 1960s onwards was a surprise to most political scientists. Their developmentalist models predicted a gradual decline in territorial-based loyalties as communications within the state brought all the population into a single community (Deutch 1961). This would be accompanied by modern functional cleavages such as class replacing traditional core—periphery ethnic cleavages (Rokkan 1970). And, in any case, this was Europe the continent whose boundaries had been redrawn after two world wars to produce nation-states. Nevertheless separatist and autonomist nationalisms have grown and survived just as political scientists were writing their obituaries. In the 1980s minority national resurgence has occurred in the USSR a state that had long seemed to have safely accommodated its ethnic diversity (Smith 1985). Clearly Europe today is experiencing yet another round of nationalist politics.

A further surprising feature of the new nationalism is that it is primarily occurring in the oldest states of Europe. Spain, Britain and France have been particularly affected. We can use these three states to illustrate the range of political practices to be found in the new nationalism (Williams 1986). The most threatening form of politics is violence against the state and its agents. This political practice dominates the Basque struggle in Spain, the Ulster conflict in Britain and the separatist movement of Corsica in France. Various forms of non-violent resistance dominate the nationalist politics of Catalonia in Spain, of Wales in Britain and of Brittany in France. Finally, party political opposition is the major strategy of the nationalists of Galicia in Spain, of Scotland in Britain and Alsace in France. The new nationalism is clearly a complex phenomenon expressed in different ways in different places. But they all have in common a challenge to the contemporary 'nation-state'.

What is the future for these various nationalist groups? Surely they are only asking for national self-determination, the principle employed to draw new state boundaries after World War I. Can this new round of nationalism produce a new round of boundary drawing and a new political map? The answer would seem to be no. The earlier case of the application of the national self-determination principle was obviously undertaken in the special circumstances of the aftermath of war. Today the states under threat show no sign of equivalent disintegration. In fact, national self-determination now seems to apply only when the so-called 'salt water theory' (Knight 1982) operates. That is to say national self-determination for overseas colonies is acceptable but not national self-determination that would undermine the territorial integrity of an existing state. Hence it seems highly unlikely that there will be a new set of nation-states created in Europe or elsewhere in the world. The new political challenge will have to be accommodated by other political means such as granting limited autonomy or devising more formal federal arrangements.

2. The rights of indigenous populations

In Nielsson's (1985, Tables 2.2 and 2.3) analysis of ethnic groups nearly half (289) reside in just one state and constitute less than ten per cent of that state's population. Some of the new nationalisms of Europe are included in this category. The indigenous populations of the European-settled states of America and Oceania make up another important example of such 'minorities'. These peoples occupied the territory before the invasion of Europeans. After defeat they were generally ignored, neglected and cheated by the new colonial states. The major source of conflict with the settlers was land and this continues to be the major practical grievance of indigenous peoples today.

In recent years indigenous peoples have found a new voice in their struggle for survival. The most striking examples are the World Council of Indigenous Peoples and the activities of the United Nations on their behalf. In 1985, for instance, over 200 representatives of indigenous peoples participated in a meeting of the UN Commission on Human Rights Working Group on Indigenous Populations (Knight 1988: 128). This provides an indication of the size and scope of this political struggle. It is difficult to find good estimates of the numbers of people involved but Burger (1987: 37) provides these figures: Canada 800,000, USA $2\frac{1}{2}$ million, Latin America 30 million, Australia 200,000 and New Zealand nearly 400,000, plus many millions more in Asia and Africa. In all cases the indigenous peoples are demanding a similar package of rights. First, they require the right to preserve their cultural identity. This requires, second, a right to their territory, to the land, resources and water of their homeland. Third, they need the right to have responsibility over the fate of their people and their environment. Finally, this leads on to the right to control their own land and people or what is commonly called in other circumstances, national self-determination.

What does all this mean for the indigenous groups? First they require recognition as 'nations' rather than mere ethnic 'minorities'. But as nations are they asking for state sovereignty? There has been some confusion over terminology in this area (Knight 1982) and it seems that most demands envisage autonomy rather than separate sovereignty. Without the demand for secession some states may grant indigenous peoples many of the rights they are striving for now that they have the United Nations as a forum for their challenge. But past treatment of these peoples does not leave much room for optimism.

Generally we can conclude with respect to all forms of nationalist struggles today that the relative stability of the world political map in the late twentieth century is not because the ideal of the nation-state has been realized. Rather any stability reflects the power of the status quo in the inter-state system. It is the realism of power-politics and not the idealism of national self-determination that matters.

MODERN THEORIES OF NATIONALISM

The ideological doctrine of nationalism presented in the first section of the chapter is what we may term the nationalist's theory of nationalism. It serves as the conceptual basis for the practice of nationalism. But it is not of any use as a framework for understanding nationalism. For a critical perspective on nation and nationalism we have to turn to modern theories that have distanced themselves from the doctrine. This allows us to look at nationalism dispassionately from outside the ideology.

The first step in separating our analysis from the doctrine is to recognize what Anderson (1983: 14) terms the three paradoxes of nationalism. First, there is an objective modernity that is built upon a subjective antiquity. This is Nairn's modern Janus analogy. Second, there is the universality of concept that covers the particularity of applications. In the world of nations every nation is unique. Third, there is the political power of the idea which contrasts spectacularly with its philosophical poverty. All theories have to come to terms with these paradoxes and explain their existence.

Modern theories of nationalism can be said to begin with the attempt of Tom Nairn (1977) to develop a new Marxist theory of nationalism. This was a highly controversial project and was severely criticized by Marxists and non-Marxists alike (Orridge 1981b; Gellner 1983; Hobsbawm 1977; and Blaut 1980, 1987). In some ways he has acted as a catalyst provoking critical but constructive reactions that have provided alternative theories. It is appropriate therefore that we begin our discussion with Nairn's theory of nationalism and uneven development. We categorize this theory as one of 'nationalism from above' because it emphasizes the role of the bourgeoisie in nationalist movements. The most cogent criticism of Nairn has come from Blaut (1987) who argues for an alternative 'nationalism from below' perspective. The two parts of this final section of the chapter deal with these two positions in turn.

NATIONALISM FROM ABOVE

Traditionally, Marxist theories of nationalism have treated this form of politics as being characteristic of a particular phase of capitalism, the rise of the bourgeoisie in Europe in the nineteenth century. Once this class had consolidated its hold on the state the need for new nationalisms would lessen. With the stage of 'rising capitalism' over, therefore, any subsequent nationalisms would be irrelevant to mainstream political struggle (Blaut 1987: 26—7) Hence Marxist theorists were ill-prepared for the outbreak of new nationalisms in Europe in the second half of the twentieth century. (Nairn (1977) was particularly concerned to understand the recent rise of Scottish nationalism.) Hence Nairn's oft-quoted remark that 'The theory of nationalism represents Marxism's great historical failure' (Nairn 1977: 329). Nairn sets himself the task of filling this theoretical void.

1. Nationalism and uneven development

Nationalism did not occur in isolation. As well as this new political phenomenon, the nineteenth century witnessed many other economic and social changes often summarized by the terms industrialization and urbanization. Of course these parallel developments are not a coincidence but adequate linkages between the various strands have been difficult to find. Nairn (1977), drawing on Gellner (1964), has provided a basic model to integrate these great processes of change. Nationalism is the result of the 'tidal wave of modernization' that swept Europe in the nineteenth century. This 'modernization', or more precisely economic development, was not evenly spread, as we know, so that western Europe was more advanced than central and eastern Europe. Nationalism is, then, a compensatory reaction to this uneven development. Beginning in the area bordering the advanced zone the new rising urban-industrial interests were unable to compete with the more efficient core producers. They had to evolve strategies to survive, to prevent their peripheralization. We have already discussed one part of their reaction — List's new economic theories which led to the *Zollverein* customs union in 1843. But economic policy alone is not enough. How can workers be persuaded that dearer food caused by tariffs is in their interests? The answer is to appeal to 'higher' values than mere material needs. The only resource available to these local capitalist interests not available to the metropolitan interests was their cultural affinity to their 'people'. By emphasizing differences between ethnic communities, local interests could form broad 'national' alliances with which to challenge the core. Hence the regions where nationalism blossomed as a major force on the European stage were central Europe and the unification nationalisms of Germany and Italy. From this beginning nationalism spread like a wave following the uneven development unleashed on the world by 'modernization'. Next came the separation nationalisms of eastern Europe to be followed by the liberation nationalisms outside Europe in the twentieth century. But nationalism became more than a reaction of semi-periphery and periphery. With the demise of British hegemony, the new vigorous nationalism spread to the core as a major force in the subsequent political competition resulting, as we have seen, in the second phase of formal imperialism. By the twentieth century nationalism was to become the dominant ideology throughout all zones of the world-economy.

Where do the two sides of nationalism fit into this theory? So far the use of 'tradition' has been made clear but what of the 'progress' side of the ideology? Although the urban-industrial interests of the semi-periphery and periphery used images of an idyllic past to mobilize the people, they could not be true conservatives and prevent progress. The whole purpose of the strategy was to close ranks with a view to catching up the core. This could only be done by borrowing the salient features of the modernization against which the movement was reacting. A 'medieval' Germany or Italy would be no match for a modern Britain or France. Hence the rhetoric of nationalism with its glorification of the past was ultimately only a cover for rapid modernization. The classic case is, of course, late nineteenth-century Germany where massive industrial growth went hand in hand with a popular German cultural 'revival'.

What of figures such as Cvijic in Serbia? The intelligentsia have played an important role in the rise of nationalist movements everywhere (Smith 1981: 81), not least by giving them a respectability they hardly deserved. The new class of intellectuals of nineteenth-century Europe, often from lower middle-class backgrounds, were able to provide the historical, philosophical, ethnographic and even geographical basis of the new nationalisms. As Nairn (1977: 100) puts it, the dilemma of underdevelopment only becomes nationalism when it is 'refracted' into a society in a certain way. The intellegentsia were the agents of refraction, the most 'advanced' part of the new national middle class. Nairn (1977: 117) postulates a social diffusion process starting with a small intelligentsia, initially reacting to the French Revolution, which he terms phase A. This is followed by phase B, from 1815 to 1848 in Europe, where the ideology spreads through the middle classes. But it is still only a minority movement and this accounts for its ultimate failure in the 1848 revolutions. Phase C occurs in the second half of the nineteenth century in Europe when it diffuses to the lower classes and modern popular nationalism is born. The intelligentsia were therefore the initial purveyors of ideas to be used for the general interests of their class. But they continued to be of use in sustaining and developing the special theories underlying each nationalism. Jovan Cvijic fits into our story as a dominant intellectual justifying and charting an expansionary minor nationalism of the early twentieth century.

Finally Gellner (1964) and Nairn (1977) point out that there is an important psychological aspect to nationalism. As Giddens (1981) observes, the dominant élites did not have to force-feed the masses their nationalism; there was a receptive public out there waiting to be mobilized. The strong sentiments that were aroused indicate a particular need for identity. As well as threatening the dominant interests outside the core, the tidal wave of modernization was undermining the everyday life of ordinary people. Many were migrating to industrial zones where their existence was routinized in ways never previously experienced. Here we have the alienation of mass society based upon the breakdown of tradition. Nationalism gave the people back their tradition and provided an identity in an alien-world. It is for this reason that nationalism is particularly associated with periods of radical disruption such as wars and, as Giddens (1981) emphasizes, strong charismatic leadership. In short nationalism acts as compensation for the alienation of mass society by producing what Anderson (1983) has termed 'imagined communities'.

2. Nations as imagined communities

Benedict Anderson (1983) argues that nationalism should not be automatically linked to self-consciously held political ideologies such as liberalism and socialism. Rather nationalism has more in common with the larger cultural systems that preceded it. Nationalism is a political ideology to be sure, but it is much more than that. This is the reason why it is constantly being underestimated by theoreticians.

Societies have always been held together by more than physical coercion. The population of the former world-empires consisted of 'imagined communities' integrated by religious ideology. In these religious 'imagined communities' a sacred language operated as a medium for creating a whole cosmology in which the people could play their part. From the Christendom of feudal Europe the early modern world-system inherited a religion that was fragmenting. In seventeenth-century Europe tens of thousands of people fought and died for their religion. In twentieth-century Europe millions of people fought and died for their country. Nation had replaced religion as the cultural system within which people could find their identity. The measure of the change was that it had become 'normal' for German Protestants to fight English Protestants and German Catholics to fight French Catholics. Religion was no longer the basis of the people's imagined communities; it had been superseded in its cultural role by nation.

Anderson (1983) argues that this new force of imagined community was made possible by the convergence of capitalism with the impact of print technology on Europe's diversity of languages. The latter ensured that the communities would be inherently limited in scope. In the seventeenth century Latin was still widely used as the medium in intellectual circles but as more books, newspapers and pamphlets came to be written and printed in vernacular languages so Europe became divided into separate language-based print markets. This made it possible to conceive of a 'nation' consisting of people existing together in space and time. The key concept is simultaneity — the new technology enabled people to appreciate that their lives ran parallel with the lives of other people like themselves. Newspapers in particular could provide a feeling of community in time and space. Since no one person can ever meet all other persons in this community it is an 'imagined' community like its more metaphysical religious precursors.

The geography of Anderson's (1983) theory of nationalism is distinctively different from Nairn's (1977). This is of particular interest because one of the main criticisms of Nairn's theory made by Blaut (1980) is its Eurocentric bias. Blaut finds the earliest examples of national liberation to occur outside Europe — in the United States in 1776 and in Haiti in 1804. Anderson accommodates Blaut's point in his identification of *creole nationalism* as the first of three types of nationalism. This first phase of nationalism, from 1770 to 1830, resulted in the creation of new American states by national independence struggles. These were not mass movements but served to promote the interests of the local-born European-settler groups (creoles) against imperial rule. The grievances of the creoles were expressed in the new print technology to produce 'creole communities'. The break-up of the Spanish empire into several new states was because of the limited geographical reach of the new technology which created creole communities at the scale of imperial administrative divisions. Notice this first 'separatist nationalism' is not based on language — the creoles used the languages of their imperial masters — but on physical separation with print technology providing the means to create new communities across the Atlantic.

It is in the second phase of nationalism, from 1870 to 1920 in Europe, that languages become important in defining new communities. In the complex cultural mixture of peoples in Europe this pluralism was being reduced by the printing press in its creation of literary languages or print languages. Rising state bureaucracies further produced a need for literacy in the 'state languages'. The end result was the creation of a whole new literate class to run affairs in both private and public sectors. As Anderson (1983: 74) observes:

> 'An illiterate bourgeoisie is scarcely imaginable. Thus in world-historical terms bourgeoisies were the first classes to achieve solidarity on an essentially imagined basis.

This literate bourgeoisie had 'by the second decade of the nineteenth century, if not earlier, a model of the independent national state available for pirating' (Anderson 1983: 78), and they proceeded to turn the nineteenth century into an 'age of nationalism'. This is the 'classical nationalism' at the heart of Nairn's theory and provides examples of the first truly *popular nationalism*.

Overlapping with this popular nationalism, but continuing beyond 1920 to the present day, Anderson identifies an *official nationalism* where the state attempts, usually successfully, to harness the popularity of nationalism to bolster its own legitimacy. In the established states this involves the nationalization of the old European dynasties. This is 'the age of the primary school' (Hobsbawm 1987: 150) where the technical need for a literate and numerate work force was supplemented by secular state and national propaganda. Geography and history became favoured vehicles for transmitting the new secular religion (Grano 1981). In its extreme form this type of nationalism involved forced language policies as in the Czarist Russification of non-Russian peoples, Germanification of Danes and Poles within the German Empire and even Macaulay's famous Anglicization in British India. Hence 'Official nationalisms were conservative, not to say reactionary, *policies* adopted from the model of the largely spontaneous popular nationalisms that preceded them' (Anderson 1983: 102). In this destruction of plurality, dialects, or what Hobsbawm (1987: 156) calls 'languages without an army or police force', are gradually eroded in a new uniformity that is the modern nation-state.

Anderson's identification of official nationalism meets another of Blaut's (1987) important criticisms of the original Nairn theory. Nairn's study, like most treatments of nineteenth century nationalism, neglects the 'large nation' nationalism at the expense of 'small nation' nationalism. Secessionist nationalism was not opposed by some 'anti-nationalist' movement but by an alternative larger nationalism. It is the latter that are the generators of the popularity of the new imperialism and the oppression of other cultures world-wide. There are two sides to every nationalist conflict and both are nationalist.

Since 1945, according to Anderson (1983), the new states have contained a mixture of creole, popular and official nationalisms. National liberation movements have been dominated by their 'youth' wings which represent the first new 'schooled' generation. When they have successfully taken control of their new states official nationalism comes to dominate the imagined community resulting in new reactionary policies. Anderson (1983: 11) considers the conflicts between China, Vietnam and Kampuchea in 1979 to be 'wars of world-historical importance' since they show the strength of official nationalism even in self-consciously revolutionary socialist regimes. For Anderson nationalism remains essentially bourgeois in nature and he remains pessimistic of the achievements of recent national liberation movements. In this he is directly opposed to the position that Blaut (1987) has developed.

NATIONALISM AS RESISTANCE

The major stimulus to Blaut's (1987) work has been to correct the serious neglect of anti-colonial struggles by mainstream writers on nationalism, both Marxist and non-Marxist. He states his position as two propositions:

1. 'You really cannot understand the modern world as a whole if you do not understand the dynamic of that part of it which has endured and struggled against colonialism'.

2 . 'There can be no adequate theory of development, of imperialism, of accumulation on a world scale, and of much more beside, if there is not an adequate theory of national liberation, of national struggle in its anti-colonial form' (Blaut 1987: 9).

But he finds that current theories of nationalism are of little use in this task, because most of them are theories of nationalism from above whereas he interprets the anti-colonial struggle as very much a case of nationalism from below. In particular he is determined to refute what he calls the 'all-nationalism-is-bourgeois-theory', first empirically by documenting the numerous examples of national liberation movements dominated by workers and peasants, and second by developing an alternative theory of nationalism in which full weight is given to anti-colonial struggles. Blaut is interested in nationalism as resistance, as a form of class struggle.

1. National struggle as class struggle

For Nairn (1977), nationalism is separate from class struggle and provides an alternative mechanism of change in the modern world. Blaut (1980) is at pains to show that nationalism is not an autonomous force but is a particular sort of class struggle. Such struggle will always be focused on the state because that is where political power lies. Class struggle then takes a particular national form when control of the state is in the hands of a foreign dominant class. A national struggle against external exploitation is just as much a class struggle as resistance to an internal dominant class. Hence nationalism is not an autonomous force.

Nationalism is not necessarily 'progressive', however. Blaut quotes approvingly Horace Davis's (1978) argument that nationalism is a neutral tool that is available to all classes or alliances of classes. Hence Nairn's (1977) identification of Nazism and Fascism as the 'archetype' of nationalism is to over-emphasize one extreme reactionary use of nationalism from among the wide range of uses in the modern world. The credibility of national liberation movements in the Third World is thereby severely undermined by an unfair link to a politics we all abhor.

Blaut (1987) recovers what he sees as Lenin's theory of nation struggle as a part of the wider theory of imperialism. As the international conflict between great-power nationalisms heightens, the exploitation of colonies is intensified. This produces a new phenomenon since members of all classes are liable to suffer within the severely exploited territory. Hence there is an essentially 'multi-class struggle' directed against imperialism (Blaut 1988: 129). This differs from the earlier nineteenth century national struggles which were basically bourgeois battles against traditional forces to produce bourgeois states. Hence the products of this new nationalism need not be a reactionary bourgeois state but can be a revolutionary socialist state such as Cuba.

In this way Blaut recognizes three forms of nationalism in the world today — the original bourgeois variety, which is lessening in importance, an intensified bourgeois nationalism of the large capitalist states and the national liberation struggles of the periphery. Hence any modern theory of nationalism must confront the current opposition between great power nationalism and the nationalism of resistance in the periphery. This is precisely what Blaut's 'Leninist' theory of 'nationalism within imperialism' achieves.

Any evaluation of this theory must be centred on the interpretation of the new states created by this latest nationalism. If we follow Anderson in his disillusionment of the behaviour of revolutionary socialist states in 1979 then we would express doubts concerning the progressiveness that Blaut finds in the nationalisms of the periphery. Frank (1984: 187) identifies the south-east Asian wars of 1979 in the same light as Anderson and talks of 'nationalist cats in socialist disguise'. Samir Amin (1987), in particular, has voiced his disappointment that radical national movements have, after all, produced national bourgeois states that seem to operate the same way as the bourgeois states produced by previous phases of nationalist movements. Hence doubt can be cast on Blaut's assertion of a new form of nationalism in the second half of the twentieth century.

2. National struggle as an anti-systemic movement

In world-systems analysis all political struggle reflects a basic ambiguity of the capitalist world-economy — political activities have focused on the state while production is based on a trans-state division of labour. The conflict and tension resulting from this structural situation has to be understood and incorporated into any theory of nationalism.

For Wallerstein (1984a), national struggle is part of what he terms the anti-systemic movements. These movements originated in the ideas and political activity of the French Revolution and developed during the nineteenth century to challenge the system. Initially they took two separate forms. The social movement grew to articulate the demands of exploited classes, especially the urban proletariate. The national movement grew to articulate the demands of exploited peoples especially in the semi-periphery. Both movements provided a forum for those dissatisfied with the status quo but they identified different causes of the system's pernicious outcomes and therefore they targeted different enemies. But they both agreed on the same political strategy — to control state structures within the system. Before 1917 the two arms of the anti-systemic movement were generally seen as opposing one another. This generated a large theoretical discussion on class versus nation as alternative bases for popular mobilization. After 1917, however, this dichotomy became far less important and after 1945 all liberation movements claimed to be both national and socialist. In the recent national struggles that Blaut (1987) emphasizes, therefore, the two nineteenth century forms of anti-systemic politics have coalesced (Phillips and Wallerstein 1986). Hence Wallerstein agrees with Blaut on the revolutionary credentials of this politics of the periphery. But he disagrees in the interpretation of the meaning of the national liberation successes.

Although Wallerstein (1984a) is supportive of national struggles as elements of anti-systemic politics he counsels that we must understand the limitations of this politics. And here we return to the antinomy of multiple politics and one economy. Winning control of a state structure whether as a socialist, nationalist or as a modern national liberation front provides the opportunity to operate within the rules and constraints of the world-economy and inter-state system. This does produce genuine possibilities for tackling urgent problems within a territory: all states have some leeway within the system, some manoeuvrability as we have argued in Chapter 4. But this politics is a very constrained politics as all revolutionary regimes have found to the cost of their ideals — hence the disappointments expressed at the behaviour of modern socialist states as in the south-east Asian wars of 1979. It is not that 'socialists have become nationalists' but rather that by taking the strategic decision to pursue a politics leading to state power in the late nineteenth century, the social movement has inevitably converged with the national movement. Nationalism is as much imbued in socialism today as it is in our political geography. The vision of a world of nations remains central to world politics.

Chapter 6

RETHINKING ELECTORAL GEOGRAPHY

THE LIBERAL HERITAGE

Quantitative electoral geography

1. Geography of voting
2. Geographical influences in voting
3. Geography of representation

A systems model of electoral geography

1. Input, throughout and output
2. Critique: liberal assumptions

Coulter's global model of liberal democracy

1. Liberal democracy and social mobilization
2. Two interpretations of a relationship

A world-systems interpretation of elections

1. Liberal democracy and social democracy
2. Corollary for a 'Free World'
3. Electoral geography contrasts between core and periphery

LIBERAL DEMOCRACY IN THE CORE

The dialectics of electoral geography

1. Organization and Mobilization
2. The two geographies of elections
3. Three types of electoral politics

The making of liberal democracies

1. The development of political parties
2. Non-congruent electoral politics: section and party in the USA before the New Deal
3. Congruent electoral politics in the Cold War era
4. Changing agendas in British politics

ELECTIONS BEYOND THE CORE

The politics of failure

1. Democratic musical chairs
2. The geographies of a politics of failure: the case of Ghana

India as 'the largest liberal democracy in the world'

1. Congress geographies of support
2. Congress geographies of power

Chapter 6

RETHINKING ELECTORAL GEOGRAPHY

If success can be measured by quantity of production then electoral geography is the success story of modern political geography. In the last two decades there have been hundreds of studies on the geography of elections, so much so that some have argued that the growth has been 'disproportionate' in relation to the general needs of political geography (Muir 1981: 204). In fact, as Muir (1981: 203) points out, ideas on the role of electoral geography in political geography range from those who imply that it is 'the very core and substance of political geography' to those who feel that it does not belong in political geography at all! Obviously the position taken in such a debate depends ultimately on the definition of political geography being employed. In our political geography elections play a key role at the scale of ideology in channelling conflicts safely into constitutional arenas. Hence we need to consider electoral geography but not necessarily in its usual form.

There is a second debate on the nature of electoral geography which is much more important. Given the rapid increase in these studies, what is it they are adding to our knowledge of political geography? It is not at all clear where electoral geography is leading. The goal of most studies seems to be nothing more than understanding the particular situation under consideration. The result has been a general failure to link geographies of elections together into a coherent body of knowledge. In short we have a 'bitty' and uncoordinated pattern of researches which have produced a large number of isolated findings but few generalizations. There are some exceptions, and these are described below, but on the whole quality has lagged behind quantity of production and few would now claim electoral geography as a 'success story' Hence the need for some rethinking.

Although electoral geography has not been explicit in its theorizing its implicit theory is easy to identify. In effect electoral geography has simply accepted the political assumptions of the core countries in which it has developed. These assumptions can be summarized by the term 'liberal democracy' and in the first section of this chapter we review electoral studies in geography as a 'liberal heritage'. Unfortunately the narrowness of these past studies has led to major omissions in coverage. In particular comparison between elections in different countries is only conspicuous by its absence in electoral geography. Hence we have to 'bolster' this liberal heritage by drawing on some work in comparative politics which enables us to appreciate more fully the global implications of the liberal assumptions. The critique of this work leads on to our world-systems interpretation of elections which forms the framework for the remainder of the chapter.

The most conspicuous omission from traditional electoral geography has been elections in Third World countries. Our world-systems interpretation helps us to overcome this deficiency by providing a framework for studying elections in both core and periphery. Hence the two substantive sections after the heritage section deal with elections in the core and 'beyond the core' respectively. The thesis presented argues that these represent two very different sets of political processes.

THE LIBERAL HERITAGE

In some ways electoral geography is like geopolitics in being represented in the work of some of the founding fathers of modern geography. In the case of electoral geography we can cite André Siegfried of the French regional school whose 1913 study of western France under the Third Republic has long been regarded as a classic of its genre. Siegfried is usually considered the 'father' of electoral geography because of his method of mapping election results and comparing them with maps of possible explanatory factors. At about the same time Carl Sauer (1918) was contributing to the perennial American debate on how to define congressional districts. As the founder of America's cultural-regional school of geography it is perhaps not surprising that his solution involved representation by geographical region. Other studies could be cited but until the 1960s electoral studies in geography were sporadic with no sustained effort except perhaps in France.

All this changed with the so-called quantitative revolution in geography. This affected human geography in particular and resulted in the decline of qualitative regional studies and the rise of quantitative systematic studies, especially in economic and urban geography. As has often been noted, most of political geography was passed by in these intellectual upheavals but this is not so for electoral geography. The regular publication of volumes of electoral data neatly organized by electoral areas provided a wealth of material for the new quantitatively orientated geographers (Taylor 1978). Hence the massive rise of electoral studies in geography and the 'disproportionate' effort that electoral geography attracted within political geography. The first part of this section describes this quantitative electoral geography, the second part describes an attempt to co-ordinate this effort in a systems framework and the final parts look beyond these electoral studies to a critique of a global model of liberal democracy that geographers never achieved.

QUANTITATIVE ELECTORAL GEOGRAPHY

There were three aspects of the new quantitative approach which were applied to electoral geography. The most common we can term 'standard statistical analysis' which was widely used to study the *geography of voting*. Within geography there was a growing interest in the role of spatial factors and this is reflected in the theme *geographical influences in elections*. Finally, probability modelling of spatial distributions was employed in studies of the *geography of representation*. This trilogy of electoral geography studies was first identified by McPhail (1971) and subsequently used by Busteed (1975) and Taylor and Johnston (1979). This last source provides a comprehensive 'state of the art' review for the 1970s and in this discussion we summarize the salient features of that study.

1. Geography of voting

The geography of voting follows in the Siegfried tradition in that its purpose is the explanation of particular voting maps. In modern geography of voting studies, however, cartographic comparisons have given way to statistical analysis. It is these studies which have borne the brunt of the criticism of electoral geography. Generally speaking the explanation of a particular voting pattern has become an end in itself with the result that many sound quantitative analyses added up to very little in terms of understanding elections. Taylor and Johnston (1979) attempted to overcome this fundamental deficiency by introducing the work of Stein Rokkan (1970) into electoral geography to provide a framework in which geographies of voting could be interpreted.

Rokkan (1970) argued that there have been four major conflicts in modern Europe which result from the two fundamental processes of modernization, the national revolution emanating from France and the industrial revolution emanating from Britain. Each of these processes produces two potential conflicts. These are subject versus dominant culture and church versus state from the national revolution, and agriculture versus industry and capital versus labour for the industrial revolution. Each conflict may produce a social cleavage within any one country. But each country has a unique history in which these conflicts are played out. Rokkan argues that the particular mixtures of cleavages that occur among European states deriving from these conflicts are reflected today in the variety of political party systems in Europe.

Rokkan (1970) terms this a model of alternative alliances and oppositions. For each European state the nation-building group made alliances with one side or other in these various conflicts forcing the opposition to forge a counter-alliance. Before the full effects of franchise extensions were felt (*c.* 1900) nation-builders in the dominant culture had a choice of secular or religious alliances and agricultural or industrial alliances. According to Rokkan (1970) the choices made in these conflicts have largely determined the great variety of political parties on the centre and right of European politics. After 1900, as franchise reforms became effective, the final capital–labour cleavage came into operation to produce much more uniformity on the left in European politics.

Let us consider some examples of the process Rokkan describes. In Britain the nation-building group allied with a national church and landed interests (the Tories and later Conservatives) against an alliance of dissenters, industrial interests and minority cultures (the Whigs, Radicals and later the Liberals). After 1900 the rise of the Labour Party produced a particular right–centre–left cleavage represented by three political parties whose pattern of support in terms of votes still reflects these historical cleavages. Although the Conservatives have eclipsed the Liberals and taken their 'industrial interest' vote, the latter party remained strong in non-conformist and particularly peripheral zones of Britain. Throughout their decline Liberals maintained MPs from Celtic Britain (Cornwall, central Wales and northern Scotland) when everywhere else rejected their candidates.

A different set of alliances developed in Scandinavian countries. Here the nation-builders allied with national church and urban interests leaving an opposition alliance of periphery, dissenters and landed interests. In Norway the latter formed the 'Old Left' which defeated the King's government alliance in 1882 to usher in a new democracy. After 1900 and the gradual rise of the Labour Party, the Old Left alliance disintegrated so that Norway has inherited a five-party system of Conservatives on the right, Liberal, Agrarian and Christian Peoples Parties from the 'Old Left' and Labour on the left. The cleavages are reflected in this party system as follows:

- Northern periphery (Labour) versus South-east Core (Conservative)

- South-west periphery (Liberal, Christian) versus South-east Core (Conservative)

- Bokmal language (Liberal) versus Nynorsk (Conservative)

- Teetotal (Christian) versus Non-Teetotal (Conservative)

- Dissenters (Christian) versus National Church (Conservative)

- Rural (Agrarian) versus Urban (Conservative)

- Rural workers (Labour) versus Landowners (Agrarian)

- Urban workers (Labour) versus Industrialists (Conservative)

Not all of these cleavages are equally important so that Labour has been the largest single party since it formed its first government in 1936. The major difference with Britain is the separation of the dissenter vote from the Liberals through the Christian People's party and the separation of rural and urban conservative interests in the Agrarian and Conservative parties. Rokkan has illustrated how these cleavages continue to be reflected in the geographical pattern of votes for these five parties (Taylor and Johnston 1979: 172–7).

Rokkan identifies eight different patterns of nation-building alliances and opposition counter-alliances all of which are reflected in at least one Western European state today. This particular model summarizes European history and is not, therefore, generally applicable outside Europe. Nevertheless the process of modernization that Rokkan describes has spread beyond Europe and similar cleavages can be identified in non-European countries. This is further explored in Taylor and Johnston (1979: 196–206).

It is the core–periphery cleavage which has attracted most geographical research attention as might be expected. Even in the longest established nation-states political mobilization may not be complete as we have seen in the discussion of the resurgence of national separatism in Chapter 5. Models incorporating a core–periphery dimension such as Rokkan's imply a lessening of the relevance of location as socioeconomic criteria come to dominate modern politics. Hence to many social scientists recent expressions of separation nationalism were unexpected. But they did not appear out of nothing. In Britain, for instance, Scottish and Welsh nationalism may have only become a significant political force in the late 1960s and 1970s but that does not mean that before then Scottish and Welsh voters all behaved as typical British citizens. Hechter (1975) has shown that sectionalism persisted in British politics throughout both of the two party systems of Conservative–Liberal and Conservative–Labour. Fig. 6.1 shows a small part of his results. Eight elections from 1885 to 1966 were analyzed by counties in terms of predicting the Conservative vote from seven socioeconomic variables. The residuals from each analysis indicate how the vote percentage in a particular county deviates from that expected due to its socioeconomic structure. Positive residuals indicate a pro-Conservative bias and negative residuals an anti-Conservative bias. The average residuals over all eight elections are distributed in Fig. 6.1a, where two distinctive 'tails' are prominent. On the pro-Conservative side there are three overwhelmingly strong counties — the three most Protestant Ulster counties which consistently voted Unionist and hence Conservative in this period. The anti-Conservative tail is larger and includes fourteen counties, all in Celtic Wales and Scotland. The geography of these extreme residuals is shown in Fig. 6.1b, which defines three contiguous sections which have not conformed to normal British voting behaviour. Quite simply, British elections were never completely nationalized and sectionalism persisted to be reactivated in part as 'nationalism' after 1966.

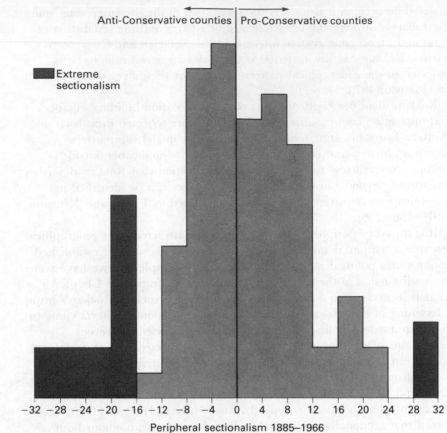

Fig. 6.1   Sectionalism in British elections, 1885–1966 (a) Distribution of residuals
(b) Geography of extreme residuals

2. *Geographical influences in voting*

For some geographers analysis of voting data by areal units is not
considered sufficiently 'spatial' to form a distinctive electoral geography
(Reynolds and Archer 1969). Standard statistical techniques, such as the
regression analysis used by Hechter above, ignore the spatial context of
the areal units which are each treated as separate and independent
observations. For this group of researchers such simple geography of
voting analyses was throwing away the geography! Hence standard
statistical analyses of voting returns were replaced by location models
which emphasized the local context within which voting occurred. In this
way simple descriptive geography *of* voting would be replaced by a more
sophisticated geographical influence *in* voting. This argument fitted in well
with the behavioural school of geography which was emerging in the late

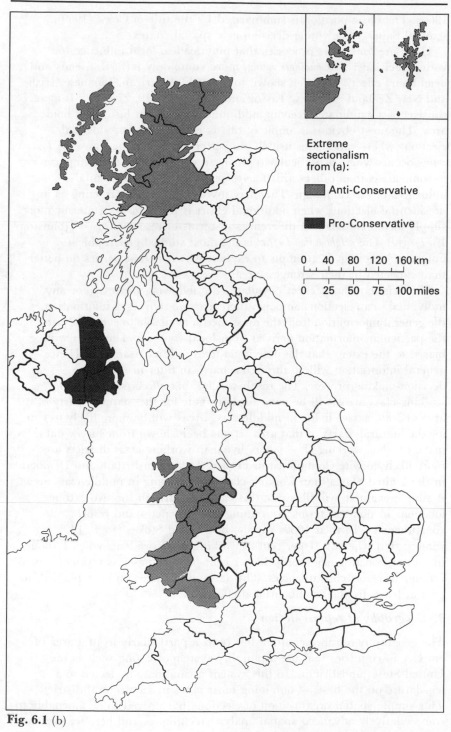

Extreme
sectionalism
from (a):

Anti-Conservative

Pro-Conservative

0   40   80   120   160 km

0   25   50   75   100 miles

Fig. 6.1 (b)

1960s. The basic position is summarized by the title of Cox's (1969) seminal paper: 'The voting decision in a spatial context'.

There are four basic processes that may lead to local influences on voting decisions: (i) *Candidate voting*, more commonly termed 'friends and neighbours effect', has been shown to occur in American, Japanese, Irish and New Zealand elections (Taylor and Johnston 1979: 274–94). It merely consists of a candidate receiving additional votes from his or her home area. The most obvious example of this is in American presidential elections where candidates usually do better in their home state. (ii) *Issue voting* occurs where a particular topic in an election is of more importance to some areas than others. (iii) *Campaign effects* reflect differential influences of the campaign. This may involve particular targeting as in presidential elections when additional effort is put into key states or more simply local campaigning differences in terms of resources used (Johnston 1977). (iv) The *neighbourhood effect* is the most studied geographical influence in voting. It attempts to explain why it is that parties do better than expected in their strongest areas.

The neighbourhood effect postulates the following process. For any individual in an election campaign there are two sources of information: the general information from the mass media available to everybody and the particular information derived from local contacts. The latter will be biased to the extent that the individual lives in a partisan area. Hence general information will go through a partisan filter in the voting decision-making process. The result will be that *all* classes living in working-class areas will be more likely to vote for the 'natural' party of the area and *all* classes living in middle-class areas will be more likely to vote for the 'natural' party of that area. It has been shown from survey data, for instance, that working-class voters living in working-class districts are more likely to vote Communist in France, Labour in Britain and Democrat in the United States than working-class voters living in middle-class areas. A simple example will illustrate this effect. In Britain the two extreme locations in political terms are mining constituencies and resort constituencies. In their 1960s survey, Butler and Stokes (1969: 183) showed that whereas 91 per cent of working-class residents voted Labour in mining constituencies, only 48 per cent of working-class residents voted Labour in resort constituencies. This large difference can be explained, in part at least, by the neighbourhood effect.

3. Geography of representation

The geography of representation has been a particularly fruitful area of enquiry in countries that use a plurality system of voting such as the United States and Britain. In this system a candidate is elected to a legislature on the basis of obtaining most votes in an electoral district. This simple spatial organization of elections has proved to be amenable to some relatively advanced spatial analysis techniques and here we present only the main findings. For further details see Gudgin and Taylor (1979).

The geography of representation has been concerned with the *districting problem*. This states that different patterns of electoral district boundaries will produce different election results in terms of legislative seats *even if the underlying pattern of voting remains the same* (Taylor 1973). Since there are very many different ways of dividing up an area into a given number of electoral districts, it follows that there are many different results even if we hold the actual voting constant. This had led to two types of electoral abuse — reapportionment and gerrymandering. In the former case districts of different populations are designed to favour one party over another. The most common form that this takes is to favour rural areas, and hence parties with rural support, which has been reported for Britain, Japan, South Africa, Australia, New Zealand, France, Chile and Canada (Taylor and Johnston 1979: 360). The most notable case, however, was in the United States before the reapportionment revolution of the 1960s when the courts insisted on equi-populous districts for elections at all levels. However it is gerrymandering which has been the main concern of recent research since it has been shown that election results can be easily manipulated without any need to resort to malapportionment.

Gerrymandering involves drawing the boundaries of electoral districts in such a way that favours one party or candidate over another. There are several strategies which may be adopted. A stacked gerrymander, for instance, is one in which an opposing party's votes are largely concentrated into just one or two districts which they win with a large majority, but which leaves them with few votes and therefore seats elsewhere. The general idea is to make your party's votes as effective as possible in winning seats while wasting the other party's votes either in surpluses in large majorities or else in losing districts. Where the drawing of district boundaries is done by politicians then governments can help perpetuate their power by careful political cartography. There have been many examples of this abuse in US and French elections (Taylor and Johnston 1979: 371–9).

There seems to be a simple solution to this abuse. Why not take it out of the hands of politicians and let a neutral body draw the boundaries? This is, of course, the situation in several countries — Britain, Australia, New Zealand, Canada and South Africa, for example. But in these countries problems remain. Neutral drawing of boundaries does not eliminate the districting problem: it merely removes the intent to discriminate against an opponent. A neutrally drawn districting plan will not necessarily be neutral in effect. To think otherwise is to subscribe to what Dixon (1968) and Taylor and Gudgin (1976a) term the 'myth of non-partisan cartography'. Such districting is merely 'innocently partisan' and employs 'the three monkey's policy — speak no politics, see no politics, hear no politics' (Dixon 1971). This is the most concrete example in political geography of Schattschneider's dictum that 'all organization is bias'.

But what is the nature of the bias instilled in election results even by neutral commissioners? This depends upon the spatial pattern of voters as reflected in the level of segregation of voters supporting different parties. Since party systems are based upon social class, religious and/or ethnic criteria which are also important in defining residential segregation, it follows that we can usually identify areas of support for different parties. In short the spatial distribution of support for particular parties is relatively uneven. When district boundaries are added to this map they produce districts with different mixes of each party's supporters. This process can be modelled to show the possible effects of the procedure. The basic result is that arbitrary (or neutral) drawing of boundaries will inevitably tend to favour the majority party in the area being districted. In Britain, for instance this means that Labour gets a higher proportion of seats than votes in urban and industrial counties whereas Conservatives obtain a higher proportion of seats than votes in suburban and rural counties. Overall the two biases tend to cancel themselves out although the majority party in the country as a whole (either Labour or Conservative depending on the election) will have a disproportionate majority in Parliament. This is sometimes known as the cube-law and results from the particular mix of social segregation and scale of constituency underlying the spatial organization of elections in Britain (Taylor and Johnston 1979: 392–6).

If partisan districting (gerrymandering) and non-partisan districting (innocent gerrymandering) are unsatisfactory why not employ bi-partisan districting where parties agree between them on the district boundaries? This solution has become quite popular in the United States where both informal and formal bi-partisan commissions have been created so that bi-partisan districting has been widespread since the reapportionment revolution (Tufte 1973). The problem is that such districting omits one important interest from the negotiations, namely that of the voter. Bi-partisan districting tends to produce sets of safe districts for each party. This means that there are few marginal seats where voters may effectively cause a seat to change hands. Bi-partisan districting takes the uncertainty out of elections! The classic case of this occurred in the 1974 congressional election in the immediate aftermath of the Watergate scandal. This hurt the Republican party in the polling booths but not so much in Congress since the existence of a relatively large number of safe Republican seats insulated the party from the worst effects of its unpopularity (Taylor and Johnston 1979: 406–7). Since bi-partisan districting lessens the influence of voters on election results it is sometimes referred to as bi-partisan gerrymandering (Mayhew 1971). This is a final confirmation that in the geography of representation all organization is bias.

A SYSTEMS MODEL OF ELECTORAL GEOGRAPHY

The organization of quantitative electoral geography is in many ways unsatisfactory. Two problems stand out. First the subject matter consists of three distinct areas of interest with little cross-reference. Second the subject matter is not integrated into the mainstream of political geography. To be sure examples of both linkages can be found — the relation between geography of representation and the segregation in geographies of voting, and the relation between geography of voting in peripheries and more general core—periphery models in political geography, for example — but such links have been no more than perfunctory and undeveloped. For all the research effort of the 1970s electoral geography had become an uncoordinated and isolated sub-discipline.

The way out of this impasse was not for more empirical research but for a new synthetic framework to integrate these various themes. Such an approach was readily available in systems analysis which had been around in political geography for more than a decade without making any important impact. Although text books (for example, Bergman 1975, Muir 1981) paid lip service to systems thinking, this did not go as far as actually influencing the presentation of most of their political geography (Burnett and Taylor 1981). The simplest model employed was Easton's (1965) political system which could be reduced to just four elements — input, throughput, output plus feed back. Such a framework seems to fit electoral geography — which is, after all, commonly thought of as dealing with electoral *systems*. Johnston (1979) attempted to use this approach to integrate studies of elections with administrative *systems* but no satisfactory overall framework was produced.

1. Input, throughput and output

The most explicit use of systems thinking in electoral geography is Taylor's (1978) use of systems concepts to order his discussion in a review of electoral geography (Fig. 6.2). Geography of voting and geographical influences in voting become the input to the system. Geography of representation becomes the throughput leaving the geographical effects of the resulting legislature/executive as the output of the system. Three implications of this reordering of the literature were identified. First, electoral geography was given a purpose and focus beyond the elections

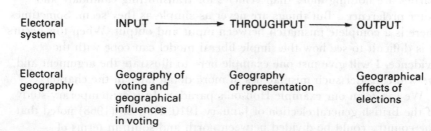

Fig. 6.2 A systems model applied to electoral geography

themselves. Second, the current emphasis on one part of the system — the input — seemed excessive in comparison with the other parts. Third, in contrast, the massive neglect of the output was highlighted. This was the reason electoral geography seemed to have no clear direction. By treating elections as an end in themselves, the actual purpose of election — the producing of legislatures and governments — had been largely forgotten. Hence the systems approach pointed towards a redirection of electoral geography beyond input and throughput.

Johnston (1980b) has taken the argument one stage further and located electoral geography as part of a systems-orientated political geography. Feedback loops between input and output round off the system and integrate electoral and political processes. This is clearly illustrated by American pork-barrel politics whereby politicians ensure the area they represent is well treated by government and they expect, in return, the gratitude of citizens to be expressed in their votes. In the US Congress, for instance, representatives and senators try to obtain places on spending committees that affect policies most relevant to their own constituents' interests. If they can achieve such committee positions, especially chairmanships, then they can usually benefit the district or state they represent. Although this process is difficult to substantiate statistically (Johnston 1982) there is no doubt that it is an important element of American politics. Although less recognized, the same process will occur in other countries such as Britain, where there are other explicitly geographical government effects such as in regional and inner city policy.

2. Critique: liberal assumptions

While providing a solution to the problems of electoral geography enumerated at the beginning of this discussion, the systems approach has proved to be more important for what it reveals rather than what it solves. Quite simply the systems approach has opened up a real Pandora's box. The assumptions upon which electoral geography has been built are laid bare. They turn out to be the classic liberal assumptions of the twentieth-century core states: a receptive government responds to an electorate that articulates its demands through its representatives. All of a sudden, conflicts have disappeared, history is forgotten and political parties are nothing more than vehicles for transmitting candidate and voter preferences. But things are never as simple as they seem. Sometimes there is a complete mismatch between input and output. When this occurs it is difficult to see how the simple liberal model can cope with the evidence. I will give just one example here to illustrate the argument and we will consider such mismatches in more detail later in the chapter.

We can term our example Hobson's paradox. In a contemporary study of the British general election of January 1910, Hobson (1968) noted that the country could be divided between north and south in terms of economic interests. The industrial north he termed 'Producer's England'

and the residential south became 'Consumer's England'. This division was reflected heavily in the voting returns with the Liberals polling strong in the north and the Conservatives likewise in the south. The interesting point, however, is that this voting pattern is inconsistent with each region's economic interests. Both parties inherited nineteenth-century traditions based upon the old urban−rural cleavage so that Liberals maintained their free-trade stance and Conservatives campaigned on a policy of tariff reform (protectionism). The paradox is that Consumer's England voted for protection and hence increased prices whereas Producer's England voted for free trade exposing its industries to American and German competition. We will not resolve this paradox here — it is difficult to see how the systems approach can cope with it beyond designating it as an historical anomaly. We will provide other paradoxes below to show that such 'anomalies' are indeed quite common.

The reason why electoral geography can get into such a muddle is that its liberal assumptions are interpreted as self-evident and innately proper. The liberal democracy model upon which it is based is a normative argument which regards itself as the rational and correct culmination of the western political tradition. But if it is so good why has the 'West' had so much trouble transplanting its parliamentary ideals to the periphery? The popular will as expressed in elections may produce changes in government in core countries but elsewhere several other procedures can be found. For example, in Fig. 6.3 all 'irregular executive transfers' as identified by Taylor and Hudson (1971: 150−3) for the period 1948−67 are plotted. Taylor and Hudson define these transfers as a change of government accomplished outside the conventional legal procedures in effect at the time of the change, and with actual or threatened violence. Their period of study covers the post-Second World War economic boom

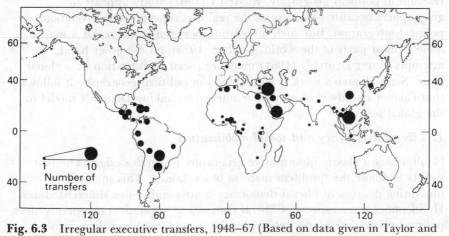

Fig. 6.3 Irregular executive transfers, 1948−67 (Based on data given in Taylor and Hudson 1971)

in the world-economy but this did not prevent 147 of these irregular transfers occurring. Only one occurred in the core — de Gaulle's return to power in France in 1958 — and there are only two other cases in Europe, in Czechoslovakia in 1948 and Greece in 1967. The remaining 144 cases are in Latin America, Africa and Asia. This is a classic case of a periphery political process which is almost entirely missing in the core. Electoral geography should no longer treat elections as an ideal; they should be seen realistically as just one of several means of choosing governments, and one with an extreme geographical bias.

The only political geographer to comment on the relative lack of liberal democracy in the periphery is Prescott (1969: 378), but he treats it merely as a data problem which prevents 'profitable geographical analysis'. Clearly the *geography* of elections as the global pattern of a particular government-creating institution is a topic sorely missing from quantitative electoral geography. Fortunately it is not a theme neglected by political scientists. Given our world-systems approach it is important that we consider global scale analyses of liberal democracy as a prelude to our own interpretation. We present one such study whose methodology is entirely consistent with quantitative approaches in modern geography.

COULTER'S GLOBAL MODEL OF LIBERAL DEMOCRACY

A major contribution of political science to the rise of modern quantitative social science was the production of large scale data sets covering almost all countries in the world (for example, Banks and Textor 1963; Russett *et al.* 1963). This allowed researchers to carry out comparative political studies on a scale never previously achieved. The comparative politics study most well-known to political geographers is Russett (1967), but in many ways Coulter's (1975) study of liberal democracy is much more relevant to political geography. Russett's (1967) study appeals to geographers because of its use of the regional concept and its relation to political integration. But such integration between states is not a major issue in most parts of the world. Coulter (1975), on the other hand, attempts to test Deutch's (1961) model of social mobilization at a global scale. Since Deutch's work is widely used in political geography it follows that Coulter's study is of particular interest in linking Deutch's model to the global scale.

1. Liberal democracy and social mobilization

Coulter uses a classic quantitative geography research design. The first step is to define the 'problem map' to be explained. This involves measuring degrees of liberal democracy across eighty-five different states. He identifies three aspects of liberal democracy — political competitiveness, political participation and public liberties — and combines them into a single index (Coulter 1975: 1–3). Multi-party elections, voter participation and freedom of group oppositions are all elements of this index so that it effectively measures the variations in the degree of importance of elections in determining governments. Variations in liberal democracy for the period 1946–66 are shown in Fig. 6.4 which can be interpreted as the obverse of Fig. 6.3.

In defining the variables to explain this map he keeps very close to Deutch's ideas on social mobilization and democracy. Deutch (1961) postulates the mobilization of people out of traditional patterns of life and into new values and behaviours. This occurs to the extent that a population is urbanized, is literate, is exposed to mass media, is employed in non-primary occupations and is relatively affluent. Coulter (1975), therefore, defines five sets of variables to produce indices of urbanization, education, communication, industrialization and economic development. These are measured both as levels for 1960 and as rates of change for 1946–66.

The global model of liberal democracy is a multiple regression analysis with liberal democracy as dependent and the five aspects of social mobilization as independent variables. The results are reasonably good, with economic development being the best explanation of liberal democracy followed by the communication index. However, these are not really separate explanations since they are very highly correlated (r = +0.94). Nevertheless Coulter (1975) has shown that liberal democracy can be statistically accounted for, in large measure, by the indices of social mobilization.

2. Two interpretations of a relationship

Coulter's results are summarized in Fig. 6.5a which shows the basic trend line whereby an increase in social mobilization is associated with an

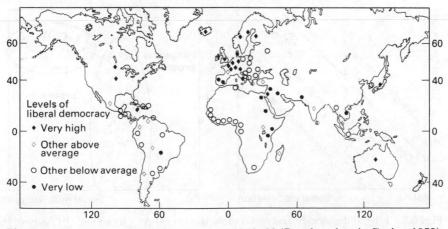

Fig. 6.4 World map of liberal democracy, 1946–66 (Based on data in Coulter 1975)

increase in liberal democracy. Also shown on this diagram is Coulter's interpretation of his results. All countries which lie within one standard error of the trend line are termed optimally democratized. By this he means that the level of liberal democracy in these countries is about as high as would be expected on the basis of their social mobilization. By using the term optimal he implies that politics in these countries is correctly adjusted to their social situation. Among this group we find all the Western European states as we might expect, but Haiti and South Africa are also designated optimally democratized. Countries which lie below the optimally democratized band in Fig. 6.5a are designated under-democratized indicating a lower level of liberal democracy than expected on the basis of social mobilization. Such countries include Spain and Portugal and so we might be tempted to argue that the democratic revolutions in these two countries after 1966 represent a move to conform with Deutch's model of political development. Countries lying above the middle band are designated over-democratized since they have 'more' liberal democracy than their social mobilization would warrant. These include Greece, Uganda and Chile and we may interpret moves against liberal democracy after 1966 by the Greek colonels, Idi Amin and General Pinochet as similarly contributing to their country's conforming to Deutch's model.

Perhaps the most surprising result of this analysis is that Coulter (1975) finds the Soviet Union to be optimally democratized and the United States to be under-democratized! This is counter to our expectations although it does not mean that the USSR is more liberal than the USA but simply that, relative to their respective levels of social mobilization, the USSR scores higher on liberal democracy. This result must make us wonder about the model, however. Either the measurements are

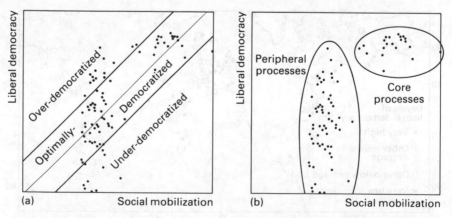

Fig. 6.5 Liberal democracy and social mobilization (a) As a trend line (b) As two clusters

unsatisfactory or else the structure of the model is incorrect. We will argue here that both are at fault. In Fig. 6.5b the same scatter of points is presented in a completely different way. Instead of concentrating on a trend line we identify two clusters of points, one defined by a vertical oval and the other by a horizontal oval. They represent separate, non-overlapping levels of social mobilization. But as we have seen, the most important component of social mobilization is economic development. We shall, therefore, interpret these two distinct levels of 'social mobilization' as representing economic core and periphery processes. Now the scatter of points begins to make some sense. *All* core countries experience liberal democracy. In peripheral countries there is a wide range of political systems showing many different levels of liberal democracy. This will depend upon the nature of the peripheral state, as discussed in Chapter 4.

This interpretation makes much more sense than Coulter's global model. It is entirely consistent with our world-systems framework in its emphasis upon two different sets of processes operating in the world-economy. Once again a world-systems interpretation has been found to be superior to a developmental one, in this case one that sees countries on an 'optimal' ladder of political development. Quite simply politics do not develop separately country-by-country but are all part of a larger unfolding system of political-economy.

A WORLD-SYSTEMS INTERPRETATION OF ELECTIONS

Of all modern social institutions elections would seem to be a set of activities that have to be understood at the scale of the individual state. Elections occur separately on a country-by-country basis and are strictly organized within one state at a time. The geography of elections, therefore, presents a particular challenge within political geography to the world-systems approach and its one society assumption. Surely here we have a case where we need a multiple-society view of the world to make sense of 'national elections'.

In fact it is relatively easy to show that the activities surrounding elections are in no way insulated from the world-economy. The remainder of this chapter is an illustration of this point. For the moment we can use the example of party labels to show how trans-state processes are directly implicated in national elections. From the period when elections moved beyond the stage of confirming local elites in power, political parties have come to dominate electoral activities. Most parties represent a set of ideas which will be linked to a political ideology however loosely conceived. Hence the plethora of Labour parties and Liberal parties, Christian Democrats and Conservatives, Communist and Social Democratic parties, etc. Every one of these parties adheres to a set of ideas that are in no sense unique to that party. Particular interpretations of these general ideas within different countries will inevitably vary, but no parties are automonous of the political world beyond their country's border. Perhaps an extreme example will help fix ideas. The power of English liberalism at the time of British hegemony is reflected in this statement by a nineteenth century Brazilian liberal politician:

> When I enter the Chamber (of Deputies) I am entirely under the influence of English liberalism, as if I were working under orders of Gladstone . . . I am an English liberal . . . in the Brazilian Parliament. (Smith 1981: 34)

As usual, hegemonic processes give us a limiting case but in general we can conclude that all electoral politics occurs within the overall political processes of the world-economy.

A world-systems approach to electoral geography has two tasks to fulfil. First, there is the need to understand the variations in the use and meaning of elections in different zones of the world-economy. We consider this topic in the remainder of this section. Second, electoral activities within states remain the prime concern of our electoral geography and make up the remainder of the chapter.

1. Liberal democracy and social democracy

The idea of liberal democracy is an even more recent phenomenon in the world-economy than nationalism. For most of the nineteenth century, for instance, liberals faced what they saw as the dilemma of democracy. A fully democratized state represented 'the great fear' that the lower classes would take control of the state and use it to attack property and privilege (Arblaster 1984). This 'liberals versus democracy' phase is the very antithesis of liberal democracy and is often forgotten in simple developmental theories about democracy. These evolutionary arguments were a product of the optimistic era of social science in the post-1945 period when liberal democracy was viewed as the 'natural' result of political progress. But as late as 1939 about half of the European liberal democracies of the 1950s had been under authoritarian rule. This was a time when pessimism about democracy reigned. We have to transcend these phases of pessimism and optimism about liberal democracy. What they tell us in world-systems terms is that liberal democracy is concentrated in time as well as place — in the core zone after 1945. But to understand this world-system location we have to return to the nineteenth century.

In Chapter 5 we concentrated on one particular problem confronting politicians in the nineteenth century: the national question. This was in reality just one of many new political questions that were competing to join the political agenda at this time. Three important questions relate to the emergence of liberal democracy. First, there was the constitutional problem posed by the liberals. They advocated the replacement of arbitrary power by constitutional checks and balances. Second, there was the political question posed by the democrats. They argued that the people as a whole should wield power in the new liberal constitutions. Third, there was the social question posed by the socialists. They asked how the new elected governments were going to deal with the new urban poverty. The answer to the first two questions was the liberal democratic state; the answer to the latter two questions was the social democratic state. We shall consider each in turn before we describe their crucial historical coalescence after 1945.

We shall interpret liberal democracy as much more than a label for a party or policy; it is a type of state. Liberal democratic states have three basic properties. First, pluralistic elections are regularly held in which there is competition between two or more parties to form the government. Second, all adult citizens are entitled to vote in these elections. Third, there are political freedoms that allow all citizens to freely associate and express their political opinions. These properties are found with only minor blemishes in all core countries at the present time. In addition these states exhibit a further important property — political stability. Since 1945 countries in the core have experienced continual liberal democracy. Hence they are liberal democratic *states*. They can be distinguished from states that have had liberal democratic interludes alternating with illiberal regimes. These more unstable states are typical of much of the world beyond the core. Analyses, such as that by Coulter (1975) reported above, confuse these two categories. It is central to any world-systems analysis to distinguish between the liberal democratic state and liberal democratic interludes in other states.

In order to understand the space and time concentration of the liberal democratic state we need to consider social democracy. Again we shall interpret this politics to represent more than a party or a policy; it is a type of state. Social democratic states have three basic properties. First, the state takes responsibility for the basic welfare of its citizens so that a wide range of social services and supports are provided. Second, there is a political consensus among all major party competitors for government that this historically large welfare expenditure is both necessary and proper. Third, the welfare is paid for through progressive taxation that involves the state redistributing income. These properties are found in all core countries to different degrees at the present time ranging from New Deal and Great Society type programmes in the United States to the more redistributive socialism of Sweden. Some of the origins of this type of state are to be found in the social imperialism processes discussed in Chapter 3. Whatever the means, however, by the 1940s 'welfare states' were being created throughout the core and they have remained as a typical characteristic of core political processes.

The three political problems from the nineteenth century have generated two forms of state in the mid twentieth century. And, of course, it is not a coincidence that these forms of state have coalesced: all liberal democracies today are social democracies. We might say that we are looking at the same state from two different angles.

From a world-systems perspective this 'liberal-social-democratic' state is the result of two processes — one economic and one political. First, the world-economy location in the core during the fourth Kondratieff cycle enabled this small number of countries to develop a politics of redistribution that was not possible in states at other times and in other places. This means that these states were rich enough to have meaningful competition between parties on the distribution of the national 'cake', where all citizens could potentially benefit. Elections matter; the question of 'who gets what' encompasses all strata. Second, in the emerging Cold War geopolitical world order, the 'liberal-social-democratic' form of state is easily the most preferable for providing an alternative 'social progressive' politics to communism. Hence the new politics of redistribution was encouraged by the United States because it provided a bulwark against communism especially in Western Europe. But notice that the ideological concept of 'free world', first coined to describe non-communist Europe, has not transferred easily to areas beyond the core.

2. Corollary for a 'Free World'

The above argument leads on to an important theoretical corollary. Since the world-economy is inherently polarized the political benefits of liberal and social democracy can never be wholly transferred to the periphery. Hence the ideal of the 'liberal-social-democratic' state that is offered to these countries is beyond their reach. But this is the only modern form in which liberal democracy has survived. Why should the vast majority of a state's people participate in an election if there is little or no politics of redistribution? This means that the simple call for 'a return to democracy' in poor countries is also not a sustainable goal. Elections turn out to be mini-civil wars with campaign deaths counted as well as votes. In short, with or without a communist threat, there can be no 'free world' in the liberal democratic sense. This conclusion has profound implications for our geography of elections.

3. Electoral geography contrasts between core and periphery

Our theory implies that elections will be substantially different in different zones of the world-economy. This will be reflected in contrasting electoral geographies. Consider the situation in the core, for instance. A viable politics of redistribution allows parties to build stable support bases as they implement policies that favour their supporters. The process that Rokkan (1970) has described for Europe has produced a stable pattern of votes based on social cleavages, for instance. This is translated into a stable geography of voting because social groups are geographically segregated. In Britain, for instance, Labour does better in working class districts and the Conservatives obtain more support from middle-class districts. In contrast, in non-core areas without a viable politics of redistribution, the basic mechanism for keeping voter loyalty is missing. A party is far less able to reward the mass of its supporters and sustain its votes. Hence we expect less stable bases for party support which will be reflected in unstable geographies of voting. We can test this basic hypothesis with a simple empirical analysis of contrasting geographies of election.

The degree of geographical stability of a party's vote can be measured by factor analyzing the geographical pattern of the vote over a series of elections. If the pattern is exactly the same in every election the first factor in the analysis will account for 100 per cent of the variance. The less geographically stable the vote over time the further the first factor will be from the 100 per cent limit. Hence the 'importance' of the first factor provides a sort of percentage geographical stability score. Such measures are reported from the major parties of ten countries in Table 6.1 covering elections between 1950 and 1980.

The countries in Table 6.1 are divided between seven core states and three periphery states to highlight the differences in the electoral politics of the two zones. In all the European core countries the geographical stability in the post-1945 period is very high. In Rokkan's (1970) terms the major parties in these countries are able to successfully 'renew their clienteles' over time. In contrast, in the three periphery states the degree of clientele renewal is very low. Jamaica seems to come closest to a level geographical stability consistent with a viable politics of redistribution but even in this case the percentage levels are well below European states with their more fully developed politics of redistribution. What this means is that in these periphery states the geographical pattern of support changes appreciably from one election to the next. Parties are unable to maintain the support of those who have supported them in the past. In short, there seems to be a very different political process going on. Even though the

Table 6.1 Geographical stability of voting patterns *c.* 1950–1980 by major parties in selected countries

Core Countries		Periphery Countries	
Italy	95	Jamaica	59
Belgium	94	Ghana	35
Netherlands	94	India	33
Britain	93		
West Germany	88		
Denmark	86		
France	83		

Source: derived from data in Johnston *et al* (1987). For all countries except Ghana and India the scores for stability are the average for the two main parties in the country. For Ghana the scores are for the pro-Nkrumah party at each election and for India the Congress Party.

Jamaican, Ghanaian and Indian elections upon which this analysis is based may be as fair and open as the European elections, this fundamentally different electoral geography is indicative of something other than a 'liberal-social-democratic' state.

We must conclude, therefore, that in order to study elections world-wide we will need to bear in mind the very different politics resulting from huge differences in material well-being between countries in the core and in the periphery. In the next section we deal with electoral geography in the core and in the final section we consider the role of elections in the far harsher politics of the periphery.

LIBERAL DEMOCRACY IN THE CORE

In traditional electoral geography political parties have been viewed as either reflections of social cleavages (Taylor and Johnston 1979) or simple vote-buying mechanisms (Johnston 1979). Parties may carry out either or both of these roles but they are much more than this. The concept conspicuous by its absence in such analysis is power. The main purpose of political parties is to gain power — to take control of a state apparatus. By adding power to our analysis we can go beyond the linear-systems model described above and create an alternative and more critical model. This is described in the first part of this section. We then apply the model to the making of liberal democracy in the core. We concentrate on the specific relations between parties and governments and the dynamic nature of the capitalist world-economy.

THE DIALECTICS OF ELECTORAL GEOGRAPHY

The source of power for any political party is two-fold. First, it has the opportunity to set or at least influence the political agenda. Second, it has the opportunity to appeal for support among the population. These two activities are closely related, of course, since success or failure in one will likely produce success or failure in the other. For instance, the demise of the Liberal Party in Britain in the first half of this century was the result of its failure to continue to dominate the political agenda as it had in the nineteenth century with a resulting loss of popular support. It was quite literally being seen as irrelevant to the needs of many newly enfranchised voters. The Labour Party, on the other hand, was much more successful in producing a new agenda with which it was able to capture much former Liberal support as well as new voters. Eventually Labour replaced the Liberal Party as a party of government. A significant transfer of power had taken place.

From the point of view of the state these two sources of party power are highly functional. First parties organize the politics of the state and then they mobilize the population behind that politics. These are major political achievements for successful parties.

1. Organization and mobilization

A competitive party system depends upon opposition groups being perceived as alternative governments rather than as threats to the state. From the nineteenth century onwards state-building groups in core countries and some peripheral countries have come to accept this position so that elections become the means of selecting governments. In the United States this fundamental position was reached in the second party system of Democrats versus Whigs which developed in the 1830s. In the first party system a generation earlier each party fought elections with the view of eliminating their rivals from the political scene — eventually the Democrat-Republicans succeeded in reducing the Federalists to political impotence. In contrast the Democrats and Whigs fought elections merely with a view to securing the presidency for their candidate (Archer and Taylor 1981: 54—61). The defeat of President Carter in 1980 was the nineteenth transfer of executive power in the USA by election.

This transfer of government office is not as open as the above discussion implies. Government formation is not a free-for-all but is a carefully controlled process. And this is where parties come in. In many countries there is a duopoly of power to form governments. In the United States, for instance, *all* presidents since the Civil War have been the nominees of the Republican or Democratic Parties. In Britain, Conservative and Liberal Parties until the 1920s, and then Conservative and Labour parties, have had a similar duopoly of power. Even in multi-party systems there remain severe constraints on voter choice with relatively few effective votes available. But this is the whole point of a party system. From the vast range of positions on a large number of topics, voters are asked to support just one of a limited number of 'manifestos' or 'platforms'. This is what Schattschneider (1960: 59) terms 'the great act of organization' with political alternatives reduced 'to the extreme limit of simplification'. The power of parties is simply that electors can vote for or against particular party candidates but they cannot vote for or against a party system (Jahnige 1971: 473).

Electoral politics as constrained by political parties is, therefore, an important control mechanism in liberal democracies. The actual organization operating at any particular election, however, is not normally designed for that election. As we have seen, parties and party systems are the product of the specific histories of their countries. The manipulation of the political agenda is not a conspiracy of ruling élites but rather reflects the relative power of different interests in the evolution of a party system.

For Schattschneider (1960) this power over choice enables parties to define the politics of a country. There are an infinite number of potential conflicts in any complex modern society. By controlling alternatives offered to voters parties decide which conflicts are organized into a country's politics and which conflicts are organized out. Hence electoral politics is defined by the party system producing massive constraints on the nature of the political agenda.

In some ways this integrating role of parties is paradoxical. 'Party' comes from the same root as 'part' and indicates a division within a political system. Political parties, therefore, have the second role of accommodating differences within a state. Hence the social conflicts and resulting cleavages that Rokkan identifies do not ultimately pull the state apart but rather become part of the state. Parties can therefore convert even potentially rebellious subjects into mere voters. The rise of Christian Democratic parties throughout Europe, but especially in Italy, represents a victory of the state over the trans-national pretentions of the Catholic Church. Devout Catholics became mobilized into state politics via their church parties. More generally we may term this process the party system's 'great act of mobilization'.

2. The two geographies of elections

The two 'great acts' that parties achieve, organizing the agenda and mobilizing the voters, can be brought together into a single argument by relating them both to the theory of the state developed in Chapter 4. In particular O'Connor's (1973) classification of the necessary functions of every modern state, promotion of capital accumulation and legitimation of the system, are pertinent here. Parties are agents which contribute to both functions with mobilization contributing to legitimation and agenda organization contributing to accumulation. We are now in a position to develop our theory of the state to incorporate political parties.

Every election incorporates two distinct processes. First, there is intra class competition within the dominant class over state tactics for promoting accumulation. Second, there is inter-class conflict over distribution issues. The former will include state relations with the rest of the world-economy, the latter will concentrate on domestic issues. Gamble (1974) terms these two processes the *politics of power* and the *politics of support* respectively. Political parties operate in both these politics by promoting special interests in their policies and mobilizing voters in their campaigns. The activities of the parties in this regard produce *two* electoral geographies, a geography of power and a geography of support. This revised model is shown in Fig. 6.6. This should be compared to the simple systems model of electoral geography (Fig. 6.2). The single linear sequence is replaced by two loops representing the two politics involved in every election.

The most important feature of this model is that the two processes occur as separate geographies. There is no general relationship between them; there are only particular relations for every state depending upon the class relations within the state, the relation of the state to the

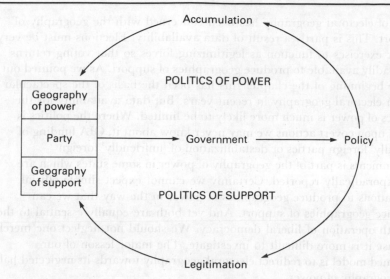

Fig. 6.6 A revised model of electoral geography

world-economy and the history of these two relations. Nevertheless, there are structural tendencies which we can identify (Taylor 1984). The following five statements provide the basic propositions of the model:

1. There is no structural need for the two processes to provide a single consistent basis for a party's actions. In fact the contradictions in the state's function will normally translate into tensions within parties.

2. There is a structural need to mystify the dual role of parties. Without this mystification the power function of the party becomes impossible. This is one of the purposes of liberal theories of the state.

3. The balance between action based on one or other of the two processes will vary in terms of whether a party is in office or opposition. Opposition parties operate more in the politics of support, for instance 'social democratic' parties become notoriously 'socialist' in periods of opposition.

4. The prime basis of action in the politics of power is class whereas there will be a variety of bases for the politics of support. In fact the mystification function is facilitated if the politics of support is *not* based upon class.

5. Parties may operate involuntarily to deflect attention on contradictions away from the state by taking the blame for the situation: a potential crisis of the state becomes a crisis of the party, for example, the Republicans in the USA in the 1930s and Labour in Britain in the 1980s.

Most of electoral geography has been concerned with the geography of support. This is partly a result of data availability. Elections must be very public exercises to function as legitimizing forces so that voting returns are readily available to produce geographies of support. As we pointed out at the beginning of the chapter this has been the basis of the spectacular rise in electoral geography in recent years. But data availability for the politics of power is much more likely to be limited. Where the politics is based upon covert actions we may never know about it. CIA funding of 'friendly' foreign parties or destabilization of 'unfriendly' foreign governments is part of the geography of power in some states which are only sporadically reported. Certainly we cannot expect simple official tabulations to produce geographies of power in the way that we can produce geographies of support. And yet both are equally essential to the smooth operation of liberal democracy. We should not neglect one merely because it is more difficult to investigate. The major lesson of our reformed model is to redirect electoral geography towards its neglected half, the geography of power.

3. Three types of electoral politics

This new model for electoral geography enables us to identify different types of electoral politics. One of the ways we criticized the linear systems model for electoral geography was to show that it could not account for Hobson's paradox. How does our revised model do? In our new interpretation the paradox is simply explicable in terms of two electoral geographies. The geography of power is represented by the contrast between Producer's England and Consumer's England. These represent two basic economic interests that were organized onto the political agenda through Liberal support for free trade and Conservative support for protectionism. The geography of support is represented by the voting map of Conservative strength in rural areas and the South and Liberal and Labour strength in urban-industrial areas and the North. This represents the mobilization of many new voters along a growing class cleavage. The paradox results from the fact that the geography of power is the very opposite of the geography of support. We will call this situation *contradictory electoral politics*.

In Fig. 6.7 we have tried to show this politics in simple abstract form. The circles representing the politics of support are standard cleavage diagrams which divide the electorate into two opposing sets of party supporters. Similarly the circles representing the politics of power divide the electorate into two but this time in terms of two sets of opposing economic interests promoted by the parties. Contradictory politics such as Hobson's paradox occur when the two divisions for one party are opposed to one another.

As can be seen from Fig. 6.7 this is just one of three types of politics that can be identified from this analysis. The opposite of contradictory

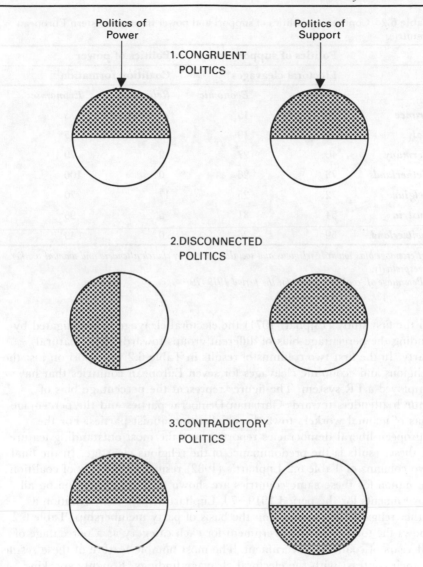

Fig. 6.7 Three types of electoral politics

politics are *congruent electoral politics* where power and support basically coincide. This is the ideal of liberal democracy that is represented by the lincar systems model (Fig. 6.2).

Between these two opposites we can find *disconnected electoral politics* where the basis of power and support are unrelated one to another. This commonly occurs under multi-party systems operating through proportional representation laws. We can illustrate this by employing the results of two surveys of liberal democracies carried out by Arend Lijphart.

Table 6.2　Contrasting politics of support and power in seven western European countries

	Politics of support		Politics of power	
	Electoral cleavages*		Coalition formation†	
	Religious	*Economic*	*Religious*	*Economic*
France	59	15	25	75
Italy	51	19	0	75
Germany	40	27	12	70
Netherlands	73	26	0	100
Belgium	72	25	17	70
Austria	54	31	5	95
Switzerland	59	26	0	49

* *Percentage bias towards religious and socialist parties by church attenders and manual workers respectively.*
† *Percentage of 'coalition years' for the period 1919–79.*

In the first study (Lijphart 1971) the electoral cleavage is investigated by finding the percentage bias of different groups towards their 'natural' party. In the first two columns of results in Table 6.2 we report on just the religious and economic cleavages for seven European countries that have employed a PR system. The figures represent the percentage bias of church attenders towards Christian Democrat parties and the percentage bias of manual workers towards socialist/communist parties. For the European liberal democracies reported here the most outstanding feature of these results is the predominance of the religious cleavage. In the final two columns of Table 6.2 Lijphart's (1982) results for a study of coalition formation for these same countries are shown. Using information on all governments for the period 1919–79, Lijphart defines each coalition as either religious or economic on the basis of party membership. Table 6.2 shows the total years of government for each category as a percentage of all years of coalition government. The most notable feature of these results is their contrast with the electoral cleavage findings. Roughly speaking religion is three times as important as the economic cleavage in voting patterns whereas economic criteria are eight times as important as religion in the process of forming governments. This is the classic case of mobilizing voters on cultural grounds while forming governments around economic coalitions to produce a disconnected politics.

THE MAKING OF LIBERAL DEMOCRACIES

With three types of electoral politics we are in a far better position to understand the making of liberal democracies than we were with the one electoral politics underlying the linear systems model. In the latter case an evolutionary history is typically produced whereby liberal democracy is a 'natural' outcome of democratizing trends over the last century or so. But from our previous introduction to a world-systems analysis of elections we know that there was no such smooth transition to democracy. Therborn (1977) in particular has recorded the extent of the political opposition to democracy in all countries that are now liberal democracies and promote democracy world-wide. Our simple typology of three types of electoral politics enables us to address both the 'dilemma of democracy' in the nineteenth century and the 'triumph of democracy' in the twentieth century.

1. The development of political parties

Liberal democracies have been created by political parties. It is hard to conceive of a fully operating liberal democracy that does not depend on parties to mobilize and organize. These two tasks have their origins in the development of two very different sorts of parties in the nineteenth century.

The acceptance of legitimate oppositions within states was reflected in the organization of parliamentary factions or 'parties'. These loose groupings of politicians represented different special interests within the dominant class. In the mid nineteenth century a distinction began to be drawn between factions serving particular interests and parties organized by principles and representing the public interest from different perspectives. In Britain Whigs and Tories are replaced by Liberals and Conservatives for instance. These parties are originally only organized in parliament and do not constitute modern political parties, according to Duverger (1954). This occurs when these parliamentary parties are forced to mobilize support in the country in the wake of suffrage extensions and competition from new parties. The formation of 'electoral committees' in electoral districts to organize campaigns converts these traditional parties into fully-fledged modern parties. They become what Blondel (1978) terms *cadre parties* since their organization is merely to find supporters and power continues to reside at the centre.

As suffrage reforms began to reach down to the direct producers another sort of political party was created outside parliament. These extra-parliamentary parties had only one source of resources — their members. Hence they were forced to mobilize direct producers into *mass parties*. The most successful were the Socialist parties who in 1889 created the 'Second International' as an alliance of socialist parties from numerous countries. Populist agrarian parties and some Christian parties also developed as mass parties in selected countries or regions.

Hence at the beginning of the twentieth century there were two sorts of parties in most of today's liberal democracies: mass parties emphasizing mobilization and cadre parties emphasizing organization. These very different political institutions based on contrasting mechanisms are a cause of the production of non-congruent politics. Hobson's paradox, for instance, represents a transition from elections organized by cadre parties to a new mass politics: the politics of power still reflected the dominant class divisions of the cadre parties while the politics of support was coming to resemble a class politics. Generally where cadre parties dominate there will be tenuous links between the politics of power and support since the latter provides little or no feedback to party policy. This is illustrated best in US politics before the New Deal which provides two classical examples on non-congruent politics.

2. Non-congruent electoral politics: section and party in the USA before the New Deal

The United States has the longest continual record of competitive elections based upon a broad franchise. As early as 1828 presidential elections were based upon white male suffrage involving millions of voters. Hence while politicians in Europe were worrying about the dilemma of democracy, the United States was practising a politics that incorporated direct producers but without their influence intruding too much on government. It is at this time that the designation of somebody as a 'politician' comes to have a derogatory meaning (Ceaser 1979). This is a direct result of the non-congruent electoral politics that was developed. This highly successful experiment in democracy warrants further investigation.

Here we briefly report on a part of Archer and Taylor's (1981) factor analyses of American presidential elections from 1828 to 1980. Using the percentage vote for all Democratic candidates, Archer and Taylor derive different patterns of party support across states. When several elections show the same pattern these are defined as 'normal votes' in the sense that a tradition of voting has been established. For the analysis of eastern states from 1828 to 1920 two such patterns dominate the analysis and we report on this finding and its relation to our previous discussion.

In Fig. 6.8 we show the strength of these two patterns over time. They clearly represent pre civil war and post civil war normal vote patterns with the first being important from 1836 to 1852 and the second from 1876 onwards. In Fig. 6.9 their respective distributions across states are shown and from this we have derived their respective names — the non-sectional normal vote and the sectional normal vote. The latter represents what was the usual pattern of voting in the United States for much of the twentieth century: solid Democratic south, less solid Democratic 'border states' and a slightly pro-Republican north with Vermont and Michigan particularly so. This is the sectional voting for which America was famous. It contrasts strikingly with what went before. In the non-sectional normal vote pattern strong Democrat states are found both north and south. The distribution seems haphazard, even random. Northerners and southerners supported both Whigs and Democrats with relatively little sectional favour. This is

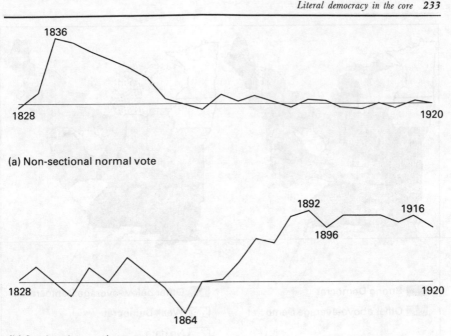

(a) Non-sectional normal vote

(b) Sectional normal vote

Fig. 6.8 Normal vote profiles: USA, 1828–1920 (a) Non-sectional normal vote
(b) Sectional normal vote

best illustrated by identifying the most pro-Whig and pro-Democrat states
of this era. Interestingly enough they turn out to be contiguous — Vermont
and New Hampshire which are as similar a pair of states in social,
economic and ethnic terms as you could expect to find in the period
prior to the US civil war. This is non-sectional voting par excellence.

There are several important aspects of this finding. First political
developmental models which assume a decline in the territorial basis of
voting over time are exposed here. In the USA the extreme sectional
voting *follows* non-sectional voting. It seems that the USA was highly
'integrated' before the civil war. This interpretation is consistent with an
emphasis on the voting pattern but must be laid aside as soon as we
consider the party system. What the non-sectional voting pattern
represents is merely a conglomeration of local alliances which come
together on the national stage to support a selected presidential candidate.
The forums for this national activity are the two political parties,
Democrats and Whigs. This local agglomeration produced 'national'
parties for the only time in American history (McCormick 1967: 109).

There is a paradox here. Just as the country was undergoing the strains
of sectional competition which was to erupt in the civil war, elections show
no sectional bias. This means that the north versus south cleavage was
being kept off the political agenda. Quite simply there was no 'north' party

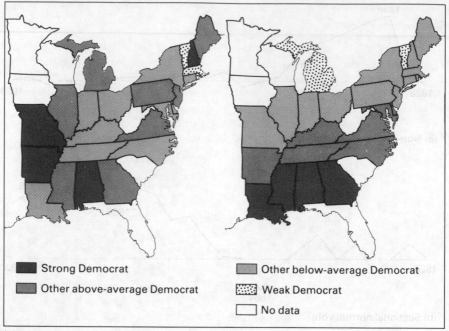

Strong Democrat

Other above-average Democrat

Other below-average Democrat

Weak Democrat

No data

(a) Non-sectional normal vote   (b) Sectional normal vote

Fig. 6.9   Normal vote patterns: USA, 1828–1920 (a) Non-sectional normal vote
(b) Sectional normal vote

or 'south' party to vote for until the 1850s. Hence the tensions developing
in the country were organized off the political agenda by a non-sectional
party system. The parties acted as an integrating force in a politics of
sectional compromise. Van Buren, President from 1836 to 1840, is
usually credited as the architect of this highly successful control of a
political agenda (Archer and Taylor 1981: 81–4). This was party versus
section and, for a generation, party won. It was in Ceasar's (1979: 138)
words 'a complete antidote for sectional prejudices'. This remains a classic
example of electoral politics being diverted from a major issue by
political parties in a disconnected politics.

The system did not survive and in 1856 the Republicans replaced the
Whigs and the Democrats split into northern and southern factions. The
upheavals of the civil war and subsequent reconstruction produced no
normal vote pattern for nearly two decades. By the late 1870s, however, a
new politics was arising based upon the sectional normal vote. This
politics of sectional dominance coincides with the establishment of the
northern section as the economic core of the state. The state's territory
becomes integrated as one large functional region serving the
manufacturing belt. And here we have a second paradox, economic
integration is accompanied by political separation. In effect north and

south become two separate political systems, the former dominated by the Republicans the latter even more so by the Democrats. This arrangement suited the industrial leaders of the country since northern states are able to outvote southern states. The presidency, therefore, becomes virtually a Republican fiefdom with only two Democratic presidents between the civil war and 1932. Hence one party was able to control the political agenda by relegating its opponents to a peripheral region.

What about the electors? What were they voting for while this control was going on? Fortunately historians have attempted to answer this question by using correlation and regression methods on voting and census data. Their findings are fascinating. The major determinants of voting in this period are always cultural variables (McCormick 1974; Kleppner 1979). Hence voters were expressing religious and ethnic identification in elections. And yet in this whole period there are only two 'cultural' policies which reach the political agenda — slavery as a moral issue at the beginning of the period and prohibition at the end. Through the whole of this period the major dividing line between the parties was protection (Republicans) versus free trade (Democrats). Hence while voters were expressing their culture in elections, party élites were competing for economic stakes in terms of US relations to the world-economy. There can be no clearer example of the separation of voters from government by parties in a disconnected politics.

3. Congruent electoral politics in the Cold War era

According to Rokkan (1970) European party systems were 'frozen' into their current structure in the first two decades of the twentieth century. Hence elections today take place between political parties most of which were competing with one another before World War I. But we should not let the similarity in party labels lead us to assume that electoral politics has not changed fundamentally between these two periods. Blondel (1978) has pointed out that the party systems in Europe before World War I were much less stable than they seem in hindsight. The mix of unresponsive cadre parties and mobilizing mass parties was a recipe for conflict rather than consensus. The latter in particular were potentially divisive since they developed political ideologies that were inclusive. Socialist ideology, for instance, looked forward to mobilizing all the working class in a country which would eventually provide the party with a permanent parliamentary majority. There was little room for pluralism here. The most extreme case was in Germany where the Social Democrats seemed to have created an alternative 'class nation'. The question is, therefore, how did this unstable and potent mix of political parties become converted into the stable liberal democracies of today?

We begin to answer this question by returning to the US case again. This country become the major exception to the party development described above since both agrarian (Populist) and socialist mobilizations

failed to produce major political parties to compete for government.
According to Burnham (1967) this is the decisive step where the American
party system diverges from the European experience. Hence US elections
remained competitions between cadre parties well into the twentieth
century. But they were forced to shed their unresponsiveness by the
economic collapse after 1929. With the coming of the New Deal we find
the generation of a new form of party which Blondel (1978) terms a
representative party. In some sense this type of party exists between the cadre
and mass types: these new parties are more responsive than traditional
cadre parties in that they attempt to appeal to the electorate by
representing the public interest but they are not mass parties since they
are not primarily concerned with mobilizing voters to accept a political
ideology. Representative parties are pragmatic and eschew ideology. In the
age of new mass communications, first radio and then TV, political leaders
can appeal to the electorate directly and we enter the world of policy
packaging, image making and the 'selling' of the candidate.

   In Europe between the two wars the cadre and mass parties continued
to exist side by side in an uneasy politics with strained party systems.
After World War II both cadre and mass parties have metamorphosed into
representative parties. For the cadre parties this was a relatively easy
transition as they extended their electoral campaigning to incorporate new
techniques. At the same time the mass parties changed fundamentally.
The old socialist parties have come to rely on pollsters and advertising
agencies just as much as their right wing rivals. Socialist parties now claim
to represent public opinion rather than guide it. Rokkan (1970) terms this
process the 'domestication of socialist parties' and distinguishes between
socialist and communist parties in Western Europe in these terms. But of
course since Rokkan's analysis, the 'Eurocommunist' tendency has
produced new 'respectable' communist parties. We can interpret this as
the final act in the conversion of mobilizing mass parties into
representative parties. The elimination of mass mobilizing parties
represents a sort of 'Americanization' of European party systems.

   This whole process of party transformation is predicated on the
possibility of a social democracy that emerged after World War II and was
able to develop in the boom phase of the fourth Kondratieff cycle. As we
have previously argued, social democracy provided the solution to the old
dilemma of democracy by buying off the lower strata. In the new politics
of redistribution the important element in elections became the
presentation of alternative baskets of public goods. This was a task for
representative parties, not aloof cadre parties or 'ideological' mass parties.
In this situation a broadly congruent politics could emerge around the
question of more or less public goods. This competitive domestic politics
was carried on within a foreign policy consensus. This was important in
the development of a Cold War geopolitical world order. In 1945 some
circles in the US government were unsure of the nature of the socialist

parties that were enjoying electoral success in Europe. They soon realized, however, that they represented the best defence against Soviet-backed communist parties. Hence Socialist Parties such as the British Labour Party were the first to be 'domesticated' and provide a 'safe' politics from the point of view of US hegemony. The British Labour Government played a leading role in forming NATO to bring the United States into Western European defence. Today, of course, even the Italian Communist Party supports the continuation of NATO, which shows how far 'domestication' has reached.

The end result of this process has been the 'liberal-social-democratic' state described above. It is the generally congruent politics of this state that has made the linear-systems model of electoral geography seem so reasonable: the dilemma of democracy is solved and elections appear unproblematic. We have to consider particular case studies in some detail to show that the simple linear model is not a good representation of elections even in conditions of congruent politics.

4. Changing agendas in British politics

Our discussion has brought the concept of power to centre stage in electoral geography. But we must not over-emphasize the power of political parties. For all their dominance of government in liberal democracies, they are still constrained by the operation of the world-economy. Although parties may be powerful within their state's boundary there is no guarantee of power beyond the borders.

The problem for all political parties is that whereas the politics of support is an internal matter within their country, the politics of power inevitably extends beyond the boundary of the state. As we have seen, the world-economy does not develop in a smooth linear fashion but is typified by major booms and recessions. Every time the world-economy moves from an A-phase to a B-phase or vice versa, the constraints and opportunities facing every individual state fundamentally change. Political parties operating within these states have to tailor their policies accordingly. The result is a series of 'new politics' within each state corresponding to the particular reactions of the political parties to the new world circumstances. The recent demise of Keynesian economic management and the return of monetarism as a guide to government policy throughout the world is an important aspect of the new politics of the current recession in all countries.

The most interesting feature of these 'new politics' is that they do not necessarily arise out of elections. Usually there is not an election whereby voters are asked to choose between 'old' and 'new' politics: this is not a matter for the politics of support, it is an issue for the politics of power. For each new politics old assumptions are swept away and new items appear on the political agenda, but all major parties accept the new politics. A new party competition arises *but takes place within the new politics,* being limited to matters of emphasis and degree. Hence the mobilizing powers of the parties are usually able to bring the voters into line with new economic circumstances. It is for this reason that the stability of voting patterns commonly found in electoral geography in core states is not a good index of the changing politics of the state.

Perhaps the best country in which to study this process is Britain. Its long-term economic decline has elicited a variety of political responses. If we consider the period from the First World War we can identify six phases of 'new politics' each developing as consecutive pairs of responses to the A- and B-phases of the world-economy. These are shown in Table 6.3 and we will consider each new politics in turn.

We begin this sequence of politics with the depression following the First World War. The initial reaction is a *politics of crisis*. The old party system of Liberals versus Conservatives crumbles and the new Labour versus Conservative system emerges. But two-party politics does not arrive straight away. Since no party has the 'answer' to the economic problems *every* election leads to the defeat of the governing party, often to be replaced by a weak minority government. This process ceases in 1931. The culmination of the political crisis is the fall of the Labour government and its replacement by a coalition 'National' government confirmed by general election. Labour retreats to the political wilderness as the National government maintains support through the 1935 election. This replaces two-party competition as the electors are mobilized to reduce their economic expectations.

The Second World War sweeps away the assumptions of the 1930s. A new *social democratic consensus* emerges and with the return of a Labour government in 1945 a 'welfare state' is created. The revision of the domestic agenda does not extend to foreign affairs. The combination of funding the welfare state and maintaining a global military presence leads to severe economic cycles — the famous 'stop-go' sequence of British economic performance. The problem becomes acute when the relative

Table 6.3 'New Politics' in Britain since 1918

Period	World-economy	'New' politics	Major events
1918–31	Stagnation B(i)	Politics of crisis I	Rise of Labour Party, National Strike
1931–40	Stagnation B(ii)	Politics of national interest I	Dominance of National Coalition
1940–60	Growth A(i)	Social Democratic Consensus	Establishment of Welfare State
1960–72	Growth A(ii)	Technocratic politics	Application to join EEC
1972–82	Stagnation B(i)	Politics of crisis II	Conflict/accommodation with Unions
1982–	Stagnation B(ii)	Politics of national interest II	South Atlantic War

performance of Britain becomes a political issue. The 'reappraisal of 1960' and the return of a Labour government in 1964 promising 'a white hot technological revolution' usher in a new *technocratic politics*. This involves widespread reform of state institutions to make Britain as competitive as its rivals. Reorganization becomes the key word as local government, the welfare state and other central state departments are 'streamlined' for 'efficiency'. In foreign affairs the retreat from global power to European power is sealed by membership of the European Economic Community — the ultimate technocratic solution to Britain's problems.

With the onset of the current recession it soon became clear that tinkering with the administration of the state was not working. Once again we enter a politics of crisis. Haseler (1976) actually identifies thirty-five events between 1966 and 1975 which he intrepets as signifying the breakdown of the political system. Once again no party is seen as having the answer and we return to electoral defeats for governing parties and even a period of minority government. The party system is under stress with the rise of nationalist parties in Scotland and Wales, increased support for the Liberal Party and finally a split in the Labour Party. All this changes with the rise of a new *politics of national interest* in the 1980s. The Conservative government is returned to power with a large increased majority as voters have learnt to mellow their demands and expectations.

Further details of these new politics can be found in Taylor (1982b). For our purpose here there are just two main points requiring further emphasis. First, the various 'new politics' have not emerged at elections. In 1931 the new political battle lines were drawn before the election. The key example, however, is probably the practice of identifying the new politics of the social democratic consensus with the 1945 Labour victory. This is incorrect. Although the Labour government was responsible for setting up the welfare state, the major policy decisions had been agreed by the Conservative-led wartime coalition government. Hence we can date the emergence of this new politics to 1940 with the creation of the new coalition government. Similarly, technocratic politics were not the result of any one election — the appraisal of 1960 came just *after* a massive government election victory which presumably endorsed past policies! I have dated the emergence of the new politics of crisis in 1972 when the Conservative government gave in to Miners' Union demands and became tarnished by their 'U-turn' image. Finally the South Atlantic War of 1982 produced a nationalistic reaction among voters represented by a turnaround in Conservative government popularity which was then consolidated in the 1983 election. 1982 obviously marks the beginning of the current politics of national interest. Hence in all cases 'new politics' have emerged independently of elections. The politics of power precedes the politics of support.

The second main point is that throughout this period of six new politics there was only one major geography of support. Generally speaking the areas voting Labour and Conservative in the first politics of crisis have continued their political biases right through to the present day: Labour maintains a northern, urban pattern of support with strongholds on the coalfields while Conservatives are the rural and suburban party. Despite electoral swings back and forth between the parties this electoral geography has remained remarkably stable. Even the rise of a centre political alliance in 1983 could not break this geographical mould. The two major political parties may not have been able to counteract Britain's steady decline in the world-economy but they have continued successfully to maintain their support pattern through thick and thin. This fascinating mixture of impotence and strength is the hallmark of political parties of all countries although the balance will differ greatly between core states and periphery states.

ELECTIONS BEYOND THE CORE

In January 1988 the Philippines under President Aquino carried out nation-wide local elections. This involved deploying 156,000 troops in 930 so-called 'election hot spots'. In the event the elections had to be suspended in 10 of the 73 provinces, and in 19 other provinces they had to be placed under the control of special commissions. The final death toll was 103 including 39 candidates. Mrs Aquino was able to claim a 'substantial reduction in blood letting' — in the previous local elections in 1971 under President Marcos, 905 people lost their lives.

What are we to make of such events? The violence of the Philippines poll was by no means untypical. Two months earlier in Haiti 150 people were killed in an election, including 14 voters at a polling station. There is no need to produce a fuller catalogue of electoral violence to make the point that elections beyond the core are qualitatively different political processes from elections in liberal democracies.

This conclusion is hardly surprising given the different historical backgrounds and material circumstances that exist between the liberal democracies and the remainder of the world. Perhaps what is surprising is how often elections are held in such unpromising situations. Even communist states feel the need to legitimate their government with periodic elections albeit with choice limited to one party. Nevertheless this does show the power that the electoral process possesses. Here we will concentrate on only genuinely competitive elections beyond the core. In these Third World countries there have been two very different routes to competitive elections. In most countries elections were a transplanted political process written into constitutions at the time of independence after 1945. Throughout Africa and Asia these constitutions failed to protect this politics and military coups have replaced elections as the most common means of changing government. Where elections do survive they are often traumatic and dangerous events, as we have seen.

In Latin America, however, with its much longer period of independence, the history of elections is very different. For instance, as Wesson (1982: 15) has pointed out:

> In 1929 every major Latin American government was civilian with some reason to claim that it was democratic; it seemed a reasonable assumption that this was the way of ever-improving civilization.

But now we know that this was not to be. Most Latin American countries have experienced military coups that have abruptly stopped this trend towards democracy. The most striking feature, therefore, is that *despite* their contrasting histories both sections of the Third World have generated a similar outcome of fragile democracy and generals commonly becoming politicians. This, of course, provides very strong evidence for materialist explanations of the relative failure of democracy since mass poverty is the one feature shared by all countries in the Third World.

What happened in Latin America after 1929 and in other Third World countries soon after their independence was that they were unable to provide the resources to sustain a viable politics of redistribution. Hence liberal democratic political processes failed because it was not possible to link them with a social democracy to produce a viable liberal-social-democratic state. Without the consensus of the latter the state reverts to a coercive mode of control.

How do parties operate in these circumstances? The first point to make is that party competition in elections is just one of several routes to power. Election campaigns and military campaigns can sometimes merge into a single process. Second, party victory in an election provides access to a state apparatus which gives two important capabilities: opponents can be persecuted and prosecuted through the legitimate agencies of the state and allies can be given access to the spoils of office. This has tended to produce a clientistic type of politics with parties controlled by 'strong men' in the battles for the spoils. Such parties consist of narrow groupings of people who support the 'boss' in return for favours. In some countries the power of these extreme cadre parties has been undermined by new mass parties of a populist variety (Canovan 1981; Mouzelis 1986). Populist parties have been successful in a few countries in bringing the rural and urban masses into a state's political system. But this mobilization could not overcome the impossibility of a large-scale politics of redistribution. It is often the ignominious failure of popularist policies, such as Peronism in Argentina, that has led to military intervention and coercion of the popular forces. In short the rural and urban masses are removed from politics once again.

THE POLITICS OF FAILURE

We can describe the processes outlined above as the politics of failure.

Given the world-system location of these countries they are unable to develop the luxury of a congruent politics. In this situation all governments in the eyes of most of their population turn out to be failures. This produces the instability of government for which the Third World is notorious. The extreme case of the politics of failure is Bolivia which has now experienced more than 200 governments in its less than two hundred years of independence. More generally, where elections continue to be used to produce governments the politics of failure is reflected in a continual turnaround in party fortunes.

1. Democratic musical chairs

Suppose that in the material circumstances beyond the core there is a country that is able to sustain competitive elections over a decade or more. What sort of political system would we expect? Whatever the particular reasons that enable elections to continue, we would predict that given that the material situation produces government 'failure', then every party government would have severe difficulties in being re-elected. In short this is an electoral situation made for opposition parties. Our expectations are, therefore, that one party would rule for one term of office, to be immediately replaced by the opposition party and so on. This process is the opposite of what we see in the USA today, in the Third World it is the incumbents who have the disadvantage and who are voted out of office.

We can observe this process operating in Latin American states in the post-1945 era. Dix (1984) has investigated what he terms 'electoral turnover' in nine states and his figures have been updated by Werz (1987). The one country with a continuous record of competitive elections is Costa Rica. In ten elections between 1948 and 1986 the government has been swept from office on eight occasions. Chile, Venezuela and Ecuador have each had five elections for just one returned government in each case. Dix and Werz find only eleven successful government re-elections out of a total of 43 elections.

The best example of this democratic musical chairs comes from outside Latin America however. Sri Lanka has been governed by elected politicians since independence in 1948. The two party politics that evolved in Sri Lanka was remarkable for its extreme changes in party fortune (Fig. 6.10). The seven parliamentary elections since 1952 have resulted in six changes of government. Subsequently, parliament has agreed a new constitution with a presidential electoral system but the country has drifted into civil war.

2. The geographies of a politics of failure: the case of Ghana

What is the electoral geography of this political instability? This question has been answered in some detail in a case study of Ghana (Osei-Kwame and Taylor 1984). We used a finding from this research in Table 6.11 to show how Ghana as a periphery country had a low level of geographical

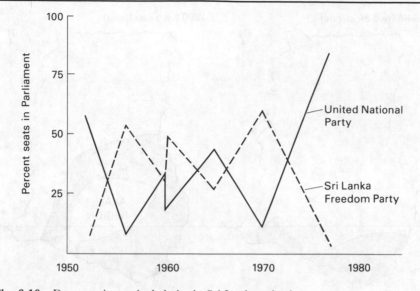

Fig. 6.10 Democratic musical chairs in Sri Lankan elections

stability in its voting patterns. This was based on the analysis of eight
elections between 1954 and 1979 which pitted one group of politicians who
supported the first president Nkrumah against his opponents centred on
his great rival Busia. The party names change over time but these two
political groupings can be easily identified. The pro-Nkrumah group are
the centralists who favoured a 'modernizing' strategy of using cocoa-based
export earnings from the central Akan region to develop modern industry.
Their early emphasis on planning and protectionism meant that they were
sometimes the 'socialists' in the party system. The opposition were
originally federalists who did not favour exploiting agricultural areas for
the benefit of the coastal ports and towns. They have been the free traders,
the 'liberals' in the party system. The analysis of voting returns concentrated
on the pattern of votes for the centralists.

Whereas in core countries of Table 6.1 there has been one major pattern
of votes since World War II, for the periphery countries low geographical
stability means several patterns of votes. In the case of Ghana the eight
elections reveal four distinct patterns. In Fig. 6.11 the changing
geographical bases of support for the centralists is shown. Starting with a
pre-independence pattern along the coast and in the south, by 1960 the
centralists spread their support inland around the Akan region but not as
far as either the northern or eastern boundary. They do reach these
boundaries in subsequent elections but at the expense of their original
support bases. In 1969 the centralists have an extreme south-eastern bias
to their voting map; a decade later this disappears to be replaced by an
extreme northern and south-western bias. Clearly there is little of

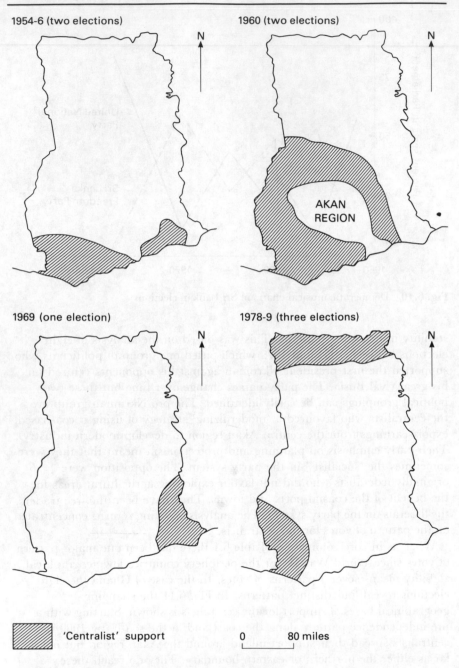

Fig. 6.11   The changing geography of voting in Ghana

Rokkan's (1970) 'renewing of clienteles' here. What is the politics behind this geographical fluidity?

The politics of support in Ghana has been dominated by ethnicity. Nkrumah's Convention People's Party led the drive to independence but never produced a national movement across the country. Its original support was among the 'modernizing' élites of the coastal area and Nkrumah's home region in the south-west. Elsewhere the party was overwhelmingly rejected. In most of the country traditional power élites were successful as either independents or candidates for small regional/ethnic parties. After independence in 1957 Nkrumah's party was able to extend its support further inland but was still firmly resisted in the Akan region (Busia's home area) and the north and east. When Nkrumah was toppled by a coup in 1966, therefore, he had not managed to become a national leader transcending ethnic rivalries.

With the departure of Nkrumah the subsequent pattern of centralist support is wholly ethnic in nature. In 1969, the only time the centralists lose an election, they are pushed back to a south-east core that is the region of origin of their new leader. His demise produces other new leaders in 1978–79 whose northern and south-western origins became yet further new support bases.

We can conclude therefore that Ghana presents a classic case of a disconnected politics. Ethnic geographies of support exist alongside a politics of power that is concerned with alternative ways of managing an economy dependent on cocoa-export revenues. Only the cocoa-growing Akan region is consistent in resisting the centralists. Otherwise different regions will support centralist policies depending on the ethnic origin of the party leader. Hence the Ghanaian political process consists of a cultural geography base that is transformed into different political geographies that provide a capability to produce alternative economic geographies.

INDIA AS 'THE LARGEST LIBERAL DEMOCRACY IN THE WORLD'

The association between political instability and elections is not found in all countries of the Third World. In Mexico, for instance, regular elections over more than half a century have resulted in the same political party being returned to office. I will argue here that these are special cases that warrant specific investigation. In Mexico, for instance, the association of the governing party with the revolution is fundamental to its ability to keep the opposition small and fragmented. Similarly, in India the Congress Party was at the head of the independence movement and has by and large been able to dominate Indian government since 1947. I describe such successful governing parties as *aggregative parties* since they display an ability to aggregate electoral support across a wide spectrum of the electorate. The discussion below focuses on the mechanisms behind this electoral strategy as operated by the Congress Party first in their politics of support and second in their politics of power.

The reason why we concentrate on the Congress Party is because of Blondel's (1978: 55) contention that India 'constitutes the largest liberal democracy in the world'. In our world-systems interpretation of elections India cannot be a liberal democratic state because it does not have the resources for a viable politics of redistribution. But it does have regular free and open elections. If Blondel is correct this would be the exception to prove our world-systems analysis wrong. Hence Indian politics represents a crucial test of our political geography. By concentrating on the electoral geographies of the Congress Party we will show that India has a very different politics from that found in the liberal democracies of the core.

1. Congress geographies of support

The geographical scale, material inequalities and cultural diversity of India provide an immense range of potential social cleavages for political parties to try and organize. It is not surprising therefore that there have been literally hundreds of parties competing in Indian elections. Most have disappeared but Congress survives and prospers. Above all the complexity that is Indian politics there is the simple fact of one-party dominance. Since 1947 Congress has been in power for all but three years. By any criterion it is a supremely successful political party. How has the Congress Party achieved this?

The Congress Party was formed in 1885 and until the end of World War I it behaved as a typical cadre party for the small Anglicized Indian middle class. After 1919 this role was taken over by the breakaway Liberal Party and Congress developed into the mass mobilizing party of the independence movement. After independence, however, it was not able to maintain either its mass mobilizing function or convert into a modern representative party. Congress never developed a single doctrine or ideology behind which it could build a national constituency of support. Hence Congress for all its dominance has not had the electoral integrative role that parties have performed in liberal democracies. Rather Congress has become an aggregative party. This means that at any particular election the party's support base is a mere aggregation of different groups. Such aggregation may be temporary since the creation of these support bases does not depend on any consistent doctrine or policy position, what Park and de Mesquita (1979: 113) refer to as Congress's 'purposive ambiguity'. The most important feature of the aggregation is that it constitutes a majority. In short, Congress has been successfully opportunist and pragmatic in its handling of the complexity of Indian politics.

The electoral geography of the aggregative strategy has been illustrated by analysis of voting patterns in the state of Punjab. In Table 6.1 the low level of geographic stability recorded for India was based on a study of

Congress voting patterns in Punjab (Dikshit and Sharma 1982). We can see the details of this geographical instability in votes for Congress in another analysis by Brass (1975). In Fig. 6.12 elections from 1952 to 1972 for the three main parties competing in Punjab are depicted. For each election a party's vote pattern is correlated against the geographical distribution of the Hindu population. For instance, the Jana Singh party campaigns as a Hindu party and its pattern of votes is always positively

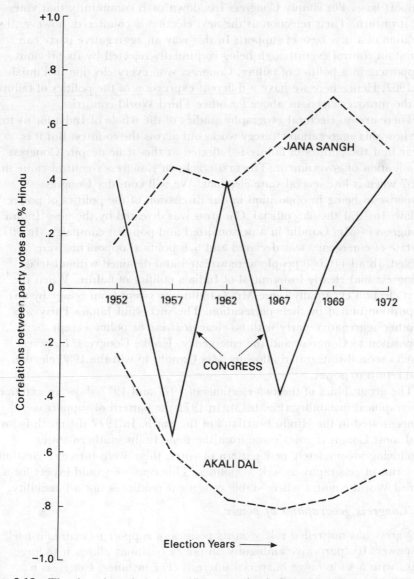

Fig. 6.12 The changing ethnic bases of party voting in Punjab

correlated with the distribution of Hindu people as we would expect. In contrast, the Akali Dal is the party of the Sikhs and this party's votes are always negatively correlated with the Hindu distribution. But Congress has no such simple correlation. In 1952 the correlation indicates largely Hindu support. At the next election, however, the correlation suggests largely non-Hindu support before reverting to Hindu support and so on back and forth between the two communities. This reflects a series of politics of failure that have been accommodated by changing the party's support base. Put simply Congress lets down each community that votes for it in turn. Their rejection at the next election is countered, however, by creation of a new base of support. In this way an aggregative party can maintain control even though being continually rejected by its previous supporters in a politics of failure. Congress won every election in Punjab to 1967. Hence here we have a different expression of the politics of failure to the turnover elections above for other Third World countries.

There are no electoral geography studies of the whole of India for us to see how this aggregation strategy works out across the country. But it is clear that the politics of failure is reflected at this scale despite Congress domination of government. The first cracks in Congress's control came in 1967 when it lost several state elections. We will consider Congress response to being in opposition in our discussion of the politics of power below. In 1971 the old 'official' Congress was defeated by the new 'Indira' Congress of Mrs Gandhi in a personalized and populist campaign. In 1975 a state of emergency was declared and 676 political opponents were gaoled. In all 110,000 people were arrested and detained without trial. Congress had clearly lost control of India's politics of failure. When the next election eventually came Mrs Gandhi was swept from power by an opposition united by their persecution. The successful Janata Party was another aggregative party with no clear doctrine or policy except opposition to Congress and the emergency. Unlike Congress, however, Janata soon disintegrated allowing Mrs Gandhi to win the 1980 election and return to power.

The geographies of the two elections of 1971 and 1977 show an extreme geographical instability (Fig. 6.13). In 1971 the pattern of support is concentrated in the Hindu heartland of the north. In 1977 the north is lost and most Congress votes come from the non-Hindu southern states producing a completely new pattern of votes: these were turnover elections in terms of geography as well as politics. This is as we would expect for a Third World country where stable congruent politics is not a possibility.

2. Congress geographies of power

Congress has not relied solely on its politics of support to maintain itself in power. Its 'purposive ambiguity' in policy positions allows it to forge links with a wide range of special interests. For instance, Congress has always claimed to be a democratic socialist party and can rely on the

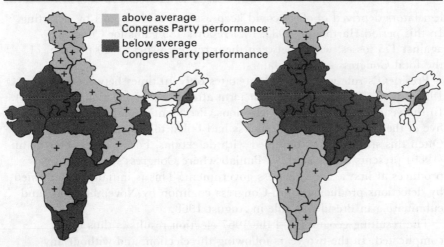

a) 1971 Election   b) 1977 Election

Fig. 6.13   Changing geographies of Indian elections

formal support of many trade unions and peasants' organizations
outflanking India's two main socialist parties. At the same time it receives
six times the amount of contributions the 'free enterprise' party,
Swatandra, obtains from big business and rich landlords (Sadasivan 1977:
307—8). Clearly a successful aggregate party depends upon a politics of
power just as much as a politics of support.

Congress's politics of power is best illustrated by the 1967 state
elections and the subsequent events. Kashyap (1969: 3) calls this the first
watershed in Indian post-independence politics because it 'exposed the
artificial level of political stability'. Prior to the election there were no
anti-Congress governments in any state. At the election Congress lost
control of 7 out of 21 states. But this was by no means the end of the
story. Losing an election in a state does not necessarily mean losing power.
There are two ways in which this can be prevented. First, opponents
can be bribed to leave the party for whom they were elected and join
Congress. Second, if political instability occurs the central Congress
government can deem the state ungovernable and declare 'Presidents
rule' which effectively means control by Congress from the centre. Both
strategies have been widely used throughout post-independence
Indian politics but became more widespread as Congress's support
base began to crumble in 1967. We shall consider each in turn.

Sadasivan (1977) reports 542 defections of legislators between 1957 and
1967. In the year after the 1967 elections there were 438 defections. Bihar
state was the foremost casualty with 85 defections among just 318
legislative seats. This was one of the states Congress lost in the election
but by January 1968 a pro-Congress coalition government had been
installed. Defections were, of course, a two-way affair as Congress

legislators deprived of office could keep a share of the spoils by defecting. In this period Hartmann (1980: 182) reports 139 gains for Congress against 175 losses, which between them represent nearly 20 per cent of the total Congress state legislators.

President's rule was imposed on states only 10 times between 1951 and 1967 but 17 times in the four-year term after the 1967 election (Dua 1979). In the year following the 1967 elections, President's rule was imposed on five of the seven states that Congress had failed to hold (Kashyap 1969). Often this strategy was combined with defections. For instance, Hartmann (1980) presents a case study of Punjab where Congress's defeat in 1967 produces at first a non-Congress government. This is initially undermined by defections producing a pro-Congress coalition by November 1967 and culminating in President's rule in August 1968.

The resulting geography of the 1967 election results is thus quite complicated. In the two years following the election, and without any further reference to the electors, there were thirteen changes of government and of the original non-Congress governments only Kerala remained untouched. The detailed geography of this politics of power is illustrated by Kashyap (1969).

Since this 'first watershed' in Indian post-independence politics these politics of power have continued to operate. Dua (1979: 19), for instance, reports a further fifteen examples of Presidential rule between 1971 and 1974. After the 'second watershed', the election of a non-Congress central government in 1977, it was defections that brought down the Janata government in 1979. Kamath (1985) reports numerous additional defections in the 1980s culminating in the outlawing of the practice in 1985. But he thinks it unlikely that defections will be eradicated since politicians will be able to get around the law (Kamath 1985: 1053). Quite simply, legislative seats are too valuable a commodity to be removed from the market. Securing election under any party label becomes a personal resource. It provides access to the state and its resources. Kamath (1985: 1048) reports prices for defectors. in the 1980s ranging from $100,000 to $250,000 plus additional inducements such as ministerial office or the dropping of criminal charges.

After only this brief exploration into Indian politics of support and power we can refute Blondel's (1978) claim for an Indian liberal democracy. The political processes operating in India are far closer to other Third World countries with their different political institutions than they are to the liberal democratic states of the core (Taylor 1986). Liberal democracy is a particular product of the history of one part of the world-economy where recent relatively abundant material circumstances have been crucial to their establishment. The attempt to diffuse this political product has explicitly failed in most countries; in some countries, however, institutions exist that look superficially like liberal democracy but which form a distinctive form of polity. India is such a case.

Chapter 7

POLITICAL GEOGRAPHY OF LOCALITIES

THE ECOLOGICAL HERITAGE

The rise and fall of urban ecology

1. Ecological theory: the hidden political dimension
2. Ecology as spatial structure: apolitical urban studies

Geography of locational conflicts

1. From ecology to pluralism
2. Locality and political economy

Recent debates in urban studies

1. Reaffirming space: Pahl's managerialism
2. Disposing of space: Castell's collective consumption
3. Disposing of 'urban': Abrams's phenomenon
4. Return of locality: Urry's special spatial effects

SOCIALIZATION IN PLACE

Neighbourhood effect revisited

1. 'The neighbourhood effect won't go away'
2. 'A process of massive indoctrination'
3. Breakdown in socialization

Ideology and locality

1. Dominant ideology for all
2. Milieux
3. Dominant ideology and Conservative success in British elections

Place and protest

1. Protest and size of place
2. A political location theory
3. Planning for harmony

A NEW THEORY OF POLITICS IN LOCALITIES

Practical politics

1. The making and breaking of places
2. Practical political strategies
3. Alternative politics of location

The local state

1. The nature of the local state
2. Local state as instrument
3. The changing potential for conflict

Chapter 7

POLITICAL GEOGRAPHY OF LOCALITIES

We have reached the scale of experience in our framework for political geography. The range of this scale is defined by the day-to-day activities of people in the ordinary business of their lives. We may start with Hagerstrand's time geography concept which treats the strict space–time constraints on an individual's behaviour. Starting from his or her 'home-base' every person's day-to-day life consists of a series of regular paths that must be organized to enable return to the home-base every night. The range of these paths depends upon the transport available to the individual. This 'physicalist' view of geography places a 'space–time' prism of constraint around every individual which is unique to that individual. Hence everybody's direct experience of the world is distinctive to that person.

Being distinct does not mean being unrelated, of course. Society does not consist of an aggregation of random 'prisms' but is a highly organized and structured phenomenon. Space–time prisms are clustered as anybody who has spent time in a city's rush hour knows only too well. In much of the modern world these clusters are the 'daily urban systems' of activities around our major cities. Although usually defined just in terms of commuting, these urban systems incorporate a wide range of people's needs in modern society including shopping, education, recreation as well as employment. In core countries, and many other parts of the world, daily urban systems are the limit of routine behaviour and therefore represent in concrete terms the scale of experience.

Before we consider the nature of this scale we must emphasize once again that our identification of scales is a pedagogic device and does not indicate any separateness of different systems at different scales. Every individual in his or her prism which is part of a daily urban system are no less members of a nation-state as citizens and participate in the world-economy as producers and consumers. Although the dependency heritage of the world-systems approach emphasizes the global scale, the second heritage we identified in Chapter 1, the French *Annales* school of history, equally emphasizes day-to-day activities of ordinary people. For Braudel (1973) it is these routine behaviour patterns which provide the long-term structures in which 'world-events' occur. The scale of experience is just as integral to the world-economy as the scale of reality.

As we have already indicated, contemporary studies of the scale of experience will normally be urban in nature. Urban studies in social science have been the largest growth area in the twentieth century. Cities have been a major concern of sociologists, political scientists and geographers for several generations. Political geography, however, apart from its treatment of capital cities, has been largely immune to this academic endeavour and urban political geography can only be said to start from about 1970. Since then studies at the urban scale have been a major growth point in political geography rivalling electoral geography as the spearhead of the sub-discipline's resurgence. Why, therefore, has this chapter not been entitled 'Urban political geography' or, in the style of past chapters, 'Rethinking urban political geography'? The reason is simply that we will argue in this chapter that attempts to produce 'urban theory' prefixed by any adjective is bound to fail. The richness of the empirical heritage of urban studies must not blind us to the poverty of the theory that has been produced to order that information.

This is the subject matter of our first section in which the 'ecological heritage' of urban studies is criticized and we conclude that there can be no urban theory. The importance of local studies is not thereby diminished however. We replace the distinctively 'urban' by the more general idea of locality and search for the nature of the relationship between experience defined by locality and the nation-state and world-economy that encompasses it. This relationship is the subject matter of the second section of the chapter when neighbourhood effects reappear as socialization in place. We explore the concept of neighbourhood effect beyond inter-personal relations and introduce culture and ideology into the argument. In the final section we introduce a new theory of politics in localities which concentrates on political practices rather than ideas and attitudes.

THE ECOLOGICAL HERITAGE

Every geography student and every researcher in urban studies is familiar with Burgess's zonal model of the city. As a spatial structure it is probably even more well-known than Christaller's central place hexagons and von Thunen's agricultural zones. But Burgess's model comes from a very different tradition to the economics of Christaller and von Thunen. It is part of the Chicago school of human ecology whose studies employed biological concepts to understand the city. The term 'ecology' now appears in geographical literature to mean analysis of areal data as in 'ecological correlation' or 'factorial ecology' so that the biological origins have all but been forgotten. In this discussion we return to this biological heritage and consider the political implications of this approach. These political implications remained when the biology was erased to leave behind confusion as to the nature of modern urban studies. We will use this debate to derive our political geography of localities.

THE RISE AND FALL OF URBAN ECOLOGY

Although E. W. Burgess's zonal model is the most well-known product of this school, the leader of the school is Robert Park. The school can be said to start from 1916 with Park's appointment to the University of Chicago's Sociology Department and the publication of his 'The City: Suggestions for the Investigation of Human Behaviour in the Urban Environment' (Park 1916). In this paper Park put forward the idea of using the city as a laboratory for investigating human behaviour and in subsequent years, with the help of Burgess and others, this suggestion developed into the first major school of thought in urban studies. This empirical basis is nicely captured in the following quotation attributed to Park (Reissman 1964: 95):

> I expect that I have actually covered more ground tramping around cities in different parts of the world, than any other living man. Out of all this I gained, among other things, a conception of the city, the community and the region not as a geographical phenomenon merely, but as a kind of social organism.

Park's vast experience was supplemented by the work of countless students in their Chicago fieldwork for Park and Burgess to produce the most sustained research effort on one city ever mounted. It is not too far off the mark to suggest that many recent geography students have known more about Chicago in the 1920s than about their own city today!

1. Ecological theory: the hidden political dimension

The interesting feature of this work, however, was that it attempted to go beyond description. The flavour of the theoretical project is glimpsed in Park's use of the term 'social organism' to describe the city. Park evolved his ideas in a period when crude social applications of Darwin's theory of evolution were still popular. This social Darwinism used biological concepts to justify social inequalities in terms of such notions as 'survival of the fittest'. In such arguments the poorest areas of the city, the slums, could be explained by the genetic inferiority of their inhabitants. One of the results of the Chicago empirical studies, however, was to show that the same areas remained slums, in Burgess's zone of transition, as different ethnic and racial immigrant groups passed through them (Faris 1967: 57). Hence slums were problems of the area and not the individuals that lived there at any one point in time. This change in focus from individual to area led to a changing biological brief, from genetics to ecology.

Ecology evolved out of Darwinian biology as the study of the relationship between an organism and its environment. These relationships defined a 'web of life' in which inter-relationship between different organisms —plant and animal —and the environment, produced an 'ecology'. Distinctive patterns of equilibrium were produced in a 'purposeless' manner by the laws of nature. These laws or processes were not 'directed' or 'planned' but nevertheless resulted in stable and clear-cut patterns of organisms. What Park did was to transfer these ideas to the organization of the city where human patterns could be similarly interpreted.

In Table 7.1 I have listed some ecological concepts and provided examples for animal/plant ecology and for human ecology. Every 'environment' must be bounded to define an ecological unit in which equilibrium can be reached. A salt marsh is a good example of such a distinctive environment. In human ecology nation-state, region or city provide such units although in practice it was the city that was the prime ecological unit. Hence human ecology was in reality only urban ecology. Within the city 'natural' processes occurred as competition for scarce resources in the same way as they occurred in other ecologies. The processes of adaption and specialization were thought of as general means by which resources were used and allocated, in biology among species, in human ecology among occupation groups and land-use classes. All are not equal in these processes and dominant species/groups will control the community as trees do in woodlands through their control on light and business does in the city through its central location. Hence the city is ordered around the central business district in Burgess's model just as shrubs, grasses and mosses are ordered with respect to trees.

Of course Park did not believe that this ecological approach could fully describe the city. The cultural components of the city had no equivalent in animal or plant ecology. Park, therefore, divided the study of society into two levels — the biotic substructure which could be described as ecology

Table 7.1 The 'Nature' and Politics of Human Ecology

Ecological concept	Animal/plant ecology example	Human ecology example	Political implications
An 'environment' as an ecological unit	e.g. salt marsh	e.g. city	Analysis is restricted to locality
Natural processes	Biological competition for scarce resources	Economic competition for scarce resources	Market processes are universal and inevitable
Adaption and specialization	Different species in different ecological niches	Occupation groups/land use classes in 'natural areas'	Class system is merely specialization which benefits all
Dominance and control of community	e.g. trees in a woodland community	e.g. Commerce and industry in the city	Dominant classes are as benign as trees

and the cultural superstructure which incorporated a moral order beyond ecology. The biotic order was based solely on the prime need for survival as expressed through competition. It is Park's version of the survival of the fittest and must not be confused with the classical Marxist base and superstructure model. Whereas the economic base in Marxism defines the structure governing society specific to a mode of production, Park's ecological processes are eternal and natural. As such they provided a new justification for the inequalities of the city to supersede the increasingly discredited genetic explanations. As Castells (1977) points out, the competition Park describes is not ecological: it is merely a particular expression of *laissez-faire* capitalism. In the final column of Table 7.1 some of the political implications of the use of ecological concepts are shown. As illustrated throughout this book, the proposition that some human behaviour is 'natural' is usually a justification for a particular status quo. Quite simply, dominant classes are not like trees, and the processes of their control are anything but natural and 'purposeless'.

2. Ecology as spatial structure: apolitical urban studies

This type of political argument did not enter urban geography until the 1970s. Urban ecology was originally criticized on empirical grounds — 'are the zones really circular?' — and then in terms of the impossibility of separating 'biotic' and 'cultural' levels. This disposed of the ecological theory but many of the ideas, especially concerning spatial structure, remained. These were incorporated into two forms of developmentalism in sociology. First, the folk—urban continuum of Robert Redfield (1941), Park's son-in-law, used human-ecology ideas to define the 'modern' end of a sequence of communities which subsequently fed into the modernization theory discussed in Chapter 1. Second, the new emphasis upon social as opposed to ecological processes generated a social-area analysis (Shevky and Bell 1955). This latter is interesting for two reasons. It represents an explicit break with human ecology's treatment of the city as separate from society. In social-area analysis modernization trends for society as a whole are extrapolated down to the city scale. General processes of urbanization and industrialization lead to specific processes such as skill differentiation and new family functions which are reflected in urban social patterns as social areas. It is these ideas which were enthusiastically taken up by urban geographers who eventually were able to show an equivalence between social-area analysis and 'ecological' structure (Murdie 1969) using the techniques of factor analysis in 'factorial ecology'. In this way urban geography was placed within the overall developmentalism of modernization theory.

Ecological theory was dead but ecological structures survived. Natural areas were replaced by social areas and purposeless processes gave way to household decision-making on where to live. The best example was Alonso's (1964) trade-off model whereby rich people chose to spend money on commuting and suburban living while poor people chose to live in overcrowded inner-city conditions, hence saving on commuting costs. Kirby (1976) has shown how this trade-off between housing costs and commuting in reality does not exist: it merely models what are structural constraints as individual choices. This point has been made more generally by Gray (1975) who argues that urban geography was both mythical and mystical in its emphasis upon choice in explaining urban spatial structures. Burgess's zones may not be due to natural ecological processes but neither are they the result of households simply choosing to live where they wished. A conservative naturalism had given way to a conservative liberalism but both had similar political implications: justification of the status quo. The inequality reflected in slums is neither an inevitable effect of natural processes nor the result of such areas being attractive to the people who live there. The idea that people might not want to live in such poor conditions but had no choice because they could afford no other locations was missing from apolitical urban geography (Gray 1975). In short, power — and hence politics — is ignored in an ideal world where the dominant classes dominate and nobody notices.

Politics has been incorporated into modern urban studies through two routes. In political geography, analysis of land-use conflicts has given rise to a new 'geography of locational conflicts.' In social science more generally, urban studies have been concerned with power and politics. The interesting point is that for both sets of literature the addition of politics into the analysis has produced a new emphasis on places. Hence they have both come to very similar conclusions which emphasize the politics of localities. We consider each route to the discovery of localities in urban politics.

GEOGRAPHY OF LOCATIONAL CONFLICTS.

The study of locational conflicts became a major theme in urban political geography in the early 1970s with the work of Julian Wolpert and his associates (Wolpert *et al.*: 1972) and Kevin Cox (1973). Initially these studies focused upon single conflicts and attempted to identify patterns of gains and losses in the local community and how these were articulated or not articulated in the conflict. This approach was subsequently extended to deal with aggregate patterns of large numbers of conflicts which could be mapped to produce a 'geography of locational conflicts'. The method was to analyze the local press over a specified period and produce a list of all 'identifiable conflicts'. In this way the geography of locational conflicts in London, Ontario for 1970–72 (Janelle and Millward 1976) and 1970–73 (Janelle 1977), Vancouver, BC for 1973–75 (Ley and Mercer 1980) and Columbus, Ohio for 1971–78 (Cox and McCarthy 1982) have been produced. The most interesting thing about this small set of studies is that whereas they all produce very similar findings on the geography, they exhibit a wide range of interpretations which encompass most of the issues we have discussed earlier in this chapter.

Between them the four studies cited above mapped nearly one thousand locational conflicts. Not surprisingly they found that the patterns of conflicts were neither evenly distributed nor merely random. A definite structure emerged with conflicts concentrated in three areas — the core of the urban region, the decaying inner city around the core and the newest developments at the edge of the city. In the 1970s these were the major areas of change in the North American city and this is reflected in these geographies of conflict. But how do we interpret this structure?

1. From ecology to pluralism

In the first study Janelle and Millward (1976) provide us with an ecological interpretation. They down-grade the influence of zoning and planning and argue that this geography represents the 'adaption of the urban environment to changing human needs and expectations' (Janelle and Millward 1976: 103). They identify different types of issues on the basis of land-use categories and summarize the patterns using a factor analysis. This produces just two general patterns of conflict — a transition zone factor relating to housing, transportation and preservation issues and a CBD redevelopment—peripheral expansion factor relating to retail, school and redevelopment conflicts. This generalized description of the geography of conflicts is therefore interpreted in terms of Burgess's concentric zone model as reflecting the 'competitive ethic operating within a free market economy' (Janelle and Millward 1976: 104).

Janelle's (1977) subsequent study moves away from identification of general aggregate processes of the ecological tradition and concentrates instead on the actors involved in each conflict. Proposers of land-use change and the objectors to the change are each identified so that the nature of the conflicts can be assessed. Using this revised methodology Janelle was able to identify major conflict-participant categories which go beyond simple ecological inferences. The basic finding was that the 'economic sector' (developers, corporations) was the most common proposer of change, followed by the public sector (planners, public institutions), with the 'household sector' (residents) a very poor third. In terms of objections, however, the reverse was true with households being responsible for nearly two-thirds of all objections, the public sector accounting for nearly one third and the economic sector hardly ever objecting to land-use change. Unlike his previous study, Janelle (1977) now emphasizes the complexity of the inter-dependencies of conflict participants in land-use change. Simple ecological interpretation is replaced by a pluralist model of the geography of conflict.

2. Locality and political economy

Ley and Mercer's (1980) interpretation is much more political. For them locational conflict represents a challenge to market equilibrium. Their study includes two new developments. First, they recognize that 'identifiable conflicts' are only a subset of all potential conflicts which appear on the political agenda. They produce, therefore, a geography of development by mapping a sample of permits awarded by the city government for land-use changes. This turns out to be a highly structured geography with a distinct concentric zonal pattern reflecting the city's zoning policy. But when this is compared to the geography of conflicts an interesting contrast emerges: the conflicts have a sectoral pattern instead of a zonal one. Whereas change permits are distributed equally between east and west sectors in Vancouver, more than eight times as much conflict is generated in the west (Ley and Mercer 1980: 100). This is explained in terms of Ley and Mercer's second new development — the linking of conflict to social cleavages and city politics. The sectoral contrast reflects a basic social cleavage in Vancouver which had become politically activated at the time of the conflict survey. In the late 1960s the ruling Non-Partisan Association, a free-enterprise business party, was challenged by a new urban reform party, The Elector's Action Movement (TEAM), offering the ideal of the 'liveable city' as an alternative to 'boosterism' and urban growth. In 1972 this new party won control of City Hall so leadership passed from business to the new professionals — university professors, teachers, lawyers, architects, and so on. The electoral base of TEAM was the affluent west sector. In fact Ley and Mercer (1980: 107) describe the party as 'a product of a distinctive urban subculture', in short a neighbourhood effect. Hence the conflict pattern is part of a larger political process that was changing the nature of Vancouver politics. A new political agenda was being devised in the west of the city which entailed resident resistance to commercial development. Ley and Mercer, therefore, provide a very political geography of conflict.

Finally, Cox and McCarthy (1982) have taken the argument one step further. In their study of variations in the resistance of residents to commercial development they have been able to show that home-owners and families with children at school had higher rates of neighbourhood activism than renters and families without school children. This suggests a 'politics of turf' centred on the different stake that families have in their localities. But Cox is unwilling to leave the matter there as a purely local phenomenon. He looks at the conflicts in which neighbourhood activism plays its part and shows that over two-thirds are concerned with a particular type of antagonism — 'between those who are interested in an expanded urban infrastructure and the conversion of land parcels to higher yielding land uses, and those whose interest in the urban environment is essentially that of use value' (Cox and McCarthy 1982: 211). This is Ley and Mercer's finding interpreted in political economy terms. The 'politics of turf' becomes the link between the private and public restructuring of space to facilitate capital accumulation and the victims of that restructuring in their neighbourhoods. The geography of locational conflict reflects adverse local experiences which have been mobilized against a changing capitalist world-economy. Since the mobilization is location-based and may therefore incorporate diverse occupational groups such conflict can cut across traditional national political cleavages. Following Castells (1977) such local challenges to the system are generally referred to as *urban social movements*.

RECENT DEBATES IN URBAN STUDIES

The debates in urban studies since the fall of urban ecology have had a strange twist to them. It all revolves around what is and what is not 'urban'. First, urban is represented by spatial structure as 'politics' are added to traditional ecological themes. Second, the spatial basis of urban is dismissed and it becomes equated with particular activities of the modern state. Third, this is taken a step further when urban is dismissed as a meaningful category for study. Finally, space, and with it urban space, is rediscovered as a neglected theme in social science.

At first glance it would seem that this debate has gone round in circles. In fact the debate is vital for understanding how the concept of locality used in this study relates to urban political geography. We do not arrive back at urban ecology, instead we find a new basis for analysis. Hence we deal with each step of the argument in turn in order finally to reach a justification for the study of locality.

1. Reaffirming space: Pahl's managerialism

The redefinition of urban sociology that came in the late 1960s did more than add politics to the processes of residential differentiation. Park had separated out the city as an 'ecological unit' and social-area analysts had treated the city as reflecting societal trends but neither had doubted the existence of a distinct phenomenon —the city. This urban entity was usually defined in opposition to rural areas but, as the latter declined, society as a whole began to resemble an 'urban society'. In such highly urbanized societies as Britain the notion of an urban sociology separate from general sociology seemed increasingly archaic. R. E. Pahl (1970) set about the task of redefining urban sociology and in the process emphasized constraints on behaviour rather than choice and so introduced power into his project.

In order to find a new urban sociology Pahl (1970) drew a parallel with industrial sociology. Although we live in an 'industrial society' the social relations of authority in the industrial system constitute a viable industrial sociology. Similarly an urban sociology should study the social relations of authority in the urban system. Pahl's (1970) schema is famous for introducing the notion of social gatekeepers — planners, social workers, estate agents, developers, and so on — who organize and control the scarce urban resources. Hence industrial managers have their counterpart in urban managers. The result is a socio-spatial system which reflects power in society as mediated by these managers. Pahl, therefore, proposes a *spatial* sociology where the organization and control of facilities, access to such resources and their effects on the life chances of individuals, replace traditional urban sociology's emphasis on the study of a particular type of place identified as 'urban'.

Pahl's approach has come to be known as the managerial thesis and has initiated a large debate. While generally praised for emphasizing the constraints that exist in the urban system over individual choices, the nature of the constraints identified by Pahl are controversial. In short, he is criticized for dealing with the 'middle dogs' at the expense of the top dogs of the system. By this it is meant that by concentrating on the immediate managers of urban resources, such as public housing managers, the ultimate constraints on their actions are neglected. Middle managers may control 'who gets what' to some degree but they have little or no say in how much there is to distribute in the first place. Unlike the industrial system where a hierarchy of managers can easily be identified pursuing a definite goal in terms of company profit, in the urban system there seems to be no equivalent pursuit. It remains an amorphous mixture of different managers controlling a wide range of resources with no overall coherent purpose in Pahl's scheme of things. But of course there are processes operating in the urban system no less than in the industrial system which define the nature of the system and the overall constraints in which it operates.

Pahl's programme of 'spatial sociology' in Britain was paralleled by a similar argument for a spatial urban political science in the United States by Williams (1971). While being more explicit in his ecological heritage, Williams attempted to move modern urban ecology away from individual choice emphasis to one in which space is socially controlled to manipulate accessibility to resources. Spatially defined interest groups rather than managers are the focus of attention but the result is similar to that of Pahl. Analysis of the urban field consists of studying the spatial organization of urban resources and facilities and the conflicts this generated. Not surprisingly these ideas appealed to geographers and it is at this time that urban political geography can be said to begin, the first substantial works being David Harvey's (1973) *Social Justice and the City* and Kevin Cox's (1973) *Conflict, Power and Politics in the City: A Geographical View*. But no sooner had geography found a spatial framework to borrow, this framework came under severe attack. With their spatial emphasis it is arguable whether these new studies represented the final death throes of the urban ecology tradition or the birth of a genuinely new urban political geography. Whichever interpretation is preferred matters little since this interpretation of urban as spatial has been largely replaced by more holistic political economy analysis. We will return to some of the themes of this work in our final section below.

2. *Disposing of space: Castell's collective consumption*

Although urban studies have been largely neglected in Marxist thought
(Tabb and Sawers 1978), the most influential urban study of the 1970s was
undoubtedly Manuel Castells's (1977) *The Urban Question* which derived
directly from the French school of structuralist Marxism. The popularity
of Castells's work was not so much due to its Marxist credentials, indeed
as we shall see his most enthusiastic followers have been non-Marxists,
but because it directly confronted the whole gamut of problems in urban
analysis from the ecologists onwards and it offered a new exciting
programme of research. In short, it represents an abrupt break in a
tradition that was being seen increasingly as an albatross. With the
publication of Castells's work urban ecology could be well and truly
buried, for the very last time.

Castells (1977) approaches the concept of the urban as an 'everyday
notion'. It is, in his words, the 'domain of experience' where people live
their day-to-day lives. Thus the urban unit is 'the everyday space of a
delimited fraction of the labour force' (Castells 1977: 445). Hence the
'domain' corresponds to the daily urban systems we identified in the
introduction to this chapter. So far, therefore, Castells's schema is entirely
consistent with our scale of experience. But Castells narrows his concern
to only certain activities within daily urban systems. In advanced capitalist
societies, he argues, the processes of production and reproduction can be
interpreted as relating to essentially different scales of operation. Whereas
production is organized at a national and international scale, the
reproduction of labour remains an urban phenomenon. This reproduction
involves consumption processes in which the state has become
increasingly involved. This is termed *collective consumption* and includes
urban planning, public transport, public housing, education, public health
care, and so on. Hence the city becomes a 'unit of collective consumption'
(Castells 1978: 148) which explains why 'urban problems' usually reduce
to local conflicts over public management of consumption in transport,
planning, housing, and so on. The result of this argument is what
Dunleavy (1980: 50) terms a 'content' definition of the urban field. This
replaces the 'urban ideology' of the ecological heritage with the equation
'urban = collective consumption'. On this basis Dunleavy has defined an
urban political analysis in which the spatial basis of 'urban' or 'city' is
entirely banished. All we are left with is a set of processes concerning the
reproduction of labour which are deemed to be 'urban' in nature.

3. *Disposing of 'urban': Abrams's phenomenon*

The final demise of the urban as a distinct object for study can be found in
the work of Philip Abrams (1978). He castigates the whole ecological
heritage as reifying the city as if it were a social object whereas in reality it
is 'nothing more than a phenomenon' (Abrams 1978: 10). Hence the

reason why we have no adequate theory of the city is because it is impossible. The city is not an entity that we can develop theory around because it is not an operating system. Here we return to Pahl's problem of the lack of a goal for his urban system. Whereas the factories, firms or companies operating in industrial systems are units that contribute to the operation of the system, there is no parallel way in which towns and cities operate in the urban system. Hence attempts to ascertain the role of cities in the rise of capitalism in the core, or in modern peripheral under-development, are misplaced. Cities and towns are merely arenas for the unfolding of social relations; they do not themselves represent social relations. In Abrams's (1978: 31) words, towns should be seen 'as battles rather than monuments'.

4. Return of locality: Urry's specific spatial effects

A major advantage of the idea of collective consumption is that it links 'urban problems' directly to increased state activities as described by, among many others, O'Connor's (1973) work on the functions of the capitalist state. It is, of course, true that the fiscal crisis of state expenditure is acutely seen in our inner city areas due to the disproportionate dependence of their populations on the state: cuts in state expenditure have been most severely felt in our cities. Dunleavy's urban political analysis is able, therefore, to harness many 'non-local' processes as necessary components in the study of urban policy. But somewhere along the way the 'urban' concept as it relates to places we know as towns and cities seems to be lost. We need to return to consideration of towns and cities as places as 'the context in which people live out their daily routine' (Mellor 1975: 277).

In the work of John Urry (1981) the argument has come full circle. He bemoans the *neglect* of the 'spatial' element in social science. In particular he criticizes Castells's (1977) argument that space has no meaning outside the social relations that define it. Although space *per se* can have no independent effect, Urry argues that the spatial arrangement of social objects *can* affect their social relations. Hence he dismisses the idea that there can be a *general* spatial social science as attempted by Chicago human ecologists in the 1920s and quantitative geographers in the 1960s, but there are specific spatial effects which are local in scope. Hence we return to the notion of a locality which in most core countries, and many periphery countries, will be the daily urban system as the local labour market. Although social classes are mobilized politically at the national scale their distribution among localities will be uneven. Different mixes of social groups or classes will lead to different patterns of social relations. These differences in experiences will not automatically be evened out by nationalizing processes. In fact, according to Urry (1981), with increasing economic control at the national and international scales we can expect more politicization of localities as particular labour markets suffer the recession. And this is not just important for reproduction of labour; it can have local effects on production processes.

We accept Urry's argument in this chapter. This is not a new position of course but a restatement of the contextual effect of localities (Filkin and Weir 1972). From our perspective localities are important since they provide different experiences for their populations and these will have political implications. But we are not trying to contribute to or develop any new 'urban' theory. The localities we deal with below are largely daily urban systems but the emphasis is upon the variety of contexts they provide in terms of class balances and resources rather than as some general notion of 'the city'. In short, we have moved on from city as ecological unit to locality as social context.

SOCIALIZATION IN PLACE

Political socialization theory has been one of the major growth areas in political science (Renshon 1977). It has come to be seen as a key process for the stability of a political system. Quite simply, political control can be by coercion or by consensus. The former is extremely dangerous and expensive and the latter is the preferred option where possible. In every society there will be a balance between coercion and consensus and this will vary throughout the world-economy. The contrast between the distribution of irregular executive transfers (Fig. 6.3) and liberal democracy (Fig. 6.4) has already illustrated the geography of the coercion/consensus balance. The consensus in the core is reproduced and sustained by political socialization processes. This involves the learning of the necessary political values through family, school, mass media and other communication. It is these processes as they operate within liberal democracies which are the concern of this section.

NEIGHBOURHOOD EFFECT REVISITED

Massive growth in a field of study does not necessarily mean any major extension of our knowledge. In the case of political socialization, attempts to develop universal theory have been unsuccessful (Renshon 1977). Political socialization does not consist of universal processes but involves particular processes operating in *concrete* social situations. It is the experiences of individuals within their specific localities which provide the context and raw material for socialization. And this process is normally termed the 'neighbourhood effect' which we described briefly in Chapter 6. In electoral geography neighbourhood effects are generally considered to be relatively unimportant. Although Cox (1969) and Reynolds and Archer (1969) attempted to develop a 'spatial' electoral geography around this concept their ideas have not been generally followed up. Explanation of voting patterns has continued to be centred upon the political cleavages among the electors with the neighbourhood effect brought in to account for minor deviations. Hence Taylor and Johnston (1979: 267) conclude that its impact is 'negligible'. Here we reverse this conclusion and bring neighbourhood effects back to the centre of the stage not as an abstract location theory but as socialization in place.

1. 'The neighbourhood effect won't go away'

One of the interesting things about studies of neighbourhood effects is that evidence for this process seems very clear-cut and firm at the aggregate scale but it has been much harder to find at the individual scale. An example of the sort of impressive findings for aggregate analysis can be found in Almy's (1973) study of 55 referenda voting patterns in 18 different American cities between 1955 and 1972. These referenda covered a wide range of topics including fluoridation of water supplies, education and public works. Almy compared voting returns for precincts with socioeconomic data to define what he termed 'electoral cohesion' within social groups. This simply means whether similar precincts in socioeconomic terms voted together on a particular referenda proposition. Almy found 19 cases of low electoral cohesion and 36 cases of high electoral cohesion. Why do these different levels of cohesion occur? Almy argued that cities with high levels of residential segregation would foster high electoral cohesion as a neighbourhood effect. Conversely in an integrated city a neighbourhood effect is cancelled out. The hypothesis is justified by his results. Sixteen of the 19 cases of low electoral cohesion occur in integrated cities and 31 of the 36 cases of high electoral cohesion occur in segregated cities. Clearly the inference that the spatial structure of these cities affects voting patterns through neighbourhood effects is a very reasonable one on this evidence.

Inferences from aggregate data may seem clear-cut but they remain only indirect 'tests' of the neighbourhood effect. Some researchers have looked at individual voters and attempted to find a neighbourhood effect in interactions among residents in local areas. Fitton (1973), for instance, surveyed 87 voters in three streets in Manchester, England during the 1970 election campaign and found some evidence for residents conforming to the pro-Labour sentiments of their neighbours but the quantity and frequency of political discussion did not suggest that the neighbourhood was a potent force in national politics. This is, of course, in line with surveys that show that most people obtain their political information from the mass media, especially TV. In fact it is becoming increasingly difficult to equate the aggregate findings for neighbourhood effects in elections with modern campaigning techniques of advertising whether 'making' presidents or prime ministers. This has led some researchers to suggest that the neighbourhood effect reflects altogether different processes.

Dunleavy (1979), for instance, argues that deviations from class voting is due to consumption issues — housing and transport — and not the neighbourhood effect. However Johnston (1983) has tested Dunleavy's ideas by adding consumption variables to class variables to his analysis and still finds evidence indicating a neighbourhood effect. In Johnston's words, despite the efforts of many sceptics, 'the neighbourhood effect won't go away'.

2. 'A process of massive indoctrination'

The only way out of this dilemma is to relate neighbourhood effects back to the overall socialization process of which they are part. This means a change of emphasis from cross-sectional studies to a longer time horizon. Instead of trying to find evidence of a process in a particular campaign as Fitton (1973) does, we consider political socialization, in Miliband's (1969: 182) words, as 'a process of massive indoctrination' from birth to death. This involves neighbourhood influences but it includes much more than that. Other findings in electoral studies soon fall into place in such a socialization perspective. In their massive survey of British electoral behaviour, for instance, Butler and Stokes (1969) found that the best predictor of a person's party preference was their knowledge of their parents voting behaviour, especially their father's. This obviously reflects socialization within the family as the prime process. But there are other factors at work relating to a voter's experiences. In particular the 'political climate' during their first voting experience seems to be subsequently important. Butler and Stokes (1969) employ a 'generational model' to show how 'pro-Labour' generations (for example, from 1945) and 'pro-Conservative' generations (for example, from 1959) have moved through time as identifiable voting cohorts.

In electoral geography the most direct evidence of this overall socialization process is not the neighbourhood effect *per se* but the stability of voting patterns. With the exception of modern USA, liberal democracies have very stable voting patterns that have lasted for several generations. We have already shown that, for instance, in post-1945 elections in core countries, most parties have a consistent pattern of support (Table 6.1). In some cases this can be traced back further. We noted in Chapter 6 that in Britain the national pattern of support for the Labour Party has remained basically the same since its first major election campaign in 1918. These stable patterns, what we previously termed 'normal votes' in our discussion of past voting stability in the United States, represent the ability of parties to mobilize support. But they do not start from scratch in every election; they build on basic socialization processes that operate either for or against them in particular localities.

3. Breakdown is socialization

We might wish to refer to this as the 'silent campaigning' of the locality. It only really appears as an observable process when it breaks down. This occurs when a change in party system operates in such a way that the 'normal' allegiance of a locality is no longer consistent with the material interests of the locality. Obviously such a change will not happen overnight. Lewis (1965) has described just such a process in Flint, Michigan in the 1930s. The black residential districts are initially solid Republican areas, still 'voting for Abraham Lincoln', but they become equally solid Democrat areas as the New Deal policies evolve. This is not an even process. In Flint there are two black residential areas and it is the northern one that converts to Democrat first. Here we have differential local neighbourhood effects operating so that in some elections, in 1942 for example, the two black districts voted in different directions.

More insights into the processes going on in localities during periods of political realignment can be found from Gregory's (1968) study of politics in mining communities in Britain before the First World War. In the late nineteenth century mining constituencies were the safest Liberal seats in the country but by the 1918 election they had become the safest Labour seats. The process of this changeover involved the miners' union and their affiliation to the Labour Party in 1907. But it was not a simple procedure of the union directing their members to vote Labour. There were different traditions of radicalisms among the coalfields which Gregory relates to working conditions. Hence the North East coalfield was relatively 'moderate' whereas South Wales was more 'radical'. This was reflected in voting so that in 1910 the Liberals maintained MPs in the North East but not in South Wales. The way in which changes occurred can be glimpsed by looking at a by-election at Houghton-le-Spring, Durham in 1913. When the sitting Liberal MP died the Liberal Association adopted a commercial traveller to defend the seat. Labour nominated the president of the Durham Miners Association to challenge. Since over half the electors were miners it might be expected that this would be a Labour gain. In the event villages and even households throughout the constituency were divided from top to bottom. Generally speaking it was the younger miners who were changing to Labour but the older miners remained loyal to the Liberals. The result was a Liberal victory with Labour remaining in third place with 22 per cent of the vote (Gregory 1968: 80–1). This was a rare competitive election for a mining constituency. Socialization between generations was breaking down as the community was adjusting to a changing national party system. After 1918 Houghton-le-Spring took its place among the safe seats in Labour's 'traditional' heartland.

IDEOLOGY AND LOCALITY

Our conclusion from the above discussion is that the neighbourhood effect is much more than a matter of inter-personal relations. It is not just whether the quantity of political contacts a person experiences are biased for one party or another; it is the fact that localities are places in which the general process of socialization occurs which is important. And this is not just a matter of favouring one party or another; it is to do with the setting up and sustaining of ideologies within which parties have to fit. These ideologies are, as we have seen, first and foremost national ideologies as individuals are socialized into becoming citizens of a particular country. This has led to the idea of different political cultures existing in different countries. The most famous study along these lines is Almond and Verba's (1963) *Civic Culture* where they used an international social survey to show that British and American citizens held attitudes more conducive to liberal democracy than German, Italian and Mexican citizens. Britain and the United States, therefore, had 'civic cultures' with the British being particularly deferential. In the discussion that follows we will develop this finding of Almond and Verba's by relating it to locality.

The problem with their concept of 'national' political culture is its unitary nature. From their sample survey Almond and Verba derive one culture per country. This precludes differences in culture within countries developing in response to material inequalities experienced in different localities. In effect Almond and Verba base their concept upon an extreme consensus model of society which assumes a homogeneous pattern of values and attitudes within countries. This is no longer acceptable. In sociological studies of local communities, for instance, there is a strong tradition of describing a 'working class' culture which is not easily accommodated in the unitary concept of political culture. In this discussion we follow Jessop (1974) in equating political culture with the notion of dominant ideology and use Parkin's (1967, 1971) scheme for identifying variety within this domination.

1. Dominant ideology for all

Starting with the basic Marxist dictum that the ruling ideas in a society are the ideas of the ruling class we will define the political culture of a country as the *dominant ideology*. This is a moral framework of ideas and values that endorse the existing system. In all countries with market economies it will endorse capitalist ideas although it will vary between countries in terms of the particular values emphasized for social control in different national contexts — in Britain there is a dominant ideology supporting the capitalist ethos but with a deferential cultural addition, according to Almond and Verba (1963).

If the dominant ideology is to be useful in avoiding the need for physical coercion to maintain the status quo it must be accepted, in part at least, by the vast majority of all the population, rulers and ruled. Parkin identifies two direct expressions of the dominant ideology in the dominated class: *deferential* and *aspirational*. In both examples the subject accepts the status quo; but in the former he also accepts his low status, in the latter he is striving *individually* to raise his position within the system. A related value system is the subordinate one which indirectly expresses the dominant system. In this case the status quo is accepted but within a moral framework which emphasizes communal improvement within the system. This is an *accommodative* set of values which amount to a 'negotiated' version of the dominant ideology (Parkin 1971: 92). The dominant ideology is filtered to day-to-day needs so that it continues to provide the abstract moral frame of reference while the subordinate value system deals with the concrete social situation involving choice and action. Parkin (1971: 95) refers to this as two levels of normative reference — ' the abstract and the situational'. Deferential, aspirational and accommodative values all contrast with *oppositional* values based upon a radical ideology which is designed to counter and replace the dominant ideology. In a stable liberal democracy the latter needs to be relegated to the status of fringe politics.

One important corollary of this argument is that we no longer have to subscribe to Almond and Verba's rather simplistic notion of Britain's 'deferential' civic culture. Such a model of the dominant ideology is unnecessary since stability can be maintained without coercion through aspirational and accommodative value systems as well as deference. This is important because Jessop (1974) has found feelings of deference less important in Britain than Almond and Verba's study would imply. The latter survey was part of a comparative politics exercise which highlighted British deference. It may well be that the British population is less aspirational than their American counterparts and less accommodative than the Swedish population (Scase 1977), but this does not mean that these two value systems are not important in Britain. In all stable Western countries ideological dominance will be reflected in various mixes of deferential, aspirational and accommodative value systems. The particular mixture in any one country will depend on the strategies of the dominant classes in the past and the concrete experiences of dominated classes in their day-to-day activities.

2. Milieux

And so we return to localities. Lockwood (1966) has explicitly linked these alternative value systems to 'the vantage point of a person's own particular milieu' and 'their experiences of the social inequality in the smaller societies in which they live out their daily lives'. Three types of locality are identified: (i) The urban-industrial milieu with large factories and a dominance of impersonal inter-class relations enables an accommodative value system to develop; (ii) the rural-agricultural milieu with small traditional industry and personal inter-class relations is conducive to the maintenance of deferential value systems; (iii) the suburban-residential milieu with its competitive conspicuous consumption is the location of the aspirational value system.

These milieux are implicit in much discussion of British politics. In quantitative electoral geography they appear as variables in attempts to explain aggregate voting patterns (Piepe, Prior and Box 1969; Crewe 1973; Crewe and Payne 1976). In the most sophisticated model, for example, Crewe and Payne (1976) add to their basic social-class model of voting, first, specific variables identifying 'agricultural' constituencies and 'mining' constituencies and, second, measures of the previous level of party voting in constituencies to take into account other abnormally 'strong' Labour or Conservative localities. The result is a highly successful model which statistically accounts for about 90 per cent of the variation in Labour voting among constituencies in 1970. But milieux imply much more than additional variables for cross-sectional statistical analyses. Milieux are living communities which have distinctive histories. The most comprehensive investigation of such communities using a long historical perspective is Newby's (1977) study of rural communities in East Anglia. He begins by using the ideas of Parkin (1971) but finds that identifying a deferential value system is more difficult than initially supposed. How far is the imputed deference of agricultural workers merely a realistic behavioural adjustment to the powerlessness of their situation? Or is it a matter of values being formed to match the constraints on the day-to-day lives of the workers? These are not problems to unravel here but the influence of locality is not in doubt.

3. Dominant ideology and Conservative success in British elections

Many observers have commented on the seeming paradox of Conservative success in British elections. As long ago as 1867 Engels lamented the success of the Conservative Party in the wake of franchise reforms which gave many working men the vote for the first time. This most traditional of political parties has shown itself most adept at mobilizing support in over a century of elections. Despite a majority of working-class voters since 1885, there have been only three anti-Conservative governments with a clear majority in Parliament in this period (Liberal 1906–10, Labour 1945–51 and Labour 1964–70). In contrast, Conservative or Conservative-dominated governments have controlled Parliament on thirteen occasions since 1885. Clearly very many working-class voters have supported the Conservative Party over these years. Such voting has been considered 'deviant' on the grounds that first Liberal and then Labour are the 'natural' party of the working class (Mackenzie and Silver 1968).

By employing a socialization and dominant ideology approach a very different picture emerges. Parkin (1967) considers *any* voting for Labour to be deviant to the extent that it is interpreted as anti-dominant class. Labour voting reflects a less than satisfactory socialization into an accommodative value system. In order for such a voting position to be maintained 'barriers' are required to insulate voters from the full weight of the dominant value system. This is where locality comes in either as a working-class community or as a large workplace. Where they are combined — dockland, mining communities — insulation is greatest and hence Labour voting highest. The least insulated members of the working class are housewives and the retired, both of whom are typically least Labour-orientated. Jessop (1974) has tested some of these ideas by devising a 'structural score' in terms of such barriers and confirms Parkin's ideas.

Clearly the neighbourhood effect when viewed as socialization in place is anything but negligible. Modern British politics can be interpreted in terms of the differential abilities of the parties to mobilize support among persons with different value systems in contrasting localities. Whereas industrial and rural milieux have consistently been Labour and Conservative orientated respectively, it is in the aspirational milieux that elections have increasingly been won and lost. In the social democratic consensus and technocratic politics phases Labour appealed to aspirational values and were relatively successful. In the two phases of national interest Conservatives have been able to push Labour back into its traditional industrial heartlands. This is, of course, the nature of the dominant ideology. In times of recession the material needs of the dominated class are accepted as being against the national interest (Miliband 1969: 207).

PLACE AND PROTEST

Ideology as it relates to voting intentions is only one part of politics. Other forms of political activity can be related to locality as many researchers have shown. Tilly (1978) has traced the changing 'repertoire' of protest from the early world-economy to the emergence of liberal democracy. Traditional parades, burning of effigies, sabotage, petitions, strikes, mass demonstrations, insurrection and revolution — all have distinctive social and ideological structures based upon experience of economic relations rooted in locality. But there is no simple relation between political activity and locality. Tilly (1978) argues that material interests alone will not produce protest but that, in addition, organization, mobilization and opportunity are required. Hence even the very plausible 'isolated mass hypothesis' of Kerr and Siegel (1954) that segregated homogeneous workforces such as miners and dockers/longshoreman are prone to high strike levels is shown to be untenable as a general process (Tilly 1978: 67).

Nevertheless there are numerous studies that have related localities to political activity. Briggs's (1963) critique of Mumford's (1938) characterization of the nineteenth-century city as the appalling 'Coketown' depends upon drawing a distinction between different locales. Although

Mumford's model fits Manchester with its large factories and resulting large social distance between classes it does not fit Birmingham with its small workshops and closer contact between classes. This idea that the industrial nature of a locality will be reflected in social relations and hence politics is similarly drawn by Read (1964: 35) when he describes Birmingham and Sheffield as 'cities of political union' and Manchester and Leeds as 'cities of social cleavage'. The most detailed study of the way local social structures are reflected in political activity is the comparison of Oldham, Northampton and South Shields by Foster (1974). These studies of social relations in place are interesting but too specific for our purposes and we will not describe them in detail here. Instead we concentrate on two topics — the relation of size of place to political activity and attempts to plan places to control political activity.

1. Protest and size of place

To many observers in the nineteenth century large cities were the centres of agitation and protest. This is certainly the opinion of Engels (1952) and of the pioneer town planners as we shall relate below. But recent statistical analysis of protest and organization has shown a remarkable regularity that disputes the militancy of large cities. In nineteenth-century Britain, Lees (1982) has shown that strikes were more likely in medium-sized towns. Similarly in late nineteenth-century USA, labour organizations and socialism were found to be stronger in medium-size towns than in large cities by Bennett and Earle (1983). Let us consider the process involved for each case.

Lees's (1982) evidence relates to strikes in Yorkshire, Lancashire, Nottinghamshire and Leicestershire in two 'strike-waves', 1842 and 1889—91. He divides these counties into settlements of different populations and computes strike rates for each of five size categories. Strike rates in small (less than 2,000) and large (over 300,000) settlements are consistently the lowest. Highest rates are usually found in his middle category of towns from 20,000 to 100,000. Lees's explanation is that different sized towns had qualitatively different forms of relations with political authority and that this changed over the two periods. In the 1840s large towns were incorporated and had their own local political authority including justices and police. In contrast other towns were controlled by outside (county) authority with policing carried out by the army. In the incorporated towns there was more likelihood of mediation and less likelihood of provocation by the authorities. By the 1890s these contrasts were even more marked. The various organs of mediation in work disputes — general trade councils for labour and chambers of commerce for capital often combined in conciliation boards — were particularly developed in the larger towns and cities. In Tilly's terms, the repertoire of protest could be extended towards more 'legitimate' politics and the single weapon of the strike blunted. The strike in nineteenth-century Britain, therefore, seems to have been a phenomenon of the social relations and authorities of medium-sized towns more than other places.

Bennett and Earle (1983) consider the two 'surges' of socialism in the USA in the late nineteenth and early twentieth centuries. In the 1880s the Knights of Labour reached a membership approaching two million and in 1912 the Socialist Party presidential candidate obtained nearly one million votes. In investigating the geography of these two movements Bennett and Earle find that size of place is important. The Knights of Labour 'displayed surprising strength in unexpected places, notably the small towns and cities of the Middle West' (Bennett and Earle 1983: 47). In the regression analysis of the 1912 Socialist Party vote by counties, population of county is found to be a significant variable. For counties with populations under 85,000 socialist vote and population size is positively correlated, whereas for counties over 85,000 the relationship is an inverse one. That is to say the Socialist Party obtained less votes in small *and* large localities. American socialism was a feature of the medium-sized settlement, localities where paternalistic social relations persisted and interfered with the domination of capital (Gordon 1976).

2. A political location theory

Gordon (1976) has incorporated the processes described above into a more general location theory of labour control. He argues that there are two forms of efficiency, quantitative efficiency related to improved technology and qualitative efficiency related to control of workforce. The latter can be indexed by strike activity. In the process of capital accumulation firms which combine both efficiencies will be the successful competitors in the market. Gordon argues that it is qualitative efficiency that has dominated location decisions for investment. Before 1870 in the USA, for instance, industrial growth was spread among towns of all sizes. After 1870, however, there is marked concentration of growth in large cities at the expense of medium-sized towns. This reflects the qualitative inefficiency of the latter as described above. Gordon takes the argument further forward in time. Concentration of workers in large cities eventually led to local commerce losing political control of their cities. This is accompanied by the suburbanization of industry symbolized by the development of Gary steelworks *beyond* Chicago. Gordon describes the 'sudden' emergence of the de-centralization strategy and relates it directly to the rise of corporate capitalism. The late 1890s are a period of phenomenal merger activity which produced large corporations able to take broad strategic decisions such as decentralization of plant. The qualitative efficiency explanation is far superior to quantitative efficiency explanations which emphasize changes in transport and land needs. Gordon is able to document that the decision-makers at the time were clear in their motives (Gordon 1978: 75). Cities had become 'hotbeds of trade unionism' and corporations were relocating investment to non-union plants in the suburbs. The final stage in this process is the regional shift from unionized North-east USA to the less-unionized South and West of the present day. The 'rise of the sunbelt' can thus be seen as the third location strategy in US capital's battle to keep control of US labour.

This process has not been documented in detail elsewhere but the general pattern seems to fit. In Britain, for instance, we have described the militancy of medium-sized towns and they certainly grew slower than large cities in late nineteenth century Britain. Similarly de-centralization and regional shifts in investment have also been inversely related to unionism in the twentieth century. The qualitative efficiency argument is clearly attractive here also. It is, of course, consistent with the 'runaway shop' process that has typified the world-economy from its inception. Wallerstein (1980a: 194) shows how the stagnation of the logistic B-phase was combated in part by a relocation strategy in many industries. Throughout central and western Europe the power of labour guilds was broken by moving industry to the countryside. This physical dispersion led to weaker labour organization and lower wages. And, of course, today's runaway shop to peripheral countries — Korea, Mexico and so on — is the latest example of the qualitative efficiency strategy. Here we have a political location theory rather than the economic location theory which has dominated geography.

3. Planning for harmony

The lesson of the above discussion is that ultimately capital, by investment, creates and destroys places. In core countries in the twentieth century this power of capital has been mediated by the state through the activity of 'town planning. 'Planning' is sometimes contrasted with 'market' and is then assumed to be anti-capitalist in some way. In fact in the theory of the state we developed in Chapter 4 planning occurs as an alternative way in which the interests of dominant classes can be safeguarded or promoted. Sarkissian (1976) has described how planning has attempted to apply the neighbourhood effect to promote social harmony.

Planners have a long history of promoting the social mixture of communities. Why should social mix be preferred to segregation of classes which the housing market left to itself would produce? Early planners argued that by mixing classes the behaviour of the lower classes would be raised by emulating their more affluent neighbours. In this way social harmony could be created and social tensions reduced. In some ways this was an anti-urban 'back-to-the-village' movement but it also encompassed ideas such as equality of opportunity for all classes and provision of leadership for the urban poor. But the emphasis upon emulation meant that social problems were reduced to individual behaviour. It was just a matter of teaching the poor to behave.

The practical application of these ideas can be traced back to George

Cadbury's building of Bourneville on the outskirts of Birmingham in the 1880s. This was a paternalistic project — it was a temperance settlement, for example — but social mix was an integral part of the plan to produce an ideal 'balanced community'. The idea of a balanced locality is most developed in Ebenezer Howard's Garden City Movement which is probably Britain's major contribution to town planning. Although his book is now well known as *Garden Cities of Tomorrow* it was originally published in 1898 as *To-morrow: A Peaceful Path to Real Reform* which clearly places the movement in a political perspective. This planning in no way challenged the basic forces operating in British society, rather it steered them into politically safe directions. Howard's motives were explicitly anti-revolutionary as his original title suggests. In fact Garden City advocates were careful to maintain segregation at the neighbourhood level because complete integration implied 'equality and hence mediocrity' (Sarkissian 1976: 236).

These ideas became popular after the Second World War. The 'classlessness' of national sacrifice became directed towards reconstruction and in Britain, in particular, this involved town planning dominated by garden city ideas. The neighbourhood unit as a small balanced community fitted into this planning ideology and was imported from the United States. The whole process was promoted in both countries by the onset of the Cold War. Balanced neighbourhoods where different classes had equal opportunities became an important element in the 'free' 'democratic' world's claim to continue to be the 'true' 'progressive' force in the world (Sarkissian 1976: 239). In the United States this inevitably led to the issue of racial segregation and ultimately to the Supreme Court desegregation victories in education and housing. There is a continuity of ideas from Bourneville, England to Little Rock, Arkansas centring on opportunity but ultimately based on containing social conflict. Originally, benevolent capitalists with foresight and then the state have used planning in an attempt to produce places of harmony to replace places of strife. It is ironic, therefore, that planning as a reformist solution to 'urban' problems should often appear today to be part of the problem.

A NEW THEORY OF POLITICS IN LOCALITIES

Debates concerning the neighbourhood effect go on unabated. In a recent exchange Johnston (1987) and McAllister (1987) have produced contrary findings for recent British elections: Johnston provides evidence for locational influences on party voting levels; McAllister, using a different analysis, shows that location variables are not required to explain party voting variations. This debate can be portrayed as an inter-disciplinary dispute with geographers developing models where location is important (for example, Johnston) and political scientists preferring to concentrate on political variables that are nation-wide in their effects (for example, McAllister). This situation is quite unsatisfactory. In recent years the debate has become transcended by an inter-disciplinary project that is creating a new theory of politics in localities. Both sides of the original debate are criticized.

The political scientists are accused of over-emphasis on the state as a political arena (Agnew 1987b). They subscribe to a nationalization of politics thesis that is no longer tenable. This thesis is that local political effects have been eroded as society has 'modernized'. Modernization was expected to produce relatively homogeneous national spaces and a national politics. Agnew (1987b) argues that this is to confuse locality or place with the concept of community. Traditional communities may have been eroded over time but this does not mean that localities have thereby disappeared. With the demise of old communities, localities remain and have generated new 'local politics'. The 'non-place realms' of modernization theory are a myth. Every place is unique and has its own politics. Political scientists, therefore, in their pursuit of the nationalization thesis, have badly neglected an important dimension of modern politics, the politics in localities. Agnew (1988) illustrates the argument most clearly for Italy where the massive political differences between localities in the north and south of the country have been lost in political scientists' search for a single Italian politics.

Localities matter in politics, therefore, but not necessarily in the way that the neighbourhood effect has been interpreted. Johnston's (1986a,b) recent attempt to use political parties as the link between localities and voting to produce the neighbourhood effect is important in getting beyond models of inter-personal contacts but still falls far short of an adequate explanation of the phenomenon. Johnston like others before him goes on to invoke the creation of local political cultures to sustain voting patterns that diverge from that expected from the composition (class structure) of a locality. Hence neighbourhood effects became products of 'culture'. The problem here is that culture is an extremely vague concept. It seems to be brought into the analysis to describe what cannot be measured in the aggregate models (Mark-Lawson and Warde 1987). Problems abound. Can similar 'cultures' produce different political actions, for instance? (Savage 1987a). What proportion of people have to subscribe to a particular 'culture' (or world view) for it to be the locality's 'culture'? And if 'cultures' do dominate a local politics how are changes ever brought about? No wonder political scientists have avoided using the concept of political cultures in recent years (Mark-Lawson and Warde, 1987).

The emphasis on ideas and attitudes, ideologies and cultures in neighbourhood effect studies has one overriding limitation: it relegates the politics of tactics and strategy within localities. And yet it is these political practices that are the very stuff of politics. The new theory of politics in localities rediscovers the political actions of people living in localities. In

this view people are not inert subjects that merely experience their locality
and who are socialized into its culture to behave accordingly. The new
theory is bringing politics back into locality studies but not in the narrow
sense of just formal political institutions such as political parties. This is a
politics of local people's power to make their localities for their own ends
and to defend their locality against outside threats.

PRACTICAL POLITICS

The emphasis on neighbourhood effects in locality studies in political
geography has produced a concentration on voting patterns at the expense
of other forms of politics. The problem with this bias is that voting for the
same party in different localities can mean very different things. Savage
(1987a) attacks the problem by distinguishing practical politics from
formal party politics. The latter involves parties competing for access to
the state as we have seen. Practical politics, on the other hand, is more
generally about people's actions in struggling to advance or defend their
own interests (Savage 1987a, 11). This need not involve direct demands on
the state of course. In this section we consider practical politics and in the
following section we return to formal politics in a discussion of the local
state.

1. The making and breaking of places

One of the attractions of the concept of political culture has been its use in
accounting for long-term continuities in political attitudes and actions.
Johnston (1986b), for instance, has shown how the Dukeries area of
Nottinghamshire in England has been a centre of 'moderate' Labour
politics for most of this century. In 1926, after the collapse of the national
strike, the Nottinghamshire miners set up a new local union in opposition
to the more militant national union; and in 1985 after a second national
strike they repeated this action. This 'moderation' has also been reflected
in voting at national, local and union elections. More commonly,
continuities in local politics have been traced for 'radical regions'. Cooke
(1985), for instance, identifies such localities in South Wales, Provence in
southern France and Emilia in central Italy. But the concept of political
culture is much less satisfactory when we come to consider political
change. No region or locality is insulated from the world around it. Hence,
as in the case of national politics, the ups and downs of the
world-economy will generate 'new politics' in the sense that the
opportunities and constraints for local people will alter. A strong local
culture may smooth out these patterns of new politics. It is more likely,
however, that the latter is interpreted within the political culture to give an
appearance of continuity when in reality very different political practices
occur. In particular, continuity in voting patterns need not indicate a
political continuity since the same political party can represent very

different politics at different times. We encountered this with 'new politics' at the national scale in Chapter 6 and there is no reason to think similar processes do not operate at the local scale. In this context Savage (1987b) talks about the different 'trajectories' of localities so that some radical regions may be declining while others are emerging. For instance, Glasgow and Liverpool can be contrasted in this respect, the former having a radical past and moderate present and the latter having the inverse of this trajectory.

Jones (1986) has provided us with a particularly clear-cut example of a changing local politics related to wider changes in the world-economy. The Michigan economy is heavily dependent on the automobile industry and the recent politics of the state has reflected changes in the fortunes of that industry. From 1965 to 1979 a liberal-labour alliance represented by the Democratic Party produced a strong welfare state program on the back of the automobile industry's prosperity. Stagnation through the 1970s was followed in 1979 by a collapse in the industry that totally changed the political scene. Corporations now had the upper hand. In the new competitive politics Michigan was deemed a high-cost state and the local welfare state alliance was no longer sustainable. Michigan's 'vigorously progressive political culture' (Jones 1986: 374) was not able to prevent the state moving along the new pro-business trajectory.

The key concept for linking localities to the processes operating in the wider world is uneven development. This is not an alternative term for the traditional geographical concept of areal differentiation. The latter merely implies diversity over space whereas uneven development posits a hierarchy of spaces. They can exist globally as in our core—periphery concepts; within countries unequal development denotes rich and poor localities or regions. At this scale places are explicitly made and broken by sequences of investments that are related to Kondratieff waves. The most famous model of this process is Doreen Massey's (1984) geology analogue. Every A-phase of the world-economy is expressed through an up-turn in investments. These are not evenly distributed over space since for any given package of new investments some places will be more suitable — provide a larger profit on the investment — than others. But different places will be favoured in the various rounds of investment over several Kondratieff cycles. Hence every locality can be viewed as having a different pattern of 'layers' of investment corresponding to the rhythms of the world-economy. For instance, in the traditional industrial zones of northern Britain many localities have investment 'layers' that signify their nineteenth-century prosperity but subsequent rounds of investment are under-represented. Their economic trajectory has taken them from 'boom regions' to 'problem regions'. The politics of all localities concerns how local politicians and people have coped with the changing world-economy and how it has impinged on their area. Local political cultures may interact with the changing economy but to fully understand the politics of a locality we need to investigate the actual political practices.

2. Practical political strategies

The most well-known model of protest activity is Hirschman's (1970) exit-voice-loyalty trilogy of responses to a problem. Exit refers to migration to overcome the problem; for instance, the movement of unemployed people to find jobs. This common strategy is the basis of the making and remaking of all places — boom regions are easily identified by high levels of in-migration, for instance, and in problem regions out-migration is usually very high. Loyalty refers to acceptance of a set of unfavourable circumstances. This need not be because of some deferential ideology or culture, it may be a rational decision on the grounds that any action is likely to fail and be counterproductive. This may represent a very realistic appraisal of the politics of a situation.

Hirschman's concept of 'voice', on the other hand, signifies protest in an attempt to change an unsatisfactory situation. Johnston (1982a: 236–40) describes three types of local protest. First, there is protest through formal channels such as giving evidence to public enquiries in Britain or fighting an action through the courts in the USA. Second, there is 'generalized protest' which involves taking the case 'to the public' for instance by organizing petitions, public meetings, marches and demonstrations. Third, direct action is to take steps to prevent an unsatisfactory situation beginning or continuing. Sit-in protests, occupying empty houses or closed down factories are typical examples.

The types of practical politics will change over time and between places. Savage (1987a) provides us with a very carefully constructed picture of the practical politics in England in the period before the welfare state. Concentrating on the problems of the working classes he defines their basic interests to be the reduction of insecurity. This is because in the industrial cities of England they had become separated from the means of subsistence. Every household therefore had to devise a survival strategy centred on the wages of its members in employment. There may have been other supplements to the wages — for example, many employers provided vegetable gardens for their employees — but the survival of the household primarily relied on swapping wages for subsistence goods. Practical politics therefore was about reducing the insecurity inherent in wage labour.

Savage (1987a) indentifies three types of equally rational responses to the problem of insecurity. *Mutualistic practical politics* involved forming collective organizations to insure against calamities and to keep control, as far as possible, of different aspects of day-to-day subsistence. Many working-class institutions were founded to lessen insecurity in this way, the most well-known being co-operative (retail) societies and friendly (insurance) societies. *Economistic practical politics* centred upon enhancing security in the workplace through trade union activities. This is not simple wage bargaining but involves negotiating for control over the work process. Demarcation agreements and control of entry into occupations represent examples of economistic solutions to insecurity. Finally, *statist practical politics* involved lobbying the state to intervene and lessen insecurity by providing social 'safety nets'. The end-result of this practical politics was the welfare state.

Savage (1987a) uses these alternative practical political strategies to show how simple reference to voting patterns can be quite misleading. In the 1920s, for instance, both South Wales and Sheffield became local Labour strongholds but this support was based on totally different practical politics. This was reflected in the different reactions to the 1919 Housing Act which promoted the construction of council (public) housing. In Sheffield a statist politics involved building houses to let at low subsidized rents. In South Wales a mutualist politics had resulted in much of the housing stock being built by 'housing clubs'. This 'self-building' tradition plus out-migration in the 1920s meant that council housing was not seen in a redistributive role and low rent schemes were uncommon. Hence popular Labour councils in different regions pursued quite different sorts of politics.

But why do different practical politics occur in different localities? Savage's (1987a) answer is a complex one involving the local social structure facilitating different politics. The pattern of skills is one important factor. Craft occupations in small-scale workshops, for instance, facilitate mutualist political struggle. In contrast, general factory skills in large organizations provide the potential for economistic struggle. Finally, casualized labour will often seek security through statist strategies. These patterns of potentials interact with local gender relations. Where the household is dependent on male wages economistic struggle is facilitated through trade unions. In contrast where the household as a whole is involved in wage labour — for instance, 'weaving families' in the textile industry — the potential for mutualistic or statist politics is produced with the demand for welfare services for the working family.

The interaction between the local social structure and the resulting politics is obviously very complex and produces a mosaic of different politics across a range of localities. Savage (1987a) illustrates this through a case study of the Lancashire textile town of Preston. Two parts of his story are of relevance here. In the late nineteenth century Preston, despite its earlier radical reputation, had become a Conservative Party stronghold. Most working people voted Conservative and Labour candidates made little headway in elections. Savage is at pains to point out that this was not a case of deferential voting but represented a rational response to working-class insecurity in a period when Preston's economic base was declining. The Conservative Party offered a 'politics of regeneration' supported by both unions and employers. Hence working-class support was purely an economistic political strategy: Conservative policy matched the practical politics. The Labour Party was only able to achieve electoral success in Preston in the 1920s when they could tap a new statist practical politics that demanded security through welfare provision. Labour's municipal socialism matched this practical politics and they reaped their electoral reward.

After 1945 the Labour Party in Britain was able to come to power on the basis of a statist political programme that produced the welfare state. This created the congruent politics of the liberal-social-democratic state described in Chapter 6. In recent years there has been an increase in the spatial polarization of voting just as levels of class voting are declining (Johnston 1985). Savage (1987b) uses a theory of locality politics to explain this phenomenon. Basically the uneven development of the downturn of the Kondratieff wave has produced additional contrasts in prosperity between localities in Britain. All residents in poorer localities have a common interest to upgrade the local labour and housing market and hence their practical politics can continue to coincide with Labour's statist approach. In prosperous areas, on the other hand, both working-class and middle-class households are gaining from the buoyant local labour and housing markets making them susceptible to the market growth policies of the Conservatives. The result is that voting contrasts between localities is cross-cutting the earlier class cleavage to generate a new congruent politics. Since poorer areas have been Labour districts and wealthier areas have been Conservative districts, the new locality-based voting can produce a neighbourhood effect pattern (accentuating Labour and Conservative stronghold support) without the need to hypothesize the vague neighbourhood effect process.

Although Savage's work applies to Britain the concepts he develops would seem to be applicable to a wide range of contexts beyond one country.

3. *Alternative politics of location*

So far our argument has concentrated on the practical politics of households. This is reasonable since households are locally dependent, their everyday life is situated within localities. Let us now add capital to our local politics. The controllers of capital must also be concerned with localities since all capital investments must also be situated. The practical political strategies of capital can be reduced to three options (Harvey 1985). First, they can meet competition from other capitalists by increasing investment in a locality to produce more efficiently. Second, they can relocate and invest elsewhere to a more favourable location — Gordon's political theory of location in the previous section describes this strategy. Third, capital can build a coalition for growth in its existing locality where it will benefit from the resulting increase in value of the locality. Cox and Mair (1988: 310) refer to this as 'enhancing the flow of value through a specific locality'. This last strategy is particularly common in the United States where locally dependent capital is encouraged by the anti-monopoly laws whereby banks and public utilities are forced to remain local.

Growth coalitions represent one of two types of 'politics of turf' that Cox has identified. The *class politics of location* is when local politics puts the needs of labour's consumption fund above capital's profit fund. This class politics depends on the local changing balance of power between capital and labour. In Jones's (1986) study referred to previously the politics of Michigan between 1965 and 1979 could be referred to as a class politics of location. In a *territorial politics of location*, on the other hand, people are mobilized as localized consumers. This enables territorial coalitions to form between locally dependent capital and households concerned with home ownership and local services such as education. These growth coalitions produce a politics of 'boosterism'. Jones describes just such a new politics in Michigan after 1979 with the Governor in a new role as lobbyist to corporations. Davies (1988) provides a superb description of a very competitive territorial politics on Tyneside, England, where 'municipal socialism' has been transformed into 'municipal capitalism'.

Cox (1988) argues that currently there is a dominance of territorial policies in localities. But whether the outcome is one or other of the location politics depends upon particular contingencies both local and non-local. It may well be that territorial politics is more common in the United States than in Western Europe (but see Davies, 1988). In Britain, for instance, local governments have attempted to devise local economic initiatives that are clearly part of a class politics (Boddy, 1984). These policies bring us to more formal political practices and the local state.

THE LOCAL STATE

The institutions of the modern nation-state exist at more than one geographical scale. All territorial states have institutions that operate at the level of the locality. A wide range of functions are typically organized at this particular scale — education, housing provision, public transport and land-use planning are all typical examples. This state activity is commonly referred to as the 'local state' to distinguish it from the activities at the scale of the state territory, commonly referred to as the 'central state'.

The concept of the local state is an ambiguous one. The use of the term 'state' in this context does not indicate sovereignty since that is vested with the territorial state. For this reason some writers have doubted the validity of the concept. It has been pointed out that the phrase 'local government' can be substituted for local state in many cases with no change in meaning (Duncan and Goodwin 1982). Hence the call to drop the concept. This would be a pity. The term 'government' merely implies imposing authority in a locality, 'state' suggests a wider set of relations in which to view the formal politics of a locality. It is for this reason that local state has come to be an important concept in the new theory of politics in localities. Let us explore this further.

1. The nature of the local state

Given the formal power of the nation-state, why is this not instituted as a single-tier structure? The fact that one-tier states are conspicuous by their absence in the world-economy suggests that extra tiers, and in particular the local state, are a necessary requirement. This need can be derived from two aspects of the modern state. First, the state's institutions consist of a large scale bureaucracy. All bureaucratic organizations operate within specific spans of control in hierarchical structures. Quite simply it is far more efficient to decentralize various functions rather than make all decisions from a remote centre: it does not make practical sense to schedule the garbage collection for a provincial city from government offices in the capital city. Second, the government function of the state requires legitimacy and this can rest to varying degrees on traditions of local autonomy. Such communalism is particularly strong in the United States but the notion that people living in localities should have some say in the running of their locality is accepted in many countries. The combination of these administrative-efficiency and government-legitimacy functions produce the local state. The balance between administration and government will vary between places and over time so that empirically the local state will differ depending on the context. Theoretically, however, the nature of the local state will remain the same.

The concept of the local state was introduced into the literature by Cockburn (1977) in a study of the political practices in a London borough. She used the term to emphasize the fact that the local government she was studying was an integral part of the capitalist state. She employs a Marxist theory of the state in which the local state is distinguished by the functions it performs, in particular 'social reproduction'. Hence the local state is an instrument of class domination managing the social needs of households for the ultimate benefit of capital. Duncan and Goodwin (1988, 34) criticize this theoretical 'top down' perspective as being too one-sided. Why is there a history of centre-local tensions within states if the local state is primarily just an agent of the central state?

The major theoretical development since Cockburn (1977) has been Saunders's (1984) 'dual state thesis' whereby the functions of the two levels of state are conceptualized into two distinct sets of political processes. At the centre a class politics based upon issues of production is to be found whereas in the local state a politics of consumption cuts across class lines. Since the central state is concerned with the needs of capital accumulation and the local state focuses more on legitimation needs then

tensions between the two scales are hardly surprising. But this thesis has
come under severe criticism. Empirically it is not very easy to show that
this division of functions actually exists. Both production and
consumption issues are to be found in the politics at both scales.
Theoretically the allocation of functions to state levels implies a rather
static pattern of social relations and the state. The dual-state thesis is
ahistorical; we need a longer term view of the local state than has been the
norm in most studies (Duncan and Goodwin 1988).

The most important characteristic of the local state is the ambiguity of
its role. Kirby (1987: 20) refers to the 'curious political position occupied
by the local state'. This is because it is both part of the state apparatus but
it can also be used to oppose the state. Duncan and Goodwin (1988: 46)
trace this idea of local state as both agent and obstacle to Miliband (1969).
They develop an instrumental theory of the local state as 'a double-edged
sword' (Duncan and Goodwin 1988: 41). Once again uneven development
is the key concept that necessitates the state to organize local agents to
manage their territorial diversity. But the very nature of this diversity will
mean that different interests from those of the national dominant groups
can dominate particular localities. Local groups can, therefore, use the
local state to promote their own policies in opposition to those of the
central state. Hence for Duncan and Goodwin (1988) it is this
contradictory role of the local state, and not its particular functions, that
enables us to specify the concept. This is the true nature of the local state.

2. Local state as instrument

The particular balance between the local state as an instrument of the
state and as an instrument of the locality will vary widely with the context
of the politics. We will describe two contrasting examples here before
considering more generally the changing potential for conflict.

The tension between central state and local state has been a prominent
feature of British politics in the last decade. The Conservative central
government has an electoral mandate to reduce public expenditure at the
same time that Labour city governments have claimed a mandate to resist
cuts in services. This has led to a classic centre-local conflict within the
state apparatus. Major clashes have occurred in all main areas of policy
including education, housing, transport and planning.

The central government's response to this challenge has been varied.
The simplest method has been to transfer functions to the centre. In
education, for instance, a 'national curriculum' has been instituted thereby
lessening local inputs to what is taught in state schools. A second simple
solution is to transfer functions from the elected public sector to new
appointed public corporations. Non-elected urban development
corporations have taken over land-use control functions in several cities,
for instance. Alternatively, functions can be transferred out of the public
sector to the private sector. This privatization strategy has been carried

out for public transport and public housing. Alternatively, the local state can be by-passed by direct appeal to residents which is part of the policy in education and housing. Far more direct controls are involved with central intervention in local government budgets. The policy of 'rate-capping' involved placing a limit on the raising of local taxes for selected local governments. There are numerous other budgetary controls operating and a new method of raising local taxes is to be implemented. Finally, the ultimate central state sanction is abolition. All seven metropolitan governments in England have been abolished. These had formed some of the major centres of opposition to the Conservative central government. We can conclude, therefore, that the attempt to use the local state as an instrument of opposition to the central government has been largely checked but at great expense to all local government practices. Hence the central Conservative policies have been opposed in many areas by local Conservative politicians as well as by the Labour Party. But in Britain the formal power of the central state is such that this major overhaul of centre-local relations was carried out with little or no delay through Parliament.

The situation in the United States is very different. Very often the local state has been an instrument for middle-class households to prevent national policies impinging on their localities. This is most clearly seen in housing and education policies within metropolitan regions. These areas are highly fragmented into many separate government units. The larger metropolitan regions such as New York and Chicago have more than a thousand governments each. In the United States as a whole Johnston (1982b) reports 80,000 municipalities and special districts, which is one for every 300 people!

This political fragmentation is particularly associated with suburbanization. The typical metropolitan region consists of a central city surrounded by numerous suburban municipalities and special districts. The major advantage of separate incorporation is to be able to control local land use through zoning. In the Connecticut section of the New York metropolitan region, for example, 75 per cent of the land is zoned for housing plots of one acre or more. Such a policy is designed to produce a social segregation which is the USA's spatial representation of the class conflict. Rich suburbs avoid any cross-subsidization with the poorer central city while at the same time free loading on city services (Cox 1973). In court cases challenging zoning these local states have always been able to maintain their discrimination policies (Johnston 1984).

The second major form of discrimination in US cities has been in education. Here the central government has used the courts to force local states to conform to national standards of non-discrimination on racial grounds. Originally this was a battle in the South as local 'separate but equal' education policies were overturned. In the North, residential segregation meant that neighbourhood schools produced *de facto*

segregated education. This was attacked by the central government in the
courts by replacing neighbourhood schools with 'mixed' schools using
bussing. This precipitated a 'white flight' to the suburbs to avoid the
policy. In 1974 Detroit tried to overcome the problem by devising a
bussing scheme to incorporate the suburbs. This was defeated in the
courts (Johnston 1984).

In these exercises in constitutional politics the local state has been the
prime instrument through which suburban households have defended their
localities. This has not really been an option for suburbanites in other
countries since it reflects use of the particularly strong American ideology
of communalism. This has provided the ammunition for the local state
victories and it illustrates the importance of the political context in any
discussion of local states.

3. The changing potential for conflict

Duncan and Goodwin (1988) are very keen that the current conflict
between central and local state in Britain be seen as part of a series of
such conflicts:

> Thus the present series of Conservative legislation should not be seen as a
> singular event, introduced as a response to the current economic crisis or to
> particular 'Thatcherite' ideology. Rather recent action and events should be
> seen as only the latest stage in a long history of central government
> restructuring in local-central relations. (Duncan & Goodwin 1988: 3).

In fact we can see that every B-phase in the Kondratieff cycles has been
associated with just such a restructuring of the local state. In the 1830s the
new Poor Law reorganized the dispensing of relief from the parish level to
'unions' of parishes in order to curb 'local excesses'. In the 1880s the
whole local government map was redrawn to take into account the growing
problems of cities. In the 1920s, in the earlier 'politics of crisis' identified
in Chapter 6, new laws were brought in to curb the activities of various
local authorities. And so we come to the new reorganization of local
government in the 1970s and the current round of legislation to bring local
states into line.

The comparison of particular interest is that between the last B-phase
and the recent situation. This is because the first 'politics of crisis'
coincided with the rise of the Labour Party as a major party. Although not
very successful nationally at this time, the uneven development meant that
inevitably Labour as a major party began winning control of local
governments. The result was centre-local conflict as Labour pursued
expenditure programmes that were incompatible with the central state's
austerity policies. 'Little Moscows' appeared in several industrial regions
(Macintyre 1980). The most serious challenge, however, came in the
London Borough of Poplar and local government rebellion is still
sometimes referred to as 'poplarism' (Branson 1979). Here the elected
members of the local state were far too generous in their dispensing of

relief to the poor for the central government's liking. New acts of parliament were passed to more tightly control expenditure. New districts were drawn and some elected authorities suspended and replaced by central government commissioners. Finally in 1934, in the period we have called the first 'politics of national interest', the abolition solution was finally used as it has been in the current politics of national interest. A new scheme of social security to be run by civil servants from the central state replaced the local systems of payments. The result was a new system that was 'centrally directed, uniformly fixed and removed from the vagaries and dissensions of party politics' (Runciman 1966: 78–9). The politics of the locality was sacrificed for the national interest then as now.

Just how powerful is the local state, therefore? Formally the answer seems to be that local governments can be easily disposed of as necessary by sovereign nation-states. Clark's (1984) analysis of local autonomy supports this view. He identifies two sources of local power, the power to initiate policy and the power of immunity from oversight by higher authorities of the state. Whether or not a local unit possesses these powers produces four types of autonomy. Where there is no initiative and no immunity the situation is one of local administration only. These are literally just agents of the central state pursuing central policies irrespective of the locality. The opposite case, where there is both initiative and immunity, produces an autonomous city-state. This ideal type does not really exist except as a sovereign state such as Singapore. Real levels of autonomy within territorial states are provided where either initiative or immunity exists. With no initiative but discretion to implement central policies for locality needs with immunity, the system can be described as 'top-down' autonomy. With initiative to pursue policies for a locality but with no immunity from central state interference, we can describe the system as 'bottom-up' autonomy. Clark's (1984) application of these criteria to local government in the USA leads him to conclude that formally they are closest to the 'local administration' type of autonomy —they have little or no initiative or immunity. We can extend this conclusion increasingly to the situation in Britain.

This 'pessimistic' view of the local state's power can be easily countered however. For all the lack of formal autonomy, local states do have a real manoeuverability that makes them potentially powerful instruments as our previous discussions have shown. The simplest evidence is the variety of expenditure on different services across local government units. The uniformity implied by local administration is simply not found. In both the United States and Britain there is a huge literature on the variability of local government 'outputs' (Newton 1981). This clearly implies some local 'choices' that are overriding the formal limitations on autonomy.

We can conclude, therefore, that uneven development will inevitably force the central state to organize control of its territory through some local autonomy. Hence abolition of the local state is never a solution to the tension of centre-local relations. In our examples of abolition above only *part* of the local state system has been removed. Complete abolition of the local state is unthinkable. And even if this policy were pursued it would not, of course, get rid of locality politics. It would remove an instrument from the locality but in doing so it would also remove an instrument of the central state. That is the fundamental ambiguity of the local state. Local states are important to central government in many ways. In times of crisis, for instance, we have seen how political problems are diverted down the state hierarchy until blame rests with the local state (Dear 1981). By abolishing the local state the central state would have no link into localities. The state would be less integrated: it would lose part of its legitimacy. Locality politics would continue but take different forms some of which have been described earlier. This might well be more dangerous than having localities firmly integrated into the nation-state through their local states.

We have concluded this book on a contradiction and that is very appropriate. Local states are not agents of the state or agents of opposition to the state. They are both simultaneously. That is their hallmark. Further the new theory of politics in localities incorporates other contradictions. This motif fits the politics of the world-economy generally as the earlier chapters have shown. The world is not a simple machine that we can understand by learning a few formulae. Our world is complex incorporating severe contradictions which translate into many difficult dilemmas for politicians. The political geography of this world must also be complex therefore. I hope I have shown in this book that a political geography perspective on the world-economy organized around geographical scales can make sense of our modern world without losing too much of the complexity of that reality.

BIBLIOGRAPHY

Abrams, P. (1978) 'Towns and economic growth: some theories and problems' in P. Abrams and E. A. Wrigley (eds) *Towns in Society*. Cambridge U.P.

Agnew, J. A. (1982) 'Sociologizing the geographical imagination: spatial concepts in the world-systems perspective', *Political Geography Quarterly* **1**: 159–66.

Agnew, J. A. (1983) 'An excess of "national exceptionalism": towards a new political geography of American foreign policy, *Political Geography Quarterly* **2**: 151–66.

Agnew, J. A. (1987a) *Place & Politics*. Allen and Unwin: London.

Agnew, J. A. (1987b) 'Place anyone? A comment on the McAllister and Johnston papers', *Political Geography Quarterly* **6**: 39–40.

Agnew, J. A. (1988) ' "Better thieves than Reds"? The nationalization thesis and the possibility of a geography of Italian politics,' *Political Geography Quarterly*, **7**: 307–22.

Agnew, J. and **O'Tuathail, G.** (1987) 'The historiography of American geopolitics', *Paper presented at ISA conference, Washington, DC, April 1987*

Ajami, F. (1978) 'The global logic of the neoconservatives', *World Politics* **30**: 450–68

Alavi, H. (1979) 'The state in post-colonial societies' in H. Goulbourne (ed.) *Politics and State in the Third World*. Macmillan: London.

Almond, G.A. and **Verba, S.** (1963) *The Civic Culture*. Princeton U.P.: Princeton, NJ.

Almy, T. A. (1973) 'Residential location and electoral cohesion: the pattern of urban political conflict', *American Political Science Review* **67**: 914–23.

Alonso, W. (1964) *Location and Land Use*. Harvard U.P.: Cambridge, Mass.

Amin, S. (1987) 'Democracy & national strategy in the periphery', *Third World Quarterly* **9**: 1129–56.

Anderson, B. (1983) *Imagined Communities*. Verso: London.

Anderson, J. (1986) 'Nationalism and Geography' in J. Anderson (ed.) *The Rise of the Modern State*. Wheatsheaf: Brighton, UK.

Arblaster, A. (1984) *The Rise and Decline of Western Liberalism*. Blackwell: Oxford, UK.

Archer, J. C. and **Taylor, P.J.** (1981) *Section and Party: A Political Geography of American Presidential Elections from Andrew Jackson to Ronald Reagan*. Wiley: Chichester and New York.

Bachrach, P. and **Baratz, M.** (1962) 'Two faces of power', *American Political Science Review* **56**: 947—52.

Banks, A. S. and **Textor, R. B.** (1963) *A Cross-Polity Survey*. MIT Press: Cambridge, Mass.

Banks, M. (1986) 'The inter-paradigm debate' in M. Light and A. J. R. Groom (eds) *International Relations: A Handbook of Current Theory*. Frances Pinter: London.

Barker, C. (1978) 'The state as capital', *International Socialism* **2**: 16–42.

Barnett, R. J. and **Muller, R. E.** (1974) *Global Reach*. Simon and Schuster: New York.

Barraclough, G. (ed.) (1979) *The Times Atlas of World History.* Times Books: London.

Barratt Brown, M. (1974) *The Economics of Imperialism.* Penguin: London.

Bartlett, C. J. (1984) *The Global Conflict, 1800–1970.* Longman: London and New York.

Bassin, M. (1987) 'Race contra space: the conflict between German geopolitik and National Socialism', *Political Geography Quarterly* **6**: 115–34.

Beard, C. A. (1914) *An Economic Interpretation of the Constitution of the United States.* Macmillan: New York.

Bennett, S. and **Earle, C.** (1983) 'Socialism in America: a geographical interpretation of failure', *Political Geography Quarterly* **2**: 31–56.

Bergesen, A. and **Schoenberg, R.** (1980) 'Long waves of colonial expansion and contraction, 1415–1969' in A. Bergesen (ed.) *Studies of the Modern World System.* Academic: New York.

Bergman, E. F. (1975) *Modern Political Geography.* William Brown: Dubuque, Iowa.

Berry, B. J. L. (1969) 'Review', *Geographical Review* **59**: 450–1.

Blake, G. (ed) (1987) *Maritime Boundaries and Ocean Resources.* Croom Helm: London.

Blaut, J. M. (1975) 'Imperialism: the Marxist theory and its evolution', *Antipode* **7(1)**: 1–19.

Blaut, J. M. (1980) 'Nairn on Nationalism; *Antipode* **12** (3), 1–17.

Blaut, J. M. (1987) *The National Question.* Zed: London.

Blechman, B. M. and **Kaplan, S. S.** (1978) *Force without War: U.S. Armed Forces as a Political Instrument.* Brookings Institute: Washington, DC.

de Blij, H. J. (1967) *Systematic political geography.* Wiley: New York

Blondel, J. (1978) *Political Parties.* Wildwood House: London.

Blouet, B. W. (1987) 'The political career of Sir Halford Mackinder', *Political Geography Quarterly* **6**: 355–68.

Boddy, M. (1984) 'Local economic and employment strategies' in M.

Boddy and C. Fudge (eds) *Local Socialism?* Macmillan: London.

Bowle, J. (1974) *The Imperial Achievement.* Secker & Warburg: London.

Bowman, I. (1924) *The New World.* World Book Company: New York.

Bowman, I. (1948) 'The geographical situation of the United States in relation to World Policies', *Geographical Journal* **112**: 129–42.

Brandt, W. (1980) *North-South: A Programme for Survival.* Pan: London.

Branson, N. (1979) *Poplarism 1919–1925.* Lawrence and Wishart: London.

Brass, P. R. (1975) 'Ethnic cleavages in the Punjabi party system, 1952–1972' in M. R. Barnett *et al.* (eds) *Electoral Politics in the Indian States.* Manohar: Delhi.

Braudel, F. (1973) *Capitalism and Material Life 1400–1800.* Weidenfield & Nicholson: London.

Braudel, F. (1984) *The Perspective on the World.* Collins: London.

Braunmuhl, C. von (1978) 'On the analysis of the bourgeois nation state within the world market context' in J. Holloway and S. Picciotto (eds) *State and Capital.* Arnold: London.

Breuilly, J. (1985) *Nationalism & the State.* Manchester University Press: Manchester, UK.

Brewer, A. (1980) *Marxist Theories of Imperialism, A Critical Survey.* Routledge & Kegan Paul: London.

Briggs, A. (1963) *Victorian Cities.* Penguin: London.

Briggs, E. and **Deacon, A.** (1973) 'The creation of the Unemployment Assistance Board', *Policy and Politics* **2**: 43–62.

Brown, L. R. (1973) *World without Borders.* Vintage: New York.

Brucan, S. (1981) 'The strategy of development in Eastern Europe, *Review* **5**: 95–112.

Brunn, S. D. (1981) 'Geopolitics in a shrinking world: a political geography of the twenty-first century' in A. D. Burnett and P. J. Taylor (eds) *Political Studies from Spatial Perspectives.* Wiley: Chichester UK and New York.

Buchanan, K. (1972) *The Geography of Empire*. Spokesman: Nottingham.

Bukharin, N. (1972) *Imperialism and the World Economy*. Merlin: London.

Bull, H. N. (1977) *The Anarchical Society: A Study of World Order*. Macmillan: London.

Bunge, W. (1982) *The Nuclear War Atlas*. Society for Human Exploration: Victoriaville, Quebec.

Burger, J. (1987) *Report from the Frontier*. Zed: London.

Burghardt, A. (1969) 'The core concept in political geography: a definition of terms', *Canadian Geographer* **63**: 349–53.

Burghardt, A. F. (1973) 'The bases of territorial claims', *Geographical Review* **63**: 225–45.

Burnett, A. and **Taylor, P. J.** (eds) (1981) *Political Studies from Spatial Perspectives*. Wiley: Chichester UK.

Burnham, W. D. (1967) 'Party systems and the political process' in W. N. Chambers and W. D. Burnham (eds) *The American Party System*. Oxford University Press: New York.

Burnham, W. D. (1970) *Critical Elections and the Mainsprings of American Politics*. Norton: New York.

Busteed, M. A. (1975) *Geography and Voting Behaviour*. Oxford U.P.: London.

Butler, D. E. and **Stokes, D. E.** (1969) *Political Change in Britain: Forces Shaping Electoral Choice*. Macmillan: London.

Canovan, M. (1981) *Populism*. Junction: London.

Castells, M. (1977) *The Urban Question: A Marxist Approach*. MIT Press: Cambridge, Mass.

Castells, M. (1978) *City, Class and Power*. Macmillan: London.

Ceaser, J. W. (1979) *Presidential Selection: Theory and Development*. Princeton University Press: Princeton, NJ.

Chase-Dunn, C. K. (1981) 'Interstate system and capitalist world-economy: one logic or two?' in W. L. Hollist and J. N. Rosenau (eds) *World System Structure*. Sage: Beverly Hills.

Chase-Dunn, C. K. (1982) 'Socialist states in the capitalist world-economy' in C. K. Chase-Dunn (ed.) *Socialist States in the World-System*. Sage: Beverly Hills.

Clark, G. L. (1984) 'A theory of local autonomy', *Annals, Association of American Geographers* **74**: 195–208.

Clark, G. L. and **Dear, M** . (1984) *State Apparatus*. Allen & Unwin: Boston.

Claval, P. (1984) 'The coherence of political geography: perspectives on its past evolution and future relevance' in P. J. Taylor and J. W. House (eds) *Political Geography: Recent Advances and Future Directions*. Croom Helm: London.

Coates, D. (1975) *The Labour Party and the Struggle for Socialism*. Cambridge University Press: Cambridge, UK.

Cobban, A. (1969) *The Nation State and National Self-determination*. Collins: London.

Cockburn, C. (1977) *The Local State*. Pluto: London.

Cohen, S. (1973) *Geography and Politics in a World Divided* (2nd ed). Oxford U.P.: New York.

Cohen, S. (1982) 'A new map of global political equilibrium: a developmental approach', *Political Geography Quarterly* **1**: 223–42.

Colls, R. (1986) 'Englishness & the political culture' in R. Colls and P. Dodd (ed), *Englishness: Politics and Culture 1880–1920*. Croom Helm: London.

Cooke, P. (1985) 'Radical regions', in G. Rees (ed.) *Political Action and Social Identity*. Macmillan: London.

Coulter, P. (1975) *Social Mobilization and Liberal Democracy*. Lexington: Lexington, Mass.

Cox, K. R. (1969) 'The voting decision in a spatial context', *Progress in Geography* **1**: 81–117.

Cox, K. R. (1973) *Conflict, Power and Politics in the City: A Geographic View*. McGraw Hill: New York.

Cox, K. R. (1979) *Location and Public Problems: A Political Geography of the Contemporary World*. Maaroufa: Chicago.

Cox, K. R. (1988) 'The politics of turf and the question of class' in M. Dear and J. Wolch (ed.) *Territory & Reproduction*. Sage: Beverly Hills.

Cox, K. R. and **Mair, A.** (1988)

'Locality and community in the politics of local economic development', *Annals, Association of American Geographers* **78**: 307–325.

Cox, K. R. and **McCarthy, J. J.** (1982) 'Neighbourhood activism as a politics of turf: a critical analysis' in K. R. Cox and R. J. Johnston (eds) *Conflict, Politics and the Urban Scene.* Longman: Harlow, UK.

Cox, K. R. and **Nartowicz, F. Z.** (1980) 'Jurisdictional fragmentation in the American metropolis: alternative perspectives', *International Journal of Urban and Regional Research* **4**: 196–209.

Cox, M. (1986) 'The Cold War as a system', *Critique* **17**: 17–82.

Cox, R. (1981) 'Social forces, states and world orders: beyond International Relations theory', *Millennium* **10**: 126–55.

Crewe, I. (1973) 'Politics of "affluent" and "traditional" workers in Britain: an aggregate data analysis', *British Journal of Political Science* **3**: 29–52.

Crewe, I. and **Payne, C.** (1976) 'Another game with nature: an ecological regression model of the British two-party vote ratio in 1970', *British Journal of Political Science* **6**: 43–81.

Davies, J. G. (1988) 'From municipal socialism to . . . . municipal capitalism?,' *Local Government Studies*, March–April: 19–22

Davis, H. B. (1978) *Towards a Marxist theory of Nationalism.* Monthly Review Press: New York.

Deacon A. and **Brigg, J.** (1974) 'Local democracy and central policy', *Policy and Politics* **2**: 347–64.

Dear, M. (1981) 'A theory of the local state' in A. D. Burnett and P. J. Taylor (ed) *Political Studies from Spatial Perspectives.* Wiley: Chichester, UK.

Dear, M. and **Clark, G.** (1978) 'The state and geographic process: a critical review', *Environment and Planning* **A** **10**:173–83.

Deighton, A. (1987) 'The "frozen front": the Labour government, the division of Germany and the origins of the Cold War, 1945–7', *International Affairs* **63**: 449–65.

Delpar, H. (1981) *Red and Blue. The Liberal Party in Colombian Politics, 1863–1899.* University of Alabama Press: University, Alabama.

Deutch, K. W. (1961) 'Social mobilization and political development', *American Political Science Review* **55**: 494–505.

Deutch, K. W. (1981) 'The crisis of the State', *Government and Opposition* **16**: 331–43.

Dikshit, R. D. and **Sharma, J. C.** (1982) 'Electoral performance of the Congress Party in Punjab (1952–1977): an ecological analysis', *Transactions, Institute of Indian Geographers* **4**: 1–15.

Dikshit, R. (1971a) 'Geography and federalism', *Annals, Association of American Geographers* **61**: 97–110.

Dikshit, R. (1971b) 'The failure of federalism in central Africa', *Professional Geographer* **23**: 27–31.

Dikshit, R. (1975) *The Political Geography of Federalism.* Macmillan: Delhi.

Dix, R. H. (1984) 'Incumbency and electoral turnover in Latin America', *Journal of Interamerican Studies* **26**: 435–48.

Dixon, R. G. (1968) *Democratic Representation: Reapportionment in Law and Politics.* Oxford U.P.: London and New York.

Dixon, R. G. (1971) 'The court, the people and "one man, one vote?"' in N.W. Polsby (ed.) *Reapportionment in the 1970's.* University of California Press: Berkeley.

Dodd, P. (1986) 'Englishness and the national culture' in R. Colls and P. Dodd (ed.) *Englishness: Politics and Culture 1880–1920.* Croom Helm: London.

Dua, B. D. (1979) *President's Rule in India.* Chand: New Delhi.

Duncan, S. S. and **Goodwin, M.** (1982) 'The local state: functionalism, autonomy and class relations in Cockburn and Saunders', *Political Geography Quarterly* **1**: 77–96.

Duncan, S. and **Goodwin, M.** (1988) *The Local State and Uneven Development.* Polity: Cambridge, UK.

Dunleavy, P. (1979) 'The urban basis of political alignment: social class, domestic property ownership, and state intervention in consumption processes' *British Journal of Political Science* **9**: 409–43.

Dunleavy, P. (1980) *Urban Political Analysis*. Macmillan: London.

Duverger, M. (1954) *Political Parties*. Methuen: London.

Easton, D. (1965) *A System Analysis of Political Life*. Wiley: New York.

Edwardes, M. (1975) *Playing the Great Game: A Victorian Cold War*. Hamilton: London.

Emmanuel, A. (1972) *Unequal Exchange: A Study of the Imperialism of Trade*. Monthly Review Press: New York and London.

Engels, F. (1952) *The Condition of the Working Class in England in 1844*. Allen and Unwin: London.

Faris, R. E. L. (1967) *Chicago Sociology 1920–1932*. Chandler: San Francisco.

Fifer, J. V. (1976) 'Unity by inclusion: core area and Federal state at American independence', *Geographical Journal* **142**: 402–10.

Fifer, J. V. (1981) 'Washington, D. C. the political geography of a federal capital' *Journal of American Studies* **15**: 5–26.

Filkin, C. and **Weir, D.** (1972) 'Locality' in E Gittus (ed.) *Key Variables in Social Research*, Vol. 1. Heinemann: London.

Finer, S. E. (1974) 'State-building, state boundaries and border control', *Social Science Information* **13**: 79–126.

Fitton, M. (1973) 'Neighbourhood and voting: a sociometric explanation', *British Journal of Political Science* **3**: 445–72.

Foeken, D. (1982) 'Explanation for the partition of sub-Saharan Africa, 1880–1900', *Tijdschrift voor Economische en Sociale Geografie* **73**: 138–48.

Foster, J. (1974) *Class Struggle and the Industrial Revolution*. Weidenfeld and Nicholson: London.

Frank, A. G. (1967) 'Sociology of underdevelopment and the underdevelopment of sociology', *Catalyst* **3**: 20–73.

Frank, A. G. (1977) 'Long live transideological enterprise! The socialist economies in the capitalist division of labour', *Review* **1**: 91–140.

Frank, A. G. (1978) *Dependent Accumulation and Underdevelopment*. Monthly Review Press: New York; Macmillan: London.

Frank, A. G. (1984) *Critique and Anti-critique*. Praeger: New York.

Gaddis, J. L. (1982) *Strategies of Containment*. Oxford U.P.: New York.

Galbraith, J. K. (1957) *The Affluent Society*. Penguin: London.

Gallagher, J. and **Robinson, R.** (1953) 'The imperialism of free trade', *Economic History Review* (2nd series) **6**: 1–15.

Galtung, J. (1971) 'A structural theory of imperialism', *Journal of Peace Research* **8**: 81–117.

Galtung, J. (1979) *The True Worlds*. Free Press: New York.

Gamble, A. (1974) *The Conservative Nation*. Routledge & Kegan Paul: London.

Gellner, E. (1964) *Thought and change*, University of Chicago Press.

Gellner, E. (1983) *Nations and Nationalism*. Blackwell: Oxford.

Giddens, A. (1981) *A Contemporary Critique of Historical Materialism Vol. 1 Power, Property and the State*. Macmillan: London.

Glassner, M. I. (ed) (1986) 'The new political geography of the sea', *Political Geography Quarterly* **5**: 5–71.

Gold, D. A., Lo, C. Y. H. and **Wright, E. O.** (1975) 'Recent developments in Marxist theories of the capitalist state', *Monthly Review* **27**: 29–43 and **28**: 36–51.

Goldfrank, W. L. (1979) 'Introduction: bringing history back in' in W. L. Goldfrank (ed.) *The World-System of Capitalism: Past and Present*. Sage: Beverly Hills.

Goldstein, J. S. (1988) *Long Cycles: Prosperity and War in the Modern Age*. Yale University Press: New Haven.

Gordon, D. M. (1976) 'Capitalist efficiency and socialist efficiency', *Monthly Review* **28**: 19–39.

Gordon, D. M. (1978) 'Class struggle and the stages of American urban development' in D. C. Perry and A. J. Watkins (eds) *The Rise of the Sunbelt Cities*. Sage: Beverly Hills.

Gordon, D. M. (1980) 'Stages of accumulation and long economic cycles' in T. K. Hopkins and I. Wallerstein (eds), *Processes of the World System*. Sage: Beverly Hills.

Gottmann, J. (1951) 'Geography and International Relations', *World Politics* **3**: 153–73.

Gottmann, J. (1952) 'The political partitioning of our world: an attempt at analysis', *World Politics* **4**: 512–19.

Gottmann, J. (1973) *The Significance of Territory*. University Press of Virginia: Charlottesville.

Grano, O. (1981) 'External influences and internal change in the development of Geography' in D. R. Stoddart (ed) *Geography, Ideology and Social Concern* Blackwell: Oxford, UK

Gray, C. S. (1977) *The Geopolitics of the Nuclear Era: Heartland, Rimlands and the Technological Revolution*. Crane, Russak: New York.

Gray, F. (1975) 'Non-explanation in urban geography', *Area* **7**: 228–34.

Gregory, R. (1968) *The Miners and British Politics, 1906–1914*. Oxford U.P.: London.

Gudgin, G. and **Taylor, P. J.** (1979) *Seats, Votes and the Spatial Organization of Elections*. Pion: London.

Hall, P. (1981) 'The geography of the fifth Kondratieff cycle', *New Society* 26th March: 535–7.

Hall, P. (1982) 'The new political geography: seven years on', *Political Geography Quarterly* **1**: 65–76.

Halliday, F. (1983) *The Making of the Second Cold War*. Verso: London.

Harbutt, F. J. (1986) *The Iron Curtain: Churchill, America and the Origins of the Cold War*. Oxford U.P.: New York.

Hardgrave, R. L. (1974) *India: Government and Politics in a Developing Nation*, Harcourt; Brace & World: New York.

Harding, T. (1971) 'The new imperialism in Latin America: a critique of Conor Cruise O'Brien' in K. T. Fann and D. C. Hodges (eds.) *Readings in US Imperialism*. Porter Sargent: Boston.

Hartmann, H. (1980) *Political Parties in India*. Meenakshi Prakasha: New Delhi.

Hartshorne, R. (1950) 'The functional approach in political geography', *Annals, Association of American Geographers* **40**: 95–130.

Hartshorne, R. (1954) 'Political geography' in P.E. James and C. F. Jones (eds) *American Geography: Inventory and Prospect*. Syracuse University Press: Syracuse, NY.

Harvey, D (1973) *Social Justice and the City*. Arnold: London.

Harvey, D. (1985) *The Urbanization of Capital*. John Hopkins U.P.: Baltimore.

Haseler, S. (1976) *The Death of British Democracy*. Elek: London.

Hawkins, A. (1986) 'The discovery of rural England' in R. Colls and P. Dodd (ed) *Englishness: Politics and Culture 1880–1920*. Croom Helm: London.

Hechter, M. (1975) *Internal Colonialism. The Celtic Fringe in British National Development, 1536–1966*. University of California Press: Berkeley.

Hechter M. and **Brustein, W.** (1980) 'Regional modes of production and patterns of state formation in Western Europe', *American Journal of Sociology* **85**: 1061–94.

Helin, R. A. (1967) 'The volatile administrative map of Rumania', *Annals, Association of American Geographers* **57**: 481–502.

Henderson, G. and **Lebow, R. N.** (1974) 'Conclusions' in G. Henderson *et al.* (eds) *Divided Nations in a Divided World*. McKay: New York.

Henige, D. P. (1970) *Colonial Governors from the Fifteenth Century to the Present*. University of Wisconsin Press: Madison.

Henrikson, A. K. (1980) 'The geographical mental maps of American foreign policy makers', *International Political Science Review* **1**: 495–530.

Henrikson, A. K. (1983) ' "A small, cozy town, global in scope": Washington, D. C.', *Ekistics* **50**: 123–45.

Hepple, L. (1986) 'The revival of geopolitics', *Political Geography Quarterly*

5 (Supplement): 21–36.

Herz, J. H. (1957) 'Rise and demise of the territorial state', *World Politics* 9: 473–93.

Heske, H. (1986) 'German geographic research in the Nazi period', *Political Geography Quarterly* 5: 267–82.

Heske, H. (1987) 'Karl Haushofer: his role in German geopolitics and Nazi politics', *Political Geography Quarterly* 6: 135–44.

Hinsley, F. A. (1966) *Sovereignty*. Watts: London.

Hirschman, A. O. (1970) *Exit, Voice and Loyalty*. Harvard U.P.: Cambridge, MA.

Hobsbawm, E. J. (1977) 'Some reflections on "The Breakup of Britain" ', *New Left Review* 105: 3–24.

Hobsbawm, E. J. (1987) *The Age of Empire, 1875–1914*. Guild: London.

Hobson, J. A. (1902) *Imperialism: A Study*. Allen & Unwin: London.

Hobson, J. A. (1968) 'Sociological interpretation of a general election' in P. Abrams (ed.) *The Origins of British Sociology 1834–1914*. University of Chicago Press.

Holloway, J. and **Picciotto, S.** (eds) (1978) *State and Capital: A Marxist Debate*. Arnold: London.

Horrabin, J. F. (1942) *An Outline of Political Geography*. N.C.L.C. Publishing Society: Tillicoultry, Scotland.

Hudson, B. (1977) 'The new geography and the new imperialism: 1870–1918', *Antipode* 9: 12–19.

Hunt, A. (1980) 'Introduction: taking democracy seriously' in A. Hunt (ed.) *Marxism and Democracy*. Lawrence and Wishart: London.

Huttenback, R. A. (1976) *Racism & Empire*. Cornell University Press: Ithaca, N.Y.

Ikporukpo, C. O. (1986) 'Politics and regional politics: the issue of state creation in Nigeria', *Political Geography Quarterly* 5: 127–40.

Inkeles, A. (1975) 'The emerging social structure of the world', *World Politics* 27: 467–95.

Isaacs, A. (1948) *International Trade: Tariff and Commercial Policies*. Irwin: Chicago.

Jackson, W. A. D. (1964) *Politics and Geographic Relationships*. Prentice Hall: Englewood Cliffs, N. J.

Jahnige, T. P. (1971) 'Critical elections and social change', *Polity* 3: 465–500.

James, A. (1984) 'Sovereignty: ground rule or gibberish?' *Review of International Studies* 10: 1–18.

Janelle, D. (1977) 'Structural dimensions in the geography of location conflicts', *Canadian Geographer* 21: 311–28.

Janelle, D. G. and **Millward, H. A.** (1976) 'Locational conflict patterns and urban ecological structure', *Tijdschrift voor Economische en Sociale Geografie*, 67: 102–13.

Jefferson, M. (1939) 'The law of the primate city', *Geographical Review* 34: 226–32.

Jessop, B. (1974) *Traditionalism, Conservatism and British Political Culture*. Allen and Unwin: London.

Jessop, B. (1982) *The Capitalist State*. Robertson: Oxford, UK.

Johnston, R. J. 1973 *Spatial Structures*. Methuen: London.

Johnston, R. J. (1977) 'The electoral geography of an election campaign', *Scottish Geographical Magazine* 93: 98–108.

Johnston, R. J. (1979) *Political, Electoral and Spatial Systems*. Oxford U.P.: London and New York.

Johnston, R. J. (1980a) 'Political geography without politics', *Progress in Human Geography* 4: 439–46.

Johnston, R. J. (1980b) 'Electoral geography and political geography', *Australian Geographical Studies* 18: 37–50.

Johnston, R. J. (1980c) *The Geography of Federal Spending in the United States of America*. Wiley: Chichester, UK.

Johnston, R. J. (1982a) *Geography and the State*. Macmillan: London.

Johnston, R. J. (1982b) *The American Urban System*. Longman: Harlow, U.K.

Johnston, R. J. (1983) 'The neighbourhood effect won't go away: observations on the electoral geography of England in the light of Dunleavy's critique', *Geoforum* 14: 161–8.

Johnston, R. J. (1984) *Residential Segregation, the State and Constitutional Conflict in American Urban Areas*. Academic: London.

Johnston, R. J. (1985) *The Geography of English Politics: The 1983 General Election.* Croom Helm: London

Johnston, R. J. (1986a) 'Placing politics', *Political Geography Quarterly* **5** (Supplement): 63–78.

Johnston, R. J. (1986b) 'The neighbourhood effect revisited: spatial science or political regionalism?', *Environment & Planning D: Society & Space* **4**: 41–55.

Johnston, R. J. (1987) 'The geography of the working class and the geography of the Labour vote in England, 1983', *Political Geography Quarterly* **6**: 7–16.

Johnston, R. J., O'Neill, A. B. and **Taylor, P. J.** (1987) 'The geography of party support: comparative studies in electoral stability' in M. J. Heller (ed) *The Logic of Multiparty Systems.* Springer–Verlag: Munich.

Jones, B. D. (1986) 'Government & business: the automobile industry and the public sector in Michigan', *Political Geography Quarterly* **5**: 369–84.

Jones, S. B. (1954) 'A unified field theory of political geography', *Annals, Association of American Geographers* **44**: 111–23.

Jones, S. B. (1959) 'Boundary concepts in the setting of place and time', *Annals, Association of American Geographers* **49**: 241–55.

Kaldor, M. (1979) *The Disintegrating West.* Penguin: London.

Kamath, P. M. (1985) 'Politics of defection in India in the 1980's', *Asian Survey* **25**: 1039–54.

Kaplan, S. S. (1981) *Diplomacy of Power.* Brookings Institute: Washington DC.

Kashyap, S. C. (1969) *The Politics of Defection.* National: Delhi.

Kasperson, R. E. and **Minghi, J. V.** (eds) (1969) *The Structure of Political Geography.* Aldine: Chicago.

Kennedy, P. (1988) *The Rise & Fall of the Great Powers.* Random House: New York.

Kerr, C. and **Siegel, A.** (1954) 'The inter-industry propensity to strike' in A. Kornhauser (ed.) *Industrial Conflict.* Wiley: New York.

Kirby, A. (1976) 'Housing market studies: a critical review', *Transactions, Institute of British Geographers* **NS1**: 2–9.

Kirby, A. (1987) 'State, local state, context and spatiality: a reappraisal of state theory', *Working Paper*: 87–07. Institute of Behavioral Science: Boulder, Co.

Kleppner, P. (1979) *The Third Electoral System: 1853–1892.* University of North Carolina Press: Chapel Hill.

Knight, D. B. (1982) 'Identity and territory: geographical perspectives on nationalism and regionalism', *Annals, Association of American Geographers* **72**: 514–31.

Knight, D. B. (1988) 'Self-determination for indigenous peoples: the context for change' in R. J. Johnston, D. B. Knight & E. Kofman (eds) *National Self-determination and Political Geography.* Croom Helm: London.

Kolko, J. and **Kolko, G.** (1973) *The Limits of Power.* Harper & Row: New York.

Koves, A. (1981) 'Socialist economy and the world-economy', *Review* **5**: 113–34.

Kristof, L. D. (1959) 'The nature of frontiers and boundaries', *Annals, Association of American Geographers* **49**: 269–82.

Laski, H. J. (1935) *The State in Theory and Practice.* Allen & Unwin: London.

Laski, H. J. (1936) *The Rise of European Liberalism.* Allen & Unwin: London.

Lees, L. H. (1982) 'Strikes and the urban hierarchy in English industrial towns, 1842–1901' in J. E. Cronin and J. Schnear (eds) *Social Conflict and the Political Order in Modern Britain.* Croom Helm: London.

Levinson, C. (1980) *Vodka Cola.* Biblios: Horsham, UK.

Levy, J. S. (1983) *War in the Modern Great Power System, 1495–1975.* University Press of Kentucky: Lexington, Ky.

Lewis, P. F. (1965) 'Impact of negro migration on the electoral geography of Flint, Michigan, 1932–62: a cartographic analysis', *Annals, Association of American Geographers* **55**: 1–25.

Ley, D. and **Mercer, J.** (1980) 'Locational conflict and the politics of consumption', *Economic Geography* **56**: 89–109.

Libby, O. G. (1894) 'The geographical distribution of the vote of the thirteen states of the federal constitution, 1787–1788' *Bulletin of the University of Wisconsin* **1**: 1–116.

Lichtheim G. (1971) *Imperialism.* Penguin: London.

Liebman, M. (1964) '1914: the great schism', *Socialist Register* 1964. 283–92.

Liebowitz, R. D. (1983) 'Finlandization: an analysis of the Soviet Union's "domination" of Finland', *Political Geography Quarterly* **2**: 275–88.

Lijphart, A. (1971) 'Class voting and religious voting in European democracies', *Acta Politica* **6**: 158–71.

Lijphart, A. (1982) 'The relative salience of the socio-economic and religious issue dimensions: coalition formation in ten western democracies, 1919–1979', *European Journal of Political Research* **10**: 201–211.

Lockwood, D. (1966) 'Sources of variation in working class images of society', *Sociological Review* **14**: 249–67.

Lowenthal, D. (1958) 'The West Indies chooses a capital', *Geographical Review* **48**: 336–64.

McAllister, I. (1987) 'Social context, turnout & the vote: Australian & British comparisons', *Political Geography Quarterly* **6**: 17–30.

McColl, R. W. (1969) 'The insurgent state: territorial bases of revolution', *Annals, Association of American Geographers* **59**: 613–31.

McCormick, R. P. (1967) 'Political development and the second party system' in W. N. Chambers and W. D. Burnham (eds) *The American Party Systems.* Oxford U.P.: London and New York.

McCormick, R. P. (1974) 'Ethno-cultural interpretations of American voting behaviour', *Political Science Quarterly* **89**: 351–77.

Macintyre, S. (1980) *Little Moscows.* Croom Helm: London.

McKay, D. V. (1943) 'Colonialism in the French geographical movement, 1871–1881', *Geographical Review* **33**: 214–32.

Mackenzie, R. T. and **Silver, A.** (1968) *Angels in Marble: Working Class Conservatives in Urban England.* Heinemann: London.

Mackinder, H. J. (1904) 'The geographical pivot of history', *Geographical Journal* **23**: 421–42.

Mackinder, H. J. (1919) *Democratic Ideals and Reality: A Study in the Politics of Reconstruction.* Constable: London; Holt: New York.

Mackinder, H. J. (1943) 'The round world and the winning of the peace', *Foreign Affairs* **21**: 595–605.

McPhail, I. R. (1971) 'Recent trends in electoral geography', *Proceedings of the Sixth New Zealand Geography Conference* **1**: 7–12.

Mansergh, N. (1949) *The Coming of the First World War: A Study in the European Balance, 1878–1914.* Longmans: London.

Mark-Lawson, J. and **Warde, A.** (1987) 'Industrial restructuring & the transformation of a local political environment', *Sixth Urban Change & Conflict Conference Proceedings.* University of Kent: Canterbury, U.K.

Massam, B. (1975) *Location & space in social administration.* Arnold: London.

Massey, D. (1984) *Spatial Divisions of Labour.* Macmillan: London.

Mayhew, D. R. (1971) 'Congressional representation: theory and practice in drawing the districts' in N. W. Polsby (ed.) *Reapportionment in the 1970's.* University of California Press: Berkeley.

Mellor, R. (1975) 'Urban sociology in an urbanized society', *British Journal of Sociology* **26**: 276–93.

Menil, L. P. de (1977) *Who speaks for Europe? The Vision of Charles de Gaulle.* Weidenfield & Nicholson: London.

Mikesell, M. W. (1983) 'The myth of the nation state', *Journal of Geography* **82**: 257–60.

Miliband, R. (1961) *Parliamentary Socialism.* Allen & Unwin: London.

Miliband, R. (1969) *The State in Capitalist Society.* Quartet: London.

Miliband, R. (1977) *Marxism and Politics.* Oxford U.P.: London.

Minghi, J. V. (1963) 'Boundary studies in political geography', *Annals, Association of American Geographers* **53**: 407–28.

Modelski, C. (1978) 'The long cycle of global politics and the nation state', *Comparative Studies of Society and History* **20**: 214–35.

Modelski, G. (1981) 'Long cycles, Kondratieffs and alternating innovations' in C. Kegley and P. McGowan (eds) *The Political Economy of Foreign Policy Behavior.* Sage: Beverly Hills.

Modelski, G. (1987) *Long Cycles of World Politics.* Macmillan: London.

Momsen, J. H. and **Townsend, J.** (1987) *Geography of Gender in the Third World.* Hutchinson: London.

Morris, J. (1968) *Pax Britannica.* Faber & Faber: London.

Mouzelis, N. P. (1986) *Politics in the Semi-Periphery.* Macmillan: London.

Muir, R. (1981) *Modern Political Geography* (2nd ed.). Macmillan: London.

Mumford, L. (1938) *The Culture of Cities.* Secker & Warburg: London.

Murdie, R. A. (1969) *The Factorial Ecology of Metropolitan Toronto, 1951–1961.* Department of Geography Research Paper; University of Chicago.

Nairn, T. (1977) *The Break-up of Britain.* New Left Books: London.

Navari, C. (1981) 'The origins of the nation-state' in L. Tivey (ed.) *The Nation-State.* Robertson: Oxford, UK.

Nelund, C. (1978) 'The national world picture', *Journal of Peace Research* **315**: 273–8.

Newby, H. (1977) *The Deferential Worker.* Allen Lane: London.

Newton, K. (1975) 'American urban politics: social class, political structure and public goods', *Urban Affairs Quarterly* **11**: 241–64.

Newton, K. (ed) (1981) *Urban Political Economy.* Pinter: London.

Nielsson, G. P. (1985) 'States and "nation-groups": a global taxonomy' in E. A. Tiryakian & R. Rogowski

(eds) *New Nationalisms of the Developed West.* Allen & Unwin: London.

O'Brien, C. C. (1971) 'Contemporary forms of imperialism' in K. T. Fann and D. C. Hodges (eds) *Readings in US Imperialism.* Porter Sargent: Boston

O'Connor, J. (1973) *The Fiscal Crisis of the State.* St Martin's Press: New York.

O'Loughlin, J. (1984) 'Geographical models of international conflicts' in P. J. Taylor & J. W. House (eds) *Political Geography: Recent Advances & Future Directions.* Croom Helm: London.

O'Loughlin, J. (1986) 'Spatial models of international conflicts: extending current theories of war behavior', *Annals, Association of American Geographers* **76**: 63–80.

O'Loughlin, J. and **van der Wusten, H.** (1986) 'Geography, war and peace: notes for a contribution to a revived political geography', *Progress in Human Geography* **10**: 484–510.

O'Loughlin, J. and **van der Wusten, H.** (1988) 'The political geography of panregions: the theory & an empirical study of Eurafrica', Paper presented at Annual Conference of I.B.G., Loughborough University, January 1988.

O'Sullivan, P. (1982) 'Antidomino', *Political Geography Quarterly* **1**: 57–64.

O'Sullivan, P. (1986) *Geopolitics.* St. Martin's Press: New York.

O'Tuathail, G. (1986) 'The language & nature of the "new geopolitics" — the case of U.S.-El Salvador relations', *Political Geography Quarterly* **5**: 73–86.

Openshaw, S. and **Steadman, P.** (1982) 'On the geography of the worst case nuclear attack on the population of Britain', *Political Geography Quarterly* **1**: 263–78.

Orridge, A. (1981a) 'Varieties of nationalism' in L. Tivey (ed.) *The Nation-State.* Robertson: Oxford, UK.

Orridge, A. (1981b) 'Uneven development and nationalism I and II' *Political Studies* **24**: 1–5 and 181–90.

Orridge, A. and **Williams, C. H.** (1982) 'Autonomous nationalism', *Political Geography Quarterly* **1**: 19–40.

Osei-Kwame, P. and **Taylor, P. J.**

(1984) 'A politics of failure: the political geography of Ghanaian elections, 1954−1979', *Annals, Association of American Geographers* **74**: 574−89.

Paddison, R. (1983) *The Fragmented State. The Political Geography of Power.* Blackwell: Oxford, UK.
Pahl, R. E. (1970) *Whose City?.* Longman: London.
Park, R. E. (1916) 'The city: suggestions for the investigation of human behaviour in the urban environment', *American Journal of Sociology* **20**: 577−612.
Park, R. L. and **de Mesquita, B. B.** (1979) *India's Political System.* Prentice Hall: Englewood Cliffs, N.J.
Parker, W. H. (1982) *Mackinder. Geography as Aid to Statecraft.* Clarendon: Oxford, UK.
Parkin, F. (1967) 'Working class Conservatives: a theory of political deviance', *British Journal of Sociology* **18**: 278−90.
Parkin, F. (1971) *Class Inequality and Political Order.* Holt, Rinehart & Winston: New York.
Paterson, J. H. (1987) 'German geopolitics reassessed', *Political Geography Quarterly* **6**: 107−14.
Pepper, D. and **Jenkins. A.** (eds) (1985) *The Geography of Peace and War.* Blackwell: Oxford.
Phillips, P. D. and **Wallerstein, I.** (1986) 'National & World identities and the inter-state system', *Millennium* **14**: 159−71.
Piepe, A., Prior, R. and **Box, A.** (1969) 'The location of the proletarian and deferential worker', *Sociology* **3**: 239−44.
Polanyi, K. (1977) 'The economistic fallacy', *Review* **1**: 9−20.
Poulantzas, N. (1969) 'The problem of the capitalist state', *New Left Review* **58**: 119−33.
Poulsen, T. M. (1971) 'Administration and regional structure in east-central and south-east Europe' in G. W. Hoffman (ed.) *Eastern Europe.* Methuen: London.
Pounds, N. J. G. (1951) 'The origin of the idea of natural frontiers in France',

Annals, Association of American Geographers **41**: 146−57.
Pounds, N. J. G. (1954) 'France and "les limites naturelles" from the seventeenth to the twentieth centuries'. *Annals, Association of American Geographers* **44**: 51−62.
Pounds, N. J. G. (1963) *Political Geography.* McGraw Hill: New York.
Pounds, N. J. G. and **Ball, S. S.** (1964) 'Core areas and the development of the European states system', *Annals, Association of American Geographers* **54**: 24−40.
Prescott, J. R. V. (1965) *The Geography of Frontiers and Boundaries.* Hutchinson: London.
Prescott, J. R. V. (1969) 'Electoral studies in political geography' in R: E. Kasperson and J. V. Minghi (eds) *The Structure of Political Geography.* Aldine: Chicago.

Randall, V. (1982) *Women & Politics.* Macmillan: London.
Ratzel, F. (1969) 'The laws of the spatial growth of states' in R. E. Kasperson and J. V. Minghi (eds) *The Structure of Political Geography.* Aldine: Chicago.
Read, D. (1964) *The English Provinces c 1760−1960. A Study in Influence.* Arnold: London.
Redfield, R. (1941) *The Folk Culture of Yucatan.* University of Chicago Press.
Reissman, L. (1964) *The Urban Process. Cities in Industrial Societies.* Free Press: New York.
Renshon, S. A. (1977) 'Assumptive frameworks in political socialization' in S. A. Renshon (ed.) *Handbook of Political Socialization.* Free Press: New York.
Research Working Group (1979) 'Cyclical rhythms and secular trends of the capitalist world-economy: some premises, hypotheses and questions', *Review* **2**: 483−500.
Reynolds, D. R. and **Archer, J. C.** (1969) 'An inquiry into the spatial basis of electoral geography', *Discussion Paper 11.* Department of Geography, University of Iowa.
Robertson, G. S. (1900) 'Political

geography and empire', *Geographical Journal* **16**: 447–57.

Robinson, K. W. (1961) 'Sixty years of federation in Australia', *Geographical Review* **5**: 1–20.

Robinson, R. (1973) 'Non-European foundations of European imperialism: sketch for a theory of collaboration' in R. Owen and B. Sutcliffe (eds) *Studies in the Theory of Imperialism*. Longman: London.

Robinson, R., Gallagher, J. and **Denny, A.** (1961) *Africa and the Victorians*. Macmillan: London.

Rokkan, S. (1970) *Citizens, Elections, Parties*. McKay: New York.

Rokkan, S. (1975) 'Dimensions of state formation and nation building: a possible paradigm for research on variations within Europe' in C. Tilley (ed) *The Formation of Nation States in Western Europe*. Princeton U.P.: Princeton, N.J.

Rokkan, S. (1980) 'Territories, centres and peripheries: towards a geoethnic-geoeconomic-geopolitical model of differentiation within Western Europe' in J. Gottman (ed.) *Centre and Periphery*. Sage: Beverly Hills.

Rumley, D. (1979) 'The study of structural effects in human geography', *Tijdschrift voor Economische en Sociale Geografie* **70**: 350–60.

Runciman, W. G. (1966) *Relative Deprivation and Social Justice*. Routledge & Kegan Paul: London.

Russett, B. M. (1967) *International Regions and the International System: A Study in Political Ecology*. Rand McNally: Chicago.

Russett, B. R. *et al.* (1963) *World Handbook of Political and Social Indicators*. Yale U.P.: New Haven.

Rustow, D. A. (1967) *A World of Nations: Problems of Political Modernization*. Brookings Institute: Washington, DC.

Ryan, H. B. (1982) *The Vision of Anglo-America*. Cambridge University Press: Cambridge, UK.

Sack, R. D. (1981) 'Territorial bases of power' in A. D Burnett and P. J.

Taylor (eds) *Political Studies from Spatial Perspectives*. Wiley: Chichester UK and New York.

Sack, R. D. (1983) 'Human territoriality: a theory', *Annals, Association of American Geographers* **73**: 55–74.

Sadasivan, S. N. (1977) *Party & Democracy in India*. Tata McGraw Hill: New Delhi.

Sarkissian, W. (1976) 'The idea of social mix in town planning: an historical review', *Urban Studies* **13**: 231–46.

Sauer, C. O. (1918) 'Geography and the gerrymander', *American Political Science Review* **12**: 403–26.

Saunders, P. (1984) 'Rethinking local politics' in M. Boddy and C. Fudge (eds) *Local Socialism?* Macmillan: London.

Savage, M. (1987a) *The Dynamics of Working Class Politics*. Cambridge University Press: Cambridge, UK.

Savage, M. (1987b) 'Understanding political alignments in contemporary Britain: do localities matter?', *Political Geography Quarterly* **6**: 53–76.

Scase, R. (1977) *Social Democracy in Capitalist Societies*. Croom Helm: London.

Scase, R. (1980) *The State in Western Europe*. Croom Helm: London.

Schattschneider, E. E. (1960) *The Semi-Sovereign People*. Dryden: Hinsdale, Illinois.

Schumpeter, J. A. (1951) *Imperialism and Social Classes*. Kelley: New York.

Semmel, B. (1960) *Imperialism and Social Reform. English Social-Imperialist Thought 1895–1914*. Allen & Unwin: London.

Shevky, E. and **Bell, W.** (1955) *Social Area Analysis*. Stanford University Press: Stanford, Co.

Short, R. J. (1982) *An Introduction to Political Geography*. Routledge & Kegan Paul: London.

Siegfried, A. (1913) *Tableau Politique de la France de l'Ouest*. Colin: Paris.

Skinner, Q. (1978) *The Foundation of Modern Political Thought* Vol. 2. Cambridge University Press: Cambridge, UK.

Small, M. and **Singer, J. D.** (1982) *Resort to Arms. International and Civil Wars 1816–1980.* Sage: Beverly Hills.

Smith, A. D. (1979) *Nationalism in the Twentieth Century.* Robertson: Oxford, UK.

Smith, A. D. (1981) *The Ethnic Revival in the Modern World.* Cambridge U.P.

Smith, A. D. (1982) 'Ethnic identity and world order', *Millennium: Journal of International Studies* **12**: 149–61.

Smith, A. D. (1986) *The Ethnic Origins of Nations.* Blackwell: Oxford, U.K.

Smith, D. (1978) 'Domination and containment: an approach to modernization' *Comparative Studies in History and Society* **20**: 177–213.

Smith, G. E. (1985) 'Ethnic separatism in the Soviet Union: territory, cleavage & control', *Environment & Planning C: Government and Policy* **3**: 49–73.

Smith, N. (1984) 'Isaiah Bowman: political geography and geopolitics', *Political Geography Quarterly* **3**: 69–76.

Smith, T. (1981) *The Pattern of Imperialism.* Cambridge U.P.

Soja, E. W. (1971) *The Political Organization of Space.* Association of American Geographers: Washington, DC.

Spate, O. H. K. (1942) 'Factors in the development of capital cities', *Geographical Review* **32**: 622–31.

Spykman, N. J. (1944) *The Geography of the Peace.* Harcourt, Brace: New York.

Szymanski, A. (1982) 'The socialist world system' in C.K. Chase-Dunn (ed.) *Socialist States in the World-System.* Sage: Beverly Hills.

Tabb, W. K. and **Sawers, L.** (eds) (1978) *Marxism and the Metropolis.* Oxford U.P.: New York.

Taylor, C. and **Hudson, M.** (1971) *World Handbook of Political and Social Indicators.* Yale University Press: New Haven, Conn.

Taylor, G. (1957) *Geography in the Mid-twentieth Century.* Methuen: London.

Taylor, M. and **Thrift, N.** (1982) *The Geography of Multinationals.* Croom Helm: London.

Taylor, P. J. (1973) 'Some implications of the spatial organization of elections', *Transactions, Institute of British Geographers* **60**: 121–36.

Taylor, P. J. (1978) 'Progress report: political geography', *Progress in Human Geography* **2**: 153–62.

Taylor, P. J. (1981a) 'Political geography and the world-economy' in A. D. Burnett and P. J. Taylor (eds) *Political Studies from Spatial Perspectives* Wiley: Chichester, UK and New York.

Taylor P. J. (1981b) 'Geographical scales within the world-economy approach', *Review* **5**: 3–11.

Taylor, P. J. (1982a) 'The changing political map' in R. J. Johnston and J. C. Doornkamp (eds) *The Changing Geography of the United Kingdom.* Methuen: London.

Taylor, P. J. (1982b) 'A materialist framework for political geography', *Transactions, Institute of British Geographers* **NS 7**: 15–34.

Taylor, P. J. (1984) 'Accumulation, legitimation and the electoral geographies within liberal democracies' in P. J. Taylor and J. W. House (eds) *Political Geography: Recent Advances and Future Directions.* Croom Helm: London.

Taylor, P. J. (1986) 'An exploration into world-systems analysis of political parties', *Political Geography Quarterly* **5** (Supplement): 5–20.

Taylor, P. J. (forthcoming) *Geopolitical Transition: Britain and the Making of the Cold War.* Frances Pinter: London.

Taylor, P. J. and **Gudgin, G.** (1976a) 'The statistical basis of decision making in electoral districting', *Environment and Planning* **A 38**: 43–58.

Taylor, P. J. and **Gudgin, G.** (1976b) 'The myth of non-partisan cartography: a study of electoral biases in the English Boundary Commission's Redistribution for 1955–1970', *Urban Studies* **13**: 13–25.

Taylor, P. J. and **Johnston, R. J.** (1979) *Geography of Elections.* Penguin: London.

Taylor, P. J. and **Johnston, R. J.** (1984) 'Political geography of Britain' in A. D. Kirby and J. R. Short (eds) *Contemporary Geography of Britain.* Routledge and Kegan Paul: London.

Therborn, G. (1977) 'The rule of capital & the rise of democracy', *New Left Review* **103**: 3−42.

Thompson, E. P. (1968) *The Making of the English Working Class*. Penguin: London.

Thompson, E. P. (1980) 'Notes on exterminism, the last stage of civilization', *New Left Review* 121: 3−31.

Thompson, E. P. (1987) 'The rituals of enmity' in D. Smith and E. P. Thompson (eds) *Prospects for a Habitable Planet*. Penguin: London.

Tietz, M. (1968) 'Towards a theory of urban public facility location', *Papers of the Regional Science Association* **21**: 35–51.

Tilly, C. (1975) 'Reflections on the history of European state-making' in C. Tilly (ed.) *The Formation of Nation States in Western Europe*. Princeton U.P.: Princeton, NJ.

Tilly, C. (1978) *From Mobilization to Revolution*. Addison-Wesley: Reading: Mass.

Tivey, L. (1981) 'States, nations and economies' in L. Tivey (ed.) *The Nation-State*. Robertson: Oxford, UK.

Trevor-Roper, H. (1983) 'The invention of tradition: The Highland Tradition of Scotland' in E. Hobsbawm and T. Ranger (eds). *The Invention of Tradition*. Cambridge University Press: Cambridge, UK.

Tufte, E. R. (1973) 'The relationship between seats and votes in two party systems', *American Political Science Review* **67**: 540−54.

Urry, J. (1981) 'Localities, regions and social class', *International Journal of Urban and Regional Research* **5**: 455−73.

Valkenburg, van S. (1939) *Elements of Political Geography*. Holt: New York.

Wallerstein, I. (1974a) *The Modern World System. Capitalist Agriculture and the Origins of the European World-Economy in the Sixteenth Century*. Academic Press: New York.

Wallerstein, I. (1974b) 'The rise and future demise of the capitalist world system: concepts for comparative analysis', *Comparative Studies in Society and History* **16**: 387−418.

Wallerstein, I. (1976a) 'A world-system perspective on the social sciences', *British Journal of Sociology* **27**: 345−54.

Wallerstein, I. (1976b) 'The three stages of African involvement in the world-economy' in P. C. W. Gutkind and I. Wallerstein (eds) *The Political Economy of Contemporary Africa*. Sage: Beverly Hills.

Wallerstein, I. (1977) 'The tasks of historical social science: an editorial', *Review* **1**: 3−8.

Wallerstein, I. (1979) *The Capitalist World-Economy*. Cambridge University Press: Cambridge, UK.

Wallerstein, I. (1980a) *The Modern World-System II. Mercantilism and the Consolidation of the European World-Economy 1600−1750*. Academic Press: New York.

Wallerstein, I. (1980b) 'Maps, maps, maps', *Radical History Review* **24**: 155−9.

Wallerstein, I. (1980c) 'The future of the world-economy' in T. K. Hopkins and I Wallerstein (eds) *Processes of the World-System*. Sage: Beverly Hills.

Wallerstein, I. (1980d) 'Imperialism and development' in A. Bergesen (ed.) *Studies of the Modern World-System*. Academic: New York.

Wallerstein, I. (1982) 'Socialist states: mercantilist strategies and revolutionary objectives' in E. Friedman (ed.) *Ascent and Decline in the World-System*. Sage: Beverly Hills.

Wallerstein, I. (1983) *Historical Capitalism*. Verso: London.

Wallerstein, I. (1984a) *The Politics of the World-Economy*. Cambridge University Press: Cambridge, UK.

Wallerstein, I. (1984b) 'Long waves as capitalist process', *Review* **7**: 559−75.

Wallerstein, I. (1988) 'European unity and its implications for the inter-state system' in B. Hettne (ed) *Europe: Dimensions of Peace*. Zed: London.

Walters, R. E. (1974) *The Nuclear Trap: An Escape Route*. Penguin: London.

Wambaugh, S. (1920) *A Monograph on Plebiscites*. Oxford U.P.: New York.

Wambaugh, S. (1936) *Plebiscites since the World War*. Carnegie: New York.

Waterman, S. (1984) 'Partition — a problem in political geography in P. J. Taylor and J. W. House (eds) *Political Geography: Recent Advances & Future Directions*. Croom Helm: London.

Waterman, S. (1987) 'Partitioned states', *Political Geography Quarterly* **6**: 151–170.

Watson, J. W. (1970) 'Image geography: the myth of America in the American scene', *Advancement of Science* **27**: 71–9.

Werz, N. (1987) 'Parties & party systems in Latin America' in M. J. Holler (ed) *The Logic of Multiparty Systems*. Springer-Verlag: Munich.

Wesson, R. (1982) *Democracy in Latin America*. Praeger: New York.

Whittlesey, D. (1939) *The Earth and the State: A Study in Political Geography*. Holt: New York.

Wilkinson, H. R. (1951) *Maps and Politics: A Review of the Ethnographic Cartography of Macedonia*. University Press: Liverpool.

Willets, P. (1978) *The Non-Aligned Movement*. Frances Pinter: London.

Williams, C. H. (1980) 'Ethnic separation in western Europe', *Tijdschrift voor Economische en Sociale Geografie* **71**: 142–58.

Williams, C. H. (1981) 'Identity through autonomy: ethnic separatism in Quebec', in A. D. Burnett and P. J. Taylor (eds) *Political Studies from Spatial Perspectives*. Wiley: Chichester and New York.

Williams, C. H. (1984) 'Ideology and the interpretation of minority cultures', *Political Geography Quarterly* **3**: 105–26.

Williams, C. H. (1986) 'The question of national congruence' in R. J. Johnston and P. J. Taylor (eds). *World in crisis?*. Blackwell: Oxford.

Williams, O. (1971) *Metropolitan Policy Analysis*. Free Press: New York

Wolpert, J., Mumphrey, A. and **Seley, J.** (1972) *Metropolitan Neighbourhoods: Participation and Conflict over Change*. Association of American Geographers: Washington, DC.

Young, C. (1982) *Ideology and Development in Africa*. Yale U.P.: New Haven.

Zinnes, D. (1980) 'Three puzzles in search of a researcher'. *International Studies Quarterly* **25**: 315–42.

Zolberg, A. R. (1981) 'Origins of the modern world system: A missing link', *World Politics* **33**: 253–81.

INDEX